T0350771

Luxury Brand Management in Digital and Sustainable Times

Luxury Brand Management

in Digital and Sustainable Times

FOURTH EDITION

Michel Chevalier
Gérald Mazzalovo

WILEY

This edition first published 2021

© 2021 John Wiley & Sons, Ltd. All rights reserved.

The right of Michel Chevalier and Gérald Mazzalovo to be identified as the authors of the editorial material in this work has been asserted in accordance with law.

Registered office
John Wiley & Sons Ltd., The Atrium, Southern Gate, Chichester, West Sussex PO19 8SQ, United Kingdom

For details of our global editorial offices, customer services, and more information about Wiley products visit us at www.wiley.com.

Wiley also publishes its books in a variety of electronic formats and by print-on-demand. Some content that appears in standard print versions of this book may not be available in other formats.

ibrary of Congress Cataloging-in-Publication
DataNames: Chevalier, Michel, 1943- author. | Mazzalovo, Gerald, author.
Title: Luxury brand management in digital and sustainable
    times : a new world of privilege / Michel Chevalier, Gerald Mazzalovo.
Description: Fourth Edition. | Hoboken : Wiley,
    2021. | Revised edition.
Identifiers: LCCN 2020029296 (print) | LCCN 2020029297 (ebook) | ISBN
    9781119706281 (hardcover) | ISBN 9781119706298 (adobe pdf) | ISBN
    9781119706304 (epub)
Subjects: LCSH: Brand name products–Management. | Luxury goods industry. |
Luxuries–Marketing. | Branding (Marketing)
Classification: LCC HD69.B7 C476 2021 (print) | LCC HD69.B7
    (ebook) | DDC 658.8/27–dc23
LC record available at https://lccn.loc.gov/2020029296
LC ebook record available at https://lccn.loc.gov/2020029297

Cover Design: Wiley
Cover Image: ©Akintevs/Getty Images

Set in 11.5/14pt, BemboStd by SPi Global, Chennai, India.

10 9 8 7 6 5 4 3 2 1

Printed and bound by CPI Group (UK) Ltd, Croydon CR0 4YY

Contents

Introduction

Why write a fourth edition of a book that was initially published in 2008?

Five reasons justify the effort:

1. **Luxury is changing.** First of all, luxury consumption and the industries related to it continue to play an increasingly important role in today's economy, societies, and ways of living, and are an important engine of innovation and fulfillment of basic human desires toward beauty and excellence. The dynamism of the luxury industries' evolution deserves constant observation just to keep up with its nature, mechanisms, and meanings and to be able to share those with our readers. In just the first months of 2020, as we were busy writing the new text, LVMH bought Tiffany's; Neimann Marcus, J.Crew, JC Penney, Brooks Brothers, Muji USA, and Barney's filed for Chapter 11; Sonya Rykiel went into liquidation and the brand was bought by two young new investors; Fenty, the new brand managed by Rihanna and co-owned with LVMH, occupied all the windows of Bergdorf Goodman in New York in February. The advent of COVID-19 has also shown numerous solidary initiatives from small and big brands.

In this catastrophic pandemic, luxury brands have also shown their resilience, not only on e-commerce but in traditional physical retail, when the conditions allow for reopening.

2. **We know more.** Since the third edition in 2015, both authors have been involved in managing and advising luxury products and services brands in personal goods, perfumery, distribution, and education. The experience garnered by being actively engaged in brand management realities in Asia, the Middle East, and Europe led us to evolve in our understanding of current and future brand management issues. The academic literature has been prolific on luxury subjects and more knowledge has emerged as a result. A lot of the lessons learned are integrated in this book.

3. **We live in digital times.** This is one of the most important factors affecting all businesses in general and luxury brands in particular. The changes brought about by digital technology are affecting the industries, the brand strategies and operations, the consumers' ways of thinking and buying, and more.

4. **Sustainability is becoming our way of living.** This is the second major factor influencing luxury brand management and consumption. Luxury brands have been somewhat late in addressing it, but are now fully on board and very often innovative leaders in the field.

5. **COVID-19 has been a major disruptor.** It will eventually be controlled, but it serves as both a revealer and an accelerator of existing trends. It will have profound effects on geopolitics as well as on everything related to mobility and, therefore, on industrial and commercial processes.

All these conditions have generated the new content that is included in this edition. Most of the examples and financial data have been updated.

Chapter 1, which delves into the notion of luxury, was completed with considerations of new luxury in which exceptionality prevails over exclusivity.

Chapter 2 explains the specificities of the luxury industry, how it can be defined, and what makes it different from other businesses, in particular from the fast-moving consumer goods and the basic fashion industry.

Chapter 3 describes the different industry sectors with their sizes and with the major players: fashion, perfumes and cosmetics, leather goods, wines and spirits, and jewelry and watches. In this edition, we have added a complete analysis of the hotel hospitality sector, and we give a size for this market, a description of the major players, and the key management issues.

Chapter 4 indicates the economic value of each luxury brand and how it can be assessed and developed.

Chapter 5 gives a description of the major luxury clients, by country and by level of income and wealth. It also describes how different segments of this population react to the idea of luxury.

Chapters 6 and 7 present brand analytical tools that we currently use. Because the number of them has increased, we split Chapter **6** of the third edition into two parts. In Chapter **6** of this edition, we introduce three tools: the brand hinge, the EST-ET$^©$ diagram, and the Brand Aesthetics Analytical Grid, the new tool that we applied to the Thai brand Jim Thompson. We introduce the three ends to any aesthetic treatment and complete the chapter with considerations of the strengths and weaknesses of the brand identity notion and position the brand identity approach within the broader field of other approaches to brand management. Chapter **7** continues with seven analytical instruments, such as the Brand Life Cycle, the prism, and the Rosewindow, and semiotic tools like the semiotic square being applied to different brands and in particular to market-centered or self-centered brands. It ends up with considerations on what constitutes a valid semiotic analysis for luxury brands.

Chapter 8 deals with creation and merchandising and has incorporated numerous new examples drawn from our latest management experiences. Real examples of reports on collection structures and calendars have been added. Considerations are made on style issues, drawing from work done for Yves Saint Laurent and Pininfarina. A whole bibliography is included for those interested in getting deeper into brand aesthetics management. The ever-growing relationship between art and brands has been addressed.

Chapter 9 deals with communication in digital times and has been completely revamped, providing the opportunity for an overall review on how digital is impacting the world, luxury brands, and consumers. The scheme of the communication chain has been updated, as have the communication plan and calendar, to consider the effects of digital media. The key performance indicators of a commercial website have been compared to those of a traditional retail one.

Chapter 10 deals with different ways to develop a worldwide brand. It describes how a brand can become completely international, sometimes through its own subsidiaries, but generally also through local importers and distributors. It also explains how online operators can become a major resource and how one must deal with them. It discusses how brands can also be present and strong in travel retail outlets. It presents pros and cons of developing a brand with licensing activities.

Chapter 11 examines different retail activities in a time of physical and digital resources. It explains how a consumer does not select one or another system of distribution, but considers these two resources as complementary. The more the client spends time with a brand on the Internet, the more likely he is to buy in a physical store, and the more the client has direct contact with a brand in a physical store, the more likely he is to purchase on the Internet. And clients must be seduced and interested and convinced when they visit a store: A client who has a bad impression or who has a negative experience in a store would never buy that brand on the Internet. Brands have to adjust to this phenomenon.

Chapter 12 deals with sustainability and authenticity. It summarizes first the future trends of luxury and then delves deeper into these two basic consumption and civilization trends. Some of the indicators of an increasing sustainability sensibility are highlighted, as well as the initiatives taken by some of the main luxury brands. We defend the complete compatibility of luxury and sustainability and introduce a possible consumer segmentation based on attitudes toward sustainability. Authenticity is considered to be a quality of a relationship between the object considered and certain referents, which can be intrinsic qualities of the object or internal to the brand, like its identity or even belonging to the consumers' mind.

We have also integrated the overall conclusion of the book in this chapter.

Appendix A presents an extract from a brand identity study led by Mazzalovo in 2020 on the Sasin School of Management, the leading Thai business school of Chulalongkorn University (Bangkok, Thailand).

Appendix B is a glossary of some of the most current expressions in the digital vocabulary.

The book, as its preceding editions, is not meant to be read as a novel. It presents a mix of macroeconomic and microeconomic considerations, and its modest ambition is to function as a reference text, where considerations can be found on specific management issues for luxury brand employees and executives, consumers, students, teachers, and anybody interested in our society's evolution, a reflection of which is given through the mirror of luxury brands.

Chapter 1

The Concept of Luxury

The word *luxury* has always been a source of discussion of what it is supposed to mean. This is the reason we added this chapter in the second edition of this book and have kept it since then. Since we are going to write about luxury along with text and diagrams, it only makes sense to explore the intricacies of what is meant by such a popular word. In this fourth edition we have added a section on the meaning of the expression *new luxury*, whose usage has been growing in the past few years.

A Problematic Definition

What is luxury? At first glance, it seems that we can answer in simple terms and to distinguish between what is luxury and what does not fall into it. But we sense, on reflection, that not everyone will agree on this distinction: luxury to one is not necessarily luxury to another.

The concept of luxury incorporates an aesthetic dimension that refers to a major theme of Western philosophy: How to characterize the notion of beauty?[1] In the twentieth century, the philosopher Theodor W. Adorno expressed the problem in these terms: "We cannot define the concept of beautiful nor give up its concept."[2] We believe that it is the same for luxury: without wanting to confuse it with the beautiful, it turns out, upon examination, no less elusive, and, perhaps, not less indispensable.

Therefore, it is probably unrealistic to seek a universal definition of luxury. But this reflection draws our attention to an initial important point: the definition of luxury has varied over time.

A Fluctuating Notion

What we commonly call *luxury* no longer has much to do with what was meant only a century ago; or, a little further back, in the years before the Industrial Revolution. We are not talking here about objects of luxury. A product like soap, for example, although a real luxury in the Middle Ages, has become largely democratic since then, and it has therefore ceased to be a luxury in our eyes. Today, the word has a very different meaning from how it was used, for example, in the seventeenth century. It connotes for us both positive and negative images; most of the negative images are derived from its historical heritage, while positive images are for the most of a recent introduction.

As we will see, the term has experienced, particularly in the past two centuries, important semantic changes that reflect the construction of our modern consumer society. These transformations are of great interest for our subject: they had direct impact on the progressive segmentation of the global luxury market and on the current positioning of brands claiming this territory.

The Paradox of Contemporary Luxury

Today's luxury market is based on a paradox. On the one hand, luxury operates as a social distinction; it is the sign of a practice reserved for the "happy few" and thus circumvents the masses. At the same time, contemporary luxury is promoted by the brands, and they remain linked

---

[1] It is a question we find in Platon's *Hippias Major* and extensively studied by Kant and Hegel.
[2] Theodor Adorno, *Äesthetische Theorie*, translated by Marc Jimenez. Paris: Klincksieck, 1982.

to the logics of volume of production and distribution. How, therefore, can we reconcile exclusivity with the industrial and commercial logics of volume? Such is the dilemma for luxury brands, which each brand will try to solve by adjusting its positioning through innovative strategies of creation, communication, and distribution.

Even though it may not necessarily appear as such at first glance, contemporary luxury, in fact, presents an extensive and highly contrasted landscape. In order to grasp this complexity, a step back is needed; this is a historical detour that will allow us to comprehend it.

Chronicle of a Semantic Evolution

Luxury is a keyword whose use is becoming more frequent in our daily lives. We read it more often in all brand communication; we use it more often in our discourses (on the Internet, Google Trends shows that its use has increased by more than 30% on average between 2004 and 2020). There are two reasons for this increase:

1. Brands have realized that this (sometimes only apparent) positioning adds to their competitiveness.
2. On the other hand, a majority of consumers have developed a positive attitude toward the products, services, or experiences connoted by this feature.

We live in a world where luxury reigns. But the word itself was not born yesterday—definitions have accumulated for centuries. Since Plato, Epicurus, Veblen, Rousseau, and Voltaire, up to today's opinion leaders, the production and use of signs of wealth have always intrigued the philosophers, sociologists, and observers of their time.

The word *luxury*, as we understand it today, inherited this accumulation of proposals, sometimes with contradictory meanings. The acceleration of the number of definitions in the past 20 years comes to prove the growing current interest for the question.

Modern Dispersion

In order to measure this abundance of meanings, we may note the growing number of expressions that, today, use it. The term now needs articles and adjectives to clarify its meanings.

Here are a few modern examples: *authentic luxury* is quite frequent as an expression and we will discuss it further; *luxury and grand luxury* was advertised by the great car designer Battista Pininfarina (*lusso e gran lusso*) on a 1931 poster where a car was presented on a pedestal like in a museum. This is an interesting segmentation, where already lies the idea of a form of an affordable luxury suitable for all budgets. More recently, the economist Danielle Allérès extrapolated the common sense of Pininfarina suggesting a distinction between accessible, intermediate, and inaccessible luxuries. Even luxury yogurt is spreading in food marketing. We hear more and more in casual talks and in advertising the expression "my luxury"—which is not yours and has the defect of not constituting a market on its own.

Ostentatious luxury or "bling-bling" has long been present in the media. It may evoke a *traditional luxury* that is opposed, of course, to the *new luxury*, and so on. Social or even academic trends regularly provide their lot of new expressions on the subject.

Two relevant points can be detected in this diversity. The first is that to each his own luxury: the concept has ceased to mark a boundary between opulence and economic discomfort—it is now a sign that needs additional specific attributes to perform its function of distinction in a human group. This ability of luxury to indefinitely segment the markets shows us how it has been able to blend, by transforming itself, in our modern civilization of mass consumption.

The second point is that this modern luxury appears to carry rather positive connotations. Obviously, it also has its excesses, its indecency; however, the fact that we can now speak of luxury in positive terms already certifies a remarkable semantic evolution. In order to measure this evolution, we must return to the etymology.

Etymology and Transformations

The word *luxury* comes from the Latin *luxus*, which means "grow askew, excess." Its root is an old Indo-European word that meant "twist." In the same family, we find "luxuriant" (yielding abundantly) and "luxation" (dislocation). In short, the term originally refers to something of the order of aberration: it is almost devoid of any positive connotation.

We have used the dictionary *Le trésor de la langue française informatisé*, which offers a brief overview of two centuries of use.

1607: "way of life characterized by large expenditures to make shows of elegance and refinement"

1661: "character of which is expensive, refined," luxury clothing

1797: "expensive and superfluous object, pleasure"

1801: "excessive quantity," a luxury of vegetation

1802: "which is superfluous, unnecessary"

Little by little, the notion of guilty excess disappears, while the ideas of distinction and refinement gain in strength. In the Classical Age, luxury is already full of ambiguities: speaking of women's toilette, La Fontaine relates the "instruments of luxury" to everything "which contributes not only to cleanness, but also to delicateness." This does not prevent him from condemning, moralistically, "these women who have found the secret to become old at twenty years, and seem young at sixty."[3] Around the same time, the grammarian Pierre Nicole wishes that "great people," by their example, deter us from "luxury, blasphemy, debauchery, gambling, libertinage."[4] In sum, the luxury already connotes sophistication, but it remains morally suspect.

At the dawn of the Industrial Revolution, the connotation of superfluous—which is not motivated by economic and utilitarian logic—begins consolidating. It becomes more nuanced with the advent of mass consumption and the civilization of leisure. The superfluous is not debauchery; it is beyond the commercial sphere, but it can also mark the promotion of a certain quality of life.

As for the price dimension, it appears very early and remains virtually unchanged over the years: luxury is something that is to be paid for.

From the same French dictionary, we see that current usages of the word "luxury" show evolutionary meanings: the original meanings are enriched by others, introducing the word into the sphere of day-to-day experience ("little luxuries") while affirming the notion of a pleasure without complex ("innocent luxury"):

1. Social practice characterized by lavish expenditures, the search for expensive amenities or refined and superfluous goods, often motivated by a taste and desire for the ostentatious and fatuous.

---

[3] Jean de La Fontaine, *Les Amours de Psyché et de Cupidon*, 1669.

[4] Pierre Nicole, *De l'Éducation du Prince*, 1670.

2. Luxury (as an adjective). Of very high quality, sophisticated and expensive. Article, object, luxury product, grand luxury, semi-luxury, luxury style, luxury animal.

3. Refers to a thing, a behavior valuable because of the enjoyment it provides. "The toothbrush still plays me tricks and also the tube of toothpaste that always breaks from the bottom. One must sacrifice these small luxuries to the great luxury of time" (Paul Morand).[5]

4. Qualify a thing, a behavior valuable because of its rarity and sometimes by the fact that it is devoid of utilitarian function. "The emerging forms of society today are not making the existence of intellectual luxury one of their essential conditions. Probably, the unnecessary cannot nor should interest them" (Paul Valéry).[6]

The adventures of the word reflect those of the concept. It shows that luxury emerged first as a licit experience—a practice of distinction—and then, when everyone wanted to distinguish himself from everyone, as a common experience. From the etymology of excess or botanical deviation, the meaning extends into excessive or unnecessary, redundant, expensive objects. The previous senses are still present, but they evolve to include scarcity. Soon the meaning attached to the valuable, rare, and expensive object will apply to the lifestyles of their owners and mean wealth, ostentation, and, therefore, power.

With the emergence of the postmodern brand—that is, the appearance of brands communicating in the registry of luxury by offering imaginary worlds associated with luxurious lifestyles, without necessarily offering expensive and certainly not rare objects—new meanings emerge and are superimposed on the previous ones.

The aesthetic treatment of objects, design, and creativity become more relevant. At the social level, luxury gathers additional values of seduction and elitism, not foreign to the values of power and prestige. Hedonism becomes the latest addition to the valences of luxury, a characteristic of our times of postmodern consumerism.

The Advent of Intermediate Luxury

This transformation of meaning is based on a contemporary sociological revolution, a direct consequence of the mass production and especially of

---

[5] Morand, *L'homme pressé*, 1941.
[6] *Regards sur monde act*, 1931.

the rise of the brands: the advent of intermediate luxury. Truly luxurious lifestyles are present, more than ever, in any modern communication: but they form only part of the equation. Intermediate luxury brands offer countless possibilities for the middle class to take part symbolically, partially, or virtually into this world.

The global luxury chessboard is therefore distributed on two levels, if not more: on the one hand, "true luxury"—which few people can afford—increases its hold on the market. The growth of the number of wealthy or well-to-do consumers (especially in the BRIC countries) combined with a bigger supply—investments in the luxury industries that have been yielding higher returns on investment than ordinary brands—have led to a strong visibility of luxurious lifestyles. The press and the media in general contribute actively by exposing the life of the rich and famous.

On the other hand, intermediate luxury brands, in applying their logic of volume of production and communication, ensure the democratization of luxury. They multiply the opportunities for consumers of the middle classes, to be in contact with the possible imaginary worlds they offer. What is more naturally human than to aspire to signs of social recognition, success, comfort, and prestige? This democratization is rampant. Nervesa, the Italian brand of men's ready-to-wear, does not hesitate to promote "low-cost prestige." The American brand Terner Jewelry promotes its products in airport shops with broad signs showing "Luxury at €12."

The ultimate symbol of this democratization could be the recent attention paid to soccer—a popular sport, anti-elitist par excellence—by some brands, much bigger than Terner and Nervesa. The kick-off had taken place in 1998 in Paris, when Yves Saint-Laurent presented a parade of some of his historic fashion models at the opening ceremony of the World Cup at the France Stadium. During the 2010 World Cup in South Africa, Louis Vuitton presented an advertising campaign where the mythical champions Pelé, Maradona, and Zidane competed in table soccer (baby-foot). Parmigiani, the Swiss watchmaker, was "the official watchmaker of the football club Olympique de Marseille" in the 2010s. Its direct competitor Hublot sponsors the soccer clubs Juventus of Torino, Chelsea, and Benfica, as well as Jose Mourinho (coach), Pele (the legendary Brazilian player), and Kylian Mbappé (an international French player at Paris-Saint-Germain). It was also the official timekeeper of the 2018 World Cup. The English Premier League is a favorite target of the luxury watches because of the widespread worldwide coverage it benefits from. Tag Heuer is with Manchester United, Jean Richard with Arsenal, and so on.

Brands are the main factor of the recent transformations of the concept of luxury. The essayist Dana Thomas traces this drift from the notions of exclusivity, quality, and tradition to those of accessibility and aesthetics in the 1960s, with the advent of a generation of young consumers anxious to break social barriers.[7] It is nevertheless in the 1990s that the modern connotations of the term *luxury* expand, as postmodern brands flourish with their multiple representations and proposals of possible worlds.

We see in any case that the concept can boast a rich history as well as a present that has never been more diverse or abundant. But if we have seen how luxury has evolved, it remains, in essence, difficult to identify. Its definitions are essentially subjective: they reflect the professional, social, and cultural trajectories of their users. Depending on whether one is an economist, brand manager, philosopher, sociologist, psychologist, or consumer, the dimensions that someone will retain will be obviously different.

However, this proliferation of representations is not devoid of meaning. There is logic to this wealth of definitions that can teach us about the overall economy and the meanings of luxury.

Classification of Existing Definitions

Beyond the tangible aspects of luxury products or services, we need to consider the phenomenon as a whole in terms of production, marketing, and communication. Luxury is a discourse, the assertion of a certain lifestyle. We can therefore distinguish between emission and perception of this discourse.

With this reading, the diversity of the current definitions and analyses of luxury can be divided into two broad categories: those relating to the supply of products or services and those related to the psychological and social implications of these products or services—in other words, consumers' perceptions.

---

[7] Dana Thomas, *Deluxe: How Luxury Lost Its Luster.* Penguin, 2008.

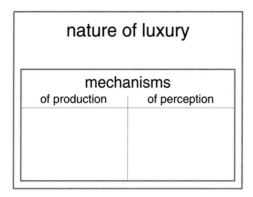

Figure 1.1   Analytical Scheme of the Definitions of Luxury

On the one hand, we therefore find definitions relating to the production of luxury; on the other, definitions relating to its perception (see Figure 1.1). Alternatively, in economic terms we could identify them as the supply and the usefulness logics.

Perceptual Approaches

Sociologists and psychologists are naturally interested in the resonance of luxury in the population—and are, therefore, on the side of the mechanisms of perception.

For some authors, such as Pierre Bourdieu, buying a luxury brand is a way to express a social position: according to him, luxury is essentially defined by its dimension of social communication.[8] The American economist Thorstein Veblen and his concept of "conspicuous waste" also belongs in this group.[9] According to him, highlighting one's consumption of pricey products is a method of building respectability for the man of leisure. Jean Baudrillard has a similar approach: for him, our objects, torn between their value of use and exchange value "are taken in the fundamental compromise to have to mean, that is to give a social sense."[10] In the same vein, Gilles Lipovetsky recently wrote: "Luxury is seen as perpetuating a form of mythical thinking at the heart of a desacralized

---

[8] Pierre Bourdieu, *La distinction et Critique sociale du jugement*. Minuit, 1979.
[9] Thorstein Veblen, *The Theory of the Leisure Class*. The MacMillan Company, 1899.
[10] Jean Baudrillard, *Pour une critique de l'économie du signe*. Gallimard, 1972.

commercial culture."[11] In other words, in a society where everything is measured and bought, luxury would reintroduce an almost magical, not strictly quantitative distinction among individuals.

Economists who have reflected upon the phenomenon of luxury are especially attached to integrating the question of its valorization into a global macroeconomic model. They are therefore positioned also on the side of the mechanisms of perception. For instance, the theory on the elasticity of demand for luxury goods is considered to be positive and greater than 1, which means that the demand, paradoxically, will increase when the price increases. This is obviously the symbolic value of the luxury product—its distinctive effect—that is the cause.

Productive Approaches

For this other category, the discourses oriented toward the mechanisms of the production of luxury are made by operational managers, executives concerned with the functioning of their brand and the conditions of production of "the luxury effect." They also need definitions, but more pragmatic ones.

Consider the case of Patrizio Bertelli, president of Prada: he defines luxury by a convergence of creation and intuition. Another example is the Comité Colbert, an association regrouping 82 French luxury houses in 2020 (plus 16 associated members and 6 European members), which stresses the alliance between tradition and modernity, know-how and creation, international reputation and culture of excellence.

For these approaches, what defines luxury is less its social implications than a set of qualifications embedded in the production of the object or service: quality of materials, technical know-how, and bold and creative talent, whose sustainability is ensured by the transmission of intangible values—tradition, artisanal exigency, quest for perfection.

The great fashion designer Coco Chanel used to define luxury simply as the opposite of vulgarity: a way to evade the question, which refers more to the mechanisms of perception, but which shows us *a contrario* how the discourses of the actors of the luxury world have become more profound in the postmodern world.

---

[11] G. Lipovetsky and E. Roux *Le luxe Eternel.* Gallimard, 2003.

We can already hold on to two universes of clearly distinct representations, whose issues diverge and even conflict. But it is possible to refine this classification further.

Social and Individual Aspects

For psychologists and sociologists focused on the perceptions of luxury, the interest is first on the paradoxical commitment to some object, apparently useless: What are the hidden reasons behind luxury consumption?

The perceptual approach reveals two types of motivations that do not overlap entirely: one can consume luxury (possibly unconsciously) in order to display it or, in a more personal approach, simply to have fun for his own pleasure. This dimension seems often neglected by the sociological discourse but cannot be reduced to the previous one. This is a more private dimension, a dimension of comfort and individual hedonism, as points out, for example, Jean-Paul Sartre in *L'Être et le Néant* (1943), when he wrote: "the luxury does not designate a quality of the object owned, but a quality of possession."

It is conceivable, for example, that I buy a luxury soap "because I'm worth it" to identify with the celebrity who makes the claim—in short, for the sake of social representation. But I also buy it because it smells good and its foam is smoother than soap from other brands. These qualities I do not need to show to anyone in order to enjoy them. The soap serves my own hedonism: it pleases me, and if I am no longer convinced that it smells better than the others, I will probably stop buying it, despite the prestige of its brand.

Still, the pleasure born from the consumption of luxury comes also from stories that can be told. Luxury makes us dream and we also can dream alone. How do I know whether my soap feels objectively better or if it is the brand advertising, the reference to a celebrity that convinced me? In this sense, social representation is never far from personal experience. This is what Jean Baudrillard stresses when writing "the private and the social are mutually exclusive only in the daily imagination."[12]

Without denying this analysis, one wonders if there is not, among sociologists of luxury, a certain moralist bias that encourages them to ignore the question of hedonism. In their discipline, social experience

---

[12] Baudrillard, *Pour une critique de l'économie du signe.*

often overwhelms pure pleasure—or, said differently, the intrinsic qualities of the product. These qualities remain, consumers will agree, constitutive of experience.

The Brand and Its Manifestations

As we just mentioned, discourses about the mechanisms of production of luxury characterize the point of view of operational executives. They are, however, structured by the phenomenon of the brand. It introduced a second and critical dimension in a productive approach to luxury. The brand generates issues that the manager cannot confuse with those of the product itself.

For example, specific qualities are expected from a Hermès scarf, the results of a know-how that can be recognized visually and tactilely and that are the indispensable and defining attributes of Hermès scarves. However, something else is expected: a more intangible supplement, an idea, a prestige that will be called "Hermès"—as a brand or, more precisely, as a brand identity.

There is a sort of "beyond the actual product," that is the brand and that the product must promote without betrayal. But the product is only one of the possible brand manifestations, making brand management issues even more complex. Advertising, points of sale, store windows, websites, social networks, sponsorships, and so forth are other forms of brand manifestations and not less essential for the promotion of its identity.

Two dimensions of brand identity are usually distinguished: the brand ethics, the intelligible part that is made up of its values, its vision of the world, and its idealized representation; and the brand aesthetics, the sensory part that affects its physical and concrete manifestations or all imaginable interfaces between the brand and its consumers. The aesthetic treatments of the sensory part of the brand participate in the sensitive experience of the brand. The emergence of "lifestyle brands" tells us that this experience spread beyond products, in other areas, such as communication, spaces, or behaviors (see Chapter 8 on creation).

Now that we have split the production side into the brand and its manifestations and the perception side into its social and individual parts, we are able to position all the authors' definitions we have mentioned so far (see Figure 1.2).

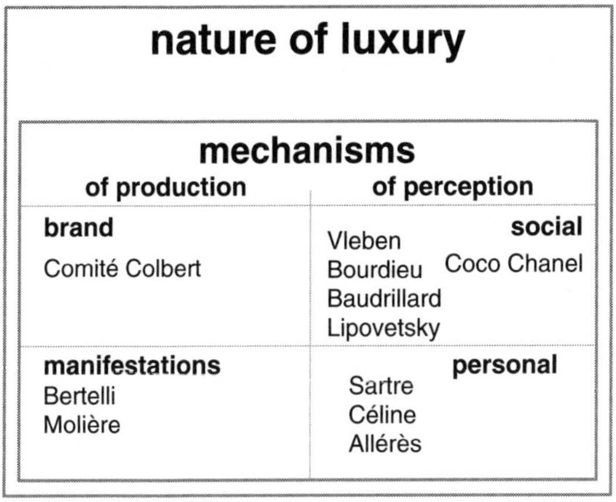

nature of luxury

mechanisms

of production	of perception
brand Comité Colbert	Vleben **social** Bourdieu Coco Chanel Baudrillard Lipovetsky
manifestations Bertelli Molière	Sartre **personal** Céline Allérès

Figure 1.2 Positioning of Some Authors on the Analytical Scheme of the Definitions of the Notion of Luxury

nature of luxury

Etymology: Excess

mechanisms

of production	of perception
brand **power**	*Lavish lifestyle* **social** splendor ostentation **status** wealth **seduction** **elitism**
manifestations *costly* sumptuous, quality *superfluous* precious, rare *useless* **design** *quantity* **creativity** *excessive* **excellence**	personal *refinement* *elegance* pleasure, exception boldness **hedonism**

Words in italic and gray: historical definitions
Words in Roman and black: modern definitions
Words in bold: postmodern definitions

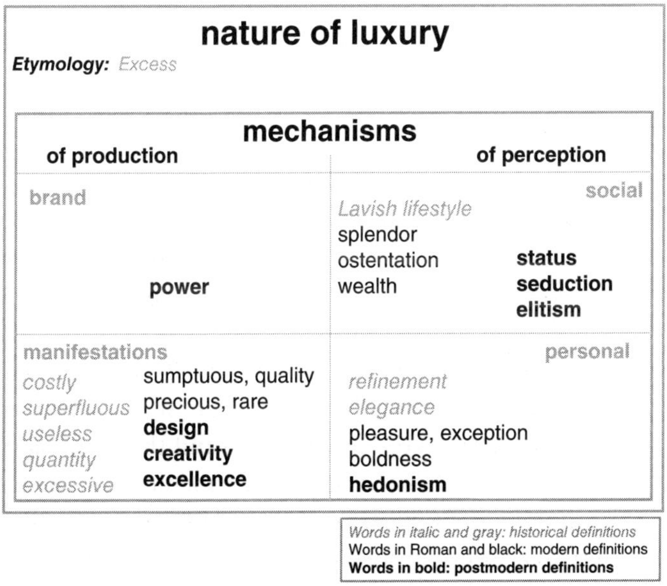

Figure 1.3 History of the Semantic Evolution of the Definitions of the Notion of Luxury

In order to close the loop, it remains to revert to the semantic history of the term *luxury* described earlier and insert the meanings identified in our analytical scheme (see Figure 1.3).

The progressive transformation of the concept becomes more noticeable. A number of modern or postmodern values (referring to lifestyle brands) that characterize contemporary luxury like elitism, hedonism, aesthetic creativity, and seduction can be regrouped within clusters. These meanings are mainly concentrated around social luxury perceptions and the positive connotations of its manifestations: it is a symptom of the growing social importance of luxury, especially through the intermediate luxury consumption, but it also reflects the rise of the brand as its main vehicle—without a doubt, the major and structuring phenomenon of this new market.

Luxury Values

Now that luxury is imposing its positive connotations to the contemporary world, how do consumers perceive it? What are the values they identify with luxury?

The Three Scales

An answer can come from a very relevant study, led by de Barnier, Falcy, and Valette-Florence, on a sample of over 500 persons in France. It allows synthesizing the values currently associated with luxury by consumers. This investigation offers the interest to compare three independent scales of value that explored the perception of luxury by consumers done by Kapferer,[13] Vigneron and Johnson,[14] and finally by Dubois et al.[15]

The statistical convergence of the three models highlights four main types of values, which we classify by order of intensity. In fact, we may recognize here four essential dimensions that consumers consider to be essential for a brand to belong to the luxury world.

---

[13] J.-N. Kapferer, "Why Are We Seduced by Luxury Brands?," *Journal of Brand Management* 6, no. 1 (1998): 44–49.

[14] F. Vigneron and L. W. Johnson, "A Review and a Conceptual Framework of Prestige-Seeking Consumer Behavior," *Academy of Marketing Science Review* 3, no. 1 (1999): 1–15.

[15] B. Dubois, G. Laurent, and S. Czellar, "Consumer Rapport to Luxury: Analyzing Complex and Ambivalent Attitudes," HEC Research Papers Series 736. HEC Paris, 2001.

1. Elitism ("distinction," "select") is the dimension most present simultaneously on the three scales. The historical social dimension of luxury still plays its role fully as an indicator of social success—or a simulacrum of that success. The creation of a sense of belonging to a selected group appears as the essential experience dimension. The creation of a feeling of belonging to a chosen group appears to be the essential dimension of the experience.
2. Unsurprisingly, product quality and high prices are also significant characteristics. The concept of quality can extend to all brand manifestations such as communication, real and virtual places, people, and so on.
3. In the third position we find personal emotional and affective elements, such as hedonism, but with a weaker correlation. This is the generation of pleasure and emotions, key components of postmodern consumption, which applies here to luxury brands.
4. Finally, the power of the brand (resulting from past decisions and actions) appears at the side of reputation and uniqueness.

Through this exercise, the consumer himself gives us his own definition of luxury. And although the fundamental intuition of sociologists (distinction) is confirmed, we discover that the consumer is not less attentive to the means of production of the luxury object and brands than to its personal and social impacts (see Figure 1.4). Yet again, luxury cannot be reduced to its sole effects of display.

Other considerations can be drawn from this study.

First, most consumers think and live luxury only in terms of brands. Could luxury be experienced outside of the brand world? We could refer to the imaginary world of two French novels, *À Rebours*[16] and *Les Choses*[17]: two portraits of characters, consumers obsessed by luxury. In both cases, the brands are absent from their universe: it is the quality of the products that holds their attention. Today, on the contrary, brands appear as the natural vehicles by which luxury plays its primary role in postmodern consumption.

Secondly, each brand develops its own specific strategies, which do not necessarily cover the four sectors of our analytical scheme.

---

[16] J.-K. Huysmans, *À Rebours*. Charpentier, 1884.
[17] G. Perec, *Les Choses*. Julliard, 1965.

nature of luxury

mechanisms

of production	of perception	
brand		**social**
power reputation	elitism	
manifestations		**personal**
quality high price	hedonism	

Finally, the study of de Barnier, Falcy, and Valette-Florence demonstrates the existence of a continuum of luxury with increasing intensity, from mass luxury to unaffordable luxury, via intermediary luxury.

The Semiotic Square of the Consumption Values

We briefly present a tool that will be described in more detail in Chapter 7. We anticipate its use because it can support some reasoning about luxury, especially with regard to the logics of consumer behavior, and thus refine our approach to a general definition of luxury.

This diagram is called a semiotic square. It is a way to present a group of contrary and contradictory concepts focusing on the manner in which they are opposed. These oppositions are dynamic, as the tension between the antagonists produces effects of meaning. (The same way as in an action movie where the opposition between "good" and "evil," between the hero and his opponent, can be the engine of the plot.)

This is also true for the discourses on the motivations of luxury consumers. The diagram of consumption values was originally developed by Jean-Marie Floch to help in the design of a supermarket layout. It covers the distribution of the definitions we have outlined earlier and allows exploring the motives of consumption luxury.

It distinguishes four types of logic (Figure 1.5), which are some of the motivations of possible purchase and who oppose each other or contradict: the logic of need ("we have no more bread"); the logic of interest ("I already have enough coffee at home, but I want to take advantage of this promotion"); the logic of desire ("an exotic dish is a way to travel"); the logic of pleasure ("I am crazy about chocolate"). It goes without saying that a purchase can perfectly obey several logics at the same time, despite their apparent contradictions: I can choose to buy organic chocolate or premium pasta.

If we seek to classify the values associated with luxury in this distribution, we realize that the logics of desire and pleasure on the right side of the square will be the predominant engines. Hedonism is in the logic of pleasure activated by diversionary/aesthetic values; elitism is located on the top right vertex, with the mythical/utopian values. As we noted, luxury brands, even more than others, must make customers dream of possible worlds and provide experiences intense in emotions, dreams, and pleasure.

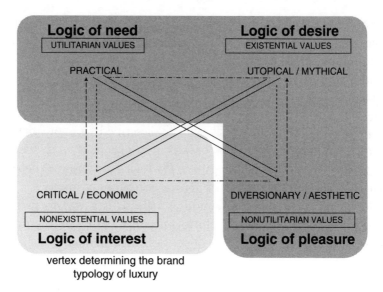

Figure 1.5 Semiotic Square of Consumption Values

But it is also possible to speak of "good deal luxury," sacrificing, partially, the logic of interest. In recent years, websites specializing in "private sales" have been flourishing on the Internet, offering luxury brand products with heavy discounts.

In fact, the economic logics are not identical for true luxury brands and those of intermediate luxury. As its name indicates, intermediate—or accessible—luxury is defined precisely by its affordable price.

In addition to private sales, luxury brands are often interested in developing more affordable collections or products, capitalizing on their notoriety. It is an obviously perilous exercise because of the risk of disrepute. However, some brands have been very successful at it. For the past 10 years, the Ferrari brand has been developing license agreements for all kinds of derivative products in areas that are carefully kept away from its core business: watches, clothes, perfumes, computer equipment, entertainment parks in the Persian Gulf and China, and so on. Ferrari manages the unusual feat of flooding the market with caps or keychains bearing its name and color without altering its true luxury image.

More significant, perhaps, is the current trend that sees middle-market brands, born in general on the left side of the semiotic square of consumption values, developing to the right side, using the codes of behavior of traditional luxury brands in terms of communication, creation, and coherence in the management of brand identity (re)oriented toward luxury. It is a typical movement of mid-range leather-goods brands such as Furla, Longchamp, Coach, Lancel, and so on. Lew Frankfurt, former CEO of the American brand Coach, used to define his brand as "a democratized luxury brand."[18]

Certainly, today, to remain competitive, all brands must excel on all four vertices of the square of consumption values. But intermediate luxury is distinguished from true luxury by its presence on the economic vertex, that is, how it positions itself within the logic of interest. Where the real luxury is not afraid of its relative expensiveness, intermediary luxury seeks minimum cost and affordable prices.

True Luxury, Intermediate Luxury

Historical and current definitions of luxury have been classified according to their receptive and productive dimensions; this has also been applied to the most common representations of consumers on luxury. Finally, some analytical instruments have been introduced.

We have seen that mass brands have learned to manage their operations by adopting the rules of traditional luxury: they seek to be present on the four vertices of the semiotic square of consumption values.

Therefore, what may differentiate a true luxury brand, in the sense that was intended 50 years ago, from a new entrant with a proper strategic understanding of the luxury industry and the talent to run an intermediate luxury positioning? One could mention longevity (the tradition, the legacy), but these criteria do not appear to have been taken into account, at least consciously, by the consumers interviewed for the study of the three scales. Are there other differentiating factors? How to distinguish, for example, Hermès from Bottega Veneta or Fendi?

We can invoke what Jean-Marie Floch calls "the refusal of an overall economic hegemony,"[19] a brand attitude focusing on other values

---

[18] Suzy Menkes, "Coach Gallops into Europe," *International Herald Tribune*, November 1, 2010.

[19] J.-M. Floch and E. Roux, "Gérer l'ingérable: La contradiction interne à toute maison de luxe," *Décisions Marketing* 9 (1996): 15–23.

than the pure logic of profit. In other words, where intermediate luxury is seeking affordability, true luxury is going to position itself not as unaffordable but as foreign to the issue: the left side of the consumption square seems deserted. The stakes are elsewhere.

Very high luxury brands cultivate this type of signal to their consumers when they guarantee their products for life (as Bally was still doing in 2000 for the men's shoe model Scribe that it was repairing when sent back to headquarters), or even when they try to suggest that there is no preferential treatment—that all their customers receive the same (exceptional) attention to service, regardless of their volume of purchases. Some very selective brands can even promote sales models based on cooptation, where purchasing power seem irrelevant, in appearance, at least. This is a way of saying "our demand for quality puts us above mercantile considerations." This confirms the differentiating role of the critical/economy vertex of the consumption square for true luxury brands (Figure 1.5).

In strict business logic, it is an irrational behavior and in fact it will naturally find its limits. But it is interesting to see that the brand claims it as a posture, that it makes it one of the keys of its identity. This is a major point of differentiation between true luxury and intermediate luxury: the latter cannot afford indifference, or even a hint of indifference, to economic imperatives. One can see also, in this somehow unnatural posture of a true luxury brand, a deviation that brings us back to the etymological sources of the word *luxury*. Luxury is an excess, a gap, a discontinuity, an eccentricity. It involves a shift from a norm, from a position retained as normal.

Eccentric Luxury

Let's position luxury as a differential with respect to a standard. Can the conditions of this eccentricity be specified? What norms or standards will real luxury brands break from?

For Jean-Marie Floch, the foil is the natural mercantile attitude seeking the optimization of profits in the short term. In fact, anything that is driven by logics of mass markets should remain outside of the realm of luxury: Is the consumer not seeking there, precisely, signs of distinction?

A definition from Jean-Louis Dumas-Hermès (late chairman of Hermès), reported by Lallement, goes in the same direction: "luxury brand is one that manages to meet three conditions: designing beautiful objects; choosing the consumer as the best vector of communication; and finally, deciding freely."[20] What a great formula! Beauty; clients as heralds of the brand; and, finally, freedom, where we meet again with the refusal of the overall economic logics.

Designing beautiful objects is not the exclusive domain of luxury anymore (think of the design of Ikea, Conran, etc.), and the concept of beauty is subjective. Choosing its consumer as a main vector of communication is already a most sought-after strategy, including for brands that aspire to lifestyle status. But it applies in areas other than luxury, for example, in the activation of social networks on the Internet.

We are left with the third part of the Dumas-Hermès statement: freedom. This independence from constraints, standards, and habits is the prerogative of a luxury that is defined by something extraordinary, a meaningful and relevant differential gap. The luxury product distinguishes us from others; it is a sign of being exceptional and freed (with respect to specific norms). Similarly, it should be distributed and promoted in an outstanding manner reflecting somehow this freedom.

Deviation from Norms.   Such would be the essence of luxury, the basis for most of the definitions we have seen, for both the productive and perceptual types.

Luxury is not only the denial of mass mercantilism, but also the refusal of certain norms, within the meaning of a convention accepted by the greatest number, a positioning reflecting the distinctive character of luxury as highlighted by sociologists. The antithesis of a standard, luxury will be rare, elitist, expensive, beautiful, original, surprising, superfluous, refined, creative, inaccessible, representative of authority, and so on. Everything will depend on the chosen norms and on the type of perceived deviation.

If one accepts this definition as the "mother" of all the others, the implications are many. Each brand will have to set its own luxury, that is, the way to be competitive as a luxury brand, specifying both the norms it intends to depart from and the differentials on which this gap will rely.

In fact, most major luxury brands carefully cultivate their originality (i.e. their differentials), which they often develop in several directions at

---

[20] O. Lallement, *Caractérisation des éléments spécifiques de la marque de luxe dans l'esprit du consommateur. Une étude des images mentales associées a un visuel publicitaire.* IAE Montpellier, 2000.

a time: a way for them to express luxury, but also to affirm the richness of their identity. This ability to mark its difference may characterize a luxury brand only if it is accompanied by a positioning on the right side of the semiotic square of consumption values: playing on the logics of desire and pleasure, respectively activating myths and dreams as well as fun and aesthetics.

Consider the case of Ferrari: the prestigious manufacturer used to be known to limit the number of vehicles it produced each year. From 2007 to 2017, the number of cars manufactured was oscillating between 5,000 and 7,000 cars per year. This Malthusianism was first a guarantee of exclusivity for the happy (few) customers of the brand. Since 2017, the policy has been altered and the volume of cars manufactured increased to around 8,500; the number of cars shipped was 10,131. It introduces also a spectacular difference from Porsche, its reference competitor, which shipped 280,800 vehicles in 2019. The other "luxury" of Ferrari obviously rests on its almost-century-old presence in the circuits of international motor racing and especially in Formula 1. Since 1950, the Scuderia Ferrari has won 238 Grand Prix races, 16 Constructor World titles, and 15 Drivers' World titles. It is a euphemism to say that the amateurs of exceptional automobiles dream about Ferrari cars: in 70 years of existence, the brand has been able to jealously preserve its status as a myth. The absolute differential belongs to the winner with respect to all the other (defeated) competitors.

The glassmaker Daum cultivates its difference by being the only European brand to produce "pâte de cristal" using the lost wax method. Its history is intimately linked to that of the Arts décoratifs and l'Ecole de Nancy in the early twentieth century. Daum appears, in this regard, to be a good example of these traditional luxury brands relying on a glorious past often linked to an artistic movement. It is an asset with which younger competitors can hardly compete; however, the prestige of tradition alone is not enough to guarantee the relevance or today's competitiveness of Daum's product offering.

Reasonable Luxury

As a counterpoint to these two examples, the Zara case can bring further light to the luxury concept. From an original business model, this brand of mainly ready-to-wear is the only one to propose, in a continuous, fast, and efficient way, the latest fashion products. Zara founded its difference on the service (new products every other week) and psychological comfort (a guarantee to be in fashion) that it provides to its clients through a logistical mastery, superior to that of its competitors. Its time-to-market (between 2D designs to product in the store) is less than two weeks.

The approach is innovative, and it is the most successful business model in that industry. This success is based on logic of volume supported by logistical excellence, which position the brand outside of the perimeter that we have qualified as true luxury. This is confirmed by Zara's positioning on the square of consumption values. The constant renewal of its products is both strength and weakness: the ever-fluctuating universe of the brand cannot offer strong representations, the possible world that consumers would dream about. Zara is weak on the utopian/mythical vertex. However, it is anchored in hedonism—pleasure and fun to be in fashion—which gives competitiveness to its offering. Moreover, the brand cultivates the research for minimum costs in order to be able to offer products at the lowest possible prices, which is the antithesis of the strategies of true luxury (see Figure 1.5).

Zara is therefore a brand of affordable (or mass) consumption, selling to the highest possible number of customers. Of course, Zara offers a distinctive feature, fashion at a reasonable price, but this distinction is a fugitive one. It is a very relevant business positioning and no doubt still promised to a rich future; however, it cannot be confused with that of real luxury.

Authentic Luxury

In opposition to Zara's positioning—mass affordable latest fashion—we can evoke the watchmaker Patek Philippe's 2018 advertising campaign for its men's collection: a video in black and white, a timeless tone, a father with his young son, a mother with her daughter in luxury contexts around the world; a watch model shown at the end of the video after the legendary slogan: "You never actually own a Patek Philippe. You merely look after it for the next generation." The slogan has been used for more than 10 years, and that makes it one with the most longevity. The advertising highlights tradition and heritage values, permanence, and uniqueness of the product, all in opposition to the logic of volume.

The key ingredients of true luxury are gathered in this communication, cleverly removing any culpability for the buyer. The economic and utilitarian dimensions are fully occulted in favor of the transmission of values: the watch is no longer a luxury in the sense of an expensive whim; it becomes a pure symbol of tradition, and a wise investment.

We have used the term *true luxury* to distinguish it from *intermediate luxury*, because the question of authenticity is decisive. True luxury never lies or pretends to be what it is not. Patek Philippe promotes its authenticity through the transparency between its brand identity and its communication. The watchmaker shows itself as a family business whose roots date back to the nineteenth century, defending a lasting legacy of excellence and innovation and intending to promote its watches through its brand values. The brand comments its own campaigns in terms that clearly refer to the existential values of the top right vertex of the semiotic square of consumption values: "our visuals show a father introducing his son to the idealized world of Patek Philippe—a world where our customers can belong and share the perennial values of our family business."

Luxury, Being and Appearing

The issue of authenticity is an obsession of our time. Very fashionable in academic circles, it concerns, rightly, most of the managers of luxury brands whether product- or service-based: it is probably the major challenge that faces brands in the twenty-first century. The online *Merriam-Webster Dictionary* gives this definition of the adjective "authentic": "True to one's own personality, spirit, or character."

The French Dictionary *Le Petit Robert* proposes: "That which expresses a profound truth of the individual and not superficial habits or conventions": one understands how luxury, in a perpetual quest for distinction and assertiveness in a world of appearances, may be trying to acquire this quality. How do brands manage to meet this requirement? Another semiotic square can help us understand it.

The Square of Veracity

The semiotic square can be applied to the meanings generated by the semantic axis "being/appearing": It is the square of veracity, proposed by the semiotician A. J. Greimas (1917–1992) and used extensively in the analysis of representations.

This scheme may initially seem abstract, but its use is simple. As in the previous model, contrary and contradictory relationships generate four types of concepts: being/appearing, not being/not appearing.

From the tensions created between these different poles emerge several categories of meaning that will allow us to classify various discourses of luxury and, hence, better identify issues that brands have to face.

Being and appearing simultaneously is truth: in other words, one is really what he seems to be. On the other hand, being and not appearing is the secret: one does not show what he really is. Not being and appearing is the lie or sham and imitation: one sets out to be something other than what he or she really is. Finally, not appearing and not being escapes the space of discourses: it shows nothing and is nothing. It is here in the category of wrong, false, or simulacrum.

Armed with this representation, we can characterize the different forms of luxury we have mentioned so far (see Figure 1.6). The sides of the square can be assimilated to axes of intensity on which we can position various categories of luxury—or, more specifically, various brands.

What we called "true luxury," to distinguish it from "intermediate luxury," is positioned around the top left vertex, in the category of the truth. However, we see that we need to introduce a separate new

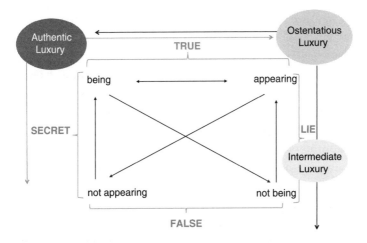

Figure 1.6 Semiotic Square of Veracity

distinction, because that genuine luxury can be either displayed, such as the bright red Ferrari car, or kept discreet, as the Patek Philippe watch.

Of course, this expensive Swiss watch is also noticeable: for many potential buyers, it will be important that it can be displayed, and Patek Philippe does not intend to discourage such buyers. We feel, however, that its watches have no vocation to be staged with the same ostentation of bright Italian luxury cars or golden Rolexes with diamonds. Patek Philippe communication respects this nuance. In the visual communication material, the product is not predominant; it appears almost inadvertently, as a symbolic detail of a scene centered on the transmission of family values. In Ferrari communication, on the contrary, the car is the inescapable star.

If Patek Philippe is positioned on the upper left vertex of the square at the intersection of the secret and truth axis, Ferrari would be more on the top horizontal line on the right side of our scheme.

No one doubts the authenticity of the luxury of Ferrari, which is based on three sources of differentiations:

1. Its innovative capacity at the level of motorization and design of high-performance cars
2. Its competence, continually renewed, to be competitive in Formula 1 racing
3. The relative rarity of its cars maintained through appropriate self-imposed productive limitations

We are thus in the presence of two brands, Ferrari and Patek Philippe, both having unambiguously established their status as authentic luxury. The fact that this real luxury is conspicuous for Ferrari and discreet for Patek Philippe derives from the use made of their products by their respective consumers. The profile of the majority of the owners of branded products influences their brand identity, but there will always be the exception of the "Ferrarista" who uses his car discreetly and the newly rich showing off with his new Patek Philippe.

Leaving the area of true luxury of the upper part of the veracity square, we find, on the right-hand side, the area of intermediate luxury. Taken in contradictory dynamics, intermediate luxury claims appearance, but it is dragged down toward the false by its economic constraints. It can be located anywhere on the axis of the lie except on the vertex of not being, where it would simply cease to exist. Intermediate luxury reflects the continuum of modern luxury: brands ranging throughout the axis of imitation (lie), from the most expensive ostentation to the low range of light and cheap imitation still able to promote a meaningful sham of distinction.

There is, of course, no judgment of value in our analysis: all positions are legitimate, and a brand can hold its identity at some point of the scale, provided that it remains aware of its positioning.

In the world of intermediate luxury, the ambition is to give a feeling of exclusivity and of true luxury, thanks to products that remain economically affordable to the greatest number. It is therefore a world of appearance and imitation, located on the right side of the veracity square. And for good reason: facing economic constraints, these brands cannot differentiate as strongly as others merely through the superior quality of their products. They cannot avail themselves of a deep authenticity and, therefore, their clients would not find any advantage cultivating discretion and secrets: they have nothing worthwhile to hide.

Intermediate luxury wants and must be seen: it will therefore find strength in mass communication, which does not forbid the preservation of some form of distinction by carefully choosing its vectors. Brands such as Dolce & Gabbana, Longchamp, and even Ralph Lauren and Michael Kors have been successful in this positioning by creating, thanks to the talent of their communicators, an imaginary world seemingly reserved for a selected few but in fact transposable to the multitude. This is the strategy of intermediate luxury: feeling of access to luxury, for everybody and at affordable prices.

The rise of a brand such as Swarovski illustrates the success of this category. Crystals substitute for diamonds that few people can afford. It is crystal, but it sparkles: it is made for display! The *strass* (or rhinestone), icon of our times, attribute of a civilization of virtual fantasy (such as costume jewelry) that cultivates superficiality. The "do as if" creates a sort of a pact between the brand and its consumers, through a playful communication where the wildest desires are encouraged through image.

Intermediate luxury (and the *strass*) is therefore distributed along the scale of the lie/imitation axis of the veracity square, which spans from appearing to not being, where reigns the need of imitation of social classes, tribes, or characters.

The veracity square highlights the continuity existing between intermediate and ostentatious luxury: it is just a question of a difference in gradation—or resources—and, to some extent, intermediate luxury can be included as a degraded version of ostentatious luxury. This opens new opportunities for segmentation. This is an area where Ferrari has become a master: in the Ferrari Stores, the general public can cultivate its passion for the brand by buying all sorts of gadgets, T-shirts, key chains, and so on, in the colors of the Scuderia, while some happy few, through a completely disjoint distribution network, may acquire its automobiles.

Five Sources of Legitimacy

If luxury is defined by an opposition to a standard, if the credibility and the competitiveness of a luxury brand are built on the choice of this norm and on the type of selected deviations, what may be the main sources that will establish the legitimacy of luxury brands?

Gilmore and Pine, in their book *Authenticity*, suggest five main sources of brand authenticity.[21] They can be extended to the world of luxury.

What the authors call *authenticity* does not correspond exactly to the notion of true or real luxury that we introduced with the veracity square. Rather, they deal with brand credibility, that is, their ability to be recognized as a genuine sign of luxury. Whether we consider authentic, intermediate, discreet, or ostentatious luxury, all brands need sources of luxury legitimacy, each of them according to their respective needs. The intermediary luxury, for example, does not escape this requirement; but because of economic constraints, it will focus its efforts in communication and marketing where they are the most efficient, rather than on the products themselves.

Here are the sources of authenticity identified by Gilmore and Pine:

- *The natural.* It is the prerogative of the brands that rely on natural materials to legitimize an ecological approach, or cultivate a *Rousseauist* simple wildlife. Luxury has always used this approach: linen, cashmere, vicuña, precious metals and woods, and plant extracts are often utilized by luxury brands in products and communication, even more so when the simplicity of the materials is

---

[21] J. H. Gilmore and B. J. Pine II, *Authenticity: What Consumers Really Want*. Harvard Business School Press, 2007.

synonymous with scarcity, thus reinforcing the true luxury symbolic value.

- *The original.* The two authors especially have in mind the creative originality of objects or visuals. This source of differential legitimacy can be extended to all the brand manifestations. To be original means to be different from everything that existed previously. In communication, intermediate luxury cultivates originality, and even provocation. But it is also a source of major legitimacy for the big couture houses created by Dior, Chanel, Ferragamo, Valentino, and Saint-Laurent; combining their values of tradition with the audacity of talented couturiers, these houses manage to cultivate their strong identity.

- *The exceptional.* This is another way to express a way to go beyond the ordinary. The authors apply it primarily to service activities, to describe an action especially sensitive to the needs of the client. In luxury, we will find hotels that base their reputation on this dimension, with a hint of extravagance—as with the famous Icelandic Ice Hotel, entirely carved in ice, or even tropical palaces of the luxury chain Aman Resorts, where staff feed fish reefs by hand. But we can add all the arts and crafts, and brands that rely on outstanding craftsmanship, such as the Hermès (Puiforcat, John Lobb, Saint-Louis) group.

- *The referential.* The authors mean evocations of other contexts, historical in general, that serve as a benchmark for their clients; for example, the golden age of Roman *Dolce Vita*. The differential in this case is temporal: the concept of luxury is emerging out of a contrast between the present and the mythical period with which the brand wants to associate, in order to make us dream. This period will be suggested by an iconic object or a historical figure. The glamour of Ferragamo is built around international divas of the 1960s or 1970s (Audrey Hepburn, Sofia Loren, Anna Magnani), while Tod's seeks representatives among a certain Anglo-Saxon elegance: Steve McQueen, Sigourney Weaver. Other brands will put forward their association with an aristocrat, an artist, or a legendary athlete of the time. This so-called sponsorship from beyond the grave is a source of legitimacy more easily used by traditional historical brands. New entrants must use more recent or less-explicit references, often with lesser success.

- *The authority*. Authority is understood as an ability to influence others based on a humanist cause. This resource is used by brands calling upon the values of solidarity, ecology, fair trade, and so on. So far, luxury has used these themes only anecdotally. Obviously, brands are careful to communicate all their social initiatives, but only a few luxury brands base their identity on these themes. There is, indeed, little correlation between luxury and ecology. The first cultivates rarity, exclusivity, and distinction, while the second reasons in terms of environment and mass phenomena. The value of selectivity places luxury at odds with any mass logic: if luxury has the means to pay its handicraft suppliers decently, it remains suspicious of environmental recklessness by its taste for rare materials.

New Luxury

The following is an extract from a Pierre Bergé *New York Times* interview in 2015.

> First, I want to say this: The time of Chanel, Balenciaga, Dior and, of course, Yves (Saint Laurent), well, that time is over. Second, so too is the era of haute couture. Completely over, gone. This is why what we call luxe today is just ridiculous. To me, that whole industry now—all money and marketing—is all something like a lie. But people's perception of what luxury is has changed in such an extraordinary way. Their conception of what is fashion is so different now from the sort of fashion that Yves created—that I created with him. That no longer exists. A handbag that a woman takes with her all over the place—to a grocery store, through the airport—I cannot imagine how that can be considered luxury. That is not luxury.[22]

Coming from someone who has been one of the major actors of the luxury industry for 40 years, this is quite an unexpected but extremely relevant statement. Pierre Bergé, co-founder of the brand Yves Saint Laurent, was only reflecting what a lot of luxury consumers are feeling too: weariness and perplexity in front of the existential paradox of most of the self-called luxury brands that propose industrial products

---

[22] Elizabeth Paton, "Pierre Bergé on Luxury, Morocco and Hedi Slimane," *New York Times*, October 28, 2015. http://www.nytimes.com/2015/10/29/fashion/pierre-berge-on-luxury-morocco-and-hedi-slimane.html?_r=0.

manufactured and distributed in great volume and marketed as luxury products in terms of communication and price.

Product and Experience Luxuries

Specific trends are showing that some parts of the market have started to escape from the most traditional acceptance of luxury toward a more accessible, more experiential, and maybe more moral attitude toward it. In fact, we have been observing for more than 20 years the emergence of a luxury of experience in parallel to what we could call the luxury of products. Besides the ownership of products, such as watches, clothes, jewelry, accessories, fragrances, and beauty products, has grown the desire and therefore the markets for adventurous or luxury travel (Mont Blanc and Everest have never seen so many visitors), space trips, haute cuisine, spas, extraordinary shows (opera, concerts, sports events), and so on. The phenomenon goes beyond the emergence of new industries proposing luxury experiences like the ones we just liste, but also the experiences built around the products including physical environment, planned consumer path (pre- and post-purchase), associations to other themes than the product itself, and so on.

The change is not a banality as it has a lot of management implications for the brands that want to be competitive in this field and, frankly, none of the traditional luxury brands can afford not to consider this new dimension. After all, retail distribution always has had an experiential dimension, fragrances too. The advent of the Internet renders pre- and after-sales services even more important. Moreover, all service brands were already involved in experiential management. It is not a major discontinuity of the consumption process because, as we saw earlier in Figure 1.4., the product purchase has to do with the personal satisfaction of ownership but also with the experience of being socially involved in association with the products ("Have they seen me with my new Rolex?"). It is a shift at the microeconomic level with product brands paying more attention to the surrounding context in terms of place and time, and the purchase process of the products, as well as a shift at the macroeconomic level, with new industries and services defining a new kind of luxury.

Most of the managerial issues raised by experiential luxury are related to creation in general. How do you create these unforgettable, exceptional, intense moments in a better way than your competitors? Designing ambiances, atmospheres, and contexts is more complex and broad than just designing a product and often requires different skills. Event management, where ambiance, atmospheres, and contexts need to be created, is becoming crucial in the luxury field.

The Vaporization of Luxury

Yves Michaud introduces an interesting metaphor in characterizing the change of focus from product to experience luxury as a *vaporization of luxury*.[23]

As experience takes precedence over product, the objects tend to dissolve themselves into a vaster and composite multisensory space. This ethereal condition that characterizes a gaseous state like vapor finds its natural place into the trend of semantization of consumption initially highlighted by Barthes when he introduces the notion of "universal semantization of usage"[24] and by Baudrillard, who states that objects have become signs belonging themselves to larger systems of meaning where symbolization, virtualization, miniaturization, and transparence are becoming characteristics of the products we purchase.[25]

We find also a correspondence between the notion of product vaporization and the concept of aura introduced by Walter Benjamin, which he defines as being what makes an art piece authentic and unique, that is, "the unique phenomenon of a distance, however close it may be."[26] We may extrapolate that some consumption objects are so exceptional that they can generate emotional shocks, and that they can qualify as having a genuine aura (an engagement ring, a vintage collection car, a famous precious stone), a sort of halo, which transfigurates them, makes them distant, apparently unapproachable—although proximate because they are accessible through purchase. This could be a definition of luxury, where the power of an object reaches beyond its functional purpose and forces the customer into a different world, due to the apparent inaccessibility, exceptionality, intensity, and, sometimes, strangeness of the product.

[23] Y. Michaud, *Le nouveau luxe: Experiences, arrogance, authenticité*. Paris: Stock, 2013.
[24] R. Barthes R. "Réthorique de l'image," *Communications* 4, no. 4 (1964): 40–51.
[25] J. Baudrillard, *Le système des objets*. Paris: Gallimard, 1978.
[26] W. Benjamin, *La obra de arte en la época de la reproductibilidad técnica*. Madrid: Taurus, 1936.

Exclusive versus Exceptional Luxuries

Rather than being constant and predictable, as we highlighted at the beginning of the chapter, the evolution of the connotation of the word *luxury* and its related perception of the phenomenon continues these days. As shown in Figure 1.7, the perception of luxury and its associated values changes according to the cultural and historical contexts.

This confirms Michaud's vaporization trend, where experience is proving to be the biggest expansion of the new luxury today. The figure highlights the fact that some of the values, such as hedonism, preciousness, memory, and sophistication, of the traditional luxury remain shared with the new one. Besides the two dichotomies, product/experience and exclusivity/exceptional, the main divide is related to the social/individual dialectic. The ostentatious nature and the sense of belonging to a restricted and exclusive group that is characteristic of the traditional luxury are essentially of a social nature, whereas new luxury is much more attached to a personal feeling where the social

Luxury market values evolution		
Traditional Luxury	**Evergreen**	**New Luxury**
Exclusivity		**Exceptionality**
Social/Political		**Individual**
Porduct Focus		**Experience Focus**
Inaccessible	Sophisticateness	Innovation
Opulence	Pleasure (Hedonism)	Authenticity
Non-essential	Preciousness	Passion
Investment	Extraordinary	Personal
Excess	Expertise	Searches
Ostentation	Precision	Newness
Elitism	Legacy	Remix
Membership	Memory	Privacy
		Skills
		Resources
		Journey
		Access

Figure 1.7   Evolution from Traditional to New Luxury

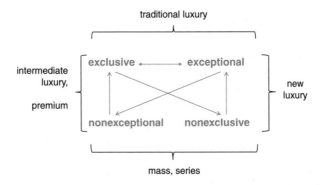

Figure 1.8   Semiotic Square on Different Types of Luxury

dimension is nonessential—even though the craze of selfies proves that when people experience something exceptional, they rush to share it on the Internet.

Within the process of analysis of Jim Thompson's brand identity in late 2015, we asked Professor Jorge Lozano (chair of theory of information at Complutense University in Madrid) to reflect on the reality and meaning of the emerging expression *new luxury*. The result of his reflection is a semiotic square (Figure 1.8) built on the semantic axis of exclusivity versus exceptionality that was published later in 2018.[27]

The notion of exclusivity implies the other qualities mentioned earlier, such as being rare, expensive, and inaccessible. The most meaningful dimension in which the notion of exceptionality can be opposed to exclusivity (and therefore considered as a contrary) lies in the fact that the latter is of the private, individual, and subjective sphere, whereas the former is in the social and public domain. Building the semiotic square by formalizing the contradictories to exclusive and exceptional, we come up with a scheme that classifies most of the luxury categories we have mentioned so far:

- Traditional luxury will combine both exclusive and exceptional. A vintage Jaguar type E could be an example.

[27] J. Lozano, *Semiótica del (nuevo) lujo. Entre lo exclusivo y lo excepcional,* in *Documentos del presente. Una mirada semiótica* (Jorge Lozano y Miguel Martín coord.). Madrid: Lengua de Trapo, 2018.

- The opposite position that combines nonexclusivity and nonexceptionality is mass luxury (an obvious oxymoron), which applies to all the brand products that are trying to trigger a luxury perception while being chain-manufactured. Marc by Marc Jacobs or Ibis hotels are relevant examples of this positioning.
- The side of the square combining exclusivity and nonexceptionality is the premium segment, or intermediate luxury. We will find there most of the wines and spirits brands, Svarowski, and Audi.
- Finally, the side of exceptional and nonexclusive defines new luxury, where accessibility becomes the main differentiating element with respect to traditional luxury.

In line with the notion of exceptionality that has been introduced, we could risk a new definition of luxury that would reflect this characteristic as well as moralize somewhat this type of consumption. Is luxury an exceptional co-investment from both parties concerned—the brand and the consumer?

> Products, services, experiences can be qualified as being of luxury nature, when both the brand and the customer have invested their resources beyond the norm(s) in the respective processes of proposing and acquiring them.

The customer investment goes beyond the acquisition price, it may involve a long research, a long study, sacrifices, and so on.

To conclude this section on new luxury, we quote Jorge Lozano, referred to earlier:

> Today, in the realm of Generalized Simulation, under the rules of big data, where the future becomes irrelevant and presentism reigns as the major tendency, emerges the authentic, which although it cannot replace the unique, the uniqueness, fundamental characteristic of the exclusive, it serves as a consolation. For its part, the exceptional of the original and genuine, of what possesses aura and belongs to the core of luxury, currently adopts other pregnant manifestations of subjectivity, expressed in cyberspace, configured with new materials. That new exceptionality can live perfectly with the non-exclusive, promoting what I consider to be the new luxury.[28]

---

[28] Michaud, *Le nouveau luxe.*

Conclusion on the Notion of Luxury

Several lessons can be drawn from this very general overview of the different dimensions of luxury.

Luxury became first an elitist and rewarding practice and then, under the impulse of brands, a market that is submitted to an ever-increasing segmentation. Today, there is not one luxury but many of them, each aimed at a specific category of population, characterized by their purchasing power, social group codes, and specific ambitions. We must get used to an acceptance of the term much broader than in the past. It has now become necessary to clarify, each time, what sort of luxury we want to talk about.

Despite their many manifestations, luxuries provide some common benefits. Luxury divides and unites at the same time; it produces distinction under the banner of brands; it blurs (with the exception of very exclusive luxury) the line between discomfort and opulence, but it promises to all social layers to escape the mass by consuming better (in the case of true luxury) or just a little better (in the case of intermediate luxury) than our peers. Luxury re-creates tribes, groups of the happy few being in the sharing of practical or symbolic qualities. This may be the excellence of a product, originality, the newness of a style, or, more informally, the manifestation of a certain state of mind. Luxury should both make us dream (logic of desire) and comfort us by communicating sensual or emotional satisfactions (logic of pleasure).

Luxury works in opposition to a norm, to a convention shared by the greatest number—the "vulgar," in the etymological sense of the term. In this sense, the lapidary definition of Coco Chanel perfectly expresses its essence: "Luxury is the opposite of vulgarity."

The challenge for luxury brands is going to be defining what kind of convention it wants to be distinguished from and by which means it will show its differences. From there follows its positioning and its strategy. Authentic and discreet luxury follows the saying that "money does not matter." It is from the mercantile norms that it intends to deviate. Economic issues are occulted in favor of the affirmation of perennial values. Its eccentricity will be modeled on the axes of aesthetic research, qualitative perfection, rejection of the ephemeral, in short, of an investment of exception. For intermediate luxury, the norms it dissociates from are those of a degraded version of daily life—the ordinary—from which it promises to escape in a fugitive whiff of distinction and fantasy, as in role playing.

There are diverse means by which luxury is distinguished: the natural, the original, the exceptional, the referential, and the authority, suggest Gilmore and Pine. But other ways can be mentioned: lifestyles, cultures, know-how (such as very high quality crafts), and technologies (e.g., it just went bankrupt the American manufacturer Tesla Motors, which aspires to become a luxury brand of electric automobiles) are all potential sources to establish true luxury brands … as long as they offer us extraordinary and exceptional experiences and continue to make us dream.

And finally, luxury is anthropological. It is a constant and natural hedonistic research of human beings of all time.

Chapter 2

Specificities of the Luxury Industry

Representatives of any business sector are usually eager to assert that their business is different from any other, but managers working in the luxury industry are possibly the only ones who are justified in claiming so. The luxury sector really *is* different. This is due partly to the amount of creative talent needed for a luxury brand to be successful, and partly to the very different way in which a luxury brand with a worldwide market needs to be run. Three major differences will be identified below. We will then briefly examine the major requirements for success in this business and conclude by identifying the main companies operating in this field.

What Is So Different About the Luxury Industry?

The three major differences between the luxury industry and the non-luxury segment are company size, financial characteristics, and the time factor.

Company Size

In almost every business, size is a major—if not the most important—element in comparing firms or industries. But in the luxury world, size doesn't seem to matter that much. In general, luxury businesses are small, but they are respected and have impressive reputations. Dior Fashion had annual sales of approximately €3,500 million in 2019, while the Peugeot Group had annual sales of €74 billion—so, in fact, Peugeot is 20 times bigger than Dior Fashion. General Motors had sales of around €135 billion, 40 times those of Dior Fashion. The number of employees in each case is probably in the same ratio, if not higher.

But if you were to ask an American, Japanese, or Chinese consumer to name a French product or a French company, they would name Dior before Peugeot. This can be explained by brand awareness: the Dior brand is better known, worldwide, than the Peugeot brand. And this very high awareness comes from the fact that consumers have a genuine interest in luxury and fashion brands. They read about them in magazines and want to know more about them.

LVMH, the luxury-goods giant with a portfolio of more than 70 brands, had total annual sales of approximately €54 billion in 2019. Compare this with Zara Inditex, with €28 billion, or Gap, with €15. In other words, the average LVMH brand—which incorporates some of the most powerful brands in the luxury industry—is about 20 times smaller than Zara or Gap, and the biggest brand in the portfolio of LVMH is probably smaller than Zara or Gap.

We can conclude, therefore, that luxury brands are rather small but with very strong awareness among consumers. So, despite their prestigious image and their advertising presence all over the world, luxury companies are generally small to medium-sized enterprises (the exceptions being the larger conglomerates of small individual firms). Some companies are very small. Cardin has worldwide annual sales of only €10 million, and Carven has sales of around €5–10 million. This is much smaller than a Volkswagen dealership in Athens or a small group of five supermarkets in Birmingham. But, of course, Cardin and Carven remain worldwide brands.

How do such relatively small businesses achieve such a strong presence in the mind of the consumer?

Sales Figures Are Difficult to Compare

In the luxury industry, comparing levels of sales across companies can be like trying to compare apples with oranges, as corporate figures may comprise very different elements. If we take the sales figures for Louis Vuitton, things are relatively simple because they include sales in the group's 450 stores worldwide. But Carven's sales figures, for example, reflect retail sales at its stores, ready-to-wear sales at wholesale outlets and department stores, export sales, and revenues from licenses given to outside enterprises. As a rule of thumb, wholesale sales are approximately half of retail sales, export sales are generally 20% of retail sales, and license royalties amount in general to 10% of billings, which can in turn come from retail, wholesale, and export sales. Thus, it just doesn't make sense to compare the two companies in terms of their sales figures.

To compare the power of two brands, one would have to multiply part of the activity by a coefficient to account for differences in export sales and wholesale sales, for example, so that everything would be computed as a final retail sales amount. But this would still be misleading, because a brand developing essentially through license agreements will be weaker than a brand that controls 100% of its activities at retail. Also, in most cases, the split between retail, wholesale, export, and license royalties isn't given, so assumptions are difficult to make.

The fact that some brands are developed through licenses, with sometimes, for example in the case of perfumes, royalties from these accounting for only 3–4% of their sales, explains why luxury businesses are sometimes very small, even when the brand has a strong presence worldwide in various stores. However, a brand such as Hermès, which (except for its perfumes) sells almost exclusively in its own stores, can still have annual sales of €6.8 billion in 2019. It may not be as big as Peugeot or Renault, but for a luxury company, it is quite impressive.

The mix of activities makes it difficult to understand exactly what is meant when executives of luxury companies declare sales targets of, say, €100 million in China or Japan. Are they referring to total sales, as will be reported in their consolidated financial statements, or do they mean retail volume, which may earn them only €3–5 million in license royalties? There is a significant difference.

As a rule, these sorts of statements should be considered carefully, given that, as we have seen, comparing businesses in financial terms can be quite difficult.

Limited Number of Staff

The fact that most luxury-goods companies are small or medium-sized enterprises has an obvious consequence: they also have a limited number of staff. In China, for example, the most successful luxury brands have staff numbers of only 100 to 1,000, most of them working in stores. The "small enterprise" element is also amplified by the fact that luxury brands must have a global presence. It is probably safe to say that there are more marketing executives in companies such as Procter & Gamble or Nestlé than in the total luxury-goods sector. Several elements contribute to this situation.

First, some companies are not just small; they can be very small. They may operate with just a small design studio that monitors trends and designs products, and may subcontract all the other activities to licensees and distributors. So, the next-most important area of activity after the studio is the legal department, or even an outside lawyer, which prepares and follows up contracts with outside partners. Some fashion companies have global headcounts that might not exceed 15 to 30 people. For example, the Nina Ricci brand has a design studio and a limited number of directly operated stores, while all its manufacturing and distribution are subcontracted.

This tendency to subcontract production activities is the second very particular aspect of the luxury field. Chanel doesn't have its own factories manufacturing all its ready-to-wear items or leather goods. Often, luxury-goods companies have just one or two factories, making prototypes and some product lines. The rest of the manufacturing is carefully controlled but is done by subcontractors. For example, the various components of most luxury-brand watches are generally produced by different companies before the final item is assembled in a fully owned workshop in Switzerland.

An automotive business is all about the factory, machinery, and equipment, but luxury brands are about design and communicating a message. Where are the products made? Who manufactures them? How many consumers know that companies in the LVMH Group, Bally, or Prada have some of their goods or, most probably, product components manufactured in China? What challenges does this pose at the production level? It seems that these questions are never raised.

Third, aside from the creative activity, the most important part of the luxury industry process is the sale. At Lancôme, probably 80% of the company's worldwide employees stand behind a counter. At Gucci, a very important part of the process happens in the stores. To make a career at Prada or Salvatore Ferragamo, it makes sense to start out working in a store—because this is where contact is made with the consumer. Very few of a luxury brand's employees will be based at headquarters, as all the investment goes into the stores. Ferragamo's group headquarters, Palazzo Feroni in Florence, also serves as the worldwide flagship store and a museum, an important tool for communicating with consumers.

So, the average luxury-goods company is small. Its sales figures include elements that are difficult to assess and to compare. A lot of activity at the level of manufacturing and distribution is subcontracted. And staff numbers are very limited.

Financial Characteristics

In studying the different luxury companies, and as we will confirm later in this book, it quickly becomes noticeable that a significant number of them are losing money. In any other industrial sector, a firm losing money is rapidly eliminated, merges with its competitors, or goes bankrupt. In the luxury-goods industry, there are brands that have been losing money for 5 or even 10 years and that survive as part of a luxury group or as a diversification within another industrial company. Bic, the writing-instruments group, owned the Guy Laroche company for a very long time and probably lost money for more than 10 years in a row before it took steps to sell out. Charles Jourdan also lost money for many years when it belonged to its previous owners (the proprietors of a large Swiss cement company). Christian Lacroix apparently never generated profits while it was in the LVMH Group and before it was sold and then ended up in bankruptcy.

Why would intelligent and reasonable executives continue to accept losing money for so long? There are probably two reasons for this: the first entails the value of the brand. Despite losing money for many years, Guy Laroche and Carven remain very attractive to consumers, and there is a tremendous brand awareness. The second reason is that successful brands are so successful and so profitable that they can compensate for many years of losses. In 1994, the research group Eurostaf conducted a study of luxury ready-to-wear companies in France. This study found that Chanel, taken alone, was more profitable than the rest of the sector combined. Of the 14 companies investigated, 10 were losing money. The fact that Chanel was so profitable could lead any other brand to think that it too had the potential to develop and generate similar returns for shareholders. Furthermore, luxury brands are a very productive path that can lead to becoming a lifestyle brand, which, in turn, can lead to enormous growth capacity through product extension. We will look more closely at this phenomenon in Chapter 6.

In this respect, the luxury business is a kind of jackpot business; not because it is unpredictable and things come only by chance, of course, but because those that are profitable become extremely profitable.

This incredible spread between unprofitable and extremely profitable companies seems to be the result of two peculiarities. First, the luxury business is a very high break-even business. Second, cash needs are quite limited.

A Very High Break-Even

In an average sector, *break-even* is a function of manufacturing invest-ments and of fixed costs. In the luxury sector, even the smaller brands have to pretend they are powerful and rich, and by doing so they end up with a very high break-even.

For example, every brand must be present everywhere in the world. If a Japanese tourist cannot find his Givenchy or Aquascutum store when he or she visits Milan or New York, he or she may well conclude that these brands are weak and decide to stop buying them in Japan.

At the outset, a brand can be in only one place, like the Café Greco in Rome. But as soon as it starts to become international, consumers expect to find it everywhere. Each store, wherever it is in the world, has fixed costs—rental, staff salaries, and other costs—before it makes its first sale.

Also, in the world of luxury brands, everything from the production process to the sale has to be of top quality. Service has to be perfect, and wherever they are in the world, customers should leave with a special and distinctive carrier bag (for Bottega Veneta, the handles are of leather) bearing the logo and the color of the brand. Even before going into the bag, the product is often expensively packaged and all of the costly glass molds, carton cases, ribbons, or bags have to be manufactured. And this is an area where cost-cutting can be extremely dangerous, because all of these factors contribute to the sense of luxury and to the individual purchase experience.

A brand's standing is often determined by expenses that rarely generate an equivalent gross margin. For example, a fashion brand must start the process by holding an expensive fashion show, twice a year, where the products that are presented are not identical to those that will be sold in the stores: for a given model, the shoulders are a bit larger, the waist a bit tighter, and the skirt a bit shorter on the runway. The cost of making this particular dress may never be recovered because the dress will probably never be sold. Haute couture, in Paris, is another activity designed to promote the image of the brand and to make it stand out, rather than to make money.

Another very expensive investment is to have flagship stores in the home town of the brand; these are invariably progressively bigger in a bid to outdo competitors. Of course, for large-volume stores, this is not so much of a problem, but for a middle-sized brand, this is a painful and unprofitable activity.

All of this adds to the very high break-even and to the difficulty for a new brand to establish itself and develop credibility before it has built sufficient volume to balance all the upfront investments.

A Limited Cash Need

As soon as a brand achieves sales above break-even, life becomes much easier. Margins are very high, and when all fixed costs are covered, a large part of the margin becomes profit.

In manufacturing, when sales develop it is necessary to invest in new factories. In luxury it is always possible to subcontract the production or the additional production. Accounts receivable are another problem area for most businesses. When the brand operates its own stores, it is paid in cash or other immediately recoverable payment methods.

What about inventory, then? In fact, as the product gross margin is quite high, inventories at cost are not too difficult to finance when the level of sales is satisfactory. The major financial difficulty is to make sure inventory is available everywhere in the world, in all of the brand's own stores or in those of its distributors. This difficulty is, of course, much greater for newly established companies than for those with a very high and growing level of sales.

Another difficulty in the area of fashion products is that of returns: at the end of a season, some items must be either sold or returned. For small brands, this is a major issue because they are obliged to start with a large number of products each season to bring variety to their customers: with a small volume of sales, bargain sales end up very big. For high-volume brands, a fashion distributor will sell 80–85% of the collection at full price and 15–20% at bargain prices. For difficult brands, the financial picture is not the same: up to 65% of total volume will be at bargain prices. So, small companies have to deal with the issue if they want to ensure that their distributors will buy the next season's products. This often entails giving special discounts to distributors if they are to avoid having to take returns, knowing that products that are returned are either sold through factory outlets or even destroyed. This is a major issue for small and medium-sized brands. For large brands, returns are a small part of the volume, and bargain sales to staff or press are usually sufficient to dispose of any outdated merchandise.

The only very important cash need relates to the opening of stores under the brand name. This need does not exist in cosmetics, wines and spirits, and in most watch brands, but it is an essential part in the development of a fashion or accessories brand.

The conclusion is very simple: luxury is a great and very profitable business for those who are successful. It is a very difficult business for the others. And it is also very easy to go from a very profitable situation to major losses as soon as the sales begin to decrease when products are no longer adapted to the consumer and, for some reason, no longer fashionable.

A luxury-goods business can therefore be summed up as either win-all or lose-all. It is great for the top profitable brands. It is difficult for those striving to make an impression. It is a nightmare for those who cannot afford a flagship store in Paris, Milan, New York, Tokyo, and Beijing and who have to keep losing money in some of their activities to maintain the dream and the glitter around their brands.

Time Frame

In the automotive business, everybody is trying to reduce the time it takes to develop a new car so that the product line can be changed more frequently. In many businesses, it is possible to turn a situation around in little more than a year. Sometimes, for fast-moving consumer-goods products, it is possible to launch a product, have an immediate and clear indication of how well it is selling in the stores, and get sales to cover the original investment costs within 6 months.

In the luxury world, launches often take much more time and investment. To launch a new perfume, it is necessary to come up with a complete line, from extracts to eau de toilette, even a "bath line," and for each item there is a need for a costly glass bottle mold and a plastic cap mold. Such molds can take up to 12 months to make. Then a large quantity of the product has to be manufactured, so that at the time of the launch the new perfume can be immediately available in a large number of countries. The lead time for a launch can be anything from 18 months to 2 years. Then in the first year, for major launches, it is not uncommon to spend an amount equal to the first-year sales forecast on advertising and promotion. It often takes 3 or 4 years to start making money.

In the watch business, too, timing is crucial. The design and manufacturing processes have to be completed in time for the Geneva or Basel watch fairs and now specific group brands jewelry fairs at the end of February or beginning of March each year. If the deadline cannot be met, the launch is delayed until the following year.

Table 2.1 Fashion Cycle for a Fall–Winter Collection

Exclusive fabric commitments	September–October, year $t-1$
Development of prototypes and matching with fabrics	September–October, year $t-1$, February, year t
Fashion show	February–March, year t
Order-taking from multibrand stores	March, year t
Delivery to the stores	July, year t
Sale at full price	September–December, year t
Bargain sale	January–February, year $t+1$

The Fashion Cycle

In the world of luxury fashion, everything boils down to the fashion cycle, as illustrated in Table 2.1.

The cycle starts when fabric manufacturers present their new samples of materials. They offer new colors, new fabric touches, and new designs. Each year, in September or October, designers visit the fabric manufacturers in Paris (Première Vision) and Italy (Idea Como) to select the colors and feel they will use for their next Fall–Winter collection. To get exclusivity on a given design, they have to commit themselves to the purchase of a minimum number of yards of the fabric that will provide the special look of their collections for the next year.

They then go back to their studios and prepare the collections for the February/March fashion shows, which will, of course, be attended by the media and by buyers from department and multibrand stores all over the world. These buyers come with specific budgets for each brand and make firm orders for the items that they believe they can sell in their stores.

The dresses are then manufactured and delivered, by July at the latest, to be presented in September as the "new Fall–Winter collection." It is only at the end of the bargain period, at the end of February of the following year, that they will know how successful they have been with a given collection, how much has been sold at full price, how much at bargain prices, and how much is left over at the very end of the process.

The fashion cycle lasts 18 months. During that same period, of course, another Spring–Summer collection will be committed, selected, presented, and delivered, and results will not be known until the very end of the cycle. This is why, when a company decides to change its designer, the new stylist will need a minimum of two years to impose a new style, to define his or her personal view of the brand, and to make it a success.

Some brands have tried to get out of this straitjacket by having additional, interim collections (the so-called cruise collections), but the system remains quite rigid. Some newcomers in the mass-market segment, such as Zara, have rejected the traditional system and develop 26 collections a year. However, unless they deal with very high volumes, they have difficulty purchasing exclusive materials and are forced to present collections produced mainly in plain or standard fabrics.

This time frame forces brands to plan a long time ahead, and it is a long time before consumers can really see major changes in styles or in brand positioning in their local stores.

Turnaround Time

For the reasons mentioned, in the luxury field there is no short-term impact of major strategic decisions. For a luxury fashion brand, for example, the results of changing the designer might not be seen until two or three years down the road.

Brands themselves cannot be modified overnight. They have a specific identity in the mind of the consumer, and it is difficult to modify this. Celine, for example, is a very feminine brand and its attempts to launch masculine products have been conspicuously unsuccessful. Paco Rabanne is, curiously, a designer for women, but the brand was mainly known for masculine perfumes until the One Million lady was a success. Some brands are modern, others are perceived as traditional. It is very difficult to change such perceptions. Chanel is a brand for women, but it also has fragrances, ties, and watches for men. At the moment, it does not have a strong men's ready-to-wear; in the long run, it probably will. But this is a major change that the brand is preparing for by presenting its masculine products at its fashion shows for women. The idea is to convince the customer that Chanel is a brand for both women and men. This may take some time, and its men's ready-to-wear products are not yet available in the stores. When the consumer changes his mind, they will be.

It takes time to turn a brand around, as the experience of Saint Laurent clearly shows. When the fashion brand was purchased by the Gucci

Group, everybody thought the turnaround in its fortunes would be rapid. However, with accumulated losses already amounting to several hundred million euros, the brand continued to lose money for a few more years before it started to turn around in 2013 and is now extremely successful.

This has major implications for investors who want to buy and redevelop a brand that has lost its image and sales. This may be possible for watches and for wines and spirits, but for fashion and perfumes it is very difficult. If a brand is not doing well, its identity must be modified over time. The paradox is that when this is done, customers have the feeling that the brand has been mishandled and its history betrayed. In the end, nobody is happy—unless a great deal of time, effort, and money are committed to the cause.

Of course, as we explain later, it has been possible to take brands such as Gucci and Burberry, which were doing relatively well, modify them over time, and increase their sales substantially. But when smaller brands such as Jacques Fath or Poppy Moreni have lost their glamour, their interest, and their reason for being, there is not much that can be done to bring them back into the limelight.

This time frame explains why private-equity specialists or private individuals seldom purchase a majority of small luxury brands. There are exceptions—Balenciaga, Balmain, or Versace—but turnarounds are seldom successful.

This is why this activity has been traditionally the field of family firms, which have time and can accept poor results for a few years before growing and making money again. There are many in this situation, including Chanel, Salvatore Ferragamo, Armani, Versace, Laurent-Perrier, and Pernod Ricard. And we should never forget that three of the major luxury groups, LVMH, Kering, Richemont, are also controlled by families. In fact, except for a few examples (Burberry, Diageo, Hugo Boss, or Helmut Lang), all luxury companies in France, Italy, the United States, China, and Japan are family controlled or belong to a group which, in turn, is also family controlled.

The Key to Success in Luxury Goods

Professor Bernard Dubois used to start on this subject by speaking of the paradox of luxury goods (see Table 2.2). To achieve success in this field,

Table 2.2   The Paradox of Luxury-Goods
Marketing

High price
High cost
Craftsmanship
Limited distribution
Low promotional activity
Advertising with no sophisticated copy strategy

Source: Bernard Dubois, *L'art du Marketing,* Paris: Village
Mondial, 1998, p. 292.

he said, it was necessary to do exactly the opposite of what was taught
in traditional marketing lessons.

At first glance, high prices, high costs, no manufacturing investment,
and a limited distribution do not seem to be normal marketing practice.
But the process is based on the creation of a well-controlled scarcity.
The product must be known and be visible, but it should also appear
expensive and slightly out of reach. Customers must go out of their way
to find it. This is a niche marketing approach that can only work when
the brand has a strong identity and a reason for being. It also requires a
specific aesthetic concept: the product must be easily recognizable and
in line with the mood of the time and with the specific fashion trends.

The Need for a Strong Name

We come back again to brand identity. It frequently starts with the name
of a person, then must be extended, and should always keep bringing
additional value and reasons for being.

Most luxury brands start with a person's name; that of a crafts-
man or a designer who was different from the crowd and who made
things differently. Louis Cartier made watches and jewelry. Sotirio Bulgari used Greek and Roman art in his pieces while giving them a contemporary touch. This became a reference for customers and a guarantee
that the products bearing the name of the founder remained exclusive
high-quality objects. It was Salvatore Ferragamo who made shoes for
actresses, and Coco Chanel who made dresses for her most sophisticated
friends. It was Giorgio Armani and Valentino Garavani who started their

own fashion collections. Boucheron, Chaumet, and Van Cleef & Arpels are all family names.

Some brands do not bear the name of a founder. This is the case of Lancôme, which was created by the Petitjean family. In the case of Ralph Lauren, the name itself is a creation of the founder, and little by little it has become his own name. This act itself is a kind of recognition of the importance of a discrete family name and identity for all luxury businesses. Those, like Aquascutum or Escada, that have no such name seem to miss something, to somehow lack identity. A family name embodies a heritage and implies that products are made for just a very small category of friends, at least at the beginning.

Brand Extension and Legitimacy

As we have seen, the process of establishing a brand often starts with a name. But the name can limit the scope of the business to the craft of the founder: Ferragamo and Prada make shoes; Gucci makes handbags; Louis Vuitton makes travel bags; Christofle makes silver-plated tableware, and so on.

To develop a fully fledged business, it becomes necessary to enlarge and diversify the product line to increase the sales volume on which to advertise. If Calvin Klein was extremely well known in the United States, he was relatively unknown in Europe and Asia until his perfume line was advertised heavily and became a success. On the back of this success, he was able to open stores for his fashion lines in Europe and Japan.

This process of line extension—moving away from one product category to another one—is particularly delicate for luxury goods. It took seven years for the first Bulgari watch to be successful. It took approximately the same time for Boucheron watches to start selling. While the psychological distance from jewelry to watches may seem very slight, it still takes a lot of time for the consumer to get used to the shift.

Some extensions have been more rapid and without apparent problems. When Prada went from shoes to handbags and then into the ready-to-wear field for women and men, it worked almost every time. The same thing happened with Gucci in its line extensions.

Other cases have been more delicate. In the 1990s, Christofle decided that tableware was not a fast-growing market. Recalling its origins as silversmiths, it decided to launch a jewelry line, opting for white gold. After the launch of its first collection, it produced a watch, also in white gold. But the company moved too far away from its traditional area of expertise and failed to make sufficient investment in advertising and promotion; the first extension did not work and proved to be a major setback for the brand. The second one is in the process today.

When Chanel decided to extend into jewelry, it was much more careful, launching a single model of watch from free-standing boutiques set up specifically for this purpose in Place Vendôme and Avenue Montaigne in Paris. The watch was a success. The company waited another four or five years before setting up a very large jewelry store in Place Vendôme, the best location for major jewelers in Paris. This, too, was a success.

Baccarat provides another interesting story. It was selling crystal glasses and facing the same problem as Christofle: difficulty in the tableware market. The company decided to concentrate on lamps and candle-holders for the home and to move into crystal jewelry pieces. It invested heavily, gave the best locations in its stores to this product line, and today, diversification products represent the majority of the brand's total sales.

The conditions governing line extensions can be summarized as follows:

- Never believe it will be easy.
- Make a major investment and a major effort.
- Do not start small as a side business.
- Do not believe that consumers will be immediately convinced. Give them time.
- Emphasize coherence and style.
- Find a credible reason why the new product line is appropriate for your brand.

Of course, with time and investment, everything is possible. But a careful review at the outset of the differences and the major issues the new product category will bring to the brand is vital.

Identifiable Products

A Mercedes sedan or BMW, whatever the model, is instantly identifiable. There can be no mistaking the design, the workmanship, or the overall appearance.

When someone makes the investment to buy a luxury product, it goes without saying that the service should be perfect, the product should be of exceptional quality, and it should be made as if it were a unique object, handcrafted or carefully prepared for the individual purchaser. But it needs something else. It needs to have a high aesthetic value. It should be part of a family of products and be clearly identified. Each brand should have its own aesthetic codes and maintain a strong coherence across its entire range of products. A Chanel perfume bottle is classic, simple, and sophisticated. A Saint Laurent jacket should look like no other, and its perfume bottles should be romantic, baroque, and feminine. There should be instant recognition.

The Primacy of Design.   Design should be considered a priority in almost every luxury activity. This is obvious for a fashion brand, but it is also the case for a watch or a perfume. In fact, in creating a perfume, two different creative teams are involved: the "nose" that develops the fragrance and the designer for the bottle in which it is presented. With perfumes, there should also be a family homogeneity of fragrances within the same brand (Guerlain fragrances, for example, are generally quite heavy, with a vanilla heart note—the fragrance that lingers an hour or two after application), and each product should bring additional value to the total picture. That is to say, a Saint Laurent men's suit should have something in common with a women's dress from the same house.

This is why, for a luxury brand, management should be able to communicate with all types of designers. They should have a common language and a common understanding that enables them to discuss all aspects of a new product.

The Raison d'Être.   Each object in the collection should add to the brand and have a reason for being. When Armani, for example, makes optical frames, they should not simply be standard glasses with an Armani label: they should have something special. For each new product line, the product category needs to be reinvented in line with the brand's ethical and aesthetic invariants, the two basic components of any brand identity, as we will explain in Chapter 6.

This is why the licensing of products without the brand studio retaining real control and real guidance is now mostly over. For many years,

Rochas, which had been a full fashion line and had become a per-fume house, had a women's ready-to-wear license in Japan. Lancel was a leather-goods company in Europe, but in Japan it had a whole col-lection of licensed products from women's ready-to-wear to panties, shoes, men's shirts and socks. This was perfectly all right in the 1960s and 1970s when luxury consumers were traveling less and when brand information was less available. Today such licensed products have a major drawback. All the customers who are knowledgeable about the brand refuse to buy them, and the products slip down to a consumer cate-gory less interested, less aware, and less demanding; they rapidly become middle-market brands.

In a way, these are simply standard positioning principles, as they apply to any marketing product analysis. For luxury items, however, we must go back to the concept of craftsmanship and what differen-tiates such items from mass-market products. A luxury object must be crafted and designed carefully. This is as true for a luxury fragrance as it is for a dress or a jacket. The sophistication of a luxury perfume should be matched by that of its presentation. Every element of the product should be carefully thought out—from the bottle to the inner and outer packaging—to give the consumer a sense of quality and perfect design every time. The distinction between a luxury product and a mass-market product is evident in the presentation of the jars of the anti-wrinkle creams of Plenitude de L'Oréal and of Lancôme. They are both manu-factured by the same company, yet the shapes, weights, and finishes are quite different.

However, given that mass-market products are gradually upgrading their appearance and approach, it is even more important for luxury goods to work harder to stay ahead of the pack.

Craftsmanship should be the hallmark of all categories of luxury goods, and any product bearing a particular luxury brand should display all the ethical and aesthetic values that belong to that brand.

The Social and Cultural Environment

This ethical and aesthetic dimension has another effect. It places the luxury industry in the realm of the arts and into the cultural trends of the moment. As it looks for new shapes, colors, feelings, or modes of consumption, this industry is much more a part of the cultural scene than any others. Thus, its advertising bypasses traditional processes and looks for a special aesthetic environment and a special artistic connivance with its consumer target. In this, luxury products must function as a cultural mirror.

Keeping Up with Social Trends.   The importance of staying in touch with changing social trends is reflected in the experiences of some of the leading brands themselves. For example, at one time the sexy-chic positioning of Gucci met with strong approval from its target customer. Versace, too, was doing very well with the sexiness of its dresses and in its communication. Today the sexy-chic theme seems to be less attractive to the consumer, and Gucci has come to a much more classic and probably much younger and much more colorful positioning. Versace, however, failed to read the mood in the same way and didn't change, with the result that its sales fell considerably until the turnaround came from very sophisticated women's cocktail dresses and men's suits.

Paco Rabanne, with his glittering metallic dresses, was an icon of the spirit of sexual liberation that was all-pervasive around 1968 and met with strong interest from the public. Jane Fonda and Brigitte Bardot had special gowns made for them as a special commitment to a given way of life. Fashion magazines were showing his models and interviewing him for his views on the new social trends. At that time, his point of view mattered to the public. Today, though, few would be interested in his thoughts on what is happening in the world.

In using a luxury product, the consumer is making a claim to being different and special, at the forefront of social trends rather than appearing to be outside of society.

This fit with social trends and the spirit of the time is a very strong aspect of luxury. When people longed for a return to nature and a simpler society, they loved Danish designer Per Spook, who was designing natural-looking heavy wool-knit jackets and beige cotton skirts. When they wanted an extremely sexy look, they went for Versace. When the times become more traditional and conservative, with the emphasis on the mature woman, Chanel has a lot to offer.

With hindsight, it is clear that some brands have developed very quickly at one time and then declined, and not necessarily because their management was less effective and their marketing was off-base. It was simply a product of the changing times. Now, of course, good marketing is supposed to remain in line with consumer trends. But how far should a company go to adjust its product and brand positioning to the changes in society?

The Response to Changing Trends.   As mentioned earlier, Paco Rabanne's appeal faded when his philosophy was deemed to be out of step with changing social trends that saw the advent of the sexy society of the late 1990s. He could have come to a sexy positioning and, indeed, many of the sophisticated metallic dresses of Versace could have been done by him. But this was not his style and he did not feel the need to do it.

Salvatore Ferragamo provides another interesting case. It developed from high-quality shoes to producing the finest silk ties and scarves on the market. A Ferragamo tie is immediately identifiable by its beautiful colors and its extremely fine prints, which could almost have come from an old Persian manuscript. But, now, the fashion is for plain jacquard silk ties. Should Salvatore Ferragamo change its product philosophy? The fact is that it has indeed introduced some jacquard silk ties, but the company is struggling to differentiate itself from its competitors.

We finish this section with a note to remind managers of the underlying uncertainty of the luxury business. Often, success (or the lack of it) is as much a product of the changing social environment as it is of individual managerial style.

The Major Operators

It is necessary to describe the major operators in the field. Various articles say that the tendency is toward large groups and that individual companies don't stand a chance in the luxury market in the long run. Is this really the case?

What Is the Size of the Luxury Market?

As we said earlier, in luxury, size is relative. As there is very little data available on the size of the total market, we are obliged to come up with our own guesstimates of this activity; we start with the very precise estimates that are published each year by consulting firm Bain & Company, and are very precise.

It all depends, of course, on whether we consider luxury in its more limited scope (fashion, accessories including leather goods, cosmetics and fragrances, wines and spirits, etc.) or if we also include luxury cars (which Bain values at €500 billion), private airplanes, and travel, including hotels (which Bain values at €190 billion) and hospitality. In the larger category, the total turnover of the corporations manufacturing products or rendering direct services could be all the way to €1,200 billion. If we take the Bain figures for what they call "personal luxury," we find the figures shown in Table 2.3.

We consider these sales statistics to be very precise and well analyzed, but we want to also include wines and spirits and tablewares (a total of €71 billion) in our tables. This is shown in Table 2.4.

Let us explain how our numbers differ from Bain's. We believe that their figures for accessories are very high but we don't want to depart from them. For wines and spirits, we considered "luxury wines" to be

Table 2.3   Bain's Estimates of Business Size, 2018 (€ billion)

Apparel	60
Accessories	75
Jewelry and watches	51
Beauty	51
Total	237

Source: Bain annual study on personal luxury, 2018.

Table 2.4   Our Estimates of Basic Luxury Products Business Sales, 2019 (€ billion)

Apparel	60
Accessories	75
Spirits and luxury wines	65
Perfumes and cosmetics	65
Watches	26
Jewelry	45
Tableware	6
Total	342

Table 2.5   Estimates of the Respective Contributions of French and Italian Companies

	Total (€ billion)	French (%)	Italian (%)	Others (%)
Ready-to-wear	60	20	30	50
Accessories	75	25	35	40
Alcohol and expensive wines	65	15	10	75
Fragrances and cosmetics	65	35	5	60
Watches	26	5	5	90
Jewelry	45	7.5	5	87.5
Tableware	6	40	10	50
Total	342			

Source: These figures are based on the authors' discussions with different industry specialists.

only wines that would retail for more than €10 a bottle. We have very different estimates for jewelry and watches because we decided to include in the jewelry those watches that were sold under a jewelry brand by a jeweler.

Based on these estimates, we compare the relative size of the French and Italian companies, as set out in Table 2.5. Again, these figures are our own estimates and have been rounded up.

In the ready-to-wear category, Italy and France have 55% of the market between them, with Italy clearly leading the way. The others category comprises countries such as the United States and England. However, if we confine ourselves to luxury, and therefore do not take into account brands such as Liz Claiborne, Gap, or Banana Republic, the United States, with the exception of Ralph Lauren or Michael Kors, is not very strong in this category.

In the watches category, which is obviously dominated by the Swiss, the French and Italians are merely secondary players.

Of the overall total, French and Italian brands account for €75 billion and €60 billion, respectively. France's strong position is built around accessories and perfumes. With the exception of Armani, Gucci, and Dolce & Gabbana, Italy seems to have been unable to impose strong perfume brands, and on top of this, those brands are not developed by Italian companies; nor does it have a strong international market in spirits.

However, Italy's strength in fashion is quite visible. Where France has 8 brands with sales of over €1 billion (Balenciaga, Cartier, Chanel, Dior, Hermès, Louis Vuitton, Saint Laurent, and Van Cleef & Arpels), with four whose core business is in the ready-to-wear world, Italy has 15 (Armani, Bottega Veneta, Bulgari, Dolce & Gabbana, Fendi, Gucci, Loro Piana, Max Mara, Moncler, Prada, Salvatore Ferragamo, Valentino, Versace, and Zegna), with 14 coming from the ready-to-wear and fashion world.

This preeminence of Italian fashion will have unexpected consequences in the long run as perfume brands are often built on the strength of ready-to-wear lines. If one day the Gucci, Prada, and Versace perfumes reach parity with those of Chanel, Dior, and Yves Saint Laurent, then Italy could become the number-one luxury operator in the world.

For reasons that will be discussed later, the French have been very slow to develop fashion and ready-to-wear brands over the past 30 years. The two major creations of French fashion brands date back to Saint Laurent and Kenzo; somehow, this looks like ancient history.

Oligopoly or Open Market?

From reading the press, it might be easy to form the conclusion that luxury has become the field of large groups and that there is no place for small operators. In fact, the real picture is quite different, as Table 2.6 shows.

As will be discussed later, small operators, if they have the critical mass to be clearly international, can do quite well in this world.

The Big Three Corporations

In the luxury business, people speak generally of the big three corporations—LVMH, Kering, and Richemont. Actually, Richemont is similar in size to Estée Lauder and L'Oréal, and similar in size to major wines and spirit companies such as Diageo and Pernod Ricard. However, in this section, we will confine ourselves to these three companies. Other companies will be described at length in the next chapter.

LVMH.   In Table 2.6, we took LVMH's sales to be approximately €39 billion because we removed the distribution activities from the total of €53.7 billion in 2019. The total picture is presented in Table 2.7.

Table 2.6   Major Luxury Operators, 2019 (or 2018/2019) (€ million)

Luxury Operators	Sales	
LVMH	38,989	Total with distribution 53,700
Kering	15,383	
Richemont	13,989	
Diageo	12,926	Total with Guinness: 15,389
Estée Lauder	12,098	
L'Oréal	11,000	Total with mass market, etc.: 29,900
Pernod Ricard	8,448	
EssilorLuxottica	8,880	Total: 16,160
Coty	8,646	
Chanel	8,400	
Hermès	5,960	
Ralph Lauren	5,704	
Capri	5,566	
Tapestry	5,409	

Source: Annual reports or authors' estimates.

Table 2.7   LVMH: Sales and Results, 2009 and 2019

	2019 Sales (€ million)	2009 Sales (€ million)	2019 Operating Profit (€ million)	Profit On Sales (%)
Wines and spirits	5,576	2,740	1,729	31.0
Fashion and leather goods	22,240	6,302	7,344	33.0
Perfumes and cosmetics	6,835	2,741	683	10.0
Watches and jewelry	4,405	764	736	16.7
Selective distribution	14,711	4,533	1,395	9.5
Miscellaneous	(67)	(27)	(383)	
Total	53,700	17,053	11,504	21.4

Source: LVMH annual reports.

As we can see, LVMH is a very impressive group, with more than half of its luxury brand business done in the fashion and leather division. It is also striking to note that this fashion business provides 64% of the group's total operating profits.

2019 was clearly a very good year for the group. From 2009 to 2019, the growth was spectacular. This is a result of operational growth, but also company purchases, and the list is long: Celine, Fendi, Loro Piana, Bulgari, and recently.

Table 2.8   Scorecard of LVMH Results (€ million)

	2019		2014		2009	
Sales	53,700	100%	30,638	100%	17,053	100%
Operating profit	11,504	21.4%	5,718	18.7%	3,352	19,6%
Net profit	7,171	13,3%	5,648	18,4%	1,973	11.6%

Source: LVMH annual reports.

LVMH's overall performance for 2009, 2014, and 2019 is summarized in Table 2.8.

The net profit of 13.3% of sales is not bad in 2019, but the operating profit of the fashion division (33% of sales) and of wines and spirits (31% of sales) is very impressive and probably one of the highest in the industry. But this percentage is interesting for another reason: Table 2.7 shows that for the perfume business, there were recorded sales of €6,835 billion, with an operating profit of €683 million. We can estimate a net profit of €137 million.[1] In other words, the perfumes and cosmetics division is providing a much lower profitability than other business sections and less than is generally expected in the perfume business.

In the luxury sectors, two segments are doing extremely well: the fashion and leather goods division, and the wines and spirits division (with its brands including Krug, Dom Pérignon, Moët and Chandon, Veuve Clicquot, and Hennessy). In the fashion and luxury division, LVMH also has many brands, including Louis Vuitton, Dior, Fendi, and Loro Piana. The question here is to determine which of these should be given priority. It seems that, based on size and potential, Celine is given major resources and development money. But Berluti, the only exclusively masculine fashion brand, seems to have an impressive business plan with the opening of many self-standing monobrand stores. The question still remains: What is the future of the other brands, if they are not profitable or only marginally contributing to the group profit?

In geographical terms, the group is well balanced, as can be seen in Table 2.9.

---

[1] Calculated as follows: The company difference between operational profit and net profit is 8% on sales. For perfumes, sales are €6,835 million and the operational profit is €683 million. If we subtract from the latter amount the average difference between operational profit and net profit (683 − 546), that gives us the net profit for the perfume and cosmetic division: €337 million.

Table 2.9   LVMH Geographical
Split, 2019

France	9%
Rest of Europe	19%
America	24%
Japan	7%
Rest of Asia	30%
Other markets	11%
Total	100%

Source: LVMH annual reports. Of course, this geographical split varies across divisions and brands.

Kering.   This group was created in 1999 by the purchase by PPR of a minority interest in Gucci and the immediate purchase of the YSL fashion and YSL beauty group. Since then, the group has purchased many other brands, including Bottega Veneta, Boucheron, and Balenciaga, and is one of the few groups that has grown by purchasing existing brands and by developing its own from scratch. This latter category includes, for example, Alexander McQueen.

The company name was changed to Kering in 2013. Table 2.10 summarizes the existing sales and operating profit data.

Gucci and Saint Laurent have outstanding performances for the past five years. The case of Bottega Veneta is quite interesting: it was at the same sales level as Saint Laurent in 2005 but grew extremely fast until 2013 when Saint Laurent was doing very poorly. Then Saint Laurent

Table 2.10   Kering Historical Sales and Results (€ million)

	Sales				Operating Profit		
	2019	**2015**	**2010**	**2005**	**2019**	**2009**	**2008**
Gucci	9,628	3,898	2,266	1,807	3926	618	625
Saint Laurent	2,049	974	237	162	552	−10	0
Bottega Veneta	1,168	1,286	402	160	207	92	101
All others	2,537	1,707	484	907	306	−75	5
Unallocated					(213)		
Total	15,383	7,865	3,389	3,036	4,778	625	731

Source: PPR annual reports.

woke up and did extremely well, and Bottega Veneta was stuck with decreasing volume and profitability. It may have woken up now, but we still have to wait to find out.

Richemont. The Compagnie Financière Richemont, based in Geneva, with sales of €13.9 billion was, for many years, the second major operator in the luxury fashion, jewelry, and watch businesses. But probably because of difficulties in the sales of watches, and little involvement in the fashion business, it has developed slower than its competitors in the past 5 years (see Table 2.11). In 2019, it integrated and consolidated the two online distribution systems: NAP (Net à Porter.com) and Y (now called YNAP).

The company's results by product lines are given in Table 2.12.

Table 2.11 Richemont Historical Sales and Profit (€ million)

	Sales	Operating Profit	Net Profit
2019	13,989	1,943	2,787
2018	10,979	1,844	1,221
2017	10,647	1,764	1,210
2015	10,410	1,339	2,387
2013	10,150	2,426	2,005

Source: Richemont annual reports.

Table 2.12 Richemont Performance by Product Lines, 2005–2019 (€ million)

	Sales			Operating Profit	
	2019	2015	2010	2005	2019
Jewelry houses	7,083	5,168	2,688	844	2,229
Specialty watches	2,980	3,325	1,437	1,750	378
Online distribution	2,105		N.A.		(100)
Writing instruments			551	297	
Leather and accessories			584	780	
Other businesses	1,881				(264)
Unallocated			46		
Total	13,989	10,410	5,176	3,671	1,943

*Starting in 2010, leather and accessories and other businesses have been merged.
Source: Richemont annual reports.

In 2019, the jewelry houses (Cartier and Van Cleef & Arpels) represented 51% of sales and 115% of operating profit, with Cartier probably being the biggest contributor, but the growth performances of Van Cleef & Arpels have certainly been extraordinary in the past 10 or 12 years. Specialty watches (which include Vacheron Constantin, Baume & Mercier, Jaeger-LeCoultre, Lange und Söhne, Officine Panerai, IWC, and Piaget) also performed quite well.

The performance of Montblanc (with Montegrappa first included in the figures then sold out) was certainly quite impressive as well. The only bad news was in the leather-goods category (which now only includes Dunhill), which has probably been losing money. Now that this category is merged with other businesses, it will be more difficult to follow.

Richemont is both a jeweler and a watchmaker. It has two star brands in Cartier and Van Cleef & Arpels. It has a very strong portfolio of watch brands, and after a few difficult years could bounce back and develop. This is what is peculiar in the luxury business.

Can the Single-Brand Company Survive?

The answer to this question is quite simple. Yes, it does make sense to be a pure player in this industry, to have only one brand and to manage it as well as possible. Armani, Hermès, Chanel, and Prada are prime examples of what can be achieved.

In multibrand portfolios with a number of star brands, management must decide where to invest, and those brands deemed to be of lower priority have a difficult time. On the other hand, brands with high potential but that are struggling cannot invest as much as they would need, because they have to balance out the losses of the smaller brands.

Clearly, large and diversified groups are not necessarily more profitable than individual brands (such as Chanel or Hermès, for example). It is true that groups provide an opportunity for small brands to find cash to finance their growth. The idea is that the new brands will one day provide future growth and profit to the company as a whole. This may well prove to be true for some but by no means all.

To sum up our findings in this chapter: the luxury business is a different business from non-luxury sectors and follows different rules. Timing, financial constraints, and the effects of size are clearly different. The keys to success are different, and even though the multibrand groups are powerful, it is possible to remain small, independent, profitable, and growing as a single-brand company.

In the next chapter, we will analyze each of the major sectors in the luxury field.

Chapter 3A

Major Luxury Sectors

Ready-to-Wear, Perfumes and Cosmetics, and Leather Goods

We are so used to the idea of luxury brands that we tend to forget that the concept of them is relatively new. For many years, businesses that we now include in the luxury sector were considered completely separate and were represented by different federations: The Federation of Ready to Wear, the Federation of Leather Goods, the Federation of Perfumes and Cosmetics, and so on. On the face of it, in the manufacturing and sales processes, a bottle of champagne and a lady's dress have very little in common. The champagne is produced through an automated system using very modern machinery. It is then sold in special wine stores but also in supermarkets and hypermarkets. On the other hand, a lady's dress is often made by hand and in very limited numbers and sold in exclusive luxury stores around the world.

The French were probably the first to understand the fact that a bottle of champagne and a sophisticated dress do have something in common, and this is why in 1954 they created the "Comité Colbert," an association to promote the concept of luxury.

The stated values of the Comité Colbert could be an introduction to the global luxury concept: its members, it informs us, "share the same ideas of a contemporary art de vivre and constantly develop and enrich this through their diversity. They have a common vision of the importance of international ambition, of authentic know-how and high standards, of design and creativity and of professional ethics." Its members are drawn from the following *métiers*, or trade activities:

- Automobile
- Crystal
- Decoration
- Faïence and porcelain
- Fragrances and cosmetics
- Gastronomy
- Gold and precious metal
- *Haute couture* and fashion
- Hospitality
- Leather goods
- Publishing
- Silver and bronze
- Sound
- Wines and spirits

When the Comité Colbert was created and the concept of *luxury business* developed, it wasn't immediately obvious that these métiers had so much in common. Now, however, the idea is commonplace, as this book can testify.

This list is quite interesting because it includes "activities" (Fashion: Does it include shoes? Or Gastronomy?: It certainly includes restaurants, but does it also include makers of upscale precious chocolates or biscuits?) and at the same time "components" (for example, gold and precious metal plus silver and bronze: This includes all jewelry activities, but does it also include complication watches?). It is interesting to note that the Comité Colbert does include luxury automobiles (with only one member: Bugatti 1909 and no DS or Alpine) and also everything that could include Hospitality, Gastronomy, and Decoration.

In the list there is no mention of airline activities (although Air France is an Associated Member) or specific or cultural travel agencies.

In this chapter, we will describe the luxury world by individual sectors, so that their characteristics and key success factors can be clearly identified.

Ready-to-Wear Activities

Under this heading we include both ladies' and men's ready-to-wear and *haute couture*, which in Chapter 2 we estimated to amount to around €60 billion in volume.

While other businesses such as perfumes and cosmetics or wines and spirits may have greater sales, in terms of image the luxury fashion business is undoubtedly the most important. Through its fashion shows, its constant renewal, and its leadership in new trends, new shapes, and new colors, it remains the sector that is most frequently mentioned in the media and that is most closely associated with the artistic world.

While the majority of students in luxury programs want to end up in the fashion business, less than 20% of the luxury jobs are in this field, in which most staff are in stores, presenting and selling the merchandise to the final consumer. As we saw earlier, marketing teams are quite small and production is very often subcontracted. Unfortunately, this is also a field in which profitability is not always easy to achieve. For many brands, the fashion business remains unprofitable, and we will try to explain why.

In this section, we will describe the specific fashion market, the key management issues, and the most common organizational structure found in this sector.

The Fashion Business and Its Operation

The Players.   The Italian business is by far the strongest, with worldwide sales (Luxury fashion and accessories) that we estimate at around €65 billion.

The Italians arrived on the luxury fashion scene later than the French, with Armani, Gucci, Prada, Valentino, and Versace, for example, coming to the fore in the mid-1970s and the 1980s. Consider also the last major Italian creations like Dolce & Gabbana in 1982, Moschino in 1983, or Moncler in 2003. In comparison, the last French luxury brands to become big and successful would be Saint Laurent in 1962, Agnès B. in 1975, and Kenzo in 1980. Since then, the French have created Alaïa, Jean Paul Gaultier, Claude Montana, and Thierry Mugler, but none of those brands have been able to create a meaningful and important fashion business. In some ways the Italians seem to be better positioned than the French in that they are still perceived as new, and they provide much diversity, opening new stores in the major cities of the world. Customers love the appearance of "newness" that the Italians have been able to build in their brands. While 30 years ago in such top luxury shopping complexes as the Imperial Tower in Tokyo or the Peninsula Hotel in Hong Kong, most stores were presenting French fashion brands, today, Italian brands are much more present and much more powerful. Customers are attracted by their sophistication and the quality of their products.

It's worth reminding ourselves that many of the top Italian brands did not start out in the fashion business. Guccio Gucci, for example, was a handbag manufacturer; Salvatore Ferragamo was a shoemaker; Edoardo and Adele Fendi were fur specialists; and Mario Prada designed and sold handbags, shoes, trunks, and suitcases. But from their craftsmanship base, they were able to start ladies' ready-to-wear lines that were interesting, creative, and fashionable.

Take Fendi, for example. As a fur brand, Fendi was much less known and less powerful than Revillon. But while Revillon stayed as a pure player, selling fur almost exclusively in a declining market, Fendi began to distribute shoes, then leather ready-to-wear, then very successful ladies' handbags. In the 1970s, it hired Karl Lagerfeld to design a ladies' ready-to-wear collection. At first it sold very little, but it persisted and now, with sales estimated at around €1,600 million in 2019, Fendi is a full-fledged brand, strong in both handbags and ready-to-wear. For its part, Revillon began to move away from fur, but not until the 1990s. Its approach lacked strength, intelligence, and consistency, however, and today the brand has almost disappeared.

As they moved away from their original businesses and into ready-to-wear, Italian brands found a very receptive local community with strong fabric creators, many ready-to-wear manufacturers and subcontractors, and a creative, open environment that was ready to take risks. For many years, Fendi ready-to-wear was produced through an outside licensing agreement and sales were very low. While it was not always profitable, it received strong and intelligent support from the company and, over time, this support has paid off.

Italy has never promoted *haute couture*, even if brands like Armani or Valentino are happy to be part of the Paris fashion shows. They believe in creative ready-to-wear lines that sell in stores, and put all their efforts into lavish twice-yearly fashion collections. And the products sell.

Though the Italians have fewer licensing deals than the French, they still have many selective licenses, as we will explain later. The market is very open, without any one brand claiming an exclusive position. The industrial sector is open and fast. For example, though Prada has been producing ready-to-wear collections for less than 30 years now, it is perceived as a very strong fashion brand, as if it has always been that way.

From the start, the Italian brands were run with a mix of creative talent and strong business competence. Franco Moschino developed his own business with a very strong manager, Tiziano Gusti; Gianni Versace first developed his brand with a strong businessman who was one of his classmates, Claudio Luti; and Giorgio Armani started his business in 1975 with the late Sergio Galeotti and has become a very rare breed—a designer who is also a businessman.

The French business is more traditional, with the strongest brands such as Chanel and Dior being created before or immediately after World War II. The French were innovators at that time, with Christian Dior inventing the licensing business that later became the *raison d'être* of many brands, including Pierre Cardin. In addition to creating *haute couture*, they were the first to develop perfume businesses, using their name and their image: first, Coco Chanel in 1921, then Carven and Dior immediately after the war. To this day, French fashion brands have a strong presence in the perfume business.

But the French, in a traditional Gallic way, also invented barriers to entry. In the 1970s and 1980s, it was quite difficult to create a new fashion brand in France. Launching a *haute couture* collection was expensive and difficult. French ready-to-wear manufacturers were very few and did not want to handle small or upcoming brands. New brands were thus obliged to subcontract their ready-to-wear lines in Italy.

The newcomers then began to position themselves as "creators," making dresses that would command immediate notice; however, this did not work well either. In the past 40 years, only Kenzo has been able to create a fully fledged brand. Thierry Mugler and Jean Paul Gaultier have developed awareness and a thriving perfume business, but not a strong, viable fashion business. Claude Montana was certainly one of the most gifted creators of his generation, but his business is no longer strong. Other gifted creators such as Angelo Tarlazzi, Myrène de Prémonville, Azzedine Alaïa, and Hervé Léger have had a reason for being but have been unable to establish lasting fashion brands.

A new generation of designers with a strong business sense, such as Regina Rubens and Paul Ka, is now emerging, but they are not considered to be luxury brands. In fact, the successful French creators for the past 20 years are probably Maje, Sandro, Claudie Pierlot, Zadig & Voltaire, and Ba&sh, but they clearly belong in the premium market and not the luxury one.

Table 3.1 highlights the brands that have achieved sales of over €1 billion. They have managed to do this because they can invest heavily in advertising, have the necessary volume to open stores almost anywhere in the world, and have the diversified product line and customer attractiveness necessary to reach break-even in those stores. These are the brands that can generally be found in the major luxury shopping galleries of the world.

Table 3.2 illustrates what we might call second-tier companies: those that have achieved sales in excess of €100 million. (Below this level, brands can be national or strong in two or three countries, but they cannot have a direct presence in the major markets of the world.) With this

Table 3.1   The Fashion Mega-Brands (Sales above €1 billion)

France		Italy
Balenciaga	Armani	Loro Piana
	Bottega Veneta	Max Mara
Chanel		Moncler
Dior	Dolce & Gabbana	Prada
Hermès	Ermenegildo Zegna	Salvatore Ferragamo
Louis Vuitton	Fendi	Valentino
Saint-Laurent	Gucci	Versace

Table 3.2   Second-Tier Fashion Brands (Sales of €100–1 billion)

France	Italy	
Agnès B.	Alberta Ferretti	Mariella Burani
Balmain	Bluemarine	Mariella Rinaldi
Berluti	Brioni	Marni
Celine	Brunello Cucinelli	Missoni
Chloé	Etro	Miu Miu
Givenchy	Ferre	Moschino
Kenzo	Krizia	Nazareno Gabrieli
Lanvin	La Perla	Roberto Cavalli
Leonard	Laura Biagiotti	Trussardi
	Les Copains	

size, it is possible to have profitable stores, perhaps not in every major city of the world but certainly in those such as New York, Beijing, and Hong Kong, where there are enough luxury specialists to make it profitable.

Unfortunately, companies with sales below €100 million cannot easily afford to open stores around the world, and even if they could, they probably don't have the awareness, the potential, or the merchandise attractiveness to make those stores profitable.

We had originally intended to include only fashion brands, but then only Balenciaga Chanel, Saint Laurent, and Dior would have been included on the French side of Table 3.1; this would have been unfair to Louis Vuitton and Hermès, which are among the most powerful French brands and which are also engaged in ready-to-wear activities.

In doing so, we clearly show the strong advantage in size, diversity, and power the Italian brands have over their French counterparts. We ought not to forget, though, that in leather goods the French have a very strong advantage, with their two major brands (Louis Vuitton and Hermès) being above anybody else in this product category. These leather goods brands are presented later.

Other nationalities are also part of this business, but they cannot be compared with either the French or the Italians. Americans Ralph Lauren, Calvin Klein, Michael Kors, Tory Burch, and Donna Karan have done quite well in developing a new concept of "lifestyle brands"—products geared to a specific style. The creator in each case is also a businessperson and has developed ready-to-wear products addressed to a specific type of clientele in their stores. Ralph Lauren does this beautifully with his Old England and New England traditional style that fits a certain type of wealthy clientele looking for nostalgic products and a country atmosphere for clothing to be worn in an urban environment.

But to be effective, the American lifestyle concept requires heavy advertising and social media budgets, and this has created a barrier to entry that makes it difficult for newcomers to be part of this very sophisticated crowd.

Perhaps because of its climate, Britain is home to two very important businesses that were first built around raincoats: Burberry and Aquascutum. It is also successful with strong men's-wear brands such as Paul Smith, Dunhill, and Daks. It also has Jaeger, a knitwear brand positioned at a middle range. Newcomers like Vivienne Westwood and Stella McCartney bring something interesting but are still small by world standards.

Germany has Escada and Hugo Boss (which used to belong to the Italian group Marzotto). Two of its brands are particularly interesting because they are different: Jil Sander, because she first developed a strong collection for executive women, and Joop, because he developed a very strong name in German-speaking countries on the basis of licensing.

Spain is home to the internationally renowned brands Loewe, Purificacion Garcia, and Adolfo Dominguez. Other creators like Pertegaz, Victorio y Luchino, Roberto Verino, and Toni Miro are strong at home but have never been able to develop outside of their own country.

Belgian designers Ann Demeulemeester, Maison Margiela, and Dries Van Noten should also be included on the list, as should Switzerland's Akris.

The reason for discussing nationalities and looking at overall business volume is because luxury fashion is a business and should be considered as such. The objective of a ready-to-wear luxury brand is to become a worldwide success. As we will discuss later, the nationality of the designers has a strong impact on the positioning of the business outside of their respective national territories.

How to Develop a Brand.   As a brand starts locally and develops, it needs to do things correctly from the outset. This process requires both a strong creator and a strong businessperson. The creator has to develop a unique style but should also have someone close by who can be relied upon to take care of business development and channel that creativity into areas that translate into sales at the cash register without constraining the designer's creativity. The partnerships of Giorgio Armani and Sergio Galeotti and of Yves Saint Laurent and Pierre Bergé are object lessons in the kind of teamwork that is required for success. A strong and trusting relationship, with complementary styles and instincts, is very important to the development of a ready-to-wear brand.

The ladies' ready-to-wear line is what gives a strong identity to many successful brands. It provides press coverage worldwide and creates an awareness in retailers and consumers alike. As brands develop the "total look" concept, ready-to-wear acts as the anchor: it is very difficult to sell branded belts, panties, or shoes without a strong image for dresses or ladies' suits.

To develop a brand, it is necessary to have a presence in many large cities around the world, and ladies' ready-to-wear is the way to go, as it enables the creation of a network of retail stores under the brand name. These stores often sell more accessories and handbags than ready-to-wear, but it is the ready-to-wear line that makes the shop window attractive and creates a fashionable store environment. It's a bit of a chicken-and-egg proposition, really: to sell accessories and handbags requires a strong name and a strong ready-to-wear line. To be able to develop and promote a strong ready-to-wear line requires the volume obtained through the sales of handbags and accessories.

How to Make Money.   The paradox is that many ladies' fashion activities are unprofitable. As we will see later, the setup of a new ladies' ready-to-wear collection requires expensive prototypes, runway products, and showroom collections that are only profitable when the volume is there. This is also the case for men's ready-to-wear lines, which are often difficult to differentiate from one brand to another one. Store activities are also very dependent on the level of sales that can be achieved. In other words, as mentioned earlier, it is not possible to make money opening a store for a brand that is not well known and not fashionable and attractive enough.

In fact, as we will discuss later, the best way to finance the start-up and development of a ladies' ready-to-wear collection is to develop license deals in other product categories.

What must be said here is that many brands are losing money in this area.

Key Management Issues

The Creative Process.   We return here to the most important element of style: the creator.

The role of management within this area is to organize a workable plan that sets out the requirements for the coming season: How many suits with pants? How many suits with skirts? How many cocktail dresses? The plan will also specify retail price targets and the target cost of the fabric to be used. The designer must then perform and create within these precise guidelines to ensure that the final product will sell at an acceptable price in the stores.

Similar planning is also required for accessories and other products, each of which must be coherent with the rest and readily identifiable with the brand. A Dior tie should be distinguishable from a Saint Laurent tie, and each product bearing a brand name should bring a specific quality and an added value to the total product group. This can only be realized through coordination and clear design directives.

While management should not be directly involved with the creative process, it must set the rules and the processes for planning and reviewing, for harmonizing the different product lines, and for analyzing what has/has not been selling. Management should also take charge of ensuring the quality of raw materials (fabrics, buttons, technical materials, lining, and so on) and of manufacturing.

The creativity of people such as Alessandro Michelle (at Gucci) or Anthony Vaccarello (at Saint Laurent) should not be controlled. It is simply a matter of setting guidelines, objectives, and reviews so that the creative process can be used to improve the brand's standing in the marketplace.

A Worldwide Presence.   The balance of activity for a fashion brand takes into account image-creation items (such as freestanding flagship stores in major cities) and image-consumption activities (such as licensing deals for secondary products).

The distribution of ready-to-wear fashion products varies in accordance with the particular needs of specific markets. In the United States,

Japan, and Australia, for example, luxury fashion brands are distributed mainly through shop-in-shops in department stores. The buyers of the different stores visit the Milan and Paris fashion shows and buy by brand in accordance with their "open to buy" budgets. This is the most important engine of brand development. But if the brand wants to create a special strength or awareness on its own, it must also build its own flagship stores in New York, Los Angeles, Beijing, Shanghai, Tokyo, Osaka, and other main cities.

In other countries, sometimes with more difficult access, European brands may use an importer or a distributor to take charge of developing sales in a given territory. This sometimes requires a showroom and a showroom collection whose products end up in multibrand stores and local department stores that do not buy direct.

In countries such as Hong Kong or Singapore, the business is run in part by individual fashion retailers such as Joyce Lane Crawford in Hong Kong or Glamourette in Singapore. These retailers are good at identifying new brands with potential and buy them before anybody else in the country.

Why Is It Difficult to Make Money?.   In this ready-to-wear activity, making money all boils down to the volume of business created and sold. In fact, when the volume is not there, the cost of manufacturing a dress becomes extremely high.

If we take the example of a women's suit sold at retail for €1,200, the wholesale price will be about €500 (that is, a mark-up coefficient of 2.4). Table 3.3 gives an indication of how manufacturing costs vary with volume.

The manufacturing cost can be multiplied by two or three if the item is to be made in small volumes. In such cases, it becomes too expensive

Table 3.3   Cost of Making a Woman's Suit in France (€)

	If Large Volume	**If Small Volume**
Manufacturing cost	100	300
Accessories (buttons, lining, etc.)	50	60
Fabric	100	110
Total cost	250	470

to use a laser cutter, and the way in which individual pieces are located on the fabric may not be as economical as with larger volumes. The process of making the suit may then become entirely manual, with no guarantee that the quality is much better at the end of it all.

The economic picture is also dependent on whether the products are all sold at full price, or some have to be sold at bargain prices, with discounts that can range from 30 to 70%. When production runs are small and most products are only sold at bargain prices, profitability is certainly no longer on the horizon, keeping in mind that for some "difficult brands" in a good season less than 50% of the collection is normally sold at full price.

This is where license deals come into the picture, as they provide the cash necessary in the early days to invest heavily in these ready-to-wear activities and to ensure that they are successful.

The Most Common Organizational Structure.   It is fairly common within many luxury fashion brands that the position of marketing manager does not exist. The reason for this is that the role of the marketing manager is to find out from the consumer what the brand should be, and that could be in direct conflict with the designer, whose job is to create what the consumer should have. Nevertheless, it is extremely necessary to have one person whose rare competence is to be able to provide unobtrusive guidelines that force the designer to look at what happens in the stores. This position is generally referred to in the US and UK fashion circles as the merchandiser.

Another specific role within luxury fashion is that of the communications and/or public relations manager. This person generally reports to the general manager and acts as a very important conduit between the GM and the designer.

Luxury fashion structures seldom have factories (there is generally a purchasing manager or supply chain manager in charge of sourcing products). So, the most important jobs fall within the field of store activities: store managers, of course, but also area managers, country retail managers, regional retail managers, and retail merchandising manager worldwide.

As mentioned earlier, the number of staff is limited, and they are in direct contact either with the designer or with the final consumer.

Perfumes and Cosmetics

As we saw in Chapter 2, perfumes and cosmetics is one of the largest luxury sectors, with total sales estimated at around €65 billion. It is also the largest in staff, as it employs probably more than 30% of all luxury-goods employees. It is also relatively concentrated, with Paris, New York, Barcelona, and Geneva being major headquarters.

This business entails selling standardized products in large quantities at low unit prices and, in this, is somewhat reminiscent of the fast-moving consumer-goods market. But, as we will discuss, this is a very different activity because the consumer expects to find a product with a very high aesthetic content and something that is special every time.

The Market

This is, strangely enough, a relatively recent market. For many years individual perfumers would extract fragrances from flowers through an alembic, as described in Patrick Susskind's novel (and subsequent film) *Perfume*.[1] Perfumers generally had another activity: they also sold gloves. This is why a French perfumer is now developing retail stores under the name Parfumeur et Gantier (Perfumer and Glovemaker). The mass-market business of selling the same standard product over time to a larger population started in the eighteenth century in the city of Köln, where "Kölnish Wasser" or "Eau de Cologne" were developed under the German brand 4711. Guerlain came into being at the end of the nineteenth century. All other brands were started in the twentieth century: Caron, then Chanel, Patou, Lancôme, and Lanvin. Most of the major brands such as Estée Lauder, Dior, Armani, and Ralph Lauren were created after 1950.

Given the fact that the average product is sold at retail for less than €100 and that the total sales of €65 billion includes products sold at wholesale and export prices, it is likely that as many as 2 to 3 billion units of luxury products are manufactured and bought every year. In major developed markets, product penetration reaches 80% of households, with a minimum purchase of one to two units a year for perfumes and much more for cosmetics. This is a very large market.

---

[1] Patrick Susskind, *The Perfume: The Story of a Murderer*. Alfred Knopf, 1986.

Consumer Expectations.   When consumers buy a perfume, they are looking for an intensely personal, sensuous, almost narcissistic, pleasure (which comes from holding and opening an aesthetically pleasing bottle and breathing in a sophisticated scent that conveys a sense of luxury and personal satisfaction). But they are also looking for social reassurance: they want to appear sophisticated and to have "good taste." Perfumes provide a personal dream of luxury at a reasonable price. It is great to be able to afford the luxury and sophistication of Chanel or Saint Laurent for less than €80.

For cosmetic products, customer expectations are quite different. Make-up, which women often carry in their handbags, has strong social connotations: there is a much greater degree of sophistication conveyed by opening a handbag and taking out a Chanel or a Hermès lipstick than there is in pulling out a mass-market product from the same handbag. For skin-care products, expectations are again different as they deal with a long-term investment in personal appearance—the need to look good and the hope of remaining good-looking for a long time.

What is clear is that consumers are looking for much more than is actually contained in the bottle. This is why knock-offs (those cheap perfumes sold for a couple of dollars in US supermarkets with a claim like "if you like Youth Dew from Estée Lauder, you will love this perfume number 17") have never done well. Of course, the fragrance is an important part of the deal, but the perceived quality of the bottle, its aesthetic value, and the social reinforcement it provides is certainly much more important.

In fact, consumers are much more interested in what we might call the environment of the product than in the product itself.

Product Types.   The mass-market segment has never really worked for perfumes. Only 20% of perfume units are sold through mass markets, and this has not changed in the past 30 years. Major mass-market merchandisers have offered extended low-price ranges, with retail prices around 10 or 15€ but without significant success. Most women, whatever their level of income, prefer to buy a €60 Dior perfume in a sophisticated perfumery or department store than spend €10 on a little-known brand in their supermarket.

The make-up category is divided into two subsegments. For social make-up (lipstick or touch-up products that they carry in their handbags and use in front of others), women buy—and will continue to buy—the right brand and in a sophisticated environment. On the other hand, for personal make-up products (such as nail polish), most of the buying is done in supermarkets or other mass-markets distributors, which represent around 75% of unit volume.

Skin-care products are a different case again. In the 1950s and 1960s, most products were sold through department stores and perfumeries, as consumers were looking for advice on which products were suited to their specific skin type. Today, consumers are much more knowledgeable about skin-care products. Most of the units purchased (around 80%) are bought through mass-market distributors. Mass-market brands such as Plénitude de L'Oréal or Procter & Gamble's Oil of Olay have done a very good job in catering to such a market.

Of course, the €65 billion we mentioned earlier relates only to the luxury part of this market. How this evolves over time remains to be seen, but it will all depend on the quality of the products and the diversity of the luxury segment. What we can say is that for a perfume or a cosmetic product, consumers are very interested in the aesthetic values of the bottle or the jar, of the top, of the outer carton box, of the specific luxury positioning of the selective products, and of the dream conveyed by the concept, which all combine to enrich the purchasing experience and the pleasure to be had from using the products.

Consumers are also very interested in the sophistication of the purchasing environment. They want the products to be available but they value an impression of scarcity, as if the products were available only to them. Of course, this is not easy to achieve for products that are sold by several billion units every year.

The concept of affordable luxury for top exclusive brands in a sophisticated environment will remain the key to the development of the market for years to come.

The Split between Niche Perfumes and Mass Selective Perfumes

Niche perfumes can be defined as low-volume upscale products generally sold outside of traditional multibrand fragrance stores and presented through blogs or world of mouth, generally without the use of media advertising.

To differentiate between niche perfumes and other luxury selective perfumes, we have coined the term *mass selective* to speak of perfumes that are obviously luxury and selective, as, for example, Gucci or Ralph Lauren, but that try to be distributed in every major department store and perfume store chains like Sephora or Douglas. Their expected presence everywhere requires a substantial mass advertising and social media budget so that the perfumes come off the shelf and have a strong awareness among a large customer base.

Niche perfume offers were developed as a complete departure from the heavily advertising traditional perfume brands like Chanel N°5, J'Adore de Dior, or White Linen from Estée Lauder. Those products are heavily advertised, distributed everywhere in the world, and, if possible, in every perfume store, including duty-free and even discount outlets, and have an impressive awareness among perfume users.

On the contrary, niche perfumes are preferred by perfume expert clients who do not want to use the same perfume as their neighbors. Niche customers are confident with their own choices and want to make sure they select a fragrance on its smell and on its basic components. They want to believe that they are not interested in the marketing messages communicated by the product and only in its basic performances.

Niche Perfumes Early Comers. Niche perfumes are not new. L'Artisan Parfumeur, for example, was founded in 1976. It developed different perfumes, which would be distinguished by their natural components like flowers, spices, or fruits. In the late 1980s, the owners of the company started to develop outside of Paris. They opened two stores in New York but could not reach their break-even sales. After a few years, they had to close their American stores. They probably did not reach the volume that was necessary to pay the rent and the staff.

Annick Goutal was created in 1981, a few years later: products were exclusively sold in their own stores in France. To satisfy the tastes of different customers, the brand had to create many different perfumes. The product line had to be wide-ranging. The brand was doing well in France but had difficulty developing abroad in its own monobrand stores, which required very heavy upfront investments. In the late 1980s Annick Goutal tried to develop in the United States through large exclusive counters in department stores, but the sales volumes they obtained could not pay the staff salaries and they almost went bankrupt. They had to retrench and to limit the sale of their perfume almost exclusively to France in a first step, then slowly try again to move out of France.

Also notable are other early brands like Serge Lutens (created by Shiseido), which was strong in France, or Penhaligon, which developed first in the United Kingdom, but which seemed, then, to have been unable to develop profitably outside of their home base.

The Early Developers.   A second category of niche brands developed in the late 1990s and the early 2000s; Frédéric Malle and Jo Malone, for example.

Compared to the early comers, these niche brands had two advantages:

1. They could develop their brand awareness through social media and, with the support of bloggers who then existed in every country, to have many followers who often had a genuine interest of the perfume world and a deep knowledge and a strong interest in new perfumes and creations.
2. They could sell their products abroad through the Internet, and the stores they opened abroad could be mainly considered as showrooms and public relations investments. In this case, the monobrand retail network had become a marketing support but not the only way to develop the business and make money.

The Reaction of Traditional Brands.   Beginning in 2000, major traditional mass selective marketing brands realized that the new niche brands offered a new perfume concept and that they could take advantage of it (see Table 3.4). Aside from their blockbuster brands, they created new collections of niche perfumes using an additional concept and a new distribution network: either a luxurious boutique corner in their own fashion stores or exclusive monobrand perfume stores.

Expected Growth of Niche Perfumes.   Gérard Delcourt, former chairman of the French Perfume Industry Association, has estimated that niche perfume sales accounted for 8% of the total selective perfume market or €1.1 billion over a total of €14 billion in 2015 (this is the part of total perfume sales in the combined perfumes, makeup, and cosmetics that we estimated at €65 billion for 2019). Gérard Delcourt predicted that the niche brands business would develop at an average of 25% a year, which means it would already reach €3 billion in sales in 2020, and

Table 3.4 Examples of Niche Collections for Major Perfume housesa

Launch Date	Brand	Number of Different Perfumes	Retail Prices (€)b	Bottle Size
2003	Armani Privé	29	180	100 ml
2003	Maison Lancôme collections	7	179	100 ml
2013	Chanel les Exclusifs	27	175	125 ml
2014	Dior Collection Privée	34	198	125 ml
2015	Saint Laurent Le vestiaire des parfums	11	210	125 ml
2016	Louis Vuitton	18	225	100 ml

[a] This table gives an example of brands that have developed their own "niche perfumes" collections. It does not include Guerlain and Hermès, both of which had developed such collections early as their way of embodying another philosophy in the development of perfume products and perfume brands.

[b] As a comparison, Chanel N°5 Eau de Toilette 50 ml retails for €75 and J'Adore de Dior Eau de Parfum 50 ml retails for €87 in France. Generally, as one moves from 50 ml to 100 ml bottles, the prices of mass selective perfumes increase by 60% or €110 for 100 ml of Chanel N°5 and €130 for 100 ml of J'Adore from Dior.

we know now that the figure for 2019 was clearly above €3 billion if it includes the new niche launches of the major mass selective perfume brands, and if it also includes a product line like the Louis Vuitton perfume line, whose sales we estimate at more than €500 million euros in 2019. The recent development of new niche brands by major operators like Dior, Saint Laurent, and Louis Vuitton have even accelerated this growth and made it a major segment of the total future perfume industry.

The Niche Perfume Economic Model.   The economics of niche retail perfumes are very different from those of mass selective perfumes. For mass selective perfumes, it is generally estimated that advertising and promotions can reach 25% of wholesale sales or close to €10 for a retail price of €100. In the case of sales through major perfume retail chains, the margin after advertising cost can become quite tight.

Contrarily, niche perfume brands are selling more expensive products or at least in bigger containers, and one of their major cost of operations is the rental cost of their stores. For niche perfumes, the critical variable is the retail store rental cost. The good news is that if those niche perfume stores must be opened in interesting and fashionable streets, they do not need to be in top luxury locations.

More good news for niche perfumes is that consumers expecting top-quality ingredients and small production runs are relatively price inelastic and in their search for top-quality and original perfumes, they view those purchases as exceptional moments for themselves or for those to whom they purchase such gifts.

In the future, these two markets will have to live separately. The mass selective products will develop first with perfumes, then makeup and skin-care products; the niche fragrances will develop in their own stores and will probably remain loyal to the only "fragrance" part of the cosmetic business.

The Financial Aspect of Perfumes and Cosmetics

The basic principle of luxury perfumes and cosmetics is that the same product, generally manufactured in one single location or, at most, in two or three locations, must be available everywhere in the world, with the same luxury presentation to the different national customers.

Products must therefore be shipped everywhere, and the necessary customs duties must be paid everywhere in the world. The same product must therefore go through different distribution phases depending on the markets in which it is to be offered, as illustrated in Table 3.5.

We have taken the example of the same product that would be sold in France and in Chile at the same retail price. In France, things are

Table 3.5 Comparison of Cost Structures for a Product Sold in Different Countries (Based on an Assumed Retail Price of €100 in the French and the Chilean Markets)

	France	Chile	Coefficients for Chile
Retail price	100.00	100.00	675.76
Wholesale price	50.00	55.00	371.62
Distributor or agent's margin		27.50	185.81
Local advertising budget		8.25	55.74
Landed cost		19.25	130.00
Paris ex-factory		14.80	100.00

simple: the company operates with its own salesforce and the billing is done at the wholesale level—the company nets €50 for each product that is sold for €100 retail. In Chile, things are a bit more complicated. The product is generally sold by a local distributor, who works on a margin of 50% of the wholesale value. Also, a special local budget of 15% of wholesale (i.e., €8.25) is set aside for local advertising and promotional activities. The landed cost is therefore €19.25, on which duties, freight, and insurance have been paid. This means that the French manufacturer will receive only €14.80 for each €100 of retail sales in Chile. Thus, the system requires very high gross margins in France for the Chilean business to be profitable. In this case, a gross margin of at least 70%, and probably 80%, is necessary.

While the figures may differ according to the country being targeted, very high margins are generally necessary in the perfumes and cosmetics category. Bear in mind, too, that advertising and promotional budgets (incorporating media advertising, samples, testers, in-store displays, and other PR activities) are very high and can be anything from 15% to 25% of wholesale prices.

The Major Operators

The Major Brands.   To be strong on a worldwide level, sales of €300 million are necessary. The brands that have achieved this level are listed in Table 3.6.

Table 3.6   Brands with Sales Above €300 Million

Armani	Hermès
Biotherm	Hugo Boss
Bulgari	Jo Malone
Calvin Klein	Kenzo
Chanel	Kiehl's
Clarins	Lacoste
Clinique	Lancôme
Dior	Nina Ricci
Dolce & Gabbana	Paco Rabanne
Estée Lauder	Saint-Laurent
Gucci	Sisley
Guerlain	Thierry Mugler

Table 3.7   Second-Tier Brands (Sales €100–300 million)

Azzaro	Kenzo
Balenciaga	Lancaster
Cacharel	Lanvin
Carolina Herrera	Montblanc
Coach	Paloma Picasso
Davidoff	Salvatore Ferragamo
Escada	Shu Uemura
Issey Miyake	Van Cleef & Arpels
Jean Paul Gaultier	Victor & Rolf
Jimmy Choo	

Of these 24 brands, 11 (Armani, Chanel, Clarins, Clinique, Dior, Estée Lauder, Gucci, Guerlain, Kiehl's, Lancôme, and Saint-Laurent) have sales above €1 billion. All, except the niche brand Jo Malone, have large advertising budgets (in most cases, above €100 million) and have established a strong presence everywhere in the world.

Also, most of these brands operate in the different segments of the industry. Half—Chanel, Clarins, Clinique, Dior, Estée Lauder, Guerlain, Lancôme, Saint Laurent, and Sisley—operate in all three segments (perfumes, skin care, and makeup); just eight—Bulgari, Gucci, Hugo Boss, Jo Malone, Lacoste, Paco Rabanne, Ralph Lauren, and Thierry Mugler—deal exclusively in perfumes.

Table 3.7 lists the second-tier brands (that is, those with sales between €100 million and €300 million) that also have a strong presence.

It is in this group that the fight for survival is the most clear-cut. Of these 19 brands, some are growing very fast while others are in decline.

The group of brands with sales below €100 million offers a different pattern. Those that make up this group are many and varied and include Boucheron, Paloma Picasso, and Salvador Dali.

The Major Corporations.   This business, despite its creative outlook and its international flavor, is really quite concentrated, with the 10 firms shown in Table 3.8 representing more than 85% of the total sector.

Estée Lauder, based in New York, began life as a unique cosmetics firm for the Estée Lauder brand. Today, it is a diversified group that has added Clinique, Aramis, Prescriptive, MAC, La Mer, and Jo Malone, among others, to its brand offerings. It is very strong in makeup and

Table 3.8 Performance (€ million) of the Major Luxury Perfumes and Cosmetics Companies (2019)

	Status	Sales	Operating Profit	Net Profit	Total Group Sales
Estée Lauder	Autonomous firm (stock market)	13,671	4,079	1,510	13,671
L'Oréal (luxury division)	A division of L'Oréal (stock market)	11,000	2,490	1,800	29,900
LVMH (perfumes and cosmetics)	A division of LVMH (stock market)	6,835	683	268 (E)	53,700
Coty Luxury products	A division of Coty (stock market)	3,030	213	N.A.	7,956
Chanel	A division of Chanel private	3,000 (E)	840 (E)	540 (E)	11,000 (E)
Puig	Private company	2,250 (E)	N.A.	250 (E)	2,100 (E)
L'Occitane	Stock market company	1,427	151	117	1,427
Shiseido fragrances	Stock market company	900 (E)	N.A.	N.A.	10,000 (E)
Clarins	Private company	998 (E)	N.A.	N.A.	998 (E)
Sisley	Private company	750 (E)	N.A.	N.A.	750 (E)

Source: Annual reports or authors' estimates. (E) indicates authors' estimates.

skin care, but also powerful in fragrances. In the past few years, it has developed new modern positioning perhaps best illustrated by what it is doing with Origins. It has also purchased several niche brands in addition to Jo Malone: Frédéric Malle, By Killian, and Le Labo, and will probably be the first group to reach sales of €1 billion in the niche business. It has come with distinctive brands, sold solely through its own stores (with only a few exceptions), rather than through department stores, using natural or active positioning. The company, still family controlled, is traded on the New York stock market and is very profitable.

L'Oréal, Produits de Luxe, based in Paris, is also a strong operator. It has brands managed from Paris (Lancôme, Armani, and Biotherm, for example), but also operates brands from New York (Ralph Lauren and Kiehl's) and Tokyo (Shu Uemura). Its Lancôme brand is very strong in cosmetics, but less so in perfume and reached €4 billion in 2019. Its other perfume lines include Paloma Picasso, Guy Laroche, Cacharel, and many others. This luxury division of L'Oréal is very profitable. In 2008, they purchased perfume brands Saint Laurent (working today as a license) and others like Alexander McQueen and Roger & Gallet from the Gucci Group, then, a bit later, the niche brand Atelier Cologne. In 2018 and 2019, they also acquired the perfume brand Thierry Mugler (with Azzaro) and several license contracts including Prada and Valentino, so, when the market recovers, they should have good sales growths in the next few years.

The **LVMH perfumes and cosmetics division** is the third-largest, thanks to Dior, which represents about half of the total. Guerlain is a great brand, but is better known in France than abroad. Though Givenchy has experienced some difficulties in recent years, these appear to have been solved. Kenzo is also an interesting growing brand. They have also purchased Makeup Forever. The fact is, though, that the overall financial performance is not great. It is fair to assume that Dior is quite profitable: this being the case, it is also fair to assume that some of the other brands are probably having financial difficulties.

Coty Prestige, based in New York, but also in Paris, is a German group of perfume brands created in 1991 by Benckiser as a diversification activity from the detergent business. It has been able to develop or acquire some of the best industry licenses, including Davidoff, Calvin Klein, Chloé, Lancaster, Jil Sander, Joop, and Vera Wang. It has licensed Marc Jacob. It has celebrity perfumes such as Jennifer Lopez and Sarah Jessica Parker. This was a rapidly growing private group that is much more involved in perfumes than in cosmetics. In 2017, they decided to purchase the luxury perfume division of Procter & Gamble, which gave them Gucci, Hugo Boss, Lacoste, Escada, and many others. But the merger between the two companies has been difficult: many strong perfume brands left the group (Dolce & Gabbana, Valentino, and others).

They have also purchased the Bourjois group from Chanel, but global results were recently quite lackluster—a good opportunity for the German family group to purchase some of their shares at the stock market to increase the family control on the operations.

Chanel, a private company based in Switzerland, mainly works for that unique brand. The business is built largely around it, but, in the fashion field, it also incorporates Holland & Holland and Erès. Just like Dior and Estée Lauder, Chanel is in the race to become the biggest perfume and cosmetic brand in the world and grow above Lancôme.

Puig is a Spanish group, very powerful at home, which owns major brands like Nina Ricci, Paco Rabanne, Jean-Paul Gaultier, and Carolina Herrera (for both fashion and perfumes) and which also handles brands under license, such as, for example, Christian Louboutin or Comme des garçons. They also own niche brands like L'Artisan Parfumeur and Penhaligon and manage celebrities' brands like Banderas.

L'Occitane has known a very impressive growth rate in the past 10 years. Products are sold almost exclusively in their 1,572 own stores, franchises, or department store shop-in-shops, with very few products in multibrand stores. It conveys a message of nostalgia and Provence tradition, but in a rather sophisticated way.

Clarins was created as a skin-care brand in Paris about 40 years ago. It has become a very strong group but in 2019, they sold their perfumes division (Thierry Mugler, Azzaro, and Montana) to L'Oréal. It also has a minority investment in L'Occitane, the figures of which are not consolidated.

Shiseido Europe is the group that started Issey Miyake perfume. They then launched Jean Paul Gaultier, which now belongs to Puig. It purchased Decleor, with which it has done very well, and Carita. It now represents Dolce & Gabbana, Issey Miyake, Narciso Rodriguez, and Alaia.

Sisley was created by Hubert d'Ornano after he sold the former family firm, Orlane. It is a private family firm that has developed consistently over the past 30 years.

These 10 companies, claiming 85% of the total volume, have very strong brands. Of them, only one group has taken many new licenses and has created a strong base from almost nowhere 30 years ago: Coty. Strangely enough the French have generally been unable to develop new license deals, with the exception of L'Oréal and InterParfums (Montblanc, Jimmy Choo, Lanvin, Coach, Rochas, S.T. Dupont, and others). However, this company, with sales of €600 million, is growing fast but is relatively small and belongs in the second-tier category.

Is There Room for Outsiders?.   In reviewing the very big groups, questions arise as to whether the barrier to entry is too high and if there is actually room for newcomers.

This really all depends on how consumers react to a new product. If the product gets early consumer interest and acceptance at the outset, it can do very well; and as the margins are very high, it is possible to start the business with a very limited cash investment.

But as the risk of failure is very high, companies with limited funds can only really afford to launch a brand once; if they are not successful, they have great difficulty trying a second time.

There are, of course, brands that were launched independently and with limited funds but that still did very well. These include Bulgari, Lolita Lempicka, Kenzo (before it was purchased by LVMH), and MAC (before it was purchased by Estée Lauder), for example, without speaking of niche brands.

The new situation is that niche perfume brands can be started and developed with relatively limited budgets, as explained earlier.

Key Management Issues

Sophisticated Marketing.   Traditionally, marketing perfumes and cosmetics is different from what happens at the mass-market level. For one thing, a perfume can be "hated" by most people and still be a great success if it is liked very strongly by 3–5% of the target audience worldwide. To be successful, a perfume must be different, and even if it is perceived as unpleasant by many people, it can still do well. In this industry, products that perform well in open tests and in blind tests are not necessarily strong performers in the marketplace. To take an extreme example, it could be said that the fragrance that would perform best in product tests would be Cologne Water: nobody would reject it, even if nobody was very excited about it. Product tests must be conducted to see if a perfume has a strong negative or a special weakness that had not been perceived, but the final product decision should never be based on test results alone.

Another difficulty in market tests is that a very great worldwide success may only have a penetration of 4%: it is very difficult to find users and to interview them. For example, in considering modifications to the packaging of its "Pour un Homme" product, Caron decided it would interview French current users, but these constituted less than 0.5% of the French male population; interviewing 200 of them would have required an original sample of 40,000. The company therefore decided to ask a group of perfume stores to take the addresses of those who bought the product and agreed to be interviewed. But, of course, the sample was not really representative of either the total population or of those who used the product. Today, this would be easy to do thanks to Internet platforms.

Unfortunately, because of such limitations, target marketing is also quite difficult. Segmentations are difficult to study, target, and measure.

Selective perfumes marketing is a bit like fashion marketing. Part of it is top down in that someone has to decide how the product fits into a given fashion trend at a given time; the shape, the fragrance, and even the colors of the packaging are not selected by chance. They often result from an analysis of major long-term fashion trends. Asking today's consumer what tomorrow's product should be would in fact miss the point.

Nevertheless, market research is a very important aspect of the tactical decisions behind such things as shapes, positioning concepts, advertising execution, or baseline slogan, for example.

Worldwide Advertising and Promotion.   Contrary to what happens with mass-market products, consumers of luxury perfumes and cosmetics expect to find the same advertising campaign and the same positioning everywhere in the world. In the mass market, it is possible to adjust positioning and communication to local needs and to local circumstances. In selective perfumes and cosmetics, the same brand platform should apply everywhere.

This does not mean that there should not be specific changes to adjust to one country or another. For example, in Japan, men's fragrance lines include numerous hair products (liquids and tonics) because those products are obviously needed there. In the same way, products for a cosmetic line must be adjusted to meet the specific needs of Asian customers, American customers, and European customers. In some markets, people prefer jars; in others, they prefer tubes or dispensing bottles. In some markets the scent should be lighter or almost nonexistent; such adjustments must be made locally, but based on a common platform.

In promotional activities in this category, we have identified three different types of countries, leading to large differences. These are as follows:

1. Those, including Spain, Italy, Argentina, and Brazil, in which small perfumery stores are the most important channel of distribution.
2. Those such as France (Sephora) and Germany (Douglas) where dealing is done through large chains of perfumeries that have centralized purchasing systems and only merchandising activities in the local stores.
3. Those such as the United States, Japan, Mexico, and Australia, where department stores produce more than 50% of the total volume.

In addition, duty-free operations provide a very large part of worldwide purchases (for perfumes, in particular), with major sales recorded in airport duty-free stores and through in-flight outlets.

For each of these, the promotional plan should be different: for department store countries, gifts with purchase or purchases with purchases are a very important part of the marketing plan. In countries with large distribution chains, merchandising becomes critical. In duty-free activities, promotional programs must be adjusted as well.

The name of the game is therefore a very strong, generalized marketing platform with specific local adjustments.

Managing Distribution Networks.   Almost everybody uses a mix of fully owned subsidiaries, local distributors, and, in some cases, commission agents, and here again marketing programs must be adjusted to these different setups. This subject will be covered in Chapter 10.

Organizational Structures

For perfumes and cosmetics, the organizational structure is very similar to what it would be for mass-market products. Marketing and sales staff are crucial for cosmetics products, making training a high-priority activity both for staff operating counters fully owned by the brand and for multibrand sales staff who also need to understand the specifics of each of the brand's products and its general brand positioning.

The Leather Goods Market

We spoke earlier of all fashion accessories but for this subsection, we wanted to concentrate exclusively on leather goods. Sometimes this definition also includes shoes, but here we have decided to keep shoes outside of our analysis: for shoes, we consider the manufacturing processes and the commercial challenges to be quite specific, so will not speak about them.

The Market

The world market, at a mix of retail and wholesale, corresponds to approximately €35 billion. It can be divided into the following three major segments.

Ladies' Handbags.   Handbags are a fashion accessory and part of a woman's total look. In fact, a beautiful dress or an impressive woman's suit can be "damaged" if worn with a cheap plastic handbag or a bag made of low-quality leather. Also, a brand-new and sophisticated dress can lose its fashion and its freshness if it is combined with an old, outdated, and shapeless bag. A handbag is clearly a fashion accessory. This is very obvious for the Japanese. It is obvious for the Italian, the Chinese, and the American, but it is not always perceived as such by French consumers. On the contrary, a branded and new-fashioned handbag can freshen up a slightly outdated dress and give it additional style. A luxury handbag can cost around €200 to €5,000, so it is a lower expense than for a sophisticated fashion dress, and it has a much longer life.

Luggage.   When people travel by car for a weekend or keep their luggage on a plane flight or on a train, they are looking for elegant, light, and convenient products. They are happy to show different luggage that can demonstrate their sophistication and their social status to their friends. In contrast, for luggage that must be checked at the airport to end up as cargo on a plane, they are looking for strong products, convenient and as standard as possible because they are afraid that an upscale suitcase, for example, may be more frequently identified, searched, or stolen by the cargo-handling team of an airport or another. A luggage collection must therefore correspond to two contradictory criteria: sophistication and an ability to stand out on one side, and anonymity and a low profile on the other.

Small Leather Goods.   Such items are the necessary complements of a handbag collection. Wallets and purses must exist in every color and every handbag style; they are a frequent complementary purchase. They have to be developed to take into account local practices. To handle US dollars, euros, or yuans, one needs a pocket of a different size. In the same way, driver's licenses or identification cards have different sizes and formats: small leather goods items, to be in line with local practices, must be diversified almost without limits.

All this calls for a very large collection, sometimes several hundreds of stock-keeping units per season. For manufacturers, leather goods provide higher gross margins than ready-to-wear, so this can be a very profitable activity. This higher margin standard comes from the fact that the consumer is looking for a much longer use of the product than is the case for ladies' ready-to-wear. A suitcase can last more than 10 years and its purchase seems like an investment rather than a seasonal wish. It is also an ideal gift and it is often given for special occasions. But for a gift to be perceived as a purchase with limited risk, the brand must be known and valued and the product must be different, recognizable, and attractive.

The Major Operators

Table 3.9 lists the major operators of the sector. The list is nevertheless not complete because we have decided, for example, to consider Prada as a leather goods brand (it started as a shoe brand then as a leather goods one) and not include Gucci (it was considered a fashion brand, which is unfair for a brand that was created by Mr. Guccio Gucci, a ladies' handbags manufacturer and distributor).

What is shown in this table is that five or six brands correspond to a very large part of this market and probably have a very high profitability.

Table 3.9   Major Leather Goods Manufacturers (2019)

	Nationality	Sales (million €)	Ownership
Louis Vuitton	French	13,000 (E)	LVMH
Hermes	French	6,883	Quoted
Coach	US	3,900	Tapestry
Fendi	Italian	1,600 (E)	LVMH
Prada	Italian	1,570	Quoted
Kate Spade	US	1,260	Tapestry
Longchamp	French	800	Private
Furla	Italian	700 (E)	Private
Hunting World	US	400 (E)	Private
Loewe	Spain	350 (E)	LVMH
Mulberry	UK	180	Quoted
Lancel	Italian	60	Private
Mandarina Duck	Italian	50 (E)	Private
Valextra	Italian	50 (E)	Private

Source: Major annual reports and management comments of the firms. (E) indicates authors' estimates.

One should also notice that apart from Longchamp, Loewe and Furla, the smaller operators on this market are relatively small and seem to have difficulty in becoming major worldwide global brands.

Key Management Issues

We will start with the creative requirements of this sector, then look at the industrial and commercial challenges.

Finding an identifiable style is a necessary requirement of this industry. Developing a new handbag is not enough. It must be different from those of other brands and two products of the brand must have something in common. For entry price products, it is not too difficult: one must develop a special canvas design, playing on the logo of the brand or on a specific pattern, playing with the letters of the brand or some other particularities, and using a mix of tone or tone colors: Louis Vuitton does that very well, but so do Gucci, Fendi, and Dior. Other brands like Lancel had developed a traditional canvas pattern but they seem to have abandoned it over time. Others like Longchamp have come out with a specific canvas pattern much more recently.

One must also create a collection of full leather handbags, immediately recognizable, that brings something new and an additional value to the brand. Dior, with its handbag Lady Dior, has perfectly reached that objective; Chanel, too, with its 1955 model. Other brands like Salvatore Ferragamo or Armani have never been able to develop their own handbag style that could make any item clearly recognizable and give a brand family look to different models. Saint Laurent was also unable to do so. This requirement is necessary for handbags, but also for luggage. For luggage, one needs a general concept, easily identifiable but that can evolve over time and be adapted to different models.

Manufacturing is also an important field. One must start with top-quality components: a strong quality canvas or top leather pieces. But the products must have an outstanding look, be sophisticated and, have a long life.

Traditionally, this upscale leather manufacturing came mainly from Italy, France, and, to a lesser extent, Spain. But the lower labor costs of China, Thailand, and Taiwan seem to have lured some brands to move their production to Asia. This is the case, for example, for Coach, which claims that most of its production is done in Asia. It is to a lesser extent the case for other brands, which must compete directly with brands made exclusively in China, as, for example, Carolina Herrera.

Although Chinese leather goods manufacturers do not reach the domain of the craftsmanship of Europe and its sophistication in the smallest details, they have improved significantly in the past 15 years and their final products can have an acceptable final quality, principally if the leather that is used comes from Italy, Spain, or France.

Distribution is also a major issue. It must be worldwide and requires directly operated stores built in the best locations and with a sophisticated and minimalist design, and communicates the craftsmanship and sophistication of the product line. But one may also sell in multibrand stores that provide additional sales volume and a higher brand visibility. Such multibrand stores must be carefully selected, so that the products of the brand do not end up in stores selling mainly plastic handbags or low-quality leather goods.

For leather goods, duty-free stores are quite important because they provide not only volume, but also visibility and image. The issue here is to make sure the brand is presented with the best merchandising conditions and, if possible, given a better brand status than its most direct competitors.

To finish, one must say that if, in this subsection, we have spoken exclusively of leather goods brands, one must not forget that for brands like Chanel, Dior, Gucci, or Dolce & Gabbana, ladies' handbags are an important part of total fashion sales. A strong leather goods collection can help a store to reach more easily its break-even. In Asia, leather goods can represent up to 40% of the sales of a given brand in its own store. Without leather goods, many Asian fashion boutiques would be losing money.

Chapter 3B

Major Luxury Sectors

Wines and Spirits, Jewelry and Watches, and Hotels and Hospitality

Wines and Spirits

This is the only luxury category in which products are sold in supermarkets (off trade) or in clubs and restaurants (on trade). Duty-free activities are also very important in this category, in some cases accounting for as much as 20% of total volume.

Despite these unusual outlets, this is still a luxury business because of the sophistication of the products and the worldwide market in which it operates. It is also a product category with very strong branding issues, which will be described later.

The Wines and Spirits Market

As mentioned earlier, this market (excluding fine wines) is estimated to be around €55 billion and is characterized by very different product types: brown products (essentially Scotch whiskies and cognacs); white products (vodka, gin, and rum); and Champagne, which is a market all its own.

The Brown Products.   This group accounts for approximately €20 billion, split approximately 75% for Scotch and 25% for cognac. Though both product categories are fundamentally strong, selling in duty-free outlets and nightclubs, they need to be sold in supermarkets and through wine specialists if they are to build a strong worldwide image.

The cognac market, which continues to do reasonably well in Europe, consists of two distinct strands. The first is the very profitable Asian market (essentially, Japan and China), where it is a status symbol and where people purchase the most aged and expensive products, such as XO. Here, though, where cognac used to be the drink of choice with meals, consumers are now turning toward imported wines. The second strand is the large-volume medium-price markets such as the United States where there is demand for lower-priced VS (Very Superior) and VSOP (Very Superior Old Pale) products.

Whisky sales, the biggest part of these products, have remained steady and have benefited from producers expanding their range of aged-malt products. But this business is not growing because its development potential is limited in an era in which consumers are looking to mix their spirits with, say, cola, but are reluctant to do so with the brown products.

The White Products.   Vodka, gin, and rum each contribute equally to a sales volume of between €5 and €10 billion, with vodka—the preferred drink of the younger generation and good for mixing—experiencing very strong growth and reaching €11 billion. Gin, on the other hand, is declining slightly, but remains a very strong category nevertheless. In the white products, one should not forget tequila, which belongs to the "other" category and which is probably the

Table 3.10   Breakdown of Major Rum Brands (in million cases of nine liters)

Tanduay	20.1
Bacardi	17.1
Captain Morgan	11.7
McDowell's	11.2
Havana Club	4.6
Barcelo	2.2
Bozkov	1.7
Old Port	1.3

Source: Statista, 2019.

smallest market, but still, with €3 billion a year, is very strong in Latin America and in some parts of the United States.

White products have a big advantage in that they are not aged. In a way they are ideal marketing products and, given that advertising is limited for all alcoholic products, sound positioning is more important than anything else in creating awareness and interest for the product category. Rum, which is famous as a mixer in drinks such as the famous Cuba Libre, sells almost exclusively in North and Latin America. Table 3.10 gives the breakdown of the major rum brand sales (many of them unknown to the European customer).

Champagnes.   This is another market of approximately €6 to €7 billion. The name *Champagne* applies exclusively to a product that has been made from grapes from a very small territory around the cities of Reims and Epernay in France. Similar products from any other part of the world must be called sparkling wines (or Prosecco). Champagne sales amount to around 320 million bottles per year. Using grapes solely from the Champagne region limits production to a maximum of 360 million bottles. Given this limitation, producers are engaged in a strong movement of trading up and bringing added value to their brands and to their products. As with cognac and whisky, Champagne must be left to age, and takes advantage of the possibility of blending different wines from different Champagne grapes.

More than half of the world consumption of Champagne is within France itself, followed by the United Kingdom and the United States.

Other Categories. Other categories, also estimated at about €5 billion, include brandies; liqueurs such as Grand Marnier and Cointreau; specific regional products such as Calvados, Armagnac, Metaxa from Greece, Bols from Holland, and so on; and the biggest of all—tequila already mentioned above.

The Major Operators

The Major Brands. A study conducted every year by Intangible Business (from the United Kingdom) defines the "most powerful spirits and wine brands." This is not calculated simply on volume or sales but through a complex score that includes:

- Share of market: volume-based measure of market share
- Brand growth: projected growth based on 10 years' historical data
- Price positioning: a measure of a brand's ability to command a premium
- Market scope: the number of markets in which the brand has a significant presence
- Brand awareness: a combination of spontaneous and prompted awareness
- Brand relevance: the capacity to relate to the brand and the propensity to purchase
- Brand heritage: a brand's longevity and a measure of how embedded it is in local culture
- Brand perception: loyalty and how close a strong brand image is to a desire of ownership

What is striking about the results of this survey (see Table 3.11) is that brands such as Jack Daniel's and Captain Morgan, for example, which are not necessarily known all over the world, still have a very strong clientele and awareness in a given part of the world.

Of this top 20, six are whiskies or bourbons, five are Chinese Maotais, three are brands of vodka, and two are brands of cognac, underlining the importance of these categories.

The Major Corporations. Table 3.12 shows the number of brands sold by the larger groups in 2019.

Table 3.11   The World's Most Powerful Spirits, 2018*

		Sales in Cases	Owner	Country of Origin	Sector
1	Maotai	19.5		China	Maotai
2	Wuilangye	13.5		China	Maotai
3	Yanglie	7.1		China	Maotai
4	Johnnie Walker	3.9	Diageo	Scotland	Whisky
5	Luzhou	3.5		China	Maotai
6	Jack Daniel's	3.2	Brown Forman	USA	Whisky
7	Hennessy	3.1	LVMH	France	Cognac
8	Smirnoff	3.2	Diageo	England	Vodka
9	Gujing Gong Ju	2.2		China	Maotai
10	Bacardi	2.2	Bacardi	Bermuda	Run
11	Absolut	N.A.	Pernod	France	Vodka
12	Grey Goose	N.A.	Bacardi	Bermuda	Vodka
13	Ruang Kao	N.A.		Thailand	Aperitif
14	Chivas Regal	N.A.	Pernod Ricard	Scotland	Whisky
15	Jameson	N.A.	Pernod Ricard	Scotland	Whisky
16	Rémy Martin	N.A.	Rémy Cointreau	France	Cognac
17	Officer's Choice	N.A.	Allied Blenders & Distillers	India	
18	Crown Royal	N.A.	Diageo	Canada	Bourbon
19	Ballantine's	N.A.	Pernod Ricard	Scotland	Whisky
20	Captain Morgan	N.A.	Diageo	Jamaica	Rum

[a] In number of nine-liter cases.
Source: Intangible Business, 2019. Spirits 50, Brand Finance.

Table 3.12   Number of Top 30 Brands Sold by Different Operators

	Number of Brands in Top 30
Diageo (UK)	7
Pernod Ricard (France)	5
Bacardi (Bahamas)	4
Beam Suntory (USA)	3
LVMH	1
Brown Forman	1

Source: Impact Databank, 2019.

Table 3.13   Performance (€ million) of the Top Nine Operators (2019/2020)

	Sales	Operating Profit	Net Profit	
Diageo	10,805	1,964 (E)	2,133 (E)	Assuming Guinness is a €2,264 million business and that profitability is identical across the board.
Pernod Ricard	8,448	2,260	1,654	
Bacardi	6,500 (E)	N.A.	N.A.	Private company not reporting any figures.
LVMH	5,576	1,729	1,283 (E)	
Brown Forman	3,934	1,052		
Beam Suntory	3,500	N.A.	768	The total group has sales of more than €10 billion and the alcoholic drink activities more than €6.5 billion.
Constellation	2,679	374 (E)	249 (E)	Total business, including distribution and beer, reaches €7,466 million.
Campari	1,842	N.A.	267	
Rémy Cointreau	1,125	264	159	

Note: (E) indicates authors' estimates, based on discussions with professionals in these fields.
Source: Annual reports and authors' estimates.

Table 3.13 gives an indication of where the major companies stand in terms of size and profitability.

Diageo, with seven brands among the top 30 and huge sales and profits, is the leader in this field. Its top brands include Smirnoff vodka, Johnnie Walker whisky, Bailey's, J&B whisky, Captain Morgan rum, and Tanqueray and Gordon's gin. The company is public and is the result of the merger between two already big operators in 1997: Guinness and Grand Metropolitan.

Remarkably, for a very powerful group, Diageo has no major cognac or Champagne brands of its own. For many years, first Guinness and then Diageo have been associated in distribution joint ventures with LVMH, which means that Diageo products are distributed with

Hennessy cognacs and some strong LVMH Champagne products. On top of this distribution cooperation, Diageo owns 25% of the LVMH wines and spirits division.

Pernod Ricard started out selling a local product, Pastis, in France. In 2001, it purchased 38% of Seagram's activities; in 2005, acquired the majority of the assets of Allied Domecq; and, in 2008, the vodka brand Absolut. To complement its traditional Pastis 51 and Ricard brands, it now has a very large number of others products with a lot of growth potential. These include Chivas Regal, Ballantine's, Campbell, and Jameson whiskies; Absolut vodka; Havana Club, and Malibu rums; Martell cognac; Seagram's and Beefeater gins; and Perrier Jouët and Mumm Champagnes.

Bacardi is a private group, on which there is very little available data. Headquartered in Bermuda, the company is the offspring of a merger between Bacardi Rum and Martini. But it also owns very impressive brands like Grey Goose vodka, Bombay gin, and Dewar's whisky.

LVMH is a very strong business. It has Hennessy cognac in its stable and is a clear leader in Champagne (with Dom Pérignon, Krug, Moët et Chandon, Veuve Clicquot, and many others). It has distribution joint ventures with Diageo for a strong worldwide presence. While confining itself largely to the cognac and Champagne sectors, it acquired Glenmorangie whisky and Belvedere vodka in 2005.

Brown Forman is a public company created in the United States by a pharmacist in Louisville, Kentucky. Its strongest brands are Jack Daniel's, Southern Comfort, Tennessee whiskies, Finlandia vodka; and many Californian, Italian, and French wines.

Beam Suntory is a division of the Suntory holding group and a sister company of Suntory and Orangina. The total Suntory group reports total sales of €6.25 billion and the international branded activities include Jim Beam and Legent Bourbon but also Courvoisier cognac.

Constellation Brand: Its spirit division recorded sales of €2.672 billion. Its beer sales (more than €1 billion) are in a different product category. The company is, nevertheless, the leader in wines, with 240 brands and 25% of the US wine market. It is also strong in vodka (Svedka), tequila (Casa Noble), whisky, gin, and rum, in particular with the Barton brand.

Campari is an Italian company listed on the Milan stock market, and still controlled by the founding family. Its products include Campari, Cinzano, and Cynar, and a spirit called Sella & Mosca. It has grown very fast in recent years thanks to the success of its Aperol cocktail done with Spritz and prosecco wines. It has recently purchased Grand Marnier and the cognac Bisquit.

Rémy Cointreau is the third French group in this sector. It manufactures Rémy Martin cognac and Cointreau. It sold its Champagne brands Charles Heidsieck and Piper Heidsieck in 2011, and the company says it has enough cash to make a major acquisition.

All of the groups just described appear to have considerable financial strength. Almost all are the result of a series of mergers, a process that is certainly not finished. In the past 10 years, external growth has been a very large part of each company's strategy.

Key Management Issues

Dealing with Mass Merchandisers.   The name of the game is to ensure that the product is available on the shelves of local supermarkets everywhere in the world. It must first be sold to very demanding purchasing managers and then carefully managed in the stores by visiting merchandisers. The fact is, though, that a single product cannot afford the cost of this local merchandising effort, making it an absolute necessity to have a local distribution system that can cover its costs by selling many complementary products. The ideal would be to distribute a brand of whisky, a strong vodka brand, a good cognac, and some Champagnes simultaneously. This in itself requires associations between the different brands or companies to be present everywhere.

This is also the case for nightclubs and restaurants, which are very important for image but difficult to reach and do not necessarily sell large volumes.

Duty-free outlets are very important for creating and maintaining product availability and a strong image for wines and spirits.

The Need for a Worldwide Structure.   Every brand needs to be present and strong everywhere in the world. This often requires joint-venture partnerships such as that between Diageo and LVMH, mentioned earlier. Another such venture, Maxxium, which has now disappeared, was created by Rémy Cointreau, Jim Beam (Beam Suntory), and Famous Grouse whisky (the Errington group from Scotland). In fact, almost every major operator has, in a given country, one or more of its brands being distributed by a friendly local competitor.

Financing Inventories.   A difficult part of this business is the need for the aging of the products before they are put up for sale. The average Champagne must wait 44 months before it is sufficiently aged to have an exclusive and strong taste. For cognac, the average is 68 months, or almost six years, and for certain whiskies it can be considerably longer. This has a financial cost, which can reach as high as 40% of the unit cost of the finished product.

As mentioned earlier, this gives white products a strong advantage because they do not have to age and therefore have a much better cost structure.

The Need for Pull Marketing.   When a product is on a supermarket shelf somewhere, it still has to be picked up by the consumer, and this requires that it is known and appreciated. It is the responsibility of the brand to make sure that the product does not stay on the shelf. It must be advertised strongly. But the advertising of wines and spirits has two limitations. First, in many countries, such advertising is not allowed on television and is often limited to magazines and billboards.

A second limitation springs from the fact that all products are quite similar and are perceived to be similar by the consumer. The only differentiating element is the perceived content of the brand. This will be discussed later. But this is without doubt a very difficult marketing and positioning challenge.

Organizational Structures

Just as for perfumes and cosmetics, marketing and worldwide sales are the most important activities in this category. Companies require a large international workforce within distribution companies, either directly or in joint ventures around the world. Here country managers, zone managers, duty-free specialists, and promoters sell the brand, or a selected number of brands, everywhere in the world.

The Watch and Jewelry Market

In this section, we will first describe the situation of the jewelry market, then deal with the watch business. In fact, the two businesses are similar, but they have different customer expectations and different marketing practices.

The Market

The Jewelry Market.   Executives in the field generally estimate the jewelry market to be worth €45 billion (excluding the Mainland Chinese luxury brands, as explained later). Approximately one third of this is accounted for by nonbranded business, which incorporates the work of all individual family jewelers, who undertake unbranded individual pieces for their customers. Here, products are sold as a function of the weight of gold or silver used in the piece. Precious stones, purchased directly on the open market and valued according to their size, purity, and shape, are often brought by the client to a trusted jeweler, who will mount them in a ring or other piece of jewelry for a reasonable price.

Family jewelers, who may work across several generations of the same family, often manufacture the pieces of jewelry themselves. They may sometimes subcontract the production, but, in every case, they have the trust of their clients and can modify the same piece several times to adapt it to the wishes of different individuals over time.

The branded market has a very different setup. The customer usually does not know anybody inside the store and the trust comes exclusively from the name that appears over the door. Such stores generally sell standard products and would seldom (except, perhaps, for very wealthy clients) recondition an old jewel or add new stones to a piece.

Customer expectations: Given the price of different jewels and the risk of buying a fake or overpriced product, customers rely on someone they can trust. This trust can come from the brand name of a famous jeweler or from individual contact, with the jeweler acting in a role similar to that of a family doctor.

A large part of the business is undertaken for special occasions. Tiffany, for example, is well known in the United States for its engagement rings. Wedding anniversaries or the birth of a baby, for example, are private, family occasions when people look for something special, visiting several stores before they decide what they want and where to buy it. The sale of a company or a piece of real estate may prompt others into buying an expensive piece of jewelry. In such circumstances, they generally know what they want and are prepared to visit several stores to get it.

As they buy jewelry, for special or standard occasions, customers expect a very high level of service from people they feel they can trust. They need to be able to feel that the store cares about them and takes as much time as necessary to satisfy their requirements.

Product ranges: Products can vary greatly, from gold to silver and from products with stones to those without them. Precious stones such as diamonds have a set market value, which is known by everybody, everywhere. Producing a diamond ring in the United States to sell in Japan through a local distributor is not that simple, as margins escalate and the final price must still be within a reasonable target. This is why, in fact, gold pieces can be more profitable and provide greater price flexibility.

One jeweler has found a way around this problem: H. Stern, which originated in Brazil, is a specialist in semiprecious stones and brings to the market jewelry pieces with stones such as aquamarine, amethyst, and yellow citrine.

Financial aspects: Pricing is a very difficult subject in this business. For precious stones, there is a limited range of possible retail prices. For gold, there is an official measure of the retail price: the cost per gram. It is possible to visit gold markets in many places. Bogotá and Lima, for example, provide a choice of many small retailers and many jewelry pieces, but the retail price is computed by weight and the different pieces are simply placed on a scale together to get the final price.

A simple way to compare the pricing level of the different jewelers would be to list their price in dollars per gram of gold. However, the major brands refuse to do this. They do not see themselves simply as sellers of gold but, rather, of artistic objects, for which the work required varies from one piece to another and that the time and skills involved cannot be compared.

Also, at the brand's headquarters, the difficulty is to ensure that the global margin can be divided between the workshop where the piece is made by specialist craftsmen, marketing and promotion, the distributor, and the final retailer or department store.

The Watch Market.   The value of this market is considered by professionals in the field to be around €26 billion. It is more heterogeneous than the jewelry market and differs from it in market segments, gender, and nationalities.

Complication watches or upscale watches have individual movements and, of course, no quartz batteries. They have a movement that is generally handmade and can be self-winding. They are called *complication* watches because of the combination of features they offer, such as time, date, position of the sun and the stars, or the seasons. They often also have a chronograph function. Sometimes, such watches are produced as a single unit or in very limited numbers, commanding prices of up to €200,000 or above.

Jewelry or specialty watches are less sophisticated and are manufactured in larger numbers. In this category, we have put all watches that sell for between €1,000 and €5,000 wholesale and €2,000 and €10,000 at retail. Most are beautifully made objects, sometimes powered by quartz batteries, although most of them are mechanical now, and are ideal expensive gifts.

Fashion or "mood" watches belong to a third category. Here, we have put those watches that sell at retail for €100 to €2,000. These include Tommy Hilfiger, Calvin Klein, and Armani watches. The idea in this category is to promote the concept of owning several watches that can match the customer's changing moods.

Men or women? Watches are one of the few luxury products that men can buy and cherish. Probably 90% of complication watches are purchased by men, many of whom collect old models as they would collect expensive stamps.

Women are important in the second segment as they purchase or are offered expensive watches for special occasions. They are also the largest segment of buyers of fashion and mood watches.

Which Nationalities? Two markets must be singled out. China is a very big market for watches: Traditionally, Chinese men were buyers of luxury products, and expensive watches were taken to be a sign of business and financial success. But when President Xi Jinping wanted to cut corruption in China, he took photos of major politicians with relatively low salaries and very expensive watches on their wrists. Overnight, the expensive watch market in China almost disappeared. In Europe, Italians buy more watches than anybody else and have been known to line up outside a Swatch store the night before a limited-edition model goes on sale. They believe that wearing an expensive, well-known watch is the ultimate in elegance and sophistication.

Other important markets are Japan and the United States, where customers buy both mood watches and more expensive brands (often, for women with a jewelry taste, small diamonds surrounding the watch face), which can become sophisticated conversation pieces.

But watches are also a very important part of men's status and dress codes in Latin America, the Middle East, and South East Asia. Preferences vary around the world: Europeans generally wear their watches with a leather strap, whereas in Asia and tropical countries people prefer steel bracelets.

The Major Operators

The Jewelry Brands.   Table 3.14 shows our estimates of the total sales and of the watch sales of the major operators in the sector. For example, watches account for approximately 33% of Cartier's total business. For Van Cleef, the figure is 10% of sales, and for Tiffany's only 2.5%. However, it is not possible to arrive at the jewelry sales estimate of a brand by simply subtracting the watch sales from the total, because for Cartier, for example, the total sales include scarves and leather goods, and those of Bulgari also include perfumes. What can also be seen from Table 3.14 is that only 10 operators have a major and meaningful level of activity. Some of the highlights are presented next.

We have decided not to put Chanel, Dior, Gucci, and Louis Vuitton in this table because our estimates of sales were too uncertain.

- **Cartier** is the largest brand and an extremely profitable one. It is very strong in watches, which has hurt them in the past few years, but it has also been able to develop an important jewelry business. It is very strong in Europe and Asia and is an important operator in the United States.
- **Tiffany's** is as big as Cartier in jewelry. It is very well known in the United States for its diamond engagement rings, but also, in particular in the United States and Asia, it is also known for such things

Table 3.14   Estimated Sales (including watches) of Major Jewelry Operators, 2019

Operator	Country	Total Sales (€ million)	Watch Sales (€ million)	Ownership
Cartier	France	5,600 (E)	1,900 (E)	Richemont
Tiffany & Co.	United States	3,900	100 (E)	LVMH
Bulgari	Italy	3,200 (E)	275 (E)	LVMH
Van Cleef & Arpels	France	1,500 (E)	150 (E)	Richemont
Chopard	Switzerland	850 (E)	450 (E)	Private
David Yurman	United States	650 (E)	N.A.	Private
L. Graff	United Kingdom	650 (E)	N.A.	Private
H. Stern	Brazil	600 (E)	N.A.	Private
Harry Winston	United States	500 (E)	300 (E)	Swatch
Tous	Spain	450 (E)	50 (E)	Private
Mikimoto	Japan	400 (E)	N.A.	Private
Pomelatto	Italy	200 (E)	N.A.	Kering
Boucheron	France	150 (E)	N.A.	Kering
Damiani	Italy	130 (E)	N.A.	Private
Chaumet	France	100 (E)	N.A.	LVMH
Mauboussin	France	80 (E)	N.A.	Galeries Lafayettes
Repossi	Italy	60 (E)	N.A.	LVMH
Buccelatti	Italy	60 (E)	N.A.	Private
Fred	France	50 (E)	N.A.	LVMH
Qeelin	China	50 (E)	N.A.	Kering
Mellerio	France	15 (E)	08 (E)	Private
Poiray	France	12 (E)	N.A.	Private
Dinh Van	France	12 (E)	N.A.	Private

Note: (E) indicates authors' estimates.

as ballpoint pens, silver-plated birth spoons, and christening medals with low entry prices of around €100 or €120. It is relatively strong in Asia, but not very well established in Europe.

- **Bulgari**, based in Rome, is a strong performer that, from its beginnings as a silversmith, has moved slowly into jewelry and watches. It is also quite strong in perfumes, has a very effective collection of ties and scarves, and is quite active in leather goods. It sold the majority of

Table 3.15   Estimated Sales of Complication/Upscale Watch Operators

Operators	Nationality	Sales (€ million)	Unit Sales	Average Unit Price per €	Wholesale
Patek Philippe	Swiss	1,375	70,000	15,000	Private
Audermars Piguet	Swiss	1,000 (E)	40,000	N.A.	Private
Bréguet	Swiss	500 (E)	30,000	N.A.	Swatch
Vacheron Constantin	Swiss	500 (E)	25,000	20,000	Richemont
Piaget	Swiss	300 (E)	N.A.	N.A.	Richemont
Harry Winston	United States	300 (E)	N.A.	N.A.	Swatch
A Lange & Söhn	German	300 (E)	N.A.	30,000	Richemont
Blancpain	Swiss	250 (E)	5,000	30,000	Private
Frank Muller	Swiss	250 (E)	N.A.	N.A.	Private
Richard Mille	Swiss	250 (E)	4,600	50,000	Private
Girard Perregaud	Swiss	200 (E)	15,000	13,000	Kering

Note: (E) indicates authors' estimates.
Sources: Discussion with industry experts and Vontobel Equity Research, 2019.

the company to LVMH in January 2011. Before this purchase, their sales were around €950 million. So, the development work that was done in this past decade, in particular in high jewelry and leather accessories and also in China, has been very impressive.

- **Van Cleef & Arpels** has also grown very fast in the last 15 years. They are strong in Europe and in the United States. They are also developing in Asia. They remain relatively weak in watches.
- **Chopard**, a family firm based in Geneva, operates 100 stores around the world and has a very impressive performance as a watchmaker. Its "happy diamond" line is well known and well considered.
- **David Yurman**, almost unknown in Asia and Europe, is moving slowly outside of the United States. It is a very strong and much-respected American retailer.
- **Lawrence Graff** started as an apprentice jeweler, then created his firm in 1960. He specializes in very expensive stones, and he generally bids for extremely beautiful stones. He is a specialist in rare diamonds and more specifically in colored diamonds. He has an extremely upscale clientele and only a few beautiful and large stores.

He is strong in England and in the United States, but also in the Middle East and in Asia; he opened a large store in Paris in 2019.

- **H. Stern** was created in Brazil in 1945 by Hans Stern, who passed away in 2007 and was replaced by his eldest son Roberto. Specializing in semiprecious stones, it now has some 160 stores, mostly in Latin America, but with boutiques in the United States, Europe, and Asia.
- **Harry Winston** is an American jeweler with headquarters in New York. It was developed by a Canadian diamond company, which sold it to the Swatch group in 2013. Since the purchase, they have developed a very impressive collection of complication and jewelry watches and opened stores in Asia.
- **Tous** is a somewhat different animal, but its rapid growth in the early twenty-first century, its relative stability for the past seven or eight years, and its creative low-price gold pieces make it an interesting case.

But this list of 23 jewelers is not complete. We must add the three major Chinese retailers:

- **Chow Tai Fook**, first, with headquarters in Shenzhen: With sales of €7.9 billion for 2019, it seems at first sight even bigger than Cartier. Very often people say that they are not a brand but a retailer, because they operate 2,250 stores in mainland China and have only 200 stores out of mainland China, most of them in Hong Kong and Macao. Nevertheless, their web site gets 130,000 visitors per day and they also rapidly integrate vertically (four factories to cut diamonds, including one in South Africa and one in Botswana). They are quoted in the Hong Kong Stock Exchange, and the Cheng family owns 90% of the shares.
- The second of the Chinese jewelry groups is also impressive: **Lao Feng Xiang**, with headquarters and a stock market registration in Shanghai, has sales of €6.0 billion for 2019 with its 3,000 stores. It is still in part state owned.
- The smaller operator, **Chow Sang Sang**, with 52% of the shares owned by the Chow family, is registered in Bermuda and has 380 stores (with 305 in mainland China and 54 in Hong Kong) and sales of €1.8 billion.

The Watch Brands.   Here, we classify the operators into three different categories, according to their price segments. While industry specialists might object that this segmentation is slightly artificial, it has the advantage of distinguishing between brands that are quite different in style and in size.

Table 3.15 shows the major operators in complication and very expensive watches. In this category, where the total sales of the leading 10 operators are €1.7 billion out of a total market in the region of €2.5 billion, everybody is Swiss. For these very expensive pieces, the business is run from Switzerland even though the consumers are scattered around the world. Some of these brands are still independent, but almost half of them belong to Richemont or to the Swatch Group.

Table 3.16 presents the jewelry and specialty watch operators.

The lesson to emerge from this segmentation into three categories is that there are three different businesses: one where units sold are measured in thousands; another where units sold range from 50,000 to almost a million; and a third where figures are measured in the hundreds of thousands.

We said earlier that total sales in the upscale segment were probably around €2.5 billion. In the jewelry and specialty watches segment, total sales are probably around €16.5 billion. In the last category, the fashion and mood segments, even if the unit figures are impressive, the overall sales level—also at around €6.5 billion—remains limited.

It is also interesting to note that aside from Cartier, Bulgari, and Harry Winston, the jewelry brands remain relatively small in the overall watch business. If watches are very important to enable a jewelry brand to develop, to reach break-even in existing stores and to finance new ones, the watch business stands on its own, is almost always Swiss made, and is back into growing after a long period of almost 10 years of decline.

In this business, three groups dominate the market: Swatch, which leads with a 30% market share; the Richemont Group is second, with 23; and Rolex is third, with 15%, standing almost on its own brand and with its lower-positioned brand Tudor. Despite this combined share of 68%, the market is also open to newcomers who can develop a good idea or a special craft skill.

Table 3.16 Estimated Sales of Jewelry and Specialty Watch Operators 2019

Operator	Natio-nality	Sales (€ million)	Unit Sales	Average Wholesale Price per €	Ownership
Rolex	Swiss	5,100 (E)	800,000	4,000	Private
Cartier	Swiss	1,900 (E)	700,000	2,500	Richemont
Omega	Swiss	1,900 (E)	800,000	2,300	Swatch
Tag Heuer	Swiss	750 (E)	750,000	1,000	LVMH
IWC	Swiss	625(E)	150,000	2,100.	Richemont
Hublot	Swiss	600 (E)	N.A.	4,000	LVMH
Chanel	French/ Swiss	600 (E)	150,000	5,000	Private
Jeager Le Coultre	Swiss	550 (E)	120,000	3,000	Richemont
Louis Vuitton	French/ Swiss	500 (E)	85,000	6,000	LVMH
Breitling	Swiss	450	N.A.	N.A.	CVC Capital
Panerai	Italian	350 (E)	N.A.	N.A.	Richemont
Bulgari	Swiss	250 (E)	75,000	4,000	LVMH
Dior	French	250 (E)	N.A.	N.A.	LVMH
Hermès	French	250	N.A.	N.A.	Private
Montblanc	Swiss/ German	200 (E)	N.A.	N.A.	Richemont
Baume & Mercier	Swiss	150 (E)	N.A.	N.A.	Richemont

Note: (E) indicates authors' estimates.

Source: Authors' estimates and Vontobel Equity Research, 2019. Table 3.17 presents the last group of watches, which are still luxury watches but with an average wholesale price around or below €1,000. This category is not particularly homogeneous in that it contains brands such as Tag Heuer and Rado, which could be considered as belonging to the second category, and others such as Calvin Klein and Tommy Hilfiger, which have completely different positioning and retail prices at around €200–800.

Key Management Issues

Retail versus Wholesale. Whereas for jewelry a large part of the business is done at the retail level, for watches most of the business used to be done at wholesale, as the products need visibility and a strong presence at different points of sale.

At one time or another, brands such as Ebel, dealing mainly in watches, have tried to open retail stores, but without much success.

Table 3.17   Estimated Sales for Fashion and Mood and Watch Operators, 2019

Operator	Nationality	Sales (€ million)	Unit Sales	Average Wholesale Price per €	Ownership
Longines	Swiss	1,200 (E)	1,000,000	1,200	Swatch
Tissot	Swiss	800 (E)	800,000	800	Swatch
Tag Heuer	Swiss	800 (E)	800,000	1,000	LVMH
Rado	Swiss	500 (E)	500,000	N.A.	Swatch
Gucci	Italian/ Swiss	500 (E)	500,000	N.A.	Kering
Calvin Klein	US/Swiss	400 (E)	N.A.	N.A.	Swatch
Armani	Italian/ Swiss	250 (E)	800,000	300	Fossil
Baume & Mercier	Swiss	150 (E)	100,000	1,500	Richemont
Raymond Weil	Swiss	150 (E)	250,000	600	Private
Hugo Boss	German	100 (E)	200,000	500	Movado
Baume	Swiss	35 (E)	100,000	350	Richemont

Note: (E) indicates authors' estimates.
Source: Discussions with industry experts and Vontobel Equity Research, 2019.

Nevertheless, brands like Rolex and Omega have been successful in this. Others have tried to sell their watches only in their own jewelry stores. This was the policy adopted at the outset by Bulgari, but the company quickly realized that it had to enlarge the distribution to create interest in the product.

As their wholesale activities flourished, jewelry brands have been tempted to enlarge their distribution with multibrand stores. However, unless they could come up with a very specific product line, this has not always been effective. Cartier had "Les Must de Cartier" for many years, but while this was probably very useful for building the brand at the beginning, it has now been removed from the catalog in 2007 and brought back in 2010, probably to face the post-2008 crisis, but canceled again three or five years later. Bulgari had a small jewelry line for multibrand jewelry stores. Tiffany's has never done it and is unlikely to do so in the future.

Pricing and Product Lines.   For jewelry, there are different customer segments: those ready to spend up to €10,000 for a small piece; those who are prepared to spend between €10,000 and €60,000; and those who are looking for exclusive pieces selling above that amount.

Different jewelers are often lacking in their offerings in one or another of these segments and are obliged to hire new designers and to develop specific skills to work on overcoming this lack.

For a given brand of watches, on the other hand, there should be only one price range, but this requires a strong commercial and marketing work.

The Risk of the Major Customer.   In the past, some small exclusive brands such as Asprey or Chaumet were heavily reliant on major orders from the likes of the Sultan of Brunei or the King of Morocco if they were to meet their annual sales budgets. When these very big orders arrived, everything was rosy and life was easy. But what happened when, for one reason or another, the major customer did not place an order for the following year? As in every business, diversification and balance in the client list are very important parts of a healthy activity.

Organizational Structures

In the jewelry business, the organizational structure is generally limited to a retailing manager and an export manager; a design office and a production workshop; and a comparatively large marketing team to deal with product positioning, brand positioning, and public relations. One also needs accomplished international salesmen to deal with extremely high-net-worth individuals.

The World of Hotels and Hospitality

Hospitality is a general term that includes not only hotels but restaurants, coffee shops, bars, and nightclubs, as well as luxury travel agencies, cruise lines, private jets or even the sales of first class and business tickets of regular airlines.

We thought it was impossible to write a book on luxury without speaking of this sector, which has all the characteristics of luxury, from craftsmanship and individual attention to the sense of service and the international dimension.

This is, of course, an activity where individual contacts and service are a must. The quality of the service can be partly measured. A luxury hotel room must have at least 450 square feet, with a nice view, and must be decorated (walls, curtains, wall-to-wall carpeting, bedspread, and armchairs, for example) with fabrics of very high quality. But the quality of service is also the quality of the welcome of the staff at the reception desk, in the rooms, in the restaurants, and anywhere else. What contributes most to the perceived quality of a stay is probably the quality of the contacts in two or three dozen interactions with the staff from different hierarchical levels and different sectors. This is how a customer perceives his stay in a given hotel.

In this hospitality sector, excellence can only be built over time. What makes the difference is not necessarily the first stay in a given hotel, but maybe the fourth or the fifth. Is the customer welcomed as a regular client? Have his own preferences been registered and satisfied (preferred room, regular newspaper and magazine, or special eating habits, for example)? It does not seem very difficult to take all these wishes into account, but what builds a strong customer preference for a given hotel is the quality of execution of these daily tasks, and the stability and duration of the excellence.

The necessary performance of a hotel or a restaurant can be divided into three steps, as described in the book *Cornell on Hospitality*: operations and service excellence, real estate and business ownership, and managerial excellence.[1]

The Major Players

If we speak exclusively of hotels (without considering restaurants, for example), the total international revenues are estimated at €485 billion for 2019, [2] with an average growth rate of 3.1% per year for the past 10 years. The hotel industry is in fact much bigger than the total luxury industry, as we define it in Chapter 2, but with a lower growth rate than other sectors of the luxury market.

---

[1] Michael C. Sturman, Jack B. Corgel, and Rohit Verma (eds.), *The Cornell School of Hotel Administration on Hospitality: Cutting Edge Thinking and Practice*. Wiley, 2011.
[2] Intercontinental Group annual report 2019: Industry Overview.

However, in this total sector, the lower-end segments (economy, midscale, and upper midscale) represent 56% of the total, when luxury amounts to only 6.2% or €33.2 billion, an amount that is not unlike figures we have mentioned earlier for watches or leather goods. It is something quite similar in size. The luxury segment of the hotel business is also probably growing at a faster rate than 3.1%.

The difficulty is that in the past 20 years, this hotel sector has been concentrating very rapidly. As digital reservation centers have become a very important customer entry into hotel service purchases, a single individual hotel has difficulties finding clients who have a strong tendency to access through Expedia, Carlson Wagonlit, or TripAdvisor reservation systems. So, the merger trend is very strong.

The Major Hotel Groups.   The largest hotel operators, as can be seen in Table 3.18, are quite impressive, but for some of them, their luxury activity is very limited compared to their total business.

In the table, one can see very impressive brands and a mix of seven groups representing a total of around €50 billion in sales, but the luxury part of their business, with the exception of Marriott and Hyatt, is not their prime source of income.

In Table 3.19, we give a list of hotel groups or brands that are generally much smaller with many fewer properties but where each location brings something very special and can provide a really outstanding stay.

We review first the major groups before discussing the top luxury hotel brands:

Marriott is interesting because of its size (200,000 employees and 1,380,000 rooms) and its number of hotel brands (21). It is certainly the group with the largest number of luxury or upper-upscale brands: Saint Regis, Ritz Carlton, Luxury Collection, Westin, Sheraton, and so on.

Hilton is also very impressive with its 970,000 rooms, very impressive brands (Hilton, Conrad, and Waldorf Astoria), and very few economy hotels.

Host Hotels & Resorts is not a hotel brand but a real estate investment trust (REIT) based in Maryland and listed in the New York Stock Exchange. They own real estate properties, and within those buildings they have 80 hotels (47,000 rooms) that they develop under outsiders' brands. This is why they have signed agreements with almost every major hotel chain (Ritz Carlton, St. Regis, Hyatt, Hilton, etc.).

Table 3.18 The Major Hotel Groups

	Sales in € Billions	Number of Properties	Number of Brands	Major Luxury Brands	Major Brand
Marriott	18.9	7,003	21	St. Regis, Ritz Carlton, Westin, Le Méridien, Sheraton, Renaissance, Marriott	N.A.
Hilton	8.1	5,405	5	Hilton, Conrad, Waldorf Astoria	N.A.
Host Hotels & Resorts*	5.0	100		Marriott, Hyatt, Hilton, St. Regis	N.A.
Hyatt	4.3	865	15	Hyatt, Park Hyatt	Destination
InterContinental	4.2	5,656	19	Regent, Crowne Plaza, Six Senses, Intercontinental	Holiday Inn
AccorHotels	3.9	4,800	11	Raffles, Fairmont	Ibis
Jin Jiang	2.6	7,537	7	Radisson	Jin Jiang

a Host Hotels & Resorts also has building and real estate property development activities.
Source: Annual reports of the different groups, 2019, 2020.

Table 3.19   Top Luxury Hotel Brands

	Sales in € Billions	Number of Properties	Ownership
Hyatt	4.3	865	Hyatt Group
Four Seasons	3.6	117	Canadian investors
Shangri La	2.2	100	Singapore and Hong Kong listing
Mandarin Oriental	1.2	41	Jardine Matheson and Hong Kong listing
Peninsula	0.75	13	Hong Kong listing
Belmont	0.55	35	LVMH
St. Regis	N.A.	16	Marriott
Rosewood	N.A.	28	Choo Tai Fook Hong Kong
Six Senses	N.A.	10	ICG
Aman	N.A.	32	Singapore

Sources: Luxury travel expert and annual reports.

Hyatt is also an upscale and luxury group (shown in Tables 3.18 and 3.19) with very impressive brands but also has some chains like Destinations Hotels and the Joie de Vivre brand that have a clear economy positioning.

InterContinental has grown (like many other groups) through acquisitions, and the Holiday Inn activity is probably not the most impressive they have in their portfolio. Just as Marriott and Hyatt, InterContinental represents the strong American hotel chains that have developed by acquisitions in the past 30 years.

AccorHotels has its headquarters in Paris and has impressive luxury brands (e.g., Raffles and Royal Monceau in Paris), but the largest part of its business is in the middle-range chains like Sofitel, Novotel, Ibis, and Hotel F1.

Jin Jiang used to be owned by mainland China (which still owns 25% of the shares) and is very concentrated in China (6,421 hotels) and Other Asia (214 hotels) of a total of 7,537. With only 15 five- or four-star hotels in the world, they are a mid-range and economy hotel group, but with a very impressive size. They also have money to purchase foreign hotel chains, which they did by purchasing the Radisson at the end of 2018. They are now a group that, in number of rooms in the world, for example, appears at the top of some hotel listings. Today, they are certainly not a luxury chain, but they have the possibility of becoming one. They also own 12% of the shares of AccorHotels.

The Major Luxury Brands.   In Table 3.19, we can see smaller groups, with slightly under €1billion in sales, or much bigger ones, like the **Four Seasons**, with total sales of €3.6 billion. We see in this list a relatively new generation of hotel companies that are using luxury codes to attract upscale customers in beautiful resorts in some larger cities of the world or some paradisiacal vacation sites such as Bali or the Maldives.

Apart from the Four Seasons, which is based in Canada, many others—**Shangri La**, **Mandarin**, **Peninsula**, and **Rosewood**—are based in Asia and are managed from Hong Kong (with the exception of the Shangri La, which is managed from Singapore). These hotel groups are all monobrand with a strong base and clientele from Asia and are now developing top hotel locations in the prestigious cities of Europe and the United States. Each new location is carefully selected for its top location and its beautiful environment.

The **Belmont** group also has outstanding locations (8 out of 35 in Italy). It was purchased by LVMH at the very end of 2018 and integrated in their activities in April 2019. It is managed from Paris.

This is probably the sector where luxury management expertise could be more effectively put to use, like, for example, the brand development and communication activities, the design and architecture of the location, the use of an up-to-date CRM system, and sophistication in the relationship with clients.

The Use of Fashion Brands to Develop Hotels.   The reader might be surprised if we didn't discuss hotels like Armani Burg Khalifa in Dubaï or the Bulgari Resort Hotel in Bali, and we should mention the use of fashion and luxury names to develop luxury hotels.

In fact, there are two very different ways of associating a fashion brand with a hotel venture. It could be through the creation of a hotel chain with 10 or 20 locations and to compete with the Four Seasons, the St. Regis, or the Shangri La. It could also be with the development of a single hotel in one location or the artistic design of one suite in a luxury hotel.

The Luxury Brand Hotel Ventures   Three brands belong in this type: Bulgari, Armani, and Versace.

For **Bulgari**, the decision was to create a fully fledged hotel chain, with the reservation platform and management support of the Marriott group. They now have nine hotels or projects: Milan, Dubai, London, Bali, Beijing, Shanghai, Paris, and Moscow (2022) and Tokyo (2023). Each hotel is designed by a talented architect and the building is generally very striking and beautiful. The service must also be outstanding and memorable, and apparently, when one reads the comments of guests, it generally is.

Armani signed an agreement with a Dubai property developer and started with a beautiful hotel in Dubai (Burg Khalifa) in 2010 and another one in Milan in 2011.

Versace has also developed several hotels: one beautiful palazzo on the Australian Gold Coast and another one in Dubai (Jaddaf Waterfront).

This can be an interesting venture for a fashion or jewelry luxury brand. But two questions must be asked:

1. Does the brand have the necessary staff to manage a hotel chain and to provide top management? Visiting hotels and decorating them is one thing. Managing them 365 days a year is altogether another. The brand must have the necessary management team to run this activity, and if they don't, at least they must be ready to hire top managers to do it.

2. Does the brand have enough investment money to purchase top-location real estate and build one or several luxury hotels? Couldn't that money be available first to build new stores in top locations and refresh and redecorate existing stores? It is only when all internal investment needs are covered that it may make sense to invest heavily in a strong hotel chain.

Managing a hotel is more than just designing and creating a beautiful building; it is also running it—not only the communication and research of guests, but also managing the day-to-day activities. For example, food services sometimes account for more than 30% of total hotel revenues. This is another business service, and it takes 24 hours a day of work and requires motivated and competent staff.

Creating a Special Suite or One Hotel   Fendi created in its home city, Rome, a special building with seven hotel suites on top of two floors of its fashion store as a way to develop something very special. The objective was not to compete with Marriott or Hilton but to add an additional communication value to the brand.

When Dior designs a single suite in the St. Regis in New York, it is again an opportunity to communicate about the brand. It is a special occasion for Dior to indicate how creative they are and to organize special events in this hotel.

Other examples of this same thing could be mentioned: a Ferragamo suite in the Lungarno hotel in Florence, a Christian Lacroix suite in the Bellechasse Hotel in Paris, a Karl Lagerfeld suite in the Schlosshotel in Berlin, or a Viviane Westwood penthouse suite in the West Hollywood Hotel in Los Angeles. Each time is an opportunity to recognize the design talent of a creative genius and the quality image of the brand. But this type of PR activity is very far from officially and thoroughly managing a chain of luxury hotels and its complicated service activities.

Organizing for Service Excellence

It is important to understand the difference between service and hospitality: service is related to assisting others or to domestic services, as well as being useful and helpful. Hospitality seems to have much deeper meaning. The following descriptions of hospitality are from *Cornell on Hospitality*, mentioned earlier:

> Making the guests feel warm and secure and that they are cared for.
> —John Sharpe, former president of the Four Seasons Hotels

> Making people feel at ease, preferably in a seemingly effortless manner.
> —Abigail Charpentier, Human Resources VP, ARAMARK

> Making the guests feel important, confident, happy, and comfortable.
> —Chef Daniel Boulud (New York City)

There is a huge difference between a *service*, which is due, almost as a formal contract, and *hospitality*, which is a welcome and a gift. In hospitality, one can notice a graciousness or, even more, an extraordinary service.

A hotel or restaurant client could only expect some respect, which is a very positive part of the service. But he or she would be pleased to also have an experience that exceeds expectation.

In this hospitality sector, one has to organize so that the client always gets an experience that exceeds expectation. The organization must be managed in a way that makes hospitality exceed expectations of the industry norm.

In a way, nothing could be as useful as this section on hospitality, because it seems that what must be the norm of behavior and client satisfaction in hotels could also be the norm of all other luxury sectors.

This service excellence can touch different moments in the relation between the client and the hotel or restaurant.

Individual Contacts and Service before the Visit.   You might think of how you can make sure people have a good impression even before they come to visit you. You can send them recommendations for places to visit and things to do and offer to help them make theater or opera reservations. You could also send them city maps or a list of most visited locations with the special offer of reserving a seat or a program. You can also send them information on visual aids.

If you manage a restaurant, you may look at the best way to make sure people are well treated as they wait to be seated. It may be possible to position the waiting area to have a view to the kitchen. It may also be possible to give guests the opportunity to look at a sample of desserts or a tank of lobsters. The idea is to make sure they have something to watch or to think about while they wait.

Quality of the Welcome.   Some hotels have conducted studies to see how clients from a given country or from a specific age group expect to be treated. Some groups of people expect a cold and very professional reception. Others may look for a warm and friendly welcome.

It is important to decide how regular customers should be treated: With complete discretion and no sign of involvement, or, on the contrary, with a "welcome back" greeting? Should their name be remembered? Should their regular practices (which newspapers, which type of pillows, which amenities, and others?) be registered and taken into account? Hotels should, of course, have a CRM system that records guests' preferences.

If you manage a restaurant, do your guests have a regular table? Do they have special expectations?

Excellence Overtime.   What guests will remember is the quality of the hospitality over their stay. They expect to be always considered important people. They may need flexibility or the possibility of changing their plan (leaving early, staying one or two days longer, asking for a departure after noon, asking for a second room to accommodate friends, or asking to change their room because the noise of the elevators prevents them from sleeping, or because it is too cold or too hot, or because they don't have a view of the sea or the river, etc.).

Motivating the Staff.   What hotel and restaurant clients expect to experience seems very obvious but it should be shared by all staff members, who represent very different activities and functions. Some of these staff (e.g., front desk, concierges, or cashiers) have regular contact with the clients. Others, like launderers, plumbers, or room service staff, only have intermittent or exceptional connections. But the clients must perceive that everybody is part of a unique team with the same values and the same discipline. They must be part of a unique family with all of them coming from the same mold,

This requires a common philosophy and very strong training, where everybody respects the same rules.

As people are trained to provide this type of service, one should make sure everybody uses the same etiquette: etiquette in dressing and behaving, etiquette in speaking to the guests, and etiquette in body language. Staff should be trained to remember names, to sell softly, to always use positive language, to know how to make eye contact, to conduct an apparently social conversation. They should know how to act to be appreciated and remembered, but in a soft and pleasant way. Is there a better training program for other luxury activities?

Managing the Real Estate and the Business Ownership

Just like for fashion stores, different aspects of the hotel experience are not always controlled by the same person. Sometimes the operator owns the hotel brand and management and respects the brand philosophy. Sometimes the major partner owns the real estate and acts as an investor. Sometimes, the two activities are managed by the same team.

We all have the experience of a pleasant hotel in a given city changing its name. Overnight, it must change its philosophy of management and client service. It must change much more than the logo outside; it should create a specific and expected atmosphere.

Managing Multicriteria Customer Choices

When a client selects a hotel, he or she can consider different criteria as, for example:

Location
Reviews of past guests
Reviews or ratings of professional organizations
Availability of specific features (swimming pool, spa, etc.) or amenities
Promotions and special events
Technological access and options.

Each hotel offers a particular bundle of services that clients might value and appreciate differently as a function of their age, their professional requisites, or the reason of their visit. Tourists and businesspeople are not interested in the same things and they value their stay differently. Individuals, couples, families, or business teams have different requirements and may also value them differently. For each customer segment, management must appreciate the strengths and weaknesses of each hotel building and each staff philosophy.

What Can Other Luxury Businesses Learn from Hotel Management Practices?

Hotel management experience can be applied to other luxury companies.

First, knowing their customers: hotels have an effective and comprehensive client database and CRM. Regular clients can be followed in their travel habits and in their ways of behaving, eating, drinking, and using the services of the hotel. They can be rewarded in different ways (free stays, room upgrades, special weekend deals, late departures, etc.). They might pay themselves for the services, or they might be there on business and their expenses have to be adjusted to specific company procedures. Just as other luxury companies do, hotels can identify a small percentage of clients that represent an important part of total revenues. How can they be analyzed and regularly followed in their behavior?

Another aspect of hotel management techniques can be used for other luxury businesses: in hotels, some regular clients have "switching inertia"; they are no longer enthusiastic or even satisfied with one hotel or one hotel brand, but they stay there because it is more convenient for them and because they don't like to change. But they are on the lookout for new hotel experiences in the same city. How can they be spotted and acquired? Only by speaking to them.

This is another part of the hospitality management: make sure that staff know and communicate with the best clients and give them a frequent opportunity to express their impressions, their satisfactions, and any displeasure. This requires a special tact and style, but is much easier when the hotel has created an atmosphere of communication and respect.

To achieve the kind of atmosphere where the customer feels appreciated and highly considered, one must make sure, as we said earlier, that 100% of the staff, from the lobby to the basement or the sunroof, understands the specific atmosphere a given hotel wishes to create for its clients and wishes to be part of this effort, which must be general, coherent, and carefully planned but still look very natural.

But doing all this is not enough: how all these efforts contribute to the improvement of the brand identity of the hotel or the restaurant must be measured. A hotel or a private jet company are just brands that must build their awareness and their preferences in the minds of regular customers and potential clients.

In these hospitality activities, it is not enough to bring a top-quality environment and service "most of the time." It must be always there—and that requires a very special effort.

Describing the hospitality sector, it appears that the qualities required to be successful are not very far from those necessary to run a point-of-sale operation. We are right at the core of the values that are necessary in the luxury environment.

Conclusion on the Major Luxury Sectors

It seems a pity to limit our analysis of luxury sectors to these six categories. It could be argued that other categories, like men's fashion and *art de la table* items, should also be analyzed. But it is necessary to draw the line somewhere. It would also be interesting to look at the still wine market, which we consider to be the biggest product category in the luxury industry. However, this is beyond the scope of this book and would probably require a study on its own.

In the rest of the book, we will give examples taken from different parts of the luxury field, but we will speak of the industry as a whole, without differentiating the segments. In this chapter, though, we hope we have presented sufficient evidence to convince the reader that there are important differences among each of the categories, but that the luxury business is a separate activity, different from other markets. We hope, too, that we have convinced the reader that these luxury segments, despite their differences, have similarities in outlook and in management needs.

Chapter 4

The Power of the Luxury Brand

S o far in this book, we have spoken more readily of brands than of businesses. In fact, the luxury business is, above all, a business of brands. When customers have a preference for a brand, they are ready to spend a little more on it. Sometimes a brand goes through periods when perhaps the creativity is a bit weak, and new products are not as good as they should be, yet it manages to keep its loyal customers. There is always a strong value attached to a strong brand for reasons that are historical and social, as well as emotional.

For luxury goods, brand identity is a very important element of the business. In certain ways, it can also be a constraint: it is not possible to launch a product that is outside its sphere of legitimacy.

How do we measure the strength of a brand? The first question to ask is: How well known is it? This can be ascertained by asking 500 target consumers what brands of luxury watches they know. Immediate answers—Rolex or Cartier, say—will give what is called *spontaneous awareness*. But from the same answer, researchers will be able to provide other information. They will record the number of times any one brand is mentioned first, which gives the *top of mind*, an indication of great strength of a given brand for a product category. For example, if we ask a group of consumers to name all the brands of scarves that they know, they are more than likely to mention Hermès first. Recording such information will give the percentage of respondents who put a particular brand first, which allows us to determine any increases or decreases over time. It also enables us to see any changes in the respective positions of the leading brands in the consumers' top-of-mind responses.

In a second phase, interviewees are presented with a list of brands and asked to say which of them they know. This will give researchers what is known as *aided awareness*, which provides an indication of the closeness of a brand with its customers.

Generally, top brands such as Chanel, Dior, and Armani have a spontaneous awareness of between 40 and 60%, depending on the country in which the test is conducted. But they probably have an aided awareness of between 80 and 90% in the perfumes or the ladies' luxury ready-to-wear categories. Smaller brands perform less well on spontaneous awareness and are generally mentioned only by those who have the product at home and use it.

Of course, as we will discuss in Chapter 6, the level of awareness is only a secondary aspect of the total picture. The most important aspect of the brand is its identity; that is to say, the specific contents of the awareness it generates.

In this chapter, we will discuss the value of a brand and how it can be assessed and then analyze the different ways of looking at the brand and what it represents for the public.

The Value of a Brand

In this section, we concentrate on a study conducted every year by the consulting firm Interbrand, the main results of which are published in *Business Week*. Interbrand rates almost every brand in the world, assigning to each an overall value.

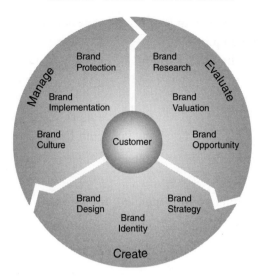

Figure 4.1   Interbrand Brand-Value Management Model.
Source: Interbrand

The Interbrand Methodology

Interbrand relies on a specific brand-value management model that summarizes all of the different elements of a brand as they relate to the customer. This is shown in Figure 4.1.

This model puts the consumer at the center and divides the brand management world into three activities: the evaluation (through research) of brand opportunities; the creative process (brand strategy, verbal identity, and brand design); and the management process (culture, implementation, and protection).

Interbrand's selection criteria for the annual study include:

- The company must be publicly traded.
- It must have at least one-third of its revenues generated outside the country of origin.
- It must be a market-facing brand. The economic value added must be positive.
- The brand must not have a purely business-to-business single audience, with no wider public profile and awareness.

The methodology Interbrand uses to assess the value of the different brands is as follows:

- It forecasts the current and future revenues specifically attributable to the branded products.
- It subtracts the cost of doing business (operating costs, taxes) and intangibles such as patents and management strengths to assess what portion of earnings is directly attributable to the brand.

In other words, the idea is to assess the flow of added revenues that come because the product has a given brand rather than no brand at all. The brand justifies a premium price, which, after subtracting the investment necessary to keep the brand where it is, can be considered the gross profit directly attributable to the brand.

Luxury Brands in the Total Brand Universe

Table 4.1 shows how the luxury field fares compared to the other industrial sectors where brands exist. This shows that the luxury sector, with a brand value of nearly €120 billion, ranks only sixth of the 100 most valuable brands. This amount is much lower than the stock market value of the major luxury groups. For example, the stock market valuation of LVMH alone is around €205 billion. This probably arises from the fact that many profitable brands are not among the top 100 and that many private family companies are not taken into account.

Table 4.1   The Place of Luxury in the Global Brand Picture (2019)

	Number of Firms	Number of US Firms	Consolidated Value (in € billions)
Computer hardware, services, and sofware	13	9	673
Internet services	14	13	259
Automotives	15	1	258
Fast-moving consumer goods	13	8	189
Financials	12	8	142
Luxury	11	2	120
Consumer electronics	5	1	53
Others	17	7	185
Total	100	54	1,879

Note: Interbrand's figures were expressed in US dollars, but for consistency we have converted these to Euros using an exchange rate of US$1 = €0.926.

Table 4.2   Interbrand's Top Luxury Brands (2019)

Brand	Interbrand Value(in € millions)
Louis Vuitton	29,856
Chanel	20,508
Hermès	16,605
Gucci	14,779
Cartier	7,590
Jack Daniel's	5,881
Dior	5,601
Tiffany & Co.	4,943
Hennessy	4,908
Burberry	4,823
Prada	4,430

Note: Interbrand's figures were expressed in US dollars, but for consistency we have converted these to Euros using an exchange rate of US$1 = €0.926.
Source: Interbrand, 2019.

Source: Interbrand, 2019. It is worth noting that the automotive sector is twice as large as that of luxury brands.

Also, luxury, like the automotive and consumer electronics segments, is a field in which there are few American brands. In fact, there are only 2 US brands among the group of 11 listed in Table 4.2, which serves to reinforce our earlier comment that, so far, this is basically a French and Italian field.

As a general comment, it is striking that most brand values are gathered around the computer hardware, software, and services and Internet and financial services fields.

The Luxury Brands in the Top 100

There are several observations arising from this list of luxury brands appearing in Interbrand's top 100 for 2019.[1]

First, the estimated brand value of Louis Vuitton is almost than double that of Hermès, and three times that of Cartier.

Another peculiarity of this list: For some reason, Interbrand does not seem to have respected its own rules. Contrary to its stated criteria, one of these brands, Chanel, is privately owned. Indeed, the privately owned

---

[1] Interbrand, Best global brands ranking. New York, 2019.

Table 4.3 Brand Value Changes Between 2001 and 2019 (€ million)

2001		2019	
Louis de Vuitton	4,863	Louis de Vuitton	29,856
Gucci	3,783	Gucci	14,779
Chanel	3,014	Chanel	20,508
Rolex	2,611		N.A.
Tiffany & Co.	2,455	Tiffany & Co.	4,943
Bacardi	2,259		N.A.
Moët & Chandon	1,826		N.A.
Smirnoff	1,715		N.A.
Polo Ralph Lauren	1,348		N.A.
Johnnie Walker	1,165		N.A.
Jack Daniel's	1,115	Jack Daniel's	5,881
Armani	1,052		N.A.
Absolut	974		N.A.

Note: Interbrand's figures were expressed in US dollars, but for consistency we have converted these to Euros using an exchange rate of US$1 = €0.7143 for 2001 and €0.926 for 2019.
Source: Interbrand, 2001 and 2019.

firms and companies that are public but still have strong family control account for 9 out of the 11 firms. Family control, either total or through a majority shareholding, is almost a peculiarity of these top brands and of the luxury industry. This probably has something to do with the need for a long-term focus in this business, as mentioned in Chapter 2, which is easier to obtain in family-controlled firms.

How has this position evolved over time? Table 4.3 gives an indication by comparing the Interbrand results for 2001 and 2019.

Only five brands appear in the results for both 2001 and 2019; two of these have experienced extremely fast growth: Chanel, which has multiplied its value by 5, and Louis Vuitton, by 6.

There are anomalies in the tables: Hermès, Cartier, and Dior should have been in the 2001 list. In the same way, Rolex, Bacardi, and Moët & Chandon, which were present in 2001, should not have been omitted from the 2019 list. The fact that two of them are private companies (and the third one does not publish sales figures by brand) may explain this, but then again, so are others that appear in the list. But the comparison between the two values gives a clear indication of how the luxury business developed during this period.

The Characteristics of the Brand

Where does the brand get its power from? A study by Bernard Dubois and Patrick Duquesne found that a brand's value comes from the following elements:

- A mythical value: This incorporates a brand's reason for being and how representative it is of its time.
- An exchange value: This refers to the best value for money, which in itself incorporates the mythical elements mentioned above and the other value components.
- An emotional value: This is quite different from the above in that it deals with emotions and impressions.
- An ethical value: This is linked to social responsibility and the way the brand reacts in the marketplace.
- An identity value: This relates to the way the brand can be used by consumers to convey something about themselves.

We'll begin by looking at the different aspects of the brand, starting with the brand as a contract. We will then look at the time dimension and finish with the role of brands in society.

The Brand as a Contract

When one company purchases a competitor for an amount above the sum of its net assets, there is a line item called "goodwill" in the consolidated balance sheet following the merger. This term designates the sum total of the intangible, but extremely valuable, positive attitudes of consumers toward the acquired company and its products.

Given the current market uncertainty that prevails at the time of writing, goodwill does not have good press. And yet, though evaluating it can be problematic, it is a genuine added value, built up gradually as consumers become convinced that a certain brand can provide them with a product whose style and quality are above that of its competitors.

When consumers buy a Burberry or an Aquascutum raincoat, they're not simply buying a raincoat; they're buying a fashion product, branded by a reputable name and one that has a strong emotional value.

In the perception of the customer, this capital is embodied above all in a name. At the beginning of the history of luxury brands, this was, as we saw in earlier chapters, generally the name of a skilled designer/craftsman, and was intended to raise the product above an otherwise standardized level and to emphasize high-quality production criteria. This seems logical enough because if, as we have said, a brand comprises first of all a capital of confidence, then putting his name on a product is, for the vendor, the simplest way of winning that confidence. We are dealing here with a fundamental structure in a great number of human exchanges.

As we will see, the name of a brand, or its logo, is an important, visible part of a more complex reality. It provides the mediation between the essential values of a luxury company—its identity—and the perceptions its customers have of it—its image.

But note that what the consumer is looking for behind the brand is the guarantee of a specific and superior quality, as well as a strong exclusivity. That long-term assurance forms the basis of the relationship between the consumer and the producer.

This holds for products and sales policies alike. The Saks Fifth Avenue department-store chain has a rule under which a customer can return any product purchased within the previous six weeks for a refund, with no questions asked. For a long time, Saks had Revillon shop-in-shops in its major stores. Every year, certain customers bought fur coats there on December 15th and returned them at the end of January. The Revillon teams, pointing out that these customers were abusing the return policy to get a free fur coat every winter, tried several times to convince the stores' management to make an exception to the policy. Saks always refused, considering that even if it left them vulnerable to abuse, the return policy was part of the store's ground rules, that it constituted a commitment, and that it was one component of its brand identity. This policy of return and refund is still at work at Saks today.

It is common for managers to speak of the brand as an expression of the company's *genetic program*—a stable structure, rich in potential, that concretizes the company's existence and can win customers' confidence, but that also imposes strict ground rules. While this is an expressive image, it is also a little unclear. We prefer to speak of *semiotic invariants* and of a brand's ethic and aesthetic. As we will see in Chapter 6, the manifestations of a brand can be seen as "meaning facts," and these invariants simply make up a basic grammar, a signature of form and content that allows the brand identity to come into being.

In fact, in ordinary discourse terms, two brands such as Armani and Gucci do not express the same values and have distinct brand identities. Giorgio Armani is a very strong proponent of the traditional woman, dressed in a conservative modern way and with a definite Italian flavor. Gucci appeals to a relatively younger and more modern woman who is independent in her choices and who wants to convey a different statement. She is also identified very much with young and slightly flamboyant creations and colorful dresses and accessories. Products and positioning must take into account these diverse representations with which they are associated in the customer's imagination. As a result, they adopt slightly different strategies in order to be recognized and to win and keep consumers' trust.

A brand is therefore a contract, one that is implicit in nature and that governs the relations between a given company and its customers. This relationship is two-dimensional: it is not only economic in nature, but also, over time, creates emotional ties that are sometimes very intense—with infidelity on both sides, momentary or permanent abandonment, and, above all, a capacity for reciprocal influence on the behavior of the two contracting parties.

The competitive dimension of the brand can be included within its contractual dimension. The brand exists only because it differentiates itself from its closest competitors. This is one of the bases of its identity. The consumer chooses a brand for the specific qualities it offers, and, in this sense, the differentiation of the brand is part of the contract between the two parties.

Because it is founded on differentiation, which is the *raison d'être* of any brand, such a contract remains implicit. As such, it cannot be confused with the standard regulations of laws governing commerce, which are the same for all. What the brand pertains to is a relationship of another nature, which is exemplified in the automatic-return policy of Saks stores. The brand implies the promise of superior quality and better service; in short, it guarantees added value.

Brands and Time

The prolongation of a contract is intrinsic to the notion of guarantee. In order to exist, a brand must not only establish its reputation, but do so durably. Thus, the chronological perspective is fundamental to understanding brands.

We will begin with a short historical sketch. In looking at brands as abstract entities, we tend to forget that, behind them, there is nothing more than a vendor who is concerned about his customers keeping him in mind. And this concern is as old as commerce itself. As early as 2700 BC, artisans were affixing a sign to their creations in order to affirm their originality.[2] In classical Greece and Rome, merchants used generic symbols to designate the business they were in: a ham for butchers, a cow for creameries, and so on. "Individual marks" in the form of seals, identifying a particular merchant, made their appearance circa 300 BC. More than 6,000 different seals used by Roman potters have been catalogued.

The large-scale explosion of brands—that is, the emergence of the brand phenomenon as we understand it—is largely a result of the Industrial Revolution. Should we view this, then, as a "mercantilization" of the world? It's more a case of a transformation of commerce itself. As exchanges became standardized, it became necessary for producers to establish a relationship of proximity with consumers by other means.

The extension of industrial property to the concept of brand appears in Europe in the second half of the nineteenth century. The US Congress enacted the first federal trademark law in the late 1800s, and between 1850 and 1890, the number of patents granted each year in the major Western nations increased by a factor of 10.

The major brands underwent sustained development between 1900 and 1945, and the development accelerated between 1945 and 1990. On the other hand—and contrary to what their omnipresence in the media might suggest—the trend since 1990 has been toward a concentration and reduction in the largest companies' portfolios of brands.

To understand these recent developments, we must look at things on a smaller scale. These fundamental trends, like the individual fate of a given business sector, can be explained by the differential between, on the one hand, the cost of maintaining and developing a brand, and, on the other, the immediate or longer-term profits to be made from it.

The fashion sector has passed through several phases. It underwent its major explosion, characterized by the emergence of the Italian brands after the Second World War. Armani, Ferré, Moschino, Trussardi, and Versace emerged in the 1970s. During the same period, slightly older brands—Fendi, Salvatore Ferragamo, Gucci—experienced

---

[2] *Des Brevets et des marques, une histoire de la propriété industrielle* (Patents and Trademarks: A History of Industrial Property), INPI (French Patent Office), Fayard 2001.

extraordinary growth. Certain provincial brands left Florence or Milan and were soon found everywhere in Italy. They quickly became international, generally with a strong presence in the United States and Japan. But at the same time or slightly later a large number of French brands, such as Phillipe Venet and Per Spook, disappeared and others, such as Grès, Courrège, and Guy Laroche, reduced their activities to a single store in Paris and some license contracts in Japan, China, or South Korea, which brought in royalties to cover the monthly expenses. The Grès store in Paris was then closed altogether, and the Grès perfumes are now part of the Lalique perfumes collection. While the luxury and fashion industry doesn't escape from the concentration of capital, the reduction in the number of brands is less evident there, perhaps because of the versatility of the markets. The novelty effect is a determining factor in consumers' choices. The result is a permanent renewal of the available brands, yet the total number has been significantly reduced.

In France, 30 years ago, 24 French firms would present a *haute couture* parade twice a year in Paris. Since Jean Paul Gaultier announced his farewell during his last January 2020 show, they are now 15 brands (Adeline André, Alexandre Vauthier, Alexis Mabille, Bouchra Jarrar, Chanel, Dior, Frank Sorbier, Giambattista Valli, Givenchy, Julien Fournié, Maison Margiela, Maison Rabih Kayrouz, Maurizio Galante, Schiaparelli, and Stephane Roland). From this list, one can see that only four (Chanel, Dior, Givenchy, and Schiaparelli) of these brands have monobrand retail stores in more than two or three countries, so at first sight, this haute couture activity seems to have been very much reduced.

Nevertheless, if we add to those brands the *membres correspondants*— Elie Saab, Fendi Couture, Giorgio Armani, Valentino, Versace, and Victor and Rolf—on one side, and the *membres invités*, including, for example, Azzaro and Guo Pei, the haute couture fashion shows are more lively today than they were in the past: they provide an opportunity for many brands, either foreign or more interested in the creative challenge than in retail sales, to present outstanding individual fashion pieces. The haute couture shows are no longer another way to present exclusive models and ready-to-wear outfits but an opportunity to create and make outstanding dresses.

Can the small fashion brands survive? The haute couture platform can help some of them, because they need visibility more than anything and this can be achieved through articles in the press.

At first sight, the best way to develop a brand is to advertise on social media and in the press. But advertising has a strong limitation for the brands that have limited advertising and social media budgets: An analysis of the effectiveness curves of fashion advertising shows the emergence of what is called a "threshold effect." Such studies show that advertising expenditures on a very broad target of consumers are only effective beyond €1 million in France, Germany, and Italy, and probably €3 million in the United States.

The costs of advertising and internationalization have clearly changed the rules of the game. Small brands will have to remain local or else disappear. The alternative to this is of course the only use of social media, which seems more accessible, but to be effective and bring clients all the way to the stores or websites, very little can be obtained for less than €500,000.

But history hasn't had the last word yet. There are brands positioned in a specific market that manage, below critical mass, to develop name recognition without advertising. In certain highly federated markets made up of devotees, word of mouth is a powerful force and even more of an advantage than advertising. In the case of fashion, a small, highly innovative brand will sometimes be extremely well received by the press, magazines, and bloggers. Fashion writers, bloggers, and influencers will adopt it as a favorite discovery, and it will be talked about for its originality. On the other hand, middle-sized and older brands, already publicized but with smaller budgets than those of the competition, will have trouble staying in the race.

While it is true that the globalization of the economy, technological progress in communications, and the volume requirements of the traditional production/distribution industries have made major brands indispensable, stronger, and less numerous, niche brands are developing extremely fast and changing the rules of the industry.

Brands and Society

When we think of the presence of brands in today's society, the first idea that comes to mind is not the quality of the products but the intensity of the messages.

On his desert island, Robinson Crusoe would not have needed his name if Friday hadn't turned up. Brands exist only because we can recognize them. And we recognize them because we perceive the messages they send, their specificities, and a certain constancy over time. We will have occasion to mention these components—communication, differentiation, and duration— throughout this book.

The communicative dimension of brands operates in two ways. First, the brand sends its messages to the consumers it targets. This is at first a shotgun type of relationship, where a wide net must be cast to be sure of pulling in the targeted consumers. Second, signs, like money, circulate. Brands, too, display this phenomenon.

Let's imagine the reaction of extraterrestrials who arrive in Times Square in New York, in the Ginza in Tokyo, or in the via Monte Napoleone in Milan. The logos and brand names on the buildings and on the clothing worn by the passersby would probably loom large in their first impressions. They would discover a civilization where brands play an important role in social communication. They would also be discovering, by comparing different places, the multitude of global brands, their systematic presence in the most famous shopping streets, and the apparent homogeneity they impose on lifestyles.

The explosion of brand communication our civilization is now experiencing would never have happened were it not for the crucial social role that brands now play. The three stripes on running shoes, the polo player embroidered on a shirt, the "swoosh" on the cap, or the Kelly bag—not to mention the cars people drive or the restaurants they go to—often say more about the personality of those who wear them than their curriculum vitae does.

It shouldn't be surprising, in a society characterized by exponential growth of communication in all its forms and contents, that brands should be at the heart of contemporary life. They guide the purchases we make, influence our judgments about products and people, and force us to position ourselves in relation to the values (or countervalues, or the absence of values) they communicate.

These effects are not limited, of course, to the isolated moment of communication (the glimpsed billboard or spot or web page). The way in which brands circulate, are copied, worn, or co-opted shows the extent and depth to which they affect our society. In fact, they have changed our way of living.

First, by claiming a conspicuous share of commercial and communication territory, they have contributed strongly to the transformation of our urban landscapes.

Further, brands convey values. As we will see in Chapter 6, a brand's identity is made up of invariants that express its vision of the world, the values it believes in, and attempts to promote. Nike is the pursuit of excellence in athletic performance; Hermès the aristocratic life; Armani relaxed elegance in the Italian style. Brands oblige us, through their presence in the commercial circuits, to position ourselves in relation to these values. The offering of products and the values associated with them have grown strongly in recent years, giving us a choice that our parents could never have dreamed of. We can choose temporary lifestyles as we see fit and reflect our moods in the way we consume.

Finally, brands are at the origin of numerous actions of solidarity. Whether under the influence of consumers or under the leadership of enlightened managers, they have greatly increased their commitments to causes in the general interest. Again, we will return to the mechanisms and the consequences of such commitments. As we will see, they are closely linked to the communicative dimension of the brands. At this early stage in our examination, we have only touched on these tangible effects on our society.

The Brand and Its Signs

With these initial analyses, we have tried to characterize the broad outlines of a brand's presence. What are the signs through which that presence asserts itself? They are of several orders, in fact, though often closely interlinked. To express itself, the brand uses these different elements, which are not interchangeable but are complementary.

The most important among them, of course, have to do with the name of the brand itself. The logo, now an unavoidable part of our urban landscape, is what immediately comes to mind. However, the name, in its literal and onomastic dimension—how it sounds to the ear—is also given a great deal of thought and attention by the brands.

We will consider this literal dimension first, before focusing on the phenomenon of the logo and other mechanisms of recognition.

Brand Names

The name remains the first sign of recognition of a brand. It is never neutral. As we have seen, many brands start with the first name and surname of their founders.

For luxury products, the first name, since it identifies the creator, remains an indispensable part of the excellence and creativity of the brand. For many years Saint Laurent never came to mind without Yves, and it took time to adjust to just "Saint Laurent." Ferragamo without Salvatore would probably be missing something. Yet there are exceptions, which have existed in their present form from the brand's origins: Gucci, the name of whose founder—Guccio—would doubtless result in an awkward alliteration; Coco Chanel always preferred to use only her surname.

But when a brand name has taken hold in the collective memory, beware of ill-advised changes. The change of the Marcel Rochas brand to simply "Rochas" was not at all lucky for the business. In the early 1990s, an attempt was made to return to the original by opening a men's clothing store by that name in Paris, but the attempt was soon abandoned.

In the field of brand-name management, one of the most interesting phenomena in recent times has been the progressive disappearance of the "Christian" from Christian Dior. Until 1995, the products and the advertising always bore the complete signature. Then, the forename progressively disappeared. For a long time, it was not shown in full size on the advertising, but on the baseline of the advertising and on the packaging. Today, the brand appears generally without the first name in, for example, the signs of the new stores and in all the advertising material. How should we view this change? Some will think that the company's directors are playing a dangerous game and are in danger of progressively diminishing the affective component of the brand among traditional European customers and creating a completely new brand, with fewer roots and more appeal to young Asian and American clients. But the brand's excellent results in the past 25 years seem to indicate that this segmentation strategy was a good one.

Strangely enough, when Dior perfumes decided to launch a new collection of fragrances in the niche category, they took a separate name—a revitalized full "Christian Dior, Paris" name. Today, the same client has the choice between a perfume like "Joy from Dior" and "Granville from Parfums Maison Christian Dior", and if she enters a Maison Parfums Christian Dior store to buy Joy, she would be told they don't have it and she could find it at Sephora or in a department store.

Changes of consolidated names and logos always generate an initial negative reaction from customers. This occurred in 2012 when Yves Saint Laurent announced its transition to Saint Laurent Paris. (They dropped the Yves from the name but maintained the three-letter logo). Then the market absorbs and gets used to the new name. Most new and younger customers will not even know of the past names.

In the history of brand creation, the name of perfumes under a luxury brand umbrella has given rise to more symbolic names. Attached to the poetics of evocation, perfume makers set the tone in the 1920s, with "Shalimar" from Guerlain in 1925 and "Shocking" from Schiaparelli in 1931.

In conclusion, what needs to be remembered is that there is no ideal name. If there were, it would be the name of a person, easy to remember in all languages, that evokes the qualities of the product or service offered, that suggests the company's philosophy, connotes intelligence and creativity, and begins with the letter "A" or "Z" to stand out in the listings.

The fact remains that the name, in itself, constitutes a vital asset. It is a source of much worry and enormous investment for companies. A good name has two characteristics: it is easy to remember and it has a significant emotional component or rational element. Yet in these two areas, the best is to be found alongside the worst. But such judgments, of course, imply a high degree of subjectivity. For that reason, we won't presume to give examples. But we're reminded of Juliet's lovely speech in Shakespeare:

What's in a name? that which we call a rose
    By any other name would smell as sweet.

That may be so for the name of a flower, but certainly not for the name of a brand.

Logos

"Logo" is the abbreviation of "logotype." It contains the Greek logos ("speech, discourse") and the suffix "-type," which in this case suggests the process of impression (as in typography).

Originally, for typographers, this word designated a group of signs that were printed all at once and that were all part of the same typographical character. Later, the term began to designate any fixed group of graphical signs representing a brand, a product, or a company.

Codification is an essential component of a logo. To be easily recognizable, it must present an invariable visual grammar, where the shape of the characters, the size of the symbol, and the colors used are rigorously defined and protected by patent. Also note that the simple fact of codifying the spelling of the name of a brand, even without accompanying visual symbols, already constitutes a logo.

The logo, then, is not the brand, but a particular way of writing the brand. It is the heraldic shield of modern times—a combination of letters or signs, an image, an ideogram, or a group of graphical elements.

The Functions of the Logo.   The logo, a unique and recognizable sign, has always served to mark an object, a work, or a building as belonging to a specific category. Logos appear to have always existed. Stone carvers placed their mark on their work, as did the great cabinetmakers. Roman slaves were tattooed with their masters' signs, and aristocrats and armies used escutcheons or standards. The word "brand" originally stood for the mark burned into the hide of cattle with a hot iron.

Communicating via symbols—language, mathematical signs, road signs—is one characteristic of humans. Logos are to modern communication and consumption activities what numbers are to mathematics or words to language: they constitute a new typology of conventional signs. In a way, logos are the new alphabet of an overcommunicating society, the symbols of our time.

The logo plays a role in social relations for two complementary reasons: on the one hand, for the informational content it communicates to the consumer before the purchase; on the other, for the perception it will create of this same consumer after the purchase, when he or she will be associated with the logo.

It's not surprising to see logos occupying such a dominant place in our overmediatized society. They often fill the need for communicative synthesis pushed to its extreme: a maximum amount of information in a minimum number of signs. The synthetic expressiveness of signs as different from each other as the Nike swoosh and the Christian cross is remarkable; independently of their referents, they accomplish an analogous semiotic function. In a few strokes, a maximum number of values or a vision of the world are summed up.

It is difficult to draw a strict typology of logos, since they borrow from a great number of expressive processes. One of the founders of semiotics, the philosopher Charles Sanders Peirce, proposed a classification of signs into three categories: icons, indices, and symbols.[3] Each of the three evokes a particular type of relation between the sign and the thing it represents.

The icon, Peirce says, is a representation of a literal type, based on the notion of similarity. For example, to represent an apple, we draw the contour of an apple.

Indices correspond to a relationship that is more mental, yet extremely strong, between the sign and the thing. It is a trace, an effect, or an element of the thing, which designates its presence without the slightest ambiguity. For example, if we see smoke on the horizon, it does not literally "draw" fire but signifies its presence very strongly ("Where there's smoke, there's fire"). In this case the association is based on objective correspondences, in the sense that they are guaranteed by laws that are identical for everyone: in Tokyo as in New York, fire generally makes smoke.

Symbols, finally, correspond to the establishment of an arbitrary link between the sign and the thing: for example, a lion for the Republic of Venice. The force of the symbol rests on the establishment of a common culture. There is no graphical similarity between one and the other, nor is there an objective link of a physical or logical nature. A foreigner confronted with the symbol would not be able to decode it; on the other hand, for all the members of a given community, its meaning is obvious. We could say that a symbol is a federating element. In Greek, *symbolon* designated the fragments of a clay tablet that had been broken.

---

[3] C. Harsborne and P. Weiss (eds.), *The Collected Papers of Charles Sanders Peirce*, vols. 1–6. Cambridge, MA: Harvard University Press, 1931–1935.

These pieces were then distributed to the members of a group, who reconstituted the tablet at each of their meetings. When Nike issues a sports advertising spot that it signs only with its swoosh, without even giving its name or slogan, it is obviously playing on the symbolic and federating dimension of its logo as well as on its fame.

These categories are abstract. In practice, logos are often hybrid, making use of all three at the same time. It might be better, then, to speak of the different functions of the sign. Let's take the example of the original Apple logo, which Jean-Marie Floch has analyzed in detail by comparing it to IBM's logo.[4] It can be called iconic, since it represents an apple; indicial (extrapolating a little), since the hollow in the outline clearly indicates that a bite has been taken out of this apple; and, above all, symbolic—the bitten-into apple is laden with rich suggestions, and the rainbow of the original logo also connotes the cultural blend that is California society.

Nevertheless, the symbolic function is by far the one most called upon. This is not surprising. To say that a logo functions as a symbol for a brand is to describe this notion of consumers' belonging to and having membership in a special and prestigious club. Note that logos that are purely typographical (a very specific way of writing the brand—font, letter size, spacing, and so on) also participate in this symbolic function. In fact, they rely on a set of visual conventions. For example, a serif character[5] will tend to connote classicism or neoclassicism, as in the case of Bulgari; a sans-serif font will connote modernity.

Ideally, a logo also seeks to take on the indicial function. The brand's dream, of course, is for its logo to represent it in a way that is as elementary as the way smoke signifies fire—even though such an ambition is utopian. Very interesting examples of this indicial function can be found on the boxes of matches given away by cigarette producers in France. Very strict regulations prohibit the display of their name, their brand, their slogan, or any other distinctive sign on the box; but they've managed to develop very abstract visual grammars, derived from their logos, which still carry meaning. It's a kind of graphical guessing game, and trying to decode them blind provides a good indication of a brand's graphical renown.

---

[4] Jean-Marie Floch, *Identités visuelles*. Paris: PUF, 1995.

[5] A serif is the horizontal line that serves as the base of the letter in certain typefaces. Fonts of more recent invention tend not to have serifs (and are referred to as "sans serif").

A Few Forms of Logo.   In this rapid overview, we claim neither to be exhaustive nor to propose a coherent typology. We devote the bulk of our efforts to logos that are strongly graphical, in an attempt to suggest the diversity of this universe.

Like the seals of the ancients, most logos consist of an image or of intertwined letters.

In the past, certain logos expressed themselves in three dimensions: Rolls-Royce chose the Winged Victory of Samothrace; Jaguar used the Leaper—a metal statuette of a leaping jaguar—as a hood ornament on its sports cars.

Certain logos have a more iconic function. In the category of images, the most frequent are those of animals. This harks back to the heraldic tradition, where animals were a prime source of inspiration for the escutcheons of the aristocracy.

Most often, we will find ourselves in the symbolic register, where the animal is an allegory for virtues that are assigned to it by convention. The choice of the brand name Jaguar, with its stylized but representational logo, is obviously associated with the aspiration to such virtues. And the list is long. There is Ferrari's rearing horse, an expression of indomitable vitality; the emblem was given to Enzo Ferrari by the family of a national hero, the aviator Francesco Baracca, who had it mounted on his plane when he was shot down over Montello during the First World War. For energy and speed, there is the shark of Paul and Shark; the elephant of Hunting World. For perseverance, there is Morabito's tortoise; for toughness and intelligence, the Lacoste crocodile. But many other representative images exist: Hermès's coach, Ralph Lauren's polo player.

Another very widespread category draws more from the history of writing and the signature. These are monogram logos, made up of the brand's initials and its derivatives. What comes to mind first are obviously the two intertwined Cs of Chanel and Cartier; Gucci's G; Yves Saint Laurent's YSL, and Loewe's "crab," with its L reflected in two axes.

Finally, there are logos of a more abstract nature, where the arbitrariness of the symbol predominates. This is not a new phenomenon. As with the choice of brand names, abstraction has been a trend for some decades. This is so with Tommy Hilfiger, with its red-white-and-blue rectangle, an extrapolation of the American flag, or Bally's red-and-white square.

Regardless of the choices made, a good logo should have the power to express and synthesize the characteristics of the brand, symbolic force, and ease of retention through a certain formal simplicity. Achieving all this is not as simple as it might seem, but success gives a brand a considerable competitive advantage.

Managing Logos.   Formal fashions change. Those within companies who are responsible for creating graphics are more sensitive than others to such issues and often ask for a logo to be transformed or rejuvenated. They rarely win out. This issue is a manager's nightmare. Many brands prefer to make do with a logo that is seen as somewhat dated rather than take the risk of damaging its fame. The graphical evolutions of logos at major brands extend over entire decades, and each stage of the process is often almost imperceptible.

Examples abound. The British brand Burberry's decided to alter its name to make it more accessible to an international clientele and, in general, to make the brand more competitive by giving it more modern connotations. This involved removing the apostrophe and the possessive "s." (This form is extremely widespread in English in the names of brands and restaurants, but it is less easily perceptible for other cultures.) Thus "Burberry's" became "Burberry." Removing the apostrophe and the "s" implies a change in the lettering as a whole, modernizing the brand, doubtless internationalizing it, but maybe slightly destabilizing part of its Anglo-Saxon clientele. These are not the kind of decisions that can be taken lightly.

Together with Jonathan Anderson's arrival as its creative director in 2013, Loewe unveiled a new visual identity by changing the typeface of its name and streamlining the heavily baroque logo. A Paris design studio revisited with much lighter lines the original anagram made of 4 L, created more than 30 years earlier by the artist Vincente Vella.

Logos are therefore always extremely sensitive to management. Their creation, their aesthetic evolution, and their utilization must be precise and organized to correspond with the general strategy of the brand.

What happens when there is no logo, or at least no graphical emblem? This is the case, for example, with Armani, Tiffany, Ferragamo, and Bulgari, among others. Generally, the company looks for one. But in the case of an established brand with a rich history, this is not easy.

In the early 1990s, Ferragamo wanted to stylize the brand name, to shorten it and make the founder's signature more legible. Also, the founder's baroque logo was very dated and was not used much. The company also wanted to attach a graphical emblem. Numerous trials were undertaken. A design with six horses, recalling the founder's six children, was studied, as was a drawing of the Feroni Palace, the company's headquarters. But the best intentions are not always successful, and the brand continues to use the Salvatore Ferragamo signature, whose calligraphy and, above all, whose length contribute to easy recognition.

Certain brands simply have no emblem and get along without one. The name of the brand, with its colors, graphics, and sometimes its calligraphy, is still the first point of recognition. The pointed Bulgari "U" has such strength as to make the search for an emblematic logo superfluous.

It may be relevant to mention the anecdoctal attempt by Gap to change its logo in 2010. The change was supposed to mark Gap's transition from classic American design to a more modern and cool version. It generated an uproar on the Internet and after one week, the brand decided to maintain the old blue box logo. This is probably the first example of a drastic decision change by a brand on the basis of market Internet expression.

Logomania.   Logos are almost omnipresent. Disseminating these totems in all the registers of communication is an easy way of universalizing the representation of the brand. They are visible on products to the point where they have become concrete signs of added value, particularly in the fashion sphere.

Logomania is also cyclical, the last craze dating back to the spring of 2000. By the 2002 Fall–Winter collections, there was a marked decrease in the number of products that were covered with logos. But, starting in 2016, logos were back, it seems. This has implications that have to be faced: fashion changes every season and can make obsolete an element that is strongly attached to the identity of the brand itself.

As for logos of public or private sponsors, they have proliferated in the past few years on posters and billboards for sports and cultural events. Their presence and, very often, their size on the poster are contractually imposed. Graphic artists often complain about this, pointing out that these additional signs, to which they are sometimes required to devote as much as 20% of the total display area, can have a negative impact on the relevance of their communication—and they have a point.

We have said that logos, as symbols, presuppose a cultural community, and taking local specificities into consideration appears to be a determining factor in establishing a threshold of tolerance.

Perceptions vary greatly from one country to another. Logos are much better received in Japan than in the United States or Europe. While a majority of Europeans refuse to wear a necktie printed with the acronym of a brand, Americans have no problem with it, and the very same necktie might well become a genuine fad in Japan. In China, things are a little bit more complicated: people living on the eastern coast have seen the logos so much that they are no longer interested in them and prefer less obvious signs of brand recognition. Conversely, people living in the west are still very interested in those simple signs of immediate sophistication.

The majority of brands with global ambitions have the wisdom to take these cultural differences into account and have integrated them. Louis Vuitton, for example, offers its Japanese clientele strongly monogrammed bags; for European consumers, the brand offers a fabric in identical colors, but with a checkerboard pattern, or else Épi or Taïga leather, where the monogram only appears episodically.

Consumers in Paris and Tokyo are very happy with their Vuitton purchases. They've made the effort of acquiring an expensive product and feel that a prestigious logo, one that reflects well on them, is the reward for that effort, provided that it remains below their own particular tolerance threshold. They feel that by carrying the bag in public, they are affirming the values they seek (a certain elegance, perhaps) without the risk of suggesting those they shun (bad taste).

The logo, as the ultimate synthesis of the brand's communication, must appeal to the eye, heart, and intelligence.

A logo is not a necessary and sufficient condition of success. However, to not have an adequate logo is to miss an incredible opportunity to communicate more effectively.

Other Signs of Recognition

Signs of recognition don't end with the name of the brand or its logo. Certain brands or products have succeeded in appropriating other elements of recognition and differentiation, often by chance or through repeated usage. Yet they manage these additional distinguishing elements closely.

Baselines have become more frequent as they come to complement a logo that is not always sufficiently explicit of the brand characteristics. Certain advertising slogans, so often heard and repeated in association with the brand, have become extensions operating like synonyms: It may be the case of De Beers's "A diamond is forever."

Faced with the difficulty of finding a logo and a name able to synthesize the brand identity, the addition of a few words often does the trick. Intel's taking advantage of a logo change to add the words "leap forward" provides a recent example of this. In luxury, brands have often used expressions such as "The art of ... ," which sounds more vintage than trendy, and seem to have abandoned the creativity theme to the technology companies.

There are examples of cult products that become emblematic of a brand, such as the Hermès Kelly bag or Gucci moccasins. There are also certain distinctive characteristics, such as the matte-metallic feel used in most Porsche design products. Color is another important element: a red sports car has to be a Ferrari. Indeed, Ferrari's monopoly on the color is so strong that it seems a little presumptuous to buy a sports car of another make in the same shade of red. Ducati has done the same with red in the motorcycle sector. Distinctive sound can even be an identifying element: Porsche, Harley-Davidson, and Ducati take great pains to maintain a very specific engine noise for their products, which they have even attempted to patent.

Packaging can also be an element of recognition. Tiffany's light-blue box and the Hermès orange box are strong aesthetic elements of their individual identity that travel with the product and are an integral part of the gift.

Labeling, too, is another element. It is more important in categories such as ready-to-wear, but it is being discovered, beyond its original informative function, as an important creative element. For instance, the hot Argentine brand La Martina is attaching—inside and out—all sorts of labels to its famous polo shirts, T-shirts, and leather accessories, and this has become a strong element (too strong?) of its brand recognition.

Whether through names, logos, or other elements, a brand's signs must be identifiable, expressive, and easy to remember. They must create a feeling of closeness, familiarity, and even humanity. They must communicate a message of belonging, not only to the brand (at the first level) but also to its universe and its values. This last point is what will distinguish between a brand that projects meaning and one whose significance is vague. Finally, they must stay in their proper place, not be a nuisance, and never give themselves over to semantic inaccuracy, which could complicate decoding. Their primary role is to speak the brand and its universe with elegance and conciseness. It is the brand's responsibility to keep a close watch over its signs, their nature, and their frequency.

The Legal Aspects and the Defense of a Brand

There are hundreds of very good books on brand protection, written by legal experts. In this book, it would be impossible for us to even summarize what has been said on the subject. Nevertheless, this is so much of a concern for luxury goods—particularly for watches, perfumes, and leather goods—that it is necessary here to at least give some indication of the operational methods available for dealing with the subject.

Brand Protection

Brand Registration.   The first step with any new brand is to register it; this registration must be done by country and by class. Table 4.4 gives a broadly accepted list of brand categories.

For registering a fashion brand, categories 25 and 24 are essential, but so is 18 for leather goods, 9 for glasses, and 16 and 34 for writing instruments and lighters. That's a total of six categories. For perfume activities, registering in class 3 is essential; and if the ultimate goal is perhaps to come up with promotional articles such as combs or brushes, then it is also advisable to look at class 21. Jewelry and watches have their own class, 14.

The ideal for a new brand would be to register in 10 categories. But this is not cheap. Brand registration in one country could cost anywhere from €1,000 to €2,000 (taking into account lawyers' fees as well as the tax levied by the national registration authorities). In 100 countries and in 10 classes, this could cost €1–2 million. This is not easy for a brand that is just starting up.

Table 4.4   Brand Registration Categories

1	Chemical products
2	Paint, varnishes
3	Perfumes, soaps, cosmetics
4	Oil, candles
5	Pharmaceutical products, disinfectants, cosmetics
6	Metal tools
7	Machine tools
8	Tools, razors
9	Technical instruments, optical products, glasses
10	Medical and veterinary products
14	Jewelry, watches
15	Musical instruments
16	Paper products, writing instruments
17	Plastic products
18	Leather goods
19	Construction materials
20	Furniture
21	Kitchenware, chinaware, combs, brushes
22	Ropes, textile and fabric bags
23	Thread
24	Fabric and textile products
25	Garments, shoes, hats
26	Embroidery
27	Rugs
28	Toys
29	Meat products
30	Food
31	Agricultural products
34	Tobacco, lighters

At the outset, it is not necessary to be registered everywhere in the world; indeed, most European countries that have signed the Madrid Convention require only one registration. But registering in the United States, Japan, and China, and in Latin American countries, is essential; not to do so is to leave the way clear for unscrupulous local companies to register the name for counterfeit activities.

Registration Renewal.   Registration does not remain active forever. It can, depending on the country and the legislation in place, last for either 5 or 10 years. This means that every year it is necessary to renew approximately 20% of all registrations at a cost of anywhere between €200,000 and €400,000 for each of the classes mentioned.

To renew the registration in a given class, local authorities will request proof of usage. If nobody takes legal action for lack of usage and forfeiture of the original registration, things should be fine. Should such action be taken, however, the courts can be very demanding.

Take, for example, a brand that was the leader in the field of men's eau de toilette in Brazil. It was heavily advertised and it had a very strong awareness locally. But as customs duties on perfumes were very high, the company's local distributor was smuggling the products into the country. When the court asked for proof of payment of import duties, these could not be presented. The court's judgment was that the brand had never been officially present in Brazil, and it enacted forfeiture in class 3. The brand was then immediately registered by someone considered by the company to be a counterfeit operator but whom the Brazilian courts continued to consider to be the genuine brand user for many years.

Very well known brands can fight this situation by pointing to the worldwide awareness of the brand and, in some cases, to the fact that the brand is the patronymic of a given individual and that the local operators knew of the brand's world status when they registered it and were thus not acting in good faith. The brand eventually succeeded in recovering its name in Brazil, but it took six or seven years to enforce this judgment.

In their main businesses, luxury companies generally do not have difficulty in protecting and renewing their brands. But in secondary product categories, it is not that simple. For example, to protect itself against actions for nonusage under classes 24 and 25, Cartier has developed a range of scarves. Very famous brands that do not have a perfume business are well advised to make a standard perfume every three to five years and to invoice it to their overseas subsidiaries or distributors to ensure that there is minimum proof of usage, in the form of receipts for payment of customs duties, in most parts of the world.

The potential dangers of not protecting registration rights are evident in another case involving Cartier. In Mexico, an individual registered the brand before Cartier itself, opened a Cartier store, and traded in Cartier watches before the company could manage to regain its full registration rights. For many years, Lacoste had problems in Hong Kong and China with a locally registered brand, Crocodile, which had a similar logo. The brands finally came to the agreement that the Chinese company would modify its logo in such a way that it would not be confused with the Lacoste crocodile.

While registration for any brand can be difficult, costly, and tedious, it is absolutely necessary, and is even more so for perfume houses. Dior perfumes, for example, has to register both its brand and each of its individual products: Joy, J'Adore, Dolce Vita, Fahrenheit, Sauvage, Capture, and many others.

The Original Registration.   It is not easy to register a new brand, not least because for perfumes with suggested names such as Romance, Romantique, or Romantic it is likely that the name has been registered and is already in use somewhere in the world. Brand names are often generated through creative group discussions or creative sessions, at the end of which maybe 50 names come up for consideration. A first run on the Internet will probably eliminate most, if not all, of these: the names are already in use or may have sufficient legally acceptable proofs of usage to discourage their adoption. Sometimes a registered letter to a company indicating a desire to start a legal action for lack of usage and forfeiture of its early brand registration may give rise to an opportunity to buy that registration. Where there is no real proof of usage, this may be done for €10,000–20,000. Where there are strong worldwide registrations and convincing proof of usage, this may rise to anywhere between €200,000 and €500,000. This is not a very easy subject.

Fighting Counterfeit Activities

Some activities are considered legal in one part of the world and illegal in others. We examine some of these first, look at the specific case of China, and then move on to what we call the lenient countries.

Knock-offs and Tables of Correspondence

In the United States, supermarkets sell cheap perfumes with labels that proclaim: "If you liked Youth Dew by Estée Lauder, you will love our No. 36," or "If you liked Chanel No. 5, you will love our No. 17." In most countries, such products—known as knock-offs—would be prohibited because they exist only by feeding off the awareness of and preference for established brands. Elsewhere they would be seen as unfair competition or, to put it more accurately, commercial parasites, but in the United States consumer advocates take the view that such products provide fair value to the customer and reduce selective luxury perfume houses to what they really are—providers of a given scent that can be copied. Each country has its own system and its own specific characteristics.

Tables of correspondence are the German equivalent of knock-offs. Here, perfumes are sold with a designated number that corresponds with the customer's usual, more expensive, brand of choice. To openly link any known named brand with a cheaper corresponding numbered brand is prohibited by law as unfair competition. But German firms have found a way around this: as long as they and their sales staff don't make such links, in writing or orally, products can be sold in this way. Again, consumer advocates are very much in favor of these products and this approach, and such sales are strong.

What can brands do about this? The answer is, with both knock-offs and tables of correspondence, absolutely nothing. In other countries, such practices would be fought very strongly.

This is not unlike the T-shirts with the name Chanel, Dior, or Prada embroidered on the front that you find on some tourist places in Asia. Such products are clearly counterfeit and are clearly perceived as such. In a way, they are the unwanted outcome of brands' success. Whether such things should be fought against is debatable, since the consumers who buy these products are well aware that they are not buying the real thing.

Chinese and Korean Counterfeits

Tourists walking around in Seoul or Shanghai will be stopped quite frequently by people offering fake watches, shoes, or handbags. If they show some interest, they are led to a store down a back street somewhere and are then presented with as many copies of luxury watches as they could hope for. It seems that every brand of watch is on offer, along with any number of handbags. While the watches sometimes never work for more than two or three minutes, the handbags are more or less no risk, even if the product finishes are not in line with those of the genuine products.

Again, some might say that it is not necessary to fight such counterfeit activities, because those purchasing the products know that they are fake and they would never have bought the genuine article. This is to put the genuine branded product and the fake into two different market segments.

A Japanese or other Asian tourist would not be interested in a fake product: they value the legitimacy of the authentic goods too highly for that. Americans, too, are not interested in anything other than the genuine article. The only ones who are really interested are the Europeans, who believe they are smart and can get a good deal and nobody would know the difference anyway—which is almost never true.

The fight against counterfeiters is never a simple task. It requires both the will and the means to tackle the whole distribution chain, from those offering the fakes in the streets, to the back-street shops, to the wholesaler, and on to the manufacturer. Even if the manufacturer is located and sued, the machinery and equipment are simply moved to another location or sold to another company, and the cycle will start all over again.

Though it may seem an endless fight, it is nevertheless a necessary one if the development of such counterfeiting trades is to be curbed and their volumes curtailed.

The Lenient Countries

In some countries, the authorities are not particularly interested in curbing counterfeiting, an activity that provides local jobs and brings in hard foreign currency. Morocco is a case in point. There, it is possible to buy copies of every type of branded leather goods, a trade that obviously provides jobs for local leather-goods specialists.

Italy provides another example of where perhaps the authorities may sometimes turn a blind eye where counterfeiting is concerned. In Rome or Ventimiglia, for example, you can find copies of every single French luxury brand—Chanel, Louis Vuitton, Dior. Strangely, though, it's much more difficult to get Gucci or Ferragamo copies. Here again the Italian government and police could be more active and more effective. We can only hope that the European Union can bring the necessary pressure to bear to counter such activities more effectively than simple bilateral discussions have been able to achieve to date.

What makes counterfeiting such an interesting activity is the fact that the margins of luxury goods are very high. The higher the power of the brand, the more interesting it is to move into the field. Counterfeit goods are, in their own way, a clear indication of the desirability and power of the original brand.

Chapter 5

The Luxury Client

I n other chapters, we speak repeatedly about the consumer. This is, in fact, something of a misnomer. A consumer, as the name implies, consumes the products he or she purchases. We have already seen in Chapter 1 that in luxury there are no products, only special objects that clients want to acquire and keep, and what matters is the experience each client discovers as he or she purchases and uses over time. Someone purchasing a Rolex watch or a Hermès handbag is not going to consume the product and then go back to the store to acquire a new one.

The client purchases iconic objects on special occasions and does so with a special mood or spirit. Even repeat purchases of objects such as a bottle of perfume or of champagne are exceptional events, charged with emotional and social content.

In this chapter we will first ask who the luxury clients are. We will then study how such clients behave, before looking at differences in national behavior. In a first subsection, we will look at who the clients are, and then in the second subsection, we will describe the X, Y, and Z generations of customers to then concentrate on the millennials and the HENRYs. In the third subsection, we will study the specificities of different luxury products and explain national differences in perfumes, wines and spirits, and fashion habits.

Who Is the Luxury Client?

Luxury clients are in fact the very rich, and, also … everybody. We will begin by looking at some quantitative analysis that has been done to see who those clients buying a bottle of champagne or an expensive watch really are.

The Rich, the Very Rich, or Everybody?

There are several studies analyzing the very rich. According to the Capgemini study of 2020,[1] there were 19,608 million individuals in the world with net financial assets exceeding US$1 million.

Of these 19.6 million, it is important to note that 37.9% are female and 45.9% are under 40.

This study also divides this group of millionaires into three segments:

1. The ultra-high-net-worth millionaires (more than US$30 million): 183,000
2. The mid-tier millionaires (US$5–$30 million): 1,758,000
3. The millionaires next door (US$1–$5 million): 17,667,000

Obviously, having a million dollars in China is not exactly the same thing as having that amount in the United States, where the cost of living is very different and where the disposable income is also quite different. But in both cases, it makes it possible to buy a relatively expensive gift.

In Table 5.1, we give the number of millionaires by nationality for 2020 as indicated in the Capgemini report.

---

[1] Capgemini, *World Wealth Report 2020*, May 2020. www.capgemini.com>fr.fr>ressources> worldwealthreport.

Table 5.1   Nationality of the Millionaires (in thousands)

United States	5,909
Japan	3,387
Germany	1,466
Mainland China	1,317
France	702
UK	591
Switzerland	438
Canada	392
Italy	298
Holland	287
Australia	284
India	263
South Korea	243

Source: Capgemini World Wealth Report, 2020.

Another report, prepared by Crédit Suisse Research,[2] analyzes the millionaires in cash as well as investments (including real estates and company shares) and reports 46.8 million millionaires or 2.5 times more.

Every year, *Forbes* magazine also publishes a list of the world's wealthiest individuals, with a special section on the richest Chinese men. The total number of billionaires was 2,095 in 2020. Table 5.2 gives the split of these wealthiest individuals by nationality.

These 2,095 billionaires control as much net worth as the 4.6 billion less-privileged individuals of the planet Earth.[3]

These millionaires and billionaires have something to do with the luxury business and they are target clients for high-end jewelry pieces or made-to-order haute couture outfits. But they are not the main source of luxury business sales and growth. Apart from very expensive items, it seems that the more than €342 billion sales done each year by luxury firms, as we mentioned in Chapter 2, are not made exclusively by the very rich. To be active, luxury flagship stores should have other regular clients. The source of luxury business comes from a much larger

---

[2] Crédit Suisse Research Institute, Crédit Suisse reports and research, Global Wealth Report, March 2020.
[3] Oxfam Report, January 20, 2020. www.oxfm.org>tags>billionaires.

Table 5.2   Nationality of Billionaires

United States	614
China	389
Germany	107
India	102
Russia	99
Hong Kong	66
United Kingdom	48
Canada	44
Brazil	41
France	39
Italy	36
Switzerland	35

Source: *Forbes* special issue, *World's Billionaires* 2020, May 23, 2020.

population, the higher middle class; it is this middle class that brings volume, repeat business, and diversity in the stores.

This is, of course, still a very far cry from the 4,000 women in the world who can afford a haute couture dress, or even from the 18 million who can afford an expensive piece of jewelry. The luxury client is almost everybody. But he or she purchases a luxury object less frequently than high-net-worth individuals.

Researchers have tried to identify luxury clients and have moved away from the very rich to those who could purchase some or many luxury objects. Don Ziccardi, in a relatively old book, showed a lot of foresight when he identified four consumer segments:

1. **Millennium money:** This is the category of those who made a fortune around the turn of the twenty-first century, all celebrities and sport stars, as well as those who became rich through the Internet business. They will be part of the subject of our next subsection.
2. **Old money:** This is the traditional category of those who have inherited their wealth and don't really work, or who manage a business they have inherited, or who perhaps have a professional life with a standard of living that is not related to their salary.
3. **New money:** This category is made up of those who have made a fortune themselves. Unlike the millennium-money category, these millionaires are not necessarily young and they did not come by

their money easily. These individuals have worked hard and are still working hard. They are careful about money and seem to know its value.

4. **Middle money:** This is the category of the upper-middle class, which is careful about money. Their main revenues are through salaries or professional income and they are reasonable spenders. This is the group that we mention all along in this book.[4]

The Excursionists

Other researchers have considered that nonfrequent luxury buyers were the main source of business volume.

When asked "Have you bought a luxury product in the past 24 months?," 63% of respondents in developed countries answered yes.[5] This is actually the real group of luxury clients: more than half of the general population in developed countries. And the rapid growth rate of this industry (an annual average of 8%) results from the fact that every year a new group of "middle class" consumers from developed or developing countries can, for the first time, afford to buy a bottle of champagne, a €2,000 handbag, or a €4,000 watch. With the increased accessibility of such goods, luxury is, for 63% of people in developed countries at least, becoming part of their regular experience.

The term *excursionist* was coined by Bernard Dubois and Gilles Laurent[6] as they looked at the frequency of luxury purchases when academic studies on luxury management were very rare. Their findings are shown in Table 5.3.

They showed that, apart from the "happy few" (12%) who had bought a luxury item more than five times in the previous two years and who obviously represented a very large volume of the total market, the largest group (51% of the population) had bought between one and five items in the last two years. What immediately leaps to mind here is the lower-middle-class group, who are very careful about their general spending and who look for special promotions in the supermarket, but

---

[4] Don Ziccardi, *Influencing the Affluent: Marketing to the Individual Luxury Customer in a Volatile Economy.* New York: MFJ Books, 2001.

[5] RISC International, The luxury market, 2003.

[6] Bernard Dubois and Gilles Laurent, *Les excursionnistes du Luxe,* Hommes et Commerce, no. 271, MW 1999.

Table 5.3   Breakdown of Luxury Clients in Developed Countries

Have not purchased a luxury product in the past 24 months	37%
Have purchased a luxury product in the past 24 months	63%
Have purchased more than five pieces	12% (i.e., 20% of purchasers)
Average number of purchases	2

Source: Bernard Dubois and Gilles Laurent, *Les excursionnistes du Luxe,* Hommes et Commerce, no. 271, MW 1999.

who can also decide to buy a Cartier watch for their daughter's graduation or a small Tiffany engagement ring for their future wife. Dubois and Laurent used the word "excursion" to describe how this group approached the purchase of luxury items. Entering a Cartier or Tiffany store was, for such consumers, a bit like taking a boat ride or visiting a museum. The interesting question Dubois and Laurent were exploring was what these "excursionists" were expecting from their "ride" to a luxury store. So, they investigated further, asking the question: "What were you looking for?" The answers they received from the excursionists were as follows:

- They expect the product to be of outstanding **quality**, in both the materials used and the service. This is not like visiting a supermarket: it is a very special experience and must be rewarding for them.
- They expect the product to be **expensive**. For the function it satisfies, the luxury product should clearly belong to another price range: the purchase is not a natural or matter-of-fact activity and the price should reflect this.
- They want to be sure that the object they acquire is **scarce and difficult to obtain**, available only to **a very few individuals**.
- They expect the shopping experience to provide a **multisensory** moment: when they walk into the store, across the thick wall-to-wall carpet, they want to be surrounded by sophisticated music, to see beautiful objects, and to know that what they are about to do will be worth it. And, of course, they expect sales staff to treat them as people who are doing something exceptional.
- They expect to come to a world that has its **roots in the past**. They want to make a purchase that is **timeless**. They want their act

to become part of an environment that has always existed and will always exist.

- They know that their purchase does not make too much economic sense and they are happy with that. They accept the fact that what they are doing is **slightly pointless or unnecessary**. They speak of jewelry or perfumes in the way, for example, others may speak of an expensive car: they are not concerned with its engine or its technical characteristics, but they speak about the luxury of the passenger space.

The excursion must be something memorable and different for them. This is why in-store service is so important in the luxury field. But having described the excursionist model, it is important to remember that this is part of a larger movement that analyzes the marketing and consumer process, not in terms of the segmentation of individuals but in terms of different situations in life and explaining the different purchasing behaviors.

The New Client

New clients will evaluate products and buy them as a function of their individual situation. For example, a woman may in the course of one day buy Zara jeans, a Celine jacket, and Wolford leggings in physical stores and buy a Lancôme skin cream on the Internet. She may also end her day shopping at Carrefour and buying, for example, a brand of coffee because of cut price promotions. This apparently changing behavior is what specialists have tried to understand: customers today have new expectations and new patterns of behavior.

New Customer Expectations

Customers are not rational when they purchase a luxury object. They don't claim to be rational. More than anything else, they value the affective and aesthetic content of their purchase and they perceive the different product offerings along such lines.

They are **affective** because they consider their own pleasure to be more important than any other rational criteria. To judge a product on rational criteria would reduce their shopping pleasure. As they compare different product offerings, they value intangible elements like the sophistication of the atmosphere in the store, or the opportunity to go to an area of the town where they can meet people—or, even better, famous people. Even the type of music they hear in a given store can condition the way they perceive products from a particular brand and, ultimately, the way they buy.

This affective component of the consumer information process is used in advertising, as we will see in Chapter 9. Luxury advertising is not only based on information; it is based on the fact that it should surprise, attract, and communicate a specific mood.

A second expectation relates to **a need for beauty**, the belief that a product should be evaluated by its shape, its special feel in the hand, the types of fashion models used by the brand, or the aesthetic value of its new advertising.

This is one of the reasons that the aesthetic elements of a brand are so important in its development. People associate different aesthetic values with different brands. Gucci and Saint Laurent belong to completely different universes. This should be reflected in the shape of the lady's perfume bottles, the concept of the ready-to-wear stores, and the shopping bags clients are given when they purchase something.

Customers are eclectic. They want to be different from the crowd and they want to indicate to everybody that they know what they are doing. They do not want to rely on a single brand: the total look (all Chanel or all Versace) is seen to be completely out of fashion today—it does not show who you are and what you have decided for yourself. But a creative mix between Givenchy and Zara shows that you are creative and that you have taste.

However, eclecticism has some limits. Customers still want to belong to a group and are rewarded by this group for the choice they have made. While 15 years ago people wanted to be identical to their group of references or their close friends (at school, students wanted to carry the same brand), this is no longer true today. Now, they want to be similar to a very small number of individuals who they have selected as part of their mini "tribal" group. The social norm still exists and is still very strong, but its base is scattered between a myriad of subgroups that are organized along different types of activities or behaviors.

Consumers are also looking for **hedonistic** values. They prize their own pleasure more than anything else. Here again, they do not look only for the functional elements of a product's attributes but to the imaginary world that they have created themselves and that becomes their own world, leading to their own vision of luxury in general and individual luxury brands in particular.

This brings us back to the cultural dimension described at the beginning of Chapter 1. Each customer's individual vision of a given brand integrates aesthetic and cultural values, often of a specific national atmosphere and of what this brand can and cannot do.

Consumers can be fragmented in their expectations and in their behavior and can change rapidly over time.

The result for luxury brand management is quite clear: sales trends are changing rapidly and brands that are successful are those that are able to give an added cultural, aesthetic, and hedonistic value to their overall identity.

In this section, we will describe the X, Y, and Z groups of customers, concentrate next on the millennials, and then on what American analysts call the HENRYs (High earners, not rich yet).

The X, Y, and Z Clients.   We are speaking of the same thing, but the vocabulary has changed. People have been classified as Baby Boomers when they were born between 1943 and 1959, but then qualified as Generation X if they were born between 1960 and 1977. This caused the next group to be called Generation Y (born between 1978 and 1994), and a new category, Generation Z, for those born after 1995. At first sight, it was very simple.

But then experts invented the term *digital natives* for those who were born with digital systems and their own computers. This term covers more or less all those born after 1978 and it is also quite simple: it includes all Y and Z groups who have the instinct to find easy solutions on mobile phones. An additional category has also been created: the millennials, or those who have become adults as they entered the twenty-first century. This covers more or less the digital natives, but it appears that apart from being very familiar with the web, they also have very different attitudes and purchase motivations.

Why would those younger groups be more interesting to watch in terms of luxury goods? A study was conducted to distinguish between a group of Americans; they were asked if they buy luxury products and for what purpose. The results, as they appear in Table 5.4, are striking.

Table 5.4 Why Are People Buying Luxury Items by Age?

	Regular Treaters	Buyin g for Gift	Occasional Treaters	Rarely Buying	Never Buying
16–24	19%	33%	25%	19%	14%
25–34	34%	23%	22%	18%	16%
35–44	33%	15%	15%	15%	15%
45–54	7%	17%	23%	26%	27%
54–64	7%	12%	15%	22%	28%

Source: Chase Buckle, "The Luxury Market in 2019: What Brands Should Know," *GlobalWebIndex*, April 1, 2019.

What comes out is that 50% or more of the respondents above 45 years old say that they seldom or never buy luxury products, as opposed to respondents between 25 and 44 years old, who are regular or occasional treaters as well as gift buyers. Also, younger respondents, under 25 years old, have an interest for this type of product, and if they are seldom regular users, they seem to be twice as interested in luxury gift purchases than the respondents above 45 years of age.

One could say that this situation is true in the United States but not necessarily everywhere. Nevertheless, when we later describe the luxury purchasing behavior of Chinese clients, the same pattern will also appear.

This is probably why the category of clients between 25 and 45 are now given top priority for many brands, and probably why people were very creative in finding new names to define them.

As explained next, creative people have invented an additional name to speak of the millennials—the HENRYs—and explain that they prioritize those American households having yearly earnings above US$100,000. This is another way of creating a subtle new segmentation. It is also a way to understand how they are different in their purchase expectations and the kind of products and purchasing experiences they expect.

The Millennials.   More has been written on the millennials than on any other population segment in the past 50 years,[7] maybe because as we entered the twenty-first century, the millennials themselves have been carefully analyzed. They are supposed to be careful with their money,

---

[7] See, for example, the best-seller by Bret Easton Ellis, *White*. New York: Knopf, 2019.

but they love to eat out. They spend a lot on their wardrobe but are careful with their money. They are also supposed to spend more on their wardrobe than on their retirement package.[8]

There is also a specificity about millennials: they are much more numerous than Generation X, at least in the United States.

They are obviously technology enthusiasts. Again, in the United States, three-fourths of millennials have created their social networking profile; 88% of them prefer to use their phone to send a text message rather than to make a call.

In the United States alone, there are 73 million millennials: 44% of them are not white (a large part is Hispanic or Black), 88% live in metropolitan areas, and 34% are university graduates (with at least a bachelor's degree).

They are more brand-loyal than their predecessors: "Millennials have the desire to make the best decision in regards to not only price and quality but give consideration to making good investment for the future. Millennial customers find great confidence and trust in the brand name of their choice."[9] In fact, 60% "want to remain loyal to their previous purchases."[10]

In their purchasing decisions, they look carefully at:

- The price
- The customer ratings and reviews
- The overall value of the product
- The recommendations from friends
- The brand values

They also want to give their opinion and want their voice to be heard (87% agree that brands should get consumers like them to give their opinion before creating new products, whatever it means).[11] They are certainly not passive clients. They want to be part of the story.

When they are asked what would they do for their next purchase, they answer:

- 32%: a desk computer
- 25%: a smartphone

---

[8] Millennials consumer trends 2019. www2.deloitte.com.
[9] Gurven Ordun, "Millennial Consumer Behavior, Their Shopping Preferences and Perceptual Maps Associated with Brand Loyalty," *Canadian Social Sciences* 11, no. 4 (2015).
[10] "45 Statistics on Millennial Spending Habits in 2020," Lexington Law, January 24, 2020.
[11] "The 5 Truths That Define Millennials," Ipsos, June 25, 2015.

- 24%: a tablet
- 11%: go to a physical store

A recent study by Somi Arian[12] defines the millennials' environment as follows:

- They have an abundance of choice: many products or experiences are available to them.
- They are used to changes and upgrades in their products.
- They are more influenced by their peers or by influencers than by their parents or by tradition.
- They are diverse (in the United States, only 56% are white). They find by themselves and their peer generation what is good for them.
- They want to learn by themselves and at their own pace.
- They want to give their support to brands that care for the environment. (They believe the Baby Boomers have destroyed the planet.)
- They are careful with their money and want to have products with value.
- They are more interested in experience than in ownership.
- They are interested in their well-being and in the well-being of the world.
- They have different entertainment practices and are often using streaming services more than television or radio.

Unfortunately, this group of millennials is not so homogeneous as it appears at first sight. A study by the Boston Consulting Group[13] divided them in six different segments:

1. The *Hip-ennials* (29%): They are cautious customers, globally aware, charitable, and information hungry. Their sentence: "I can make the world a better place."
2. The *Millennial Moms* (22%): They are wealthy, family oriented, and confident. Their sentence: "I love to work out, travel, and pamper my baby."

---

[12] Somi Arian, "The Millennials' Mind Set: Factors That Drive Millennials' Consumer Behavior," Smart Cookie Media, May 2, 2019.
[13] Christine Barton, Jeff Fromm, and Chris Egan, "The Millennial Consumer," Boston Consulting Group, April 16, 2012. bcg.com/publications/2012/millennial-consumer.

3. The *Anti-millennials* (16%): They are locally minded, conservative, and would not spend more for green products. Their sentence: "I am too busy to worry."
4. The *Gadget Gurus*: (13%): They are confident and at ease. Their sentence: "It's a great day to be me."
5. The *Clean and Green Millennials* (10%): Their sentence: "I take care of myself and the world around me."
6. The *Old-School Millennials* (22%): They believe that connecting on Facebook is too impersonal; "let's meet up for a coffee instead." They are not wired or prefer direct contacts.

According to this listing, in fact the "real" millennials represent only 62% of this generation. However, they play an important part in the attitudes of this generation.

The question is to see how they all behave when they consider buying a luxury product. A study conducted in France on a sample of 856 millennials gives some indications.[14]

For them, luxury relates to desire, pleasure, and merit. They are not apologetic about buying luxury products (81% consider buying a luxury product during a period of crisis to not be shocking). They have no misconceptions about this industry and believe that if they can pay for it, there is really no problem.

They have real interest in the fashion business, in the brands and their positioning, and in what they are doing, but they seem interested in the luxury ambassadors or the creative genius. For them, the luxury world is not a business. It is a creative activity that is fun to watch and to be part of—that is to say, to buy and dispose of nice and interesting products.

For them, there is nothing problematic about buying luxury goods if one can afford it and use the money that one has been able to earn. Millennials show an interest in beautiful objects and are interested in shapes and design.

These young adults have grown up in a period where children were pampered by their parents, for whom nothing was too much, too beautiful, or too expensive. At a very young age, they were already used to the very best products.

---

[14] Gregory Casper and Eric Briones, *la Génération Y et le Luxe*. Dunod, 2014.

In that sense, the Chinese millennials, as we will see later, have had a similar experience of living in an economy developing rapidly and where salaries and purchasing power have increased regularly and created the feeling that they deserve everything they can afford.

A typical example of this is the client who says, "I don't care about what others may think. I dress the way I want and if people are not happy about it, that's their problem."

But this acceptance of fashion because it is creative and beautiful still has a drawback: to please the millennials the brand must remain creative and beautiful and it must always bring new ideas and new things.

The HENRYs[15].   It is quite easy to describe what the HENRYs are: they are just millennials with money. But because they have money, they buy more and account for a very large percentage of total sales.

Those who have invented the concept of the HENRYs have probably looked at Table 5.4, where we see that American people above 45 are less inclined to buy luxury goods, so they have identified a population segment with a similar spending pattern but a much higher interest in luxury. Table 5.5 shows how this is possible and confirmed.

At first sight, the best segment is those clients between 45 and 54, with average income above $104,415, although the younger age group has about the same average income ($97,569) and a similar luxury purchasing behavior.

As Pamela Danziger says in her book, the HENRYs are the most interesting purchasing category:

1. With their age starting at 26 and finishing at 45 and a high income , it is a compelling segment.
2. They are probably financially well-off. They probably own their home or will purchase one, and they are loyal and may stay loyal for a long time to their preferred luxury brands.
3. There are starting to acquire high-quality goods and services and are very careful about superior materials and workmanship.

François-Henry Pinault, the chairman of Kering, speaks about the millennials in a way that could also apply to these customers: "About

---

[15] Pamela N. Danziger, Meet the HENRYs: The Millennials That Matter Most for Luxury Brands. Rochester: Paramount Market Publishing, 2019.

Table 5.5 Household Income and Household Expenditures by Age in the United States

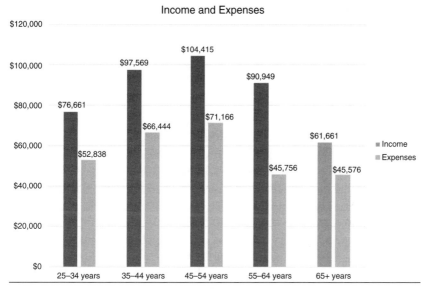

Source: Pamela N. Danziger, *Meet the HENRYs: The Millennials That Matter Most for Luxury Brands*, Rochester: Paramount Market Publishing, 2019.

50 percent of Gucci sales are coming from Millennials, the cohorts of 35-years-old and younger, a generation that has been particularly troubling for luxury brands. That means we have a core category of customers that are between 25 and 35. … The attractiveness of couture and ready-to-wear is much higher for that clientele than it used to be for older people."[16]

The president of Gucci, Marco Bizzari, has the same words: "Millennials tend to have an appetite for new things and they are driven by content, emotions, and personal connections. They value self-expression and they value sustainability."[17]

Of course, they both speak of millennials, but HENRYs are actually a special category of millennials and are the most active customers of the total group.

---

[16] François Henry Pinault, in an interview with CNBC in 2018.
[17] Danziger, *Meet the HENRYs*, 33.

How Much Should Luxury Goods Marketing Programs Adapt to Millennials' and HENRYs' Expectations?

A study by Deloitte has tried to answer this question:

> Luxury brands have started to initiate and sustain longstanding relationships with a new customer class who is likely to become or remain affluent or ultra-affluent in the future.
>
> The reality is that "new" luxury consumers only care about the brands that have created value for them in the last 24 hours. [The Millennials and the HENRYs] regard brand history and heritage as much less important attributes when making purchasing decisions, ranking them sixth after quality, customer service, design, craftsmanship, and product exclusivity … if the brands continue to depend heavily on heritage without radically reinventing, they will be destined to be rejected by the growing global affluent millennial population.[18]

So, the game is to put the priority on social platforms and developing relationships with influencers and niche bloggers, but, as Deloitte says, it is also to try to keep the brand value intact.

Customer Attitudes by Product Category and Nationality

The Major Customer Zones

At this stage, we must answer one question: Is there a worldwide luxury customer or, on the contrary, are there very different behaviors of customers coming from different countries?

One issue is the specific weight of the different nationalities in the total luxury business. Table 5.6 gives the percentage of luxury purchases made in 1995, 2005, 2015, and 2018 by different national groups. The difference is very striking: in 1995, three national groups were making the largest part of the purchases: Japan represented 30% of the total, America 29%, and Europe also 29%. As this time, mainland China represented only 1%. In 2018, the most recent year these percentages are

---

[18] "Global Powers of Luxury Goods 2019: Bridging the gap between the old and the new." Deloitte, 2019.

Table 5.6   Purchases of Luxury Goods by Geographical Groups

PURCHASES OF LUXURY GOODS BY
GEOGRAPHICAL GROUPS

	1995	2005	2015	2018
Other	4.0%	7.0%	6.0%	7.0%
European	29.0%	28.0%	22.0%	18.0%
American	29.0%	27.0%	22.0%	21.0%
Other Asia			9.0%	11.0%
Chinese	7.0% / 1.0%	7.0% / 4.0%	28.0%	33.0%
Japanese	30.0%	27.0%	13.0%	10.0%

Source: Claudia d'Arpizio and Joelle de Montgolfier, Bain Luxury Studies for Fondazione Altagamma, 1996 to 2019.

available, mainland China represented 33%, America 22%, and Europe 18%. Japan was then only 10%.

A very important element of this table must be mentioned: in 2018, the total purchases of mainland China (33%), Japan (10%), and other Asia (11%) reached 54%, or a large majority of purchases.

This information, gathered by Bain and Altagamma, pertains to Chinese or American purchases and not to purchases made in each of the specific countries. This means that part of the 54% of purchases made by Asian customers can be done in Paris, New York, or London.

The Differences in Attitudes for Jewelry

The question now is to know if there is such a thing as a worldwide client—if people from different nationalities behave in the same way.

When we discuss this with a marketing specialist from Cartier, we can get some specific details:

> The Italians like watches that are slightly flashy and insist on a mechanical movement. They collect them and may change their watches several times per day. The Germans prefer quartz watches with a very simple design: rigor and effectiveness. The French have a strong preference for the "Engineer's" watch: sporty and full of several chronometer dials.

Different European nationalities also have different ways of wearing a piece of jewelry.

In Germany, women who have a management job purchase their jewelry pieces themselves and wear them in a triumphant way. In the style, they look for the purity of the raw materials and they like the stone to be set up in a very natural way. The Italians are looking for movement so they like "baroque" pieces. They are interested in the curves of the jewel and the way gold is set up. Ring shapes are moving like a piece of fabric. In Japan, but also in France or in Spain, group pressure is stronger than individual taste. The French, afraid of social critics, are looking for "reasonable" jewels, which must be "balanced" and appear "in good taste."

So, even within the European continent, there are large differences. Extend this to the world at large and the differences become even more pronounced.

The Different National Interest for Accessories, Ready-to-Wear, and Perfumes

Ready-to-Wear.   The ready-to-wear category is, in a way, the specialty of the Chinese and the Japanese. They both purchase more than 50% of the worldwide volume of French and Italian upscale fashion brands, making the Asian market the leading market in the world for those products.

But products sold in China are quite different from those sold in Japan, where women purchase goods themselves. In China, men are the main purchasers. This is why men's brands are generally doing very well there and developed earlier than women's fashion in mainland China. Now, when men purchase fashion items for their wives or their friends, they buy much less ready-to-wear and generally confine themselves to buying simple tops or jackets, for example. They also buy a larger percentage of accessories and handbags, with a strong preference for iconic products that appear in advertising and that they know will be the ideal gift.

European markets are strong in fashion, with a large part of the purchases being made by executive women. This is where brands like Armani and Jil Sander have a strong following.

Perfumes and Cosmetics. Unlike ready-to-wear, perfumes are not very important in Japan, with sales representing just 1% of worldwide consumption. In Japan, perfumes are often viewed as products to cover up and hide the natural smell of the body, or as unnecessary. They are sometimes perceived as an intrusion, something that a woman imposes on her environment. In many companies, there is an official or informal rule prohibiting the use of perfumes in the workplace, and they are also not well received in the subway or in other public places. Teenagers wear perfumes as a way to express themselves, but many lose the habit when they start working. In some areas of Japan, the belief persists that perfumes are unhealthy for young babies, causing many mothers to stop using perfumes altogether.

Perfume brands in Japan try to develop usage by promoting the sophistication of the products and as a means of self-expression at parties or special events.

The United States and the American continent at large are strong perfume markets, with approximately 30% of worldwide consumption. The Middle East is also an area where perfumes are much appreciated and consumed in large quantities.

Cosmetics are a different matter and Japan is a very strong market. The Chinese market, too, although still small, is both a perfume and a cosmetic market.

The challenge in launching a new perfume with global ambitions is to find a note that is light enough to please Japanese women, strong enough to satisfy American or German women, and fresh and floral enough to satisfy Latin women. Products that are globally successful are those that find a way to cut across these preferences and come up with a completely new note. This is not easy.

Wines and Spirits. In consolidated terms, the wines and spirits markets are more or less balanced equally, with approximately one-third of the total business done in each of the three major markets: the Americas, Europe, and Asia. But as we saw in Chapter 32, there are considerable differences in the types of products favored in each.

Rum is mostly consumed in the Americas, while gin is essentially a British and American drink. More than 50% of the worldwide volume of champagne is consumed in France, with a very strong additional volume in other European countries. In contrast, whiskies and vodka are sold everywhere in the world and are thus relatively balanced.

Cognac is a product that is also sold everywhere in the world, but with clear differences in types of product consumed in different locations.

What is clear at this stage is that consumer behavior differs from one part of the world to another.

The Analysis of Clients by Nationality

In this last section, we describe the specificities of the different luxury clients. We mentioned earlier differences by categories of luxury products, but, in their purchase behavior, clients also have different expectations and practices.

Table 5.7 shows that customers do not expect the same type of product experiences when they consider luxury. It describes those differences for Chinese, American, French, and Italian clients.

In this study, respondents were asked to tell everything that came to their mind when they heard the word "luxury," and their answers were clustered into different concepts. What is amazing is that for Americans,

Table 5.7   Expectations of Luxury for Different Nationalities

China		United States	
High-end watches	53%	Mobility	71%
Mobility	47%	Connecting to nature	50%
Jewelry	47%	Warm interior	46%
Beautiful people	47%	Aquatic and summer holidays	45%
Fashion and accessories	46%	Urban intensity	39%
France		**Italy**	
Mobility	64%	Mobility	72%
High-end watches	42%	Connecting with nature	52%
Warm interior	41%	Aquatic and summer holidays	43%
Connecting with nature	41%	High-end watches	42%
Jewelry	37%	Warm interior	38%

Source: Françoise Hernaez, "Affluent Paradoxical Expectations." Paris: IFOP, 2020.

luxury was related to travel, connecting to nature, summer holidays, interior decoration, and beautiful city centers. They never thought about products or fashion.

The Chinese, on the contrary, mentioned watches (probably men), jewelry, fashion, and "beautiful people," who are probably a part of fashion in their mind. They also mentioned mobility (travel and tourism), but their focus was very much around luxury products and services. The French and Italian think about products and vacation environment.

It is not simple to use the same arguments to convince everybody of the attractiveness of a beautiful handbag.

The Case of Mainland China

Clients from mainland China amount today to 34% of personal luxury purchases,[19] representing by far the first worldwide clients, even if these clients buy a large percentage of the products in China but another part in Hong Kong and South Korea, another part in worldwide duty-free shops, and a last part in Europe or in the United States. As import duties are quite high, it is logical that local retail prices are higher in mainland China than in Europe. In Chapter 2, we spoke about a Chinese retail price often 35% higher than in Europe. This price difference covers only a part of the import duties; the other part is compensated for by a gross margin reduction from the manufacturers.

In the case of watches, for example, when they retail above 10,000 yuan (around €1,400) the import duty is 50%; below 10,000 yuan (less than €1,400), it is 30%. On this, one must pay a luxury consumption tax of 20% and a value-added tax of 13%.

The Chinese reporter Yiling Pan explains: "It is a way to curb the younger generation's irrational spending on luxury brands."[20] If this "irrational spending" is partly cut by duties paid on high prices, it certainly motivates a little trip to Hong Kong or South Korea or it even rapidly reimburses part of a vacation week in Paris.

---

[19] Claudia d'Arpizio and Joelle de Montgolfier, Bain Luxury Studies for Fondazione Altagamma, 1996 to 2019.
[20] "China Proposes Luxury Tax Increase to Rein in Millenial Debt," *Jing Daily*, March 11, 2019.

Who are the Chinese clients buying luxury goods? The very rich, but mainly the middle class. A report by McKinsey & Company identifies two groups of potential Chinese luxury clients:

1. The *upper middle class*, individuals with households earning between €2,400 and €3,600 per month. They will become 350 million by 2025.
2. The *affluent class*, individuals with households earning more than €3,600 per month. They will become 65 million by 2025.[21]

This group of 415 million well-to-do Chinese (taking into account the cost of living in China) is the prime target of luxury products. In the next few years, 70% of those well-to-do Chinese will travel abroad. The mix of their luxury purchases is carefully monitored by the Chinese authorities: as one reduces the import duties and additional taxes, one increases part of the purchases made at home. On the contrary, for the manufacturers, there is a fluctuating balance between the purchases in Milan, Paris, and New York and the purchases made at home, based on price elasticity and on what seems to be a logical and fair price at home and abroad.

As we mentioned earlier, a large part of those purchases is made by millennials, who have a very generous spending pattern, as we can see in Table 5.8.

It is certainly not expected to find that those 24 million Chinese customers, a relatively small part of the Chinese population, are so important for the luxury activities. Some brands have probably registered an important part of these individuals in their CRM database.

Those customers have another characteristic: 31.5% of those 24 million clients, or 7.5 million, have started buying luxury only last year and 6.5 million among those who were born after 1980: the millennials.

If we compare the top reasons why those Chinese millennials are buying luxury, we must analyze the main reasons for their purchase decision. This can be seen in Table 5.9.

---

[21] McKinsey & Company, "China Luxury Report 2019: How Young Chinese Consumers Are Reshaping Global Luxury," April 2019. https://www.mckinsey.com/~/media/mckinsey/featured%20insights/china/how%20young%20chinese%20consumers%20are%20reshaping%20global%20luxury/mckinsey-china-luxury-report-2019-how-young-chinese-consumers-are-reshaping-global-luxury.pdf.

Table 5.8 Number of Chinese Luxury Consumers and Total Spending by Age Group (2018)

	Post–1965s/ 1970s (from 40 to 55 years old)	Post–1980s (between 30 and 40 years old)	Post–1990s (less than 30 years old)	Total
Numbers of luxury consumers	7.0 (29%)	10.2 (43%)	6.7 (28%)	23.9 (100%)
Total spending in 2017	€1.44 billion (22%)	€3.23 billion (56%)	€1.3 billion (23%)	€5.97 billion (100%)

Source: McKinsey & Company, "China Luxury Report 2019: How Young Chinese Consumers Are Reshaping Global Luxury," April 2019.

Table 5.9 Reasons for Buying Luxury Products

	Brand	Design	Fabric	Production	Price
Post–1990s (less than 30 years old)	68%	11%	6%	8%	7%
Post–1980s (between 30 and 40 years old)	72%	9%	8%	8%	4%
Post 1960s/1970s (from 40 to 55 years old)	94%	3%	1%	1%	1%

Source: McKinsey & Company, "China Luxury Report: How Young Chinese Consumers Are Reshaping Global Luxury," April 2019.

The non-millennials of this table gave the brand a 94% weight in their decision. For the millennials (the top two lines in Table 5.9) it is still very important, but the product itself (design, fabric, etc.) counts for almost one-third of this weight.

One might say that this is because the millennials are in large part new buyers and they first have to be convinced by the products themselves. But what is certain is that the product (and the price) must be carefully adapted to these new consumers.

There is another finding in this report: The post–1980s were very loyal (54% claimed they bought exclusively from five brands or less, and always the same ones). The post–1990s are much less loyal (only 29% buy exclusively from five brands or less): these customers must be convinced every time they buy a new item.

Still, according to this McKinsey report, Chinese customers are different in the way they get information about a brand or a product: they use the official brand channels (on- and off-line), then word of mouth and key opinion leaders. Out of nine items, the one they value the least is traditional ads.

The communication program must take that into account, as we will describe in Chapter 9. But there is for the Chinese a very particular specificity: the credibility of the key opinion leaders. These leaders can be celebrities, bloggers, or beautiful people. In China, the brand ambassadors are more important than anywhere else.

As the new Chinese consumers are very loyal to a small number of brands, social media marketing people are very interested in the Hurun Report's list of brands that well-to-do Chinese would be "happy to purchase to make a gift to a friend." The list of Hurun Report brands for 2019 is given in Table 5.10.

In China, we are in front of a new generation, and the purchasing habits of the number-one market in the world are changing very fast.

US Customers

Representing 22% of purchases and the second-biggest market behind mainland China, the United States has always been important.

Table 5.10 Preferred Brands for Gift-Giving in China

Men	Women
Apple	Bulgari
Louis Vuitton	Louis Vuitton
Cartier	Apple
Chanel	Chanel
Dior	Bottega Veneta
Maotai (liquor)	Cartier
Gucci	Gucci
Dream blue	Hermès
Burberry	Hugo Boss
Bottega Veneta	Coach

Source: Hurun Report. Shimao Shenkong International Center, September 2019.

As mentioned by Carol Ryan, their purchasing weight has grown by at least 10% per year from 2010 to 2019,[22] which has helped strong European brands to do well and invest during this period. It has also helped American brands to develop and take advantage of their domestic market to make money and invest more outside.

Americans like to customize their products. They are also careful about the quality of their products.

How should one communicate with them? A study by Carol Ryan gives some indications (see Table 5.11).

The US luxury market must deal with a new way to communicate with its clients, relying heavily on digital activities and still using television advertisements, which has never been a strong European luxury medium.

Japanese Customers

The slide of the Japanese customer on the total luxury business from 30% to less than 10% is really disturbing. During more than 20 years, sales of luxury goods in Japan have not grown, when the worldwide market has been multiplied by 3. And still, if one divides the total sales by number of inhabitants (126 million compared to 1.4 billion), the Japanese are still buying two to three times more than the Chinese. So, they deserve a lot of attention.

Japan is a country of cultural and social sophistication, and a place where the concepts of beauty and aesthetics are very much a part of everyday life; beautiful dresses or handbags crafted with care have a reason for being.

Table 5.11 Advertising Spending in America in 2019

Television	Digital	Magazines	Newspapers
40%	31%	24%	2.1%
Outdoor	Radio	Cinema	Total
1.2%	0.8%	0.5%	100%

Source: Carol Ryan, "America Is a Land of Equal Opportunity for Luxury Brands," *Wall Street Journal*, December 24, 2019.

---

[22] Carol Ryan, "America Is a Land of Equal Opportunity for Luxury Brands," *Wall Street Journal*, December 24, 2019.

Starting in 2015, luxury sales in Japan have grown again. It may be because a new generation of Japanese (the Japanese millennials?) have become more important, financially and socially. What is definite is that the special interest of the Japanese for what is happening in France and in Italy in terms of fashion, design, and culture is still very present.

South Korean Customers

South Korea is often overlooked and it is generally included in "Other Asia," which represents 11% of customer spending. But this category mainly includes South Korea, Hong Kong, Taiwan, Singapore, and other countries of Southeast Asia.

It could be estimated that South Korea represents 4 or 5% of the total, and it would be a major performance, because with a country of 50 million inhabitants (or 40% of Japan with its 126 million), this is a spending that is equal or superior to Japan's, per inhabitant.

South Koreans buy fashion like almost everybody in Asia, but they are also heavy users of perfumes and have a strong interest for European wines. Department stores or liquor stores are often stocked with a large selection of very expensive and excellent wines, another specificity in a zone that still has a lot to offer.

European Customers

There is no European customer as such, but a British style, an Italian fashion, a French way of dressing and being, a German attitude toward luxury, which is slightly similar to that of the Scandinavian customers, and so on.

Europe, as far as luxury is concerned, is certainly a land of diversity, but this diversity explains why Europe could be a major source of original fashion styles and creation. Compared to China and America, it is a major luxury place, given its population. It is also a place with a tradition of painting, decoration, sculptures, craftsmanship, and international diversity. It is at the same time a source and an outlay for luxury activities.

The Fallacy of the BRICs

If there is a place where the BRICs (Brazil, Russia, India, China) don't seem to work, it is the luxury sector. Putting together China and India,

Russia, and Brazil (without mentioning South Africa) may give the feeling that Russia or India would be the next source of luxury growth after China. But the growth of China, as we said earlier, comes from the creation of a strong middle class, which seems to be nonexistent in Russia so far. Also, India, to a certain extent, will probably develop a middle class in the long run, but the country often changes its import duties, and the market's lack of stability and the difficulty for a foreigner to fully own his retail network, at least in most of the cases, works in the wrong way.

The source of growth for luxury may come, instead, from Brazil, Indonesia, or part of the Middle East, but it would probably be a slow development rather than the extremely fast modification that has happened over the past 25 years.

Conclusion

In this diversity of nationalities, attitudes, and expectations of consumers, one should keep a set of positions and basic rules to develop and perform in this sector:

- Do not try to sell a product, but an experience and a service.
- Make sure that in every trade-off, quality will be given the full priority.
- Keep an open line with the clients.
- Organize a community of clients who can communicate about the brand and engage in being part of the brand support.

When clients consider themselves to be part of the brand story, then it is much easier to convince others that there is something to look at.

Chapter 6

Brand Identity: Concepts and Analytical Semiotic Tools

Brand Identity

In the past 50 years a lot of ink has been and continues to be dedicated to the concept of identity. Philosophy, sociology, psychology, psychoanalysis, phenomenology, structuralism, culturalism, biology, and more disciplines and schools of thought have tried to give the ultimate definition of that familiar yet elusive concept. We start realizing that the meaning of the concept of identity is not settled (Mucchielli 1986)[1] and that every author is dependent on his chosen theoretical framework to construct the intelligibility of the phenomenon.

---

[1] A. Mucchielli, A. (1986). *L'identité*. Paris: Presses Universitaires de France, 1986.

On our side we have chosen structural semiotics as our theoretical framework, conscious that it may look like a *parti-pris*, but the choice has been confirmed throughout the years of application to brands. The semiotic tools applied to brand identity have proved to be among the most versatile analytical and management instruments for most of the brand categories.

Structural semiotics, which intends to analyze the conditions under which meaning can be produced and perceived, produced a certain number of instruments that allow us to at least partially rationalize the brand identity field, and provide very concrete solutions about the issues related to brand management. During our careers, we have had occasion to use them in the field from the pragmatic point of view of managers, with tangible results. That started with the first study on Salvatore Ferragamo in 1992 with the semiotician Jean-Marie Floch and was still going on in 2020 with the Sasin School of Management. During almost 30 years we have refined brand identity analytical and management tools stemming from semiotics and applied them to tens of brands. The instruments we present in the next two chapters have proved their versatility in fields as different as product, design, and education services.

A Concept That Is Gaining Ground

The term *brand identity* is being encountered more frequently in business jargon. It really took off in the 1990s (Heding, Knudtzen, and Bjerre 2016)[2] but it is far from being a universally accepted notion. It is probable that an in-depth and systematic consideration has been undertaken of the identity of few brands today. To formalize this concept further, we might refer to Merriam-Webster's *Collegiate Dictionary*, tenth edition, which gives the following definition of identity:

1. (a) sameness of essential or generic character in different instances; (b) sameness in all that constitutes the objective reality of a thing: ONENESS
2. (a) the distinguishing character or personality of an individual: INDIVIDUALITY; (b) the relation established by psychological identification

---

[2] T. Heding, C. F. Knudtzen, and M. Bjerre, *Brand Management: Research, Theory, and Practice.* New York: Routlege, 2016.

3. the condition of being the same with something described or asserted.

What we call brand identity corresponds to an extension of this definition, with a strong human dimension. But the term suits our purposes because two necessary (though not sufficient) elements are present in it: on the one hand, differentiation; on the other, permanence, or durability. We may attempt a more precise initial definition of brand identity:

> The capacity of a brand to be recognized as unique, over time, without confusion, thanks to the elements that individualize it.

One might think that an attachment to these criteria of individuality is somehow natural to managers, but the history of brands is full of examples to the contrary, as a result of either ignorance or else a voluntary disregard for the virtues of reflection on the identity of brands.

An example, not very recent but still very relevant, encountered in the banking sector serves as a good illustration of the absence of consideration of brand identity in such important undertakings as the definition of a new graphic identity. Banco Sabadell is a bank of Catalan origin, extremely dynamic, that was successfully introduced on the Madrid stock exchange a few years ago. In 1998 the bank decided to transform its corporate image, notably by adopting a new graphic identity. It called in Mario Eskenazi, an Argentine architect based in Spain, the winner of numerous awards and the creator of several logos for major Spanish companies. He was put in charge of designing a new graphics charter, with a new logo to be used on all communication media, and also of redecorating the bank's agencies. Once the job was done, the designer gave an interview, which the bank itself published. Here is an excerpt:

> What does the new image of Banco Sabadell try to get across?
> That's a very difficult question to answer without falling into excessively pompous phraseology. I think that, when you create a new image for a company, it's very rare that you start by considering what you are trying to communicate. It's very difficult for a corporate image, in and of itself, to transmit something. Its role is to facilitate clear identification of the company. In this sense, the new image of Banco Sabadell is not trying to get anything across.[3]

---

[3] Banco Sabadell newsletter, first quarter 1998, no. 11.

This may have been provocation on the part of the designer; it might have been his way of asserting the primacy of his intuitive creativity over the careful calculations of the communicators. Or maybe it was a way of discreetly expressing his disdain for the idea that a commercial brand can actually produce meaning. Whatever the case, a statement like this one does a disservice to the extensive collaborative and deliberative effort that must be inherent in any renovation of a corporate identity. It shows that the notion of brand identity is not sufficiently widespread in the corporate world and in corporate communication. Otherwise such a statement, made in the name of the bank itself, would be unthinkable.

The logo created by Mario Eskenazi is quite original (a white B within a blue circle and a bigger black S separated on the right), graphically much more modern than the one it replaced (a blue S enlaced in a blue B encircled by a blue circle, with white background) and more easily recognizable, qualities that many brands might envy. But what a loss of an opportunity to reflect on the specific and unique characteristics of the Catalan bank and create a corporate image that produces meaning!

The case of the French bank Crédit du Nord, however, is a good counterexample of careful reflection on the identity of a brand. In 1984, Crédit du Nord, the fifth-ranking French banking group at the time, introduced a new image, involving a redesign of the logo, the graphics of the name, the architecture of the branches, and advertising. The image was entirely founded on the concept of clarity. For 10 years, the bank had suffered from an indistinct image as an old, serious, provincial bank. Its merger with the Banque de l'Union Parisienne, a business bank active in high finance, had not helped clarify the situation.

The detailed history of the development of a new logo and all the elements of communication, starting with the concept of light or clarity, has been recounted in a book by the semiotician Jean-Marie Floch.[4] In it, he explains how the communication agency Creative Business, with whom he collaborated, developed, using semiotic tools, all the elements of the new communication, beginning with the blue star, which replaced the orange cube as the brand's logo. In the banking field, the concept of light was analyzed as the choice of a certain type of relationship between the banker and the client. This relationship was based on the recognition

---

[4] J.-M. Floch, *Sémiotique, Marketing et Communication. Sous les signes, les stratégies*. Paris: Presses Universitaires de France, 1990.

of the competence and sovereignty of the client. The idea of light thus crystallized a value involved with the very essence of what any relationship with a bank should be: confidence. This concept led, first of all, to the choice of a code—that is, a style: a brand aesthetic resolutely classical in nature, wherein the logo had to convey frankness and personalized attention. The star was chosen because it represents a visible element in open space; it is also a navigational reference point with rich symbolic connotations.

The creative function, like all other functions necessary to a brand's operation, must be part of an overall strategy. The brand's identity is a major resource and a frame of reference for the development of that strategy. It influences not only creation and communication but also logistics, production, distribution, human resources management, information processing, and so on. At all levels of its activity, a brand aspires to become what it truly is. And, in fact, concrete tools exist for capturing and managing that individuality.

A Brief History of the Emergence of the Brand Identity Notion

Naomi Klein[5] rightly refers to the work of Bruce Barton, who incidentally was the second B of the BBDO advertising agency. In the 1920s, this advertiser began to seek out the "corporate soul," demonstrating an awareness of the fact that a brand could have meaning beyond the products themselves. As the advertising industry developed, the vocabulary was enriched with concepts such as the essence, raison d'être, consciousness, soul, and genetic code of a brand. However, it was not until the 1970s that the word *identity* made its appearance in the specialized literature, generally linked to the concept of corporate identity.

Brand identity appeared in the early 1980s and spread quickly among professionals in advertising agencies.[6] Originally, the term designated, in a limited sense, everything that can identify the brand by linking it to the content of the advertising material. It soon evolved toward a real personification of brands. The words personality, individuality, and identity became common. The French advertiser Jacques Séguéla speaks of the perception of brands through the intermediary of their physicality, their character, and their style. In 1980, he developed this new methodology

---

[5] N. Klein, *No Logo: Taking Aim at the Brand Bullies*, Knopf Canada, 2000.
[6] "Chrysler Sharpens Its Brand Identity," *International Business Week*, November 1983.

under the name "brand person," which later became known as the star strategy. The concept of identity began, in an indistinct way, to be joined with that of image.

In 1984, David Bernstein, in his book *Company Image and Reality*, devoted a chapter to brand identity.[7] Little by little, the specialized literature began to study this area. David Aaker (1991) attempts a classification, still quite heterogeneous, of brand equity.[8] This includes brand loyalty, name awareness, perceived quality, brand image, and other assets. The word personality appears briefly in the book, which, however, maintains a certain confusion between the concept of brand image and that of brand identity. This confusion remains common today. In our view, these two concepts do not coincide.

The images (rather than "the image") correspond to the perceptions induced in the different consumers who make up the market segments. They are receptive in nature. The identity is the substance of the brand, expressed via all the methods of communication used by the brand. It is emissive in nature. To avoid misunderstanding, we avoid using the word image when working on the emission side. On the other hand, when we want to refer to the markets representations induced, we will speak not of image but of perception of the brand's identity.

The brand identity tools we present in the next two chapters are by no means an exhaustive review. We intend to present those that have been used effectively by the authors in their various brand management projects.

The Brand Hinge: Ethics and Aesthetics

Of all the analytical disciplines available today, semiotics is, in our opinion and based on our experience, the best suited to aiding a manager in understanding, defining, formalizing, and communicating the identity of a brand. From our perspective as convinced and experienced users, we would like to take a moment to discuss this discipline.

---

[7] D. Bernstein, *Company Image and Reality: A Critique of Corporate Communications*. New York: Holt, Rinehart and Winston, 1984.

[8] D. A. Aaker, *Managing Brand Equity: Capitalizing on the Value of a Brand Name*. New York: Free Press, 1991.

The aim of semiotics, according to Greimas and his disciples like Floch, Bertrand, Semprini, Ceriani, Fontanille, and Marrone (all referred to in this book), is to describe, as objectively as possible, the process of production of meaning, and generally of all the practices of signification that make up cultures.

If we accept the validity of applying semiotics to the study of brand identities, we are asserting the following basic premise: brands are systems that produce meaning. We even go beyond that particularly broad and somewhat abstract brand definition by believing that brands increase their competitiveness along with the sense they produce.

The semiotic tools we present require a certain degree of formalization, so we should assure the reader at the outset of their operational viability. We have used and refined them ourselves in the field for almost 30 years, and while they can't, of course, solve every problem, we know by experience that their usefulness is undeniable.

The first of the semiotic tools we present is the Hinge, a simple framework developed by Jean-Marie Floch to bring out the different levels of analysis of a brand universe.

If Jean-Marie Floch did not publish it himself in its schematic form (it can be found in several of Mazzalovo's publications),[9] the hinge of the brand has been a leitmotif since its first publications, where it takes up the Saussurian approach to the sign (signifier and signified), then theorized by Hjelmslev. Semioticians, following Ferdinand de Saussure, introduce a distinction between the signifier and the signified. The signifier is the material part of a sign; the signified is the representation with which that material part is associated. For example, the succession of letters T_R_E_E written on a blackboard corresponds to the mental image a reader of those letters produces: that of a tree, a woody plant having a trunk, and so on. However, these two dimensions are the two sides of a single coin or, as Saussure put it, a single sheet of paper: one side cannot be separated from the other.

All signs, then, are articulated at a hinge between the signifier (or level of expression) and the signified (or level of content). The same is true, by extension, of groups of signs, and thus of the creation and physical manifestations of brands.

---

[9] G. Mazzalovo and D. Darpy, "Gestion expressive des marques dans un contexte de baroquisation," *Décisions Marketing* 74 (April–June 2014): 83–96.

Floch's most significant contribution was to introduce the concept of invariance on these two plans.

> In other words, the brand has constants of expression and constants of content that give it its own identity.
>
> —Jean-Marie Floch in 1990

Schematically, the hinge distinguishes the plan of the signifier (sensory world) from the signified (intelligible world), and this articulation also extends to the permanent and variable elements of any physical expression of a brand.

The advantage of this methodological approach is twofold. First, it brings out the two fundamental levels of a brand's discourse, clearly separating content and container. Then, it places the accent on the invariant elements of the brand. These invariants are precisely what make it possible for the brand to be recognized as itself over time. They constitute the very foundation of its identity.

The hinge aims at characterizing the brand's identity through its expression and its content, that is, at giving a formal definition of its aesthetic and its ethic. We can now adopt a semiotic definition of a brand identity. It is made of its ethics and aesthetic invariants. The brand ethics is composed of all the invariant elements of the intelligible world it expresses, i.e., all the abstract and immaterial permanent components of the brand (values, world vision, founding myths associations, benefits, promises, and so on). The brand aesthetic is made up of all the invariant elements of its approach to the sensory world, i.e. all the elements perceivable by the five senses (taste, touch, sound, music, smells, vision, colors, forms, lines, textures, light, and so on).

A meaningful example can be found in Figure 6.2, which shows the application of the hinge to the analysis of Pininfarina's brand identity in 2007. The company, created by Battista "Pinin" Farina in 1930, has been a leader among traditional Italian car body makers. In 2007, it offered a full range of services from conception, design, engineering, and niche production of automobiles for third-party brands like Alfa Romeo, Ferrari, Fiat, Lancia, Maserati, Peugeot, Cadillac, GM, Bentley, Volvo, Mercedes, and so on, and recently Chinese brands such as AviChina, Chery, Changfeng, Brilliance, and JAC. After a long process

---

[10] Floch, *Sémiotique, Marketing et Communication.*

of restructuring, it was acquired by the Indian Mahindra group in 2016 and is focusing now on auto, industrial, and interior design, as well as engineering.

Late 2006, we were called by then-president Andrea Pininfarina to develop the basis for Pininfarina monobranded products and services, moving from the realm of B2B design into B2C activities. The challenge raised was related to the fact that B2B designers are supposed to interpret the identity of their client and are not necessarily showing any personal aesthetics. Some famous designers manage to let some of their *coup de patte* emerge from their creation anyway, as in the case for Pininfarina. See Mazzalovo's 2016 article for more information on that work.[11]

The Brand Identity as a Main Strategic Component

If Figure 6.1. shows the various components of the hinge, Figure 6.3 integrates the concept of brand identity into a more current business vocabulary and familiar notions.

The sign, as far as brands are concerned, is in fact a set of numerous signs more or less organized into a system. We call them brand

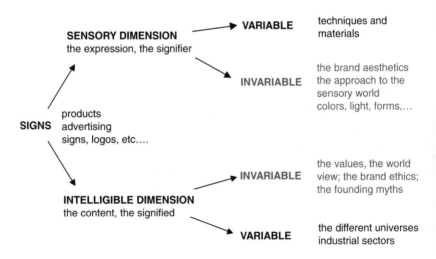

Figure 6.1 The Brand Hinge. Analytical levels of a brand universe

---

[11] G. Mazzalovo, "Resolving Tensions Among Creative Departments Through Brand Identity Definition: The Case Study of Pininfarina," *Business and Management Studies* 2, no. 1 (March 2016).

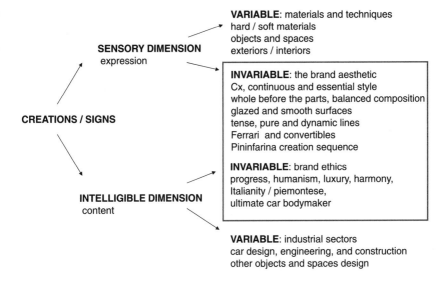

Figure 6.2   The Hinge Applied to Pininfarina Brand Identity

manifestations, that is, all the brand elements that can be grasped by the senses and that we will cover in more detail in Chapter 9. The sign essence being twofold (made of a signifier and a signified), a frequent question arises as what happens when the signified does not exist or is so tenuous or blurred as to not be perceived. In that case we are no longer in the presence of a sign but of a pure stimulus.

The dark rectangle of Figure 6.2 encompasses the invariant elements of the brand, i.e., its identity. If we add the variable elements of both intelligible and sensory plans, we enter into the brand strategy field, which by definition needs to adapt over time to the competitive context.

Shell is a good example of a company belonging to an industry that is not known for being on the frontline when it comes to brand management. In 2010, we assisted at a conference where Shell's communication director declared very explicitly that the brand strategy was an inseparable part of the company overall strategy, fostering collaboration and alignment among functions. The brand no longer belonged exclusively to the marketing department, but was in all aspects a company organizing principle. In fact, we will illustrate throughout this chapter the strategic nature of the brand identity.

Using the Brand Identity Hinge

The use of the hinge may seem relatively simple. It requires, however, a bit of practice, especially on the aesthetic side. The exercise aims at formalizing the brand's identity through its expression and its content, that is, at giving a formal definition of its aesthetics and of its ethics. The aesthetic study is relatively easy to put into practice if the brand in question is a very "typed" one, where the colors, shapes, and materials or any type of stylistic features are used in a repetitive way.

In this domain, the contribution of Jean-Marie Floch in reactualizing the work of Heinrich Wölfflin on classical and baroque expressions has been essential. He has shown how the properly plastic dimension of the expression plan is closely correlated, at the same time, with the thematic dimension of the plan of content.

To realize the relevance of these two styles, one can observe that, generally, northern European brands—such as Jil Sander, IKEA, Helmut Lang, and BMW—and North American brands—such as Calvin Klein, Donna Karan, and Coach—have an aesthetic of the classical type, characterized pictorially by:

- Clearly defined lines and contours, emphasizing individually recognizable elements
- Space divided into easily identifiable zones, each with its own autonomy
- Closed shapes, visible in their entirety, planes, no depth
- Impressions of stability, symmetry
- Saturated colors

However, Mediterranean brands such as Loewe, Ferragamo, Dolce & Gabbana, Rubelli, Majorica, Lamborghini, Versace, and Roberto Cavalli have a tendency toward the baroque, characterized pictorially by:

- Lines delineated by shadow effects: curves and crisscrosses
- Open forms, which can appear accidental
- Each part losing its autonomy and taking on meaning only in association with the rest of the work
- Movement treated in depth: volumes
- "Chiaroscuro" and deep colors

As expressed by Bertrand and Mazzalovo (2019),[12] Floch's merit has been to formalize the great difference between the two so-called baroque and classical visual regimes by explaining that Wölfflin's five categories were absorbed into a more fundamental opposition distributed on two levels: the classical vision, on the plane of expression, values the non-continuous (the contour line, the clear separation of the foreground and background, the delimitation of the frame, etc.) while it promotes, in terms of content, nondiscontinuity (long duration, permanence, stability at the expense of change). The opposite happens with the baroque vision: this magnifies, on the level of expression, the nondiscontinuous (morphing of forms, sinuous connections, deep volumes, disappearing edges), whereas, at the content level, it exalts the noncontinuous (the instant of an emotion, the climax of an action, the force of an event, the tireless transformation of a changing world, etc.).

The study conducted on Loewe in 1996 by one of the authors, who was its president at the time, in collaboration with Creative Business and Jean-Marie Floch, led to the development and the communication of the concept of a *minimalist baroque* aesthetic. These apparently contradictory terms met with much success in the press. In the late 1990s, this Spanish fashion brand—a century-and-a-half old and often referred to by the French as the "Spanish Hermès," had good name recognition, associated with quality and a strong presence in Spain and Japan, but was still weak in the other markets. Struggling to achieve international status, and also suffering from the absence of a charismatic founder in its history, unlike many French and Italian fashion brands, Loewe had the appearance of a slightly tired brand. The characterization of the brand's aesthetic effectively transmitted the message of a brand that was faithful to its roots (the baroque) and had a strong desire for modernity (minimalism, which at the time was still in vogue). That message was coherent with the recruiting of designer Narciso Rodriguez, who was himself a blend of modernity and respect for its cultural roots.

As far as brand ethics are concerned, certain brands so clearly express their values that the investigating task is relatively easy. Take Nike, for example, in the mass market sector. Since the introduction of its initial

---

[12] D. Bertrand and G. Mazzalovo, "Méthode sémiotique: de la structure au sensible," chap. 11 in *Méthodes de recherche qualitatives innovantes*, edited by Pierre Romelaer and Lionel Garreau. Paris: Economica, 2019.

slogan "Just do it," Nike has cultivated the universal values associated with sports and the Olympic movement: surpassing oneself, determination, competition, accomplishment. Nike added a good measure of universality when it doubled down with the slogan "Everybody is an athlete." Moreover, Nike in Greek mythology is the goddess of victory. This is where the brand's ethics, its vision of the world, and what it believes are situated; "what it stands for," to use Jean-Marie Floch's expression. Many brands like Dove, The Body Shop, and Victoria's Secret are easily readable. The good slogans and first page of the brand websites generally give clues to understanding what the brand believes in. As examples, the brand Toms would match every pair of shoes purchased with a new pair of shoes for a child in need (One for One ® project); Stella McCartney mentions sustainability in every aspect of its website.

The study of brand ethics may end up more problematic, above all for brands that were not founded by a creator with a strong personality and creative point of view, or that have squandered their heritage by a succession of creative directors and no continuity in the values expressed. Camper may be an appropriate example. In the 1990s, the Spanish shoe manufacturer expressed very clearly which brand ethics it wanted to promote through its slogan "Walk don't run": a whole philosophy of life. Unfortunately, the initial slogan was later abandoned for "imagination walk," then "invents your reality," "extraordinary craft," and in the Fall/Winter 2019 campaign, there are references to "fearless innovation and precision performance of motor sports." We find sentences like "the campaign brings racing subculture to life, blending fierce colors and aerodynamic details in a custom-built collection that craves speed and accelerates out of the curves." This seems incompatible with to the original philosophical and existential "walk don't run" when we know that identity is created through invariants.

In certain cases, setting about finding the permanent values a brand has expressed since its inception is a frustrating process. It sometimes leads, as was the case with Loewe in 1996, to the recognition of the nonexistence of a brand ethic. Such a situation has an advantage in that it leaves a very broad field for the choice of credible and legitimate values.

Brand Ethics Analytical Process: Some Practical Clues

We came to realize that nothing can replace the practice of actual brand identity analysis in order to use the semiotic hinge in an appropriate and efficient way, and to its fullest extent. Real work on real brands allows for the discovery of incremental tips and deeper analysis. We will give here one new example of Thai brands analyzed recently: Jim Thompson, mainly active in creating, manufacturing, and distributing silk products. Another example, on the Sasin School of Business, the leading Thai business school, part of Chulalongkorn University, is described in Appendix A.

Jim Thompson Brand Ethics

The company was founded by James H.W. Thompson in 1951, when he undertook the task of reviving the Thai silk industry. The "King of Silk" was a man of multiple dimensions: a visionary entrepreneur, great marketer, art collector, aesthete, and man of conviction and action (former OSS and military man in World War II). Above all, he was driven by a great love for the Thai people and their rich culture. Unfortunately, he disappeared without any trace in 1967 in the Malaysian jungles of Cameron Highlands, adding thus to its mysterious legend. Since then the Jim Thompson brand has expanded from around 100 employees to over 2,500 and currently boasts 36 retail stores and 5 fabric showrooms on three continents, as well as a string of first-class restaurants both in Thailand and abroad.

Often labeled "the Thai Hermès," the brand is active in fashion, home furnishings, art, and cuisine. In the retail network it offers personal goods like scarves, neckties, women's and men's ready-to-wear, leather and silk accessories, handbags, small leather goods, and finished home products like cushions, tablecloths, and more.

The technologically advanced production facilities in Pak Thong Chai (Korat province, northeast of Bangkok) are the most integrated in the world for silk production, starting from the silkworm sericulture farm up to the finished products.

One of the authors was the CEO of Jim Thompson Group from 2015 to 2019 and led a full-blown brand identity analysis with the support of several semioticians and creative professionals. This resulted in the formalization of Jim Thompson's brand identity in the terms described below.

We can find in a 2017 corporate brochure a succinct summary of the brand ethic (see Table 6.1), which was thus communicated to the public and various stakeholders.

The main methodological innovation resides in the introduction of the dialectics into the brand ethic. Brands, like human beings, need to

Table 6.1   Jim Thompson Brand Ethic (2017)

1.

Jim Thompson, the man, continues to be a source of inspiration.

2.

Elements of **Southeast Asian cultures** are subscribed to repeatedly when designing and developing products and services.

3.

Silk remains at the forefront of the brand and was one of the first global luxury materials used for textiles. Jim Thompson silks have been adopted for iconic films like *The King and I* and have been worn by royals and celebrities. These factors contribute to Jim Thompson's status as a **luxury brand**. Today, the brand strives to also achieve a contemporary definition of luxury in its products and services.

4.

Jim Thompson cultivates its sense of **Authenticity** in multiple ways: heritage; Southeast Asia; Bangkok, the Jim Thompson house; the Isan region; the jungle; and the masterful weaving process of silk. Our authenticity allows us these themes in our design and branding in an ethically authentic way.

5.

Mystery is a prominent theme, relating in a direct way to Jim Thompson's dramatic disappearance in 1967. Mystery is inspired by the allure of Southeast Asia's jungle terrain and perilous expeditions, including precarious journeys and adventures. This element casts an aura over Jim Thompson's creative activities and spaces created in our stores, restaurants, and showrooms.

6.

While some brands may define themselves through various paradoxes, Jim Thompson has a particularly significant set of juxtapositions that we like to refer as **Dialectics**. The brand seeks to resolve apparent contradictions relating to nature vs. culture; East vs. West; handcrafted vs. high-tech; tradition vs. innovation; and absence vs. presence.

resolve apparent contradictions in their lives. For example, we all need to deal with the dialectic of tradition vs. innovation as we have to go through life integrating the innate background and the learned knowledge with our creative and disruptive impulses. The choices made in resolving these apparent contradictions reveal a great deal about the values guiding one's life.

If some dialectics are shared by most brands, some may remain very specific. For instance, the dialectic East vs. West is determinant for Jim Thompson. The coexistence of both worlds is already announced in the full name of the company:

Jim Thompson
The Thai Silk Company Limited

Jim Thompson's mission has been to select elements of the Thai cultures and, after aesthetic treatment, present them to the world. There is also a stronger legitimacy at using the fauna and flora of southeastern Asia jungles in the products. A Jim Thompson tiger on a scarf expresses elements of the Thai culture. A tiger on a Gucci garment is an exercise in *chinoiserie*, a borrowing of an element extraneous to the original brand culture. Next season will be something else. These are two different ways of dealing with the East vs. West dialectics.

We will find the same dialectic, East vs. West, in the Sasin School of Management's brand identity. A complete analysis of the brand identity as of the beginning of 2020 is shown in Appendix 1.

Brand Aesthetics Analytical Process: Some Practical Clues

We have seen that notions like baroque and classical may help in understanding a brand's aesthetics and therefore identity. Continuing with our two recent Thai brand examples, we will illustrate now the aesthetic part of the analysis.

Table 6.2   Jim Thompson Brand Aesthetics (2017)

7.

Silk remains at the heart of the brand and is complemented by other luxury fibers including cashmere and linen.

8.

A set of **Institutional Colors** have been developed which is reflected in our Siam Paragon store, where multiple shades of green and brown prevail.

9.

The brand is **Mixing and Borrowing** from multiple stylistic and cultural references.

10.

While we respect the brand's unique heritage, Jim Thompson is **Resolutely Contemporary**. Staying true to customers means continuing to develop new products and services which reflect our brand identity, but also reflect the fast changing moods of our time.

Jim Thompson's Brand Aesthetics

In the process of formalization of Jim Thompson's brand identity that we mentioned in section 6.1, we have also defined the specificities of the brand aesthetics. In the same publicly available 2017 corporate brochure we added four aesthetics items to the six ethical components (see Table 6.2).

This is another example on the multiple correlations existing between the two plans of signified and signifying. The jungle theme is anchored on the brand ethic in terms of mystery, authenticity, the place of Jim's disappearance, and Southeast Asia. The theme also drives the parts of the brand aesthetics specific to the jungle flora and fauna and their resulting colors and encompasses also the notion of mixing, chaos with no immediately apparent logic.

A meaningful work was carried out by the then-creative director Jean-Christophe Vilain on the brand chromatic approach, which started from a mosaic of 36 pictures, very much centered on jungle colors in greens and browns with accents of ocher and yellow and some very light touches of contrasting light purple. The overall orientation was toward dark values.

Not every brand can benefit from a clear ownership of a specific color like Ferrari's red cars, the blue of Tiffany's packaging, the orange of Hermès's packaging, or the purple and gold of Thai Airways' logo. A straight association to a single hue is not always an advantage. It may often be better to define a set of chromatic combinations and precise rules of utilization. In the work we did on Loewe in 1995, the only qualification of the brand aesthetics was to define it as minimalist baroque, leaving thus a very large autonomy to the creatives and infinite interpretations possibilities. We also launched some research on the main Spanish painters, extracting their main chromatic combinations to help in the color development of the scarf collections. It was a sort of insurance that the colors would maintain a Spanish baroque flavor in the many variations needed to continue renewing the best-selling scarves.

Brand Aesthetics Analytical Grid: Application at Jim Thompson

A semiotic study was made in 2015 by Denis Bertrand on the identity of the Jim Thompson brand.[13] As its name (Thai Silk Company) suggests, its emblematic material is a textile and it was imperative to run a deep and decisive analysis of the expression plan. Indeed, it governs all the content: the clients feel the fabrics, they associate the tactile, visible, and audible dimensions, playing with the light, the sound of the fabrics, and the falling of their drape.

To take into account the richness of all these different dimensions of the expression plan, the following general summary table was developed (Table 6.3). This modelization may apply to any brand.

These three levels of the substantial, plastic, and figurative dimensions follow a "generative logic," going from the simplest to the most complex. The figurative level presents recognizable things and creatures

Table 6.3   Brand Aesthetics Analytical Grid

Expression Level	Form and Substance
Figurative	Form of content
Plastic	Form of expression
Substantial	Substance of expression

---

[13] Bertrand and Mazzalovo, "Méthode sémiotique: de la structure au sensible."

Table 6.4 Brand Aesthetics Analytical Grid Applied to Jim Thompson (2015) Synthesis of the Brand's Various Expressive Levels

Expression Level	Form and Substance	Jim Thompson Characteristics		
Figurative	Form of content	Realist Naïve Stylized Abstract	Iconic ↓	
Plastic	Form of expression	Geometrization Flamboyant Shading	Space Shapes Colors	
Substantial	Substance of expression	Material	Tactile	
		Weaving Iridescence	Tactile/visual Visual	

of the world. In Table 6.4, we see the application of the grid to Jim Thompson expression. Three different aesthetic treatments (or styles) are being applied by Jim Thompson's designers at the figurative level: realist (highly iconic representation of animals, flowers, villages, etc.), naive (mainly for kid's products, simplified representations), and stylized (tending toward more abstract treatment). There is a gradually diminishing figurativeness, going from the most iconic to the most abstract.

The plastic dimension regroups the elements constituting the form of expression of visual objects beyond any represented figure: colors (chromatism), and shapes and lines (eidetism) and their spatial disposition (topological). Denis Bertrand often quotes the painter Eugène Delacroix to define the plastic dimension:

> There is a kind of emotion that is very special to painting. […] There is an impression that results from arrangements of colors, lights, shadows, etc. This is what we call the music of the painting. Before you even know what the picture represents […] often you get caught by this magical harmony.
> —E. Delacroix

Jim Thompson often structures the spatial disposition by geometrization of patterns, as we find in many traditional Thai sarongs; it reactivates a Thai plastic tradition by playing the flamboyance of the shapes (as with fighting fish, for instance, or the rising extremities of Thai roofs) and plays with the chromatic work of nuances (as with *moirés*, tone on tone, opposable to linear or chromatic contrasts).

Finally, the substance of the expression deals with the sensorial materiality of objects. It focuses on the perceptual properties of the materials (tactile, visual, auditory). Three processes are deployed by Jim Thompson: the use of raw materials such as silk, linen, cotton, and leather, which favor tactility; weaving (such as ikat special weaving techniques of tie-dye), which calls on both tactility and vision; and the iridescence that is so characteristic of Thai silk, which through its play with light calls only the vision.

The analytical grid of the aesthetics of a brand extends the hinge of identity presented in Table 6.2. It gives weight to the specific articulations of the plane of expression. The extension of such a model will preferentially concern the luxury world, which has the semiotic property of precisely exalting the plane of expression: selection of materials, substances chosen for their rarity, their genesis, or their intrinsic quality. It is obviously complementary to the other content models used elsewhere in semiotic studies (semiotic square, generative model, narrative schematization, hinge of identity, etc.). This analysis therefore isolates the universe of aesthetic values from their substance and form of expression to show the specific architecture of the meaning they build.

Other Ways to Get into Brand Aesthetics

Without having to become an art history expert or a reknowned designer or artist, there are a number of publications that may help rationalize parts of brand aesthetics. Far from being exhaustive, as so much has been published on art and design, we will mention only a few references that we find quite relevant to our topic, keeping in mind that the analysis of the expression plan has interest only inasmuch as it serves the purpose of understanding the intelligible plan, that is, how the sense is generated and how consistent the brand manifestations are with respect to the formalized identity.

We can classify this literature according to specific aesthetic visual elements:

- Light
  - Baroque and classical expressions by Heinrich Wölfflin in *Principles of Art History* (Dover Publications)
- Forms/lines
  - The serpentine or beauty line by William Hogarth in *The Analysis of Beauty* (Yale University Press)
  - Four linear typologies (the SINC square) by G. Mazzalovo in *Brand Aesthetics* (Wiley)
  - Literature on the Gestalt school
- Composition
  - The golden mean, written about by many authors
  - Rudolf Arnheim in *The Power of the Center* (University of California Press)
- Colors
  - The rule of simultaneous contrast by Michel Eugene Chevreul in *The Principles of Harmony and Contrast of Colors* (Shiffer Publishing Limited).
  - The chromatic square by G. Mazzalovo in "La Sémiotique de Jean-Marie Floch et la Gestion des Marques," published in the Italian academic journal *Fictions*

The EST-ET© Diagram

This diagram is an immediate offshoot of the brand identity hinge. Two axes are made from the two components of the identity (ethics and aesthetics), which form a two-dimensional diagram that allows specific brand manifestations to be positioned on the created surface. This is the EST-ET© diagram, a diagnostic tool applicable to any brand manifestation in order to measure its adequacy with respect to the desired brand identity.

For example, the diagram shown in Figure 6.4 was applied in 2007 to a number of cars designed by Pininfarina in a study where the ethical and aesthetic dimensions of a project of the Pininfarina brand were formalized.

The concept car, Sintesi, presented at the Geneva International Motor Show in 2008 and developed according to the aesthetic and ethical invariants formalized by the study, is thus placed at the top right-hand corner of the EST-ET© diagram. Sintesi is a mythical car, full of innovations, where technology has guided a design respectful of the brand values and aesthetic sensibility. At the other end, at the lower left-hand corner of the EST-ET© diagram we find the design made for some Chinese brands, where cars have very few recognizable features of the car bodybuilder's style. A precise definition of the axes is necessary because it determines the result. For example, the axis of aesthetics can measure:

- Consistency with the brand aesthetics
- Efficiency in the transmission of ethics
- Originality of design
- Pleasure provided
- And so on

The ethical axis can measure:

- Coherence with the brand identity
- Competitive relevance
- Originality
- And so on

The choice of the axes is based on the relevance of the issues raised.

The EST-ET© diagram is one of the rare tools that allow for a rational approach to a relevant diagnosis of consistency between a newly created brand manifestation and the brand identity. In the case of Pininfarina, the diagram was applied to all manifestations of Pininfarina throughout its 90 years of history (ads, trade-show-booth design, objects, nonautomobile object design, logo, calligraphy of the name, etc.) to make a full diagnosis of the brand expression consistency. It was a major help in streamlining the coordination of the design work among the various departments as described in the article of one of the authors (2016) referred to earlier.[14]

---

[14] G. Mazzalovo, "Resolving Tensions among Creative Departments."

Brand Identity Strategic and Operational Implications

In order for the concept of brand identity to give its full effectiveness in brand management, it needs to be applied to its fullest extent and have a chance to become the federating principle upon which to guide and measure all creative and communication activities.

Once formalized, the brand identity represents a framework that will serve to manage nearly all of the brand's manifestations. Figure 6.5, applied to Jim Thompson, illustrates the influence of the brand identity, once formalized, on the main brand manifestations. In that particular example, the brand manifestations have been classified in five categories:

1. Communication in a broad sense, including traditional paper publications, Internet and PR, and events.
2. Products, including packaging, merchandising, and pricing.
3. The signature system in general, including signage, labels, stationery, and so on.
4. The architecture and functioning of all facilities (stores, offices, and factories). Retail, including window and internal displays, salespersons' uniforms, and salesmanship.
5. Behaviors of employees and also of customers.

In short, it is a federating framework to aid in eliminating, at the outset, all elements that are incompatible with the defined identity. It is also the basis for any creative briefs made to external and internal resources working on aesthetic matters.

We have seen in Figure 6.3, the brand identity represented the invariant part of the overall company strategy; the other parts constantly adapted to the competitive and environmental context. If it is true that brand identity plays a central role in any communication and creation strategy, its influence is less obvious on the choices companies make in terms of structure of the product offering, determination of prices and margins, choice of target customers, or organizational, industrial, and retailing choices. These choices, which also have an impact on the brand's perception, must of course be taken into consideration; however, it is clear that a formalized brand identity alone is not sufficient to guarantee that the best strategic decisions are made.

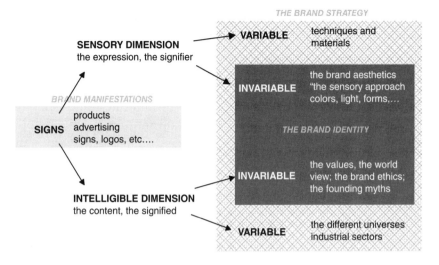

Figure 6.3   Brand Manifestations, Identity, and Strategies

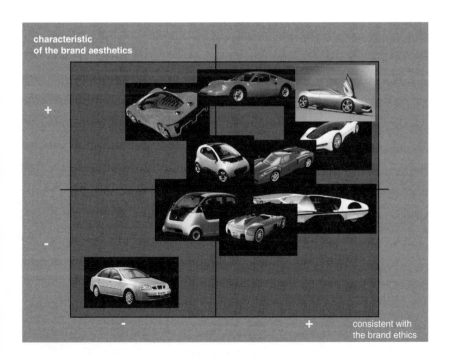

Figure 6.4   The EST-ET© Diagram Applied to Some Pininfarina Cars

brand identity
operational implications

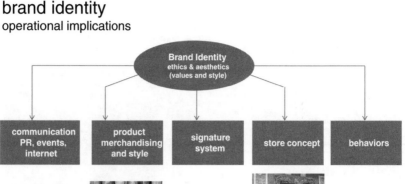

Figure 6.5   Applying the Brand Identity to All the Brand Manifestations (Jim Thompson example)

The overall strategy of a company can be broken down into functional strategies (products, customers, retailing, communication, production, logistics, and organization). While the brand identity plays a central role in any strategy of communication, it is also affected in turn by decisions made by other functions. There is no activity in a company that does not affect or reflect, in one way or another, the brand's identity. Figure 6.6 shows the degree of influence the logic of the brand identity should exert in the functional strategies of a company. The degree of influence of the brand identity will also depend on the industries. It will be of more importance in the luxury industry than in mass markets or in purely business-to-business industrial sectors.

General Considerations on the Brand Identity Concept

What is involved in the passage from identity to image? As we have indicated earlier, identity is emissive in nature, while perception is receptive.

		INFLUENCE OF BRAND IDENTITY
PRODUCTS	- categories	
	- offering structure	partial influence
	- price	partial influence
	- style	decisive influence
	- functionality	partial influence
	- quality	partial influence
CLIENTS	- targets	decisive influence
DISTRIBUTION	- network	partial influence
	- architecture / aesthetics	decisive influence
	- service	decisive influence
COMMUNICATION	- advertising	decisive influence
	- PR / events	decisive influence
PRODUCTION		partial influence
LOGISTICS		minimal influence
ORGANIZATION	- structure	minimal influence
	- personnel	decisive influence
	- culture	decisive influence
FINANCE & ADMIN.		minimal influence

decisive influence / partial influence / minimal influence

Figure 6.6 Place of Brand Identity in Company Functional Strategies

The two notions are related but between what one wants to say about oneself and what gets across to the recipient, a lot of shifting, pollution, interference, omission, and unconscious revelation go on. These unavoidable alterations represent some of the dynamic aspects of any communication process. Consequently, the messages of the brand identity undergo multiple interpretations depending on who is on the receiving end. The relevance and interpretation of the brand discourses depend strongly on the lifestyle, customs, values, and tastes of the consumers. Like any speaker, the brand must take into account the identity of its recipients. And since a brand hopes not only to be heard but also to be adopted by the consumer, to become one of the signs of his or her identity, the issue takes on crucial importance. Between the brand and individuals' identities, there is necessarily a cultural identity, structured by the cultural codes of given social groups. In communicating their identities through their various manifestations, brands will generate what could be called social and individual representations. This has two important consequences for brand management:

First, it must be accepted that perceptions of the brand will always be multiple, and that their diversity will only increase as brand awareness increases.

Second, society changes, and so does the identity of the individuals and the cultures that make it up. To continue to speak to them, brands must also renew themselves, alter somewhat their own identity, without losing their fundamental substance. They must be able to change without getting lost in the process.

Single Identity / Multiple Perceptions

Codol and Tap give the following definition of an individual's identity:

> Identity is a structured, differentiated system, anchored both in a past temporality (roots, permanence), in a coordination of current behavior, and in a legitimated perspective (projects, ideals, values, and style).[15]

This definition applies closely to a brand identity; the vocabulary is largely the same. Psychoanalysis, anthropology, and psychosociology have all studied the notion of individual's identity, bringing out the intrinsic duality on which it is founded: on the one hand, personal judgment; on the other, comparison with others—in other words, the purely individual dimension versus social existence. Most psychoanalysts hold that identity is constructed both by the internalization of cultural and social models and by the imagination of the body and its impulses. Cultural anthropology places the accent on the collective dimension of identity. It sees each culture as tending to produce personality models. In more semiotic terms, these approaches have in common the fact that they temper the idea of universal communication: I can't really say the same thing to everyone, at least not if I hope to be understood by everyone in the same way. The perception of a brand identity (values, signs) is conditioned by the values, judgments, and models developed personally and in a specific environment by each individual.

---

[15] J. P. Codol and P. Tap, "Dynamique personnelle et identités sociales," *Revue internationale de psychologie sociale* 2 (1988): 169.

Of course, we can't take the position that each individual's subjectivity is irreducible either. Human society appears to be layered by many determinisms depending on culture, region, age, income level, and so on that can in part be elucidated. However, no matter how refined the analysis, the perception of a given message by the individual members of a given group cannot be unique. Therefore, this duality inherent in identity must be dealt with.

The generation of multiple perceptions from a single brand identity is an absolutely normal phenomenon. All brands face this reality, particularly when it comes to geographical extension. In terms of communication and creation, there are two extremes in dealing with it. First, there is monolithic management, which deals with a standardized consumer. This is the case of most luxury brands, which produce a single communication campaign and collection for the entire world. Even in this case, there is still an implicit segmentation. The brand aims at an urban public who have a high income level and are fond of traveling. It relies on these strong determinisms to eclipse geographical specificities. Then there is a more flexible form of management that adapts products or advertising campaigns to local cultures. L'Oréal, in their mass market activities, is probably the best example of how cosmetic products and their relative communication can be adapted to different cultural markets. Another example that could be cited is certain liqueurs (such as Cognac) for which modes of consumption vary greatly from one country to another.

Such a range of individual and cultural identities makes all segmentations possible. The criteria are geographical, demographic, economic, and psychosocial. Mood segmentation, which breaks potential markets down according to consumers' moods, has recently appeared. It should be mentioned that the Internet and particularly the sophistication reached by data analysis have empowered enormously a brand's capability to segment any type of market up to the individual customer.

Ms. Consumer is walking down Fifth Avenue. She feels successful and seductive, or wants to; she buys an ensemble at Christian Dior. Or she's a little depressed, feels like a victim, not at ease with herself; Prada offers her the refuge she needs. She's at the top of her form physically and mentally, exuberant, in love with life; Loewe can provide her with the products that reflect Spanish energy and joie de vivre. A few days later, feeling a little guilty about all the money she spent, she feels she needs to find a bargain, a product she'll use every day, in good taste and at a reasonable price; she goes to Max Mara on West Broadway and, to soothe her shopping-tortured feet, buys a good pair of Ferragamo shoes. This example of mood marketing is extracted from a time when the Internet was in its infancy. Imagine the multiplying effect of the Internet on this hypothetical customer: not only does she not need to strain her feet by walking the streets, she has a much broader choice directly on her screens at home. She can satisfy a wider range of moods than before and be delivered the goods at home.

Consumers have become multifaceted and therefore more difficult to catch. What's interesting in this example is that all these images are aimed at the same consumer, who will choose one or another according to her mood. The choice of Christian Dior, for example, will appear daring to some and clearly outdated to others. We are looking there at the difference between brand identity and brand images. The same identity crystallizes into a multitude of perceptions depending on place, social milieu, personality, or mood.

There's nothing to be gained by fighting this diversity. On the contrary, it represents a form of wealth. It constitutes a portfolio of images, each of which enables different reactions to innovations. Perceptions are multiple, but they are not unstructured or accidental. Semiotics, by analyzing the mechanisms by which meaning is produced, is fully aware of the polysemy of its subjects. But this multiplicity of perceptions does not contradict the need to guarantee, upstream, the coherence of the message. The more coherent the identity, the more it lends itself to a wealth of interpretations. Messages that are vague, on the other hand, either through structural weakness or because of a desire to cover all the bases, to be an aggregate of all trends, melt away under the light of interpretation. An identity that borrows from too many categories runs the risk of collapsing under the weight of its referents.

The Need to Evolve

Coherence of identity does not mean rigidity. A brand's identity must evolve. How many brands have disappeared because they haven't responded to that need? Sexual liberation in the 1970s was the basis for the initial success of Paco Rabanne, with his metal dresses; that same liberalization of lifestyles took the polish off his image, and very quickly made him more marginal than original. The recent difficulties encountered by Victoria's Secret is the latest example of the need to evolve. The image of women transmitted by the brand is reflecting a completely outdated US machismo that is at the antipode of the current mood symbolized by the Me Too movement against sexual harassment that took form around 2006.

A brand's decline is an inevitable phenomenon if nothing is done to counteract it. The reasons, both internal and external, are numerous. First of all, errors in the brand management such as loss of relevance in a market, inefficient operations, incoherent strategies, inappropriate or insufficient investments, and so on. Then there is the competition, ever stronger and more battle-hardened. There is also what we call the entropy of brands. Any brand, through the wide use of its products and the repeated broadcasting of its advertising, engenders a certain demystification. It loses some of its mystery, and, thereby, part of its attraction. In the contemporary context of the race toward novelty, this wearing effect of success is more rapid than ever.

Finally, there is the evolution of the fundamental trends of our civilization: needs, fashions, technology, tastes, and so on. Obviously, the rise of the Internet is the obvious example. However, there are interesting examples in history too. We often cite the example of the history of the color blue, brilliantly told by Michel Pastoureau.[16] In Greco-Roman times, blue did not play a role in social, religious, or artistic life. It was hardly used by the Barbarians. It was not until the thirteenth century and the stained glasses of the windows of the cathedral of Chartres that blue took on more importance in liturgical and then in social life. A new theology of light had made its way and, after many debates, was seen as an emanation of God, the ineffable made visible. The thesis that light and color were identical in nature won out over the idea that colors are only a material artifice. Blue and gold were used to represent that light. Within a few decades, blue became an aristocratic color; it was seen in clothing, artistic creations, and religious life. It became the color of the sky, then of the Virgin Mary, and finally that of kings. Blue was never to lose that importance. From the uniforms of soldiers, policemen, and postmen in the nineteenth century to the blue jeans of today, blue became the most-worn color in the Western world. It is also, before

---

[16] M. Pastoureau, *Bleu: histoire d'une couleur*. Paris: Seuil, 2000.

green, the favorite color of Westerners. The Japanese, on the other hand, prefer first white, then black. Tastes change with time and from country to country.

For all these reasons, a brand identity that is too rigid, defined with too many constraints, or with too much detail hampers the ability to move rapidly with the market. However, this does not necessarily suggest renewing the brand's ethics and aesthetics invariants. In fact, the need for change is greater on the aesthetic level. More than changing invariants, the need is for keeping an aesthetic in step with the tastes of the time. We could use the metaphor of showing the same object or character under different lights or angles. The identity remains the same, but the highlights vary. The exercise is easier when in the presence of a rich brand identity.

As for brand ethics, there is no question of changing the basic values of the brand, but rather on stressing those values best in step with the mood of the markets. Evolution does not mean ill-advised transformation of the invariants, but rather making marginal corrections, variations in focus that will stay on good terms with the markets without altering the brand's substance. Rather than of permanent invariants, we can speak in terms of a stable continuity of brand aesthetics and ethics.

Finally, we would point out that the need for change is greater for brands whose ethics are based on fashionable values, which by definition are not permanent. In this area, there is old money and there are the nouveaux riches: Bentley or Hermès will be able to rely on a brand ethic that focuses on elitist and aristocratic values for some time to come. However, experience has shown that evolution will very probably be more difficult for brands like Roberto Cavalli or even Prada.

From Brand Discourses to the Sum of Discourses About the Brand

The approach, so far, has been to consider exclusively all the discourses that the brand emits through its manifestations, like a flow of signs created by the creators and communicators of all the brand-perceivable elements. This is an obvious simplification and does not represent the complexity of the entire brand phenomenon.

We cannot remove all of the perception part of the brand, probably constituting the most "voluminous" part of its reality, which is made up of all the customers' representations of the brand and of the resulting discourses emitted by them.

Production and perception have to be considered as the two essential and necessary parts on how the brand comes into existence. We even have to go beyond Semprini's (2005) statement that the brand identity is determined by "the sum of all the discourses about it." [17] As Jean-Michel Bertrand (2020) states, brands are entities in permanent interdependence with their environment and the sense they generate is the result of encounters and negotiations between the enunciators and the recipients.[18]

It will still be the brand manager's responsibility to initiate the brand projects and constantly take into account the perception side, the non-directly controlled manifestations of the brand that customers' opinions, discourses, and ways of using of the brand product or services represent. We have to be clear on what instruments of influence both the brand managers and the markets respectively have at their disposal. The former is supposed to adapt the offer and the communication in general to the markets' expectations, within the boundaries of the desired brand identity. The latter contribute to the emergence of the meaning of the brand through their discourses and acts of purchase.

These circulating and evolving discourses about the brand, added to the brand's own discourses, constitute a set of signs in movements but with boundaries determined by the subject in question: the specific brand. This virtual space where processes of signification are born, emerge, grow, disappear, and are exchanged corresponds to the definition of a semiosphere, a term originally coined in 1998 by Yuri Lotman, the semiotician of cultures, to define metaphorically a virtual space within which emerge and evolve processes of meaning.[19] This goes beyond this book's purpose and will be developed further in other instances.

The Internet allows the brand manager now to monitor in real time and closely the vast amount of discourses that are held on the brand. Semantic analytical methods, reputation monitoring, feedback on new products, or ad campaigns proposed by the web operators do just that.

[17] A. Semprini, *La marque, une puissance fragile*. Paris: Vuibert, 2005.

[18] J.-M. Bertrand, "Retour critique sur la théorie de la marque," *Modes de recherche*. Paris: IFM, 2020.

[19] Y. Lotman, *The Semiosphere: Semiotics of Culture, the Text, of the Conduct and the Space: II* (Spanish Edition). Catedra Ediciones, 1998.

Limitations of the Concept of Identity

Difference versus Sameness.   Another limitation of the concept of identity has to do with the paradox inherent in the definition of identity itself. Merriam-Webster's *Collegiate Dictionary* mentions identity as being not only the distinguishing character or personality of an individual, but also "sameness of essential or generic character."

Sameness and generic. Identical and unique. The individual and the multitude.

Is identity, then, the state of being both unique and like another? It swings back and forth between the tendencies of the mass market toward uniformity and radical uniqueness and probably exists only in terms of this dialectical tension.

These considerations take us back, indirectly, to the difficulty of defining and formalizing an identity that is completely independent of the way in which it is perceived, or, more precisely, of the brand director's perception of the way in which the brand is seen by the target market segments. To try to define a brand's identity in a closed circle, independently of considerations related to trends and to the dominant perceptions of the brand in the most significant markets, is a dangerous oversimplification.

We have seen that one of the conditions of a brand's existence is the differentiating of its identity. This implies that a brand exists in relation to other brands from which it is different. Pepsi would not exist without Coca-Cola; Coca-Cola would probably not be as important without Pepsi. The right balance must be found between the general conditions of the market and the degrees of flexibility of the ethical and aesthetic invariants.

Providing the return on investment that shareholders demand, satisfying the expectations of existing customers, but also the expectations expressed by customers of the competitors of reference, all without losing the brand soul: such are the dilemmas brand directors face every day. Ours is an anthropomorphic approach, applying the principles of identity to systems like brands, whose objectives are essentially economic. It opens up an area for more detailed research into the nature of the interfaces between brand identity and cultures and consumers' identities, and into the mechanisms that trigger the act of purchasing.

The goal of brand management being to lead consumers to buy the brand's products, consumers must position themselves in a positive way in relation to values and an aesthetic they can perceive. Are these values that are aspired to, or ones already acquired? Is a purchase an act of affirmation, of compensation, of protest? The projection of an image of the self that is desired, or actual? We leave this field of research to other disciplines and other books.

Three Purposes of Aesthetic Treatments. Most of the frustration experienced by persons newly exposed to the concept of brand aesthetic invariants as a constitutive element of brand identity is that it is not automatic to think of design as expressing a world vision. Indeed, this is only one of the purposes of the design process.

Art history literature can help rationalize the various roles of aesthetic treatment applied to objects, places, persons, and so on. Aloïs Riegl (1899) defines three purposes for any aesthetic treatment whether applied to artworks or day-to-day objects:

1. Representation, which is what we have studied so far (values, world vision, ethics, and so on)
2. Decoration (i.e., *making it nice*), which we find particularly relevant in the fashion industry
3. Functionality, where we will find all the aerodynamic shapes and ergonomically driven designs[20]

From this point of view, the concept of identity demonstrates some of its limits by covering only one of the three purposes of aesthetic treatment, which often complicates the task of the semiotic analysis. Table 6.5 summarizes Riegl's approach and its adaptation to brands.

The Relative Weakening of the Brand Identity Concept

Two prevailing factors contribute to the weakening of the brand identity concept's reputation and usefulness. The first is that less customers' time and curiosity are dedicated to understand brands beyond the immediate benefits a product or service can provide.

The advent of the Internet has had a radical impact on the way brand identities are being perceived. On the one hand, brand information is

---

[20] A. Riegl, *Historische Grammatik der Bildenden Künste*. French translation, 1978: *Grammaire Historique des Arts Plastiques. Volonté Artistique et Vision du Monde*. Mayenne: Klinckseick.

Table 6.5   Three Purposes of Aesthetic Treatments

Purpose	Riegl's Version	Adaptation to Brands
Representation	Response to desires of spiritual order	Promoting a brand's ethics, its world vision, its values
	Religion, relationships of man and nature, morals, ethics	Developing the founding concepts of a project, a product, or a brand presenting possible worlds
Decoration	Response to desires of visual order	Purely aesthetic objectives Making it nice
	Reaction to *horror vacui*	Exercises in style
	Rivalry with nature	Generating visual pleasure
Functionality	Response to desires of nonvisual and nonspiritual Utilitarian	Functional or utilitarian objectives for the object or service
		At communication level: • Memorization • Recognition • Readability

Source: G. Mazzalovo, *Brand Aesthetics*. Palgrave Macmillan, 2012.

readily and immediately available, even for less-known brands. On the other hand, the exponential growth of the amount of data available has had an impact on people's capacity to spend time and focus on specific topics. To know and understand a brand, one needs to be interested, read about it, experience it through products and services, discuss it, and so on. However, there is a consumption tendency toward superficiality and immediacy; two trends in complete opposition to the time, attention, and experience necessary to know and understand the identity of a brand.

One of the most meaningful phenomena in the sense of superficiality developed to the detriment of depth can be found in the success of Instagram stories, launched in August 2016 and now used by more 500 million Instagrammers daily. This is basically a Snapchat-like feature that allows one to create sequences of photos and videos that will disappear after one day. Videos or photos and therefore texts may be linked together to form a slideshow. Various tools are available to unleash everybody's creativity, like augmented reality filters, various links to other friends' lists, and so forth. Facebook, Instagram's owner, has introduced a similar feature. We are in a race for content. There is a real frenzy to create more content more rapidly to feed social media, blogs, websites, communication, and e-commerce platforms—and this goes head-on against the possibility of cultivating an authentic and well-managed brand identity. How much analytical depth can be applied in these circumstances? The trend is not toward understanding; it is more on immediate consumption and experience with giving more weight to a close circle of social opinions than to the authenticity of the act of consuming.

The second factor contributing to weakening the usefulness of the notion of brand identity is that some brands are having success with clear disruptive aesthetic approaches. Brands like Gucci and Loewe, for example, with Alessandro Michele and Jonathan Anderson, respectively, as creative directors, have decided in recent years to develop an aesthetic in a radical departure from the long history of the brands, with great commercial success. These are counterexamples to the benefits of a rationalized brand identity approach to a brand. Not all brands, however, have a creative genius able to read the moods of their contemporary target customers.

The Consequential Emergence of Two Distinctive Brand Positioning

This leads to the emergence of two drastically different types of brand positioning corresponding also to two different visions of the world for their respective consumers.

On one side, timelessness and heritage are irrelevant to brands and their managers. The most blatant example is Gucci's approach, which can be characterized by its research for the unconventional, where efforts are made to move away from what has defined the brand so far, investing in a new paradigm. The journalist Rachel Sanderson writes in the *Financial Times* in December 2015 about Gucci's collection in these terms: "Fashion media have been largely ecstatic over Mr. Michele's 'fashion with no rules' ethos."[21] This is clearly creation without roots, without meaning, with no justification other than pleasing or even just surprising; that is, this is *gratuitous design*, which has been anticipated and theorized by Jean Baudrillard (1983) in what he called "hyper-reality," where an image or product is its own referent without representing anything else

---

[21] Rachel Sanderson, "Gucci Sets Out on Quest for Better Times," *Financial Times*, October 21, 2015.

(the content is all in the appearance; in semiotic terms, the signifier is also the signified).[22] For Gucci's Milan AW 2020 fashion show, the *Financial Times* review mentions: "There were some new elements here, for sure—but the vintage-eclectic, everything-but-the-kitchen-sink aesthetic that Michele brought to Gucci in 2015 has come to feel a bit tired, faded,"[23] making it clear that professionals are clearly aware of his gratuitous approach. Incidentally, the source of inspiration for this last collection were vintage children's clothes, of which Michele has amassed an archive from the 1930s through the 1970s.

In this brand approach, out of the three purposes of any aesthetic treatment introduced in Table 6.7, there is no pursuit of the representation purpose. All the creative efforts are essentially on decoration, or on creating completely new values. It is not easy to create aesthetic invariants when each season has little to do with the previous one. That certainly creates expectations—"What is Michele going to do next?"—but if the only constant is the change, the unexpected, the surprise, how do you really differentiate your brand from your competitors' in a recognizable way over time?

Loewe and Etro are also riding this trend to renew their offer and enter a new wave of luxury based on disruptive codes. In that particular positioning, there is no need for a rationalized and formalized brand identity; all the brand expression is driven by the creative director of the moment and is at the mercy of his/her talents.

The second brand approach could be qualified as *research for authenticity*. In that case, the brand focus is on serving its target customers while remaining true to its identity in terms of values and aesthetics. Brands with a rich heritage normally leverage this asset that is at the root of their differentiation in the market and takes years to accumulate. Cartier, Vuitton, Chanel, Ferragamo, Loro Piana, Coach, Tod's, and Rubelli are following this trend with more or less success according to the relevance of their responses to customers' needs. The need for authenticity prevails with customers who are sensitive to the truth and consistency of the brand discourses and manifestations. "Authenticity is the new quality,"

---

[22] J. Baudrillard, *Simulations* (Foreign Agents Series). Semiotext, 1983.
[23] Lauren Indvik, "Gucci's Alessandro Michele Takes the Fashion Crowd Behind the Seams," *Financial Times*, February 19, 2020.

declare James Gilmore and Joseph Pline (2007).[24] We will delve deeper into authenticity in Chapter 14.

We will see in the next chapter how we can represent these strategic choices on a semiotic square.

Other Approaches to Brand Management

An interesting book by Tilde Heding, Charlotte F. Knudtzen, and Mogens Bjerre (2016) provides a thorough overview of all the meaningful brand management approaches spanning from the 1960s until now.[25] They identify the following seven schools of thought:

1. The economic approach (before 1985)
2. The identity approach (mid 1980s)
3. The consumer-based approach (1993)
4. The personality approach (1997)
5. The relational approach (1998)
6. The cultural approach (around 2000)
7. The community approach (2001)

We recommend the book to understand the wealth of thought and analysis related to the ways of managing brands. Even though nothing is specifically mentioned about a semiotic-based brand identity methodology, the authors' work illustrates some of the advantages of the identity approach that they qualify as being "the most far-reaching brand approach." They recognize that the early approach of the early 1990s, where a sender perspective prevailed, has been progressively altered and refined since the early 2000s, taking into account the increasing role of consumers in building the brand identity (as we will see in the next chapter). They also note that the evolution of the method has been essentially led by practitioners using the brand identity concept.

They go on to highlight some of the advantages of the method:

- The method provides answers to basic existential questions such as: "Who are we? What do we stand for? What are we recognized by? What do we want to become?"

---

[24] J. Gilmore and J. Pline, *Authenticity: What Customers Really Want*. Brighton, Mass.: Harvard Business Review Press, 2007.
[25] Bertrand and Mazzalovo, "Méthode sémiotique."

- The approach addresses both strategic and operational aspects of brand positioning and communication.
- The whole organization is mobilized into the brand identity management; i.e., company functions and behaviors contribute to send messages. Therefore, the method helps coordinate all of the company organization and provides day-to-day management tools.
- The brand identity approach contributes to creating strong brands through consistent and reliable communication, avoiding the pitfalls of a natural functional fragmentation of brand management.

Meanwhile, the notion of brand identity is gaining ground, and is being used more and more in the industry, advertising agencies, media, distribution brands, politics, and the cultural world. Specialized university education and research programs on brand identities and their meanings are increasing rapidly. The growth of the brand identity approach is also closely related to the social and international identity-related issues the world is experiencing (racism, immigration, exclusion, etc.).

We will see in the next chapter some additional analytical tools not necessarily directly related to the identity concept. Appendix A has been prepared to illustrate the application of the tools introduced in this chapter to the case of the Sasin School of Management, part of Chulalongkorn University in Thailand.

Chapter 7

Additional Brand Analytical Tools

S ince our previous edition, we have been involved in directly managing luxury brands, and we naturally have had opportunities to refine and improve the analytical tools presented in previous versions, but also to develop new ones. This is the reason for the addition of a supplementary chapter on brand analytical tools.

Brand Life Cycle

The brand life cycle, despite its apparent simplicity, remains a basic strategic management instrument. It is not of a semiotic nature and is not related to the meaning brands generate, but it provides meaningful strategic inputs on the position of the brand within its own evolution trajectory. A brand's history is not quite one and the same as that of the company that brought it into existence. Brands have an independent

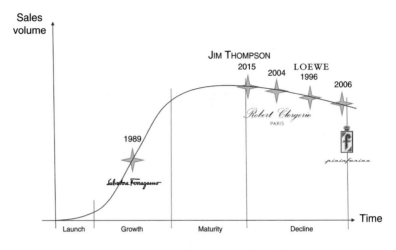

Figure 7.1   The Brand Life Cycle

life and, having become part of our imagination, sometimes survive in the markets long after the original company has disappeared.

A brand's history comprises phases of strong expansion alternating with phases of relative stagnation, and perhaps rapid decline. This is not really different from what occurs in the traditional life cycle of a product or a company. As shown in Figure 7.1, the life of a brand can be represented on a graph, with time mapped against a chosen indicator of the brand's strength.

The graph follows the same phases—launch, growth, maturity, decline (which can be followed by a relaunch), and disappearance—that characterize the life cycle of a product. At each of these stages, the luxury brand's director is faced with specific problems.

Figure 7.1 shows the stages of some of the brands that one of the authors has managed, at the time of their involvement. Most of these brands were in a declining phase. The fashion and luxury sectors are particularly concerned with the relaunching phase, which is the main issue for brands that have reached maturity or decline.

The most spectacular example of successive relaunchings is that of Gucci, as illustrated in Figure 7.2. The curve looks a bit like a roller coaster, but it reflects the brand's strength and ability to rebound with different management teams. The brand's first major relaunch took place in 1995–1996. Its results for 2002 were affected by 9/11, as well as

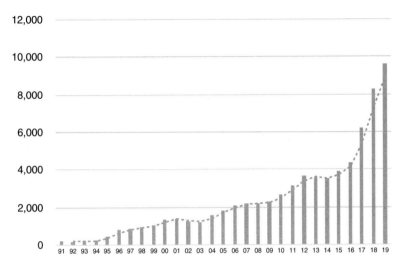

Figure 7.2   Gucci Turnover, 1991–2019 (in € millions)

by the struggle between the LVMH and Kering (named PPR at the time) groups for the control of the brand, which PPR eventually won in 2003. Even after the departure of Tom Ford and Domenico de Sole, who were, respectively, the creative director and the chairman, 2004 and 2005 results were very good, and continued to be under the direction of Patrizio di Marco (CEO since 2009 after the leaderships of Giacomo Santucci and Mark Lee) as well as with Frida Giannini as creative director since 2006.

Then sales decreased for two years in a row, 2014 and 2015. Giannini and di Marco had to step down in December 2014; Marco Bizzarri was appointed CEO of the brand. Gucci's offer had become somewhat less relevant in the fashion market. The classic looks were not sufficient to create enough excitement around the brand; edgier designs were needed. Alessandro Michele became Gucci's creative director in early 2015, and he managed one of the biggest rebounds ever seen in the luxury business. The growth of the years 2016 to 2019 is exponential. A small deceleration occurred in 2019, perhaps indicating a path to a new maturity. We can expect 2020 to show a major negative effect, as for all other luxury brands, due to the economic impact of COVID-19.

Besides this extraordinary Gucci performance, other brands in Kering's portfolio follow their own track. As can be seen in Figure 7.3,

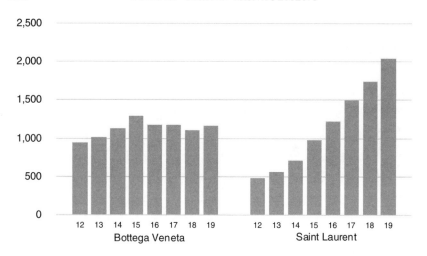

Figure 7.3   Saint Laurent and Bottega Veneta Turnover, 2012–2019 (in €
millions)

Saint Laurent is finally taking off and showing a clear growth pattern,
reaching the €2 billion mark in 2019, while Bottega Veneta is stagnating
and even declining in the €1.1–1.2 billion range.

Saint Laurent sales, which were half those of Bottega Veneta in 2012
and had stagnated for almost 15 years, are now almost double.

As illustrated in Figure 7.4, Hermès, a brand that is more than a
century old, had relatively steady growth from the early 1990s until 2009,
when its sales started to increase at a much higher rate. It is not affected
by the different economic slumps, as if the attraction of authentic luxury
was preserving the brand from any economic crises.

There was a slight decline in 2003, but in 2010 there was a yearly
growth of 25.4% and the pace is continuing. The aristocratic French
brand is far from maturity; it is still in an extraordinary growth phase.
Hermès's success is based on a completely different strategy than Gucci's:
it does not depend on a designer's talent, because the market has probably
matured to the point that the brand epitomizes genuine luxury.

The brand life cycle allows us to gain insight into the different aspects
of the brand's evolution and illustrate that success may be achieved with
different strategies.

Ferragamo, on the other hand, has had a more eventful story. Until
2009, its curve for yearly business volume was, in fact, very close to the

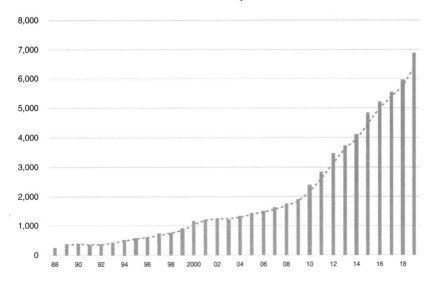

Figure 7.4   Hermès Turnover, 1988–2018 (in € millions)

theoretical profile of the life cycle. After two years of a lull in 1998 and 1999, it rebounded in 2000 with the consolidation of sales that followed the purchase of its Japanese retailing subsidiary. Then followed 10 years of maturity with sales stagnating around €600 million until the outstanding results in 2010 with a growth of 24%, as illustrated in Figure 7.5. In fact, most prime luxury brand sales increased rapidly starting in 2010 due to the positive effect of Chinese luxury customers.

Since 2015, Ferragamo again experienced maturity and decline until 2018, which seem to be coming under control in 2019, as the sales level is reversing the declining trend and coming back to the 2017 level.

Roger Vivier is an example of a much smaller brand that has the characteristic of being probably the most successful example of the revival of a "sleeping beauty." It was created by the French shoe designer Roger Vivier (1907–1998). Contrary to Ferragamo, Mr. Vivier never really developed his brand, which had only two stores (Paris and New York). It had been completely absent from the market since 1998 when the Italian entrepreneur Diego Della Valle, owner of the brands Tod's, Hogan, Fay, and so on, bought it in 2001 and relaunched it in 2003. Sixteen years later, in 2019, the brand invoiced more than €200 million. The majority of its range consists of women's shoes at prices above €1,500. The best-selling shoe model is the pilgrim, with an easily

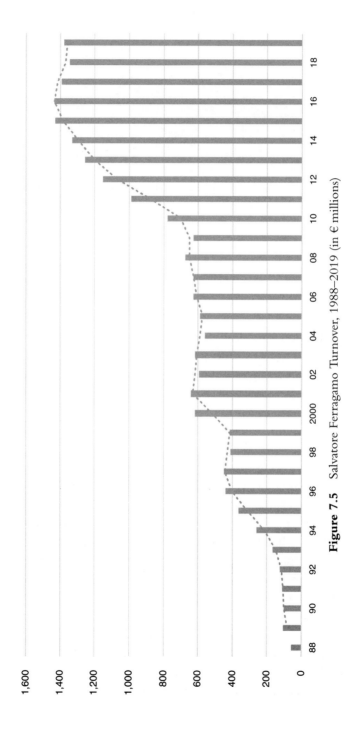

Figure 7.5 Salvatore Ferragamo Turnover, 1988–2019 (in € millions)

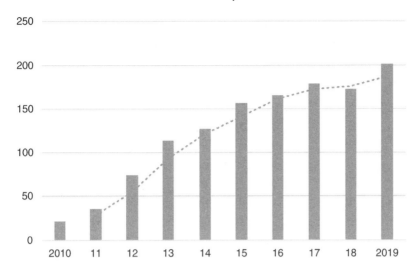

Figure 7.6   Roger Vivier Turnover (in € Millions

recognizable (and intensively exploited) metallic rectangular buckle. These are the shoes that the actress Catherine Deneuve wore in the movie *Belle de jour*, directed by Luis Buñuel. Yves Saint Laurent had designed her wardrobe.

Without a huge communication budget, the development strategy has been based on creativity, exclusivity, highest luxury, and a direct and franchised network of stores. They started opening one store per year until 2009. They had 14 stores in 2012 and 68 in 2020. The brand life cycle illustrated in Figure 7.6 shows that the brand is continuing its selective expansion while maintaining its exclusive positioning. After a slight sales decrease in 2018, the brand follows its growth period.

The Birth of a Brand

How are brands born? We are talking here of strong brands, ones destined to make their mark. One thing is sure: fame can't be planned. This is as true of brands as it is of individuals. Certain measures and resources can aid their ascent, but success is never guaranteed.

Very often a strong brand has its origins in an ambitious project supported by the faith of a talented individual. This will often be the founder of the company, whose confidence in his or her underlying vision and ability to make it a reality are determining advantages. Boldness, vision, and determination are indispensable qualities.

Innovation is the second essential factor. Creative genius consists of reading the mood of the times and offering products that respond to it in novel ways, be it at the level of style, technology, or in the identification of a new need. In the category of stylistic innovation, we find all the great names of haute couture, ready-to-wear, and accessories: Coco Chanel, Christian Dior, Yves Saint Laurent, Salvatore Ferragamo, Giorgio Armani, Miuccia Prada, and, more recently, Jimmy Choo, Michael Kors, Marc Jacobs, and so on. These creators were able to express new ideas that captured the interest of sufficient numbers of people to justify the launch of a durable economic activity.

In the area of technological innovation, there are all the great pioneers of the automobile industry: Ford, Ransom Olds, Bugatti, Panhard, and Renault. Of course, the likes of Thomas Edison, Guglielmo Marconi, William Hewlett, Dave Packard, Bill Gates, and Steve Jobs also belong on this list, as does Walt Disney. Steve Jobs occupies a special position, as he innovated technologically as well as aesthetically. Some of the founders of Internet-related brands like Jack Ma (Alibaba), Jeff Bezos (Amazon), and Larry Page and Sergei Brin (Alphabet/Google), for example, have created some of today's most valuable brands.

The innovation we are speaking of is rarely synonymous with invention because it is integrated with the conditions of distribution of the product. It often operates through appropriation or extrapolation of techniques already worked out on the theoretical level, to which it gives concrete industrial reality. It is true, for example, that Bill Gates was not an inventor of software, but it is also true that this visionary businessman understood, before most people, the potential of the microcomputer and was able to turn it to his advantage.

Consequently, there are many dimensions of innovation. They can be in the development of a specific production tool that makes mass production of a new product possible. Innovation can also consist of revolutionizing the production or distribution of an existing product, or the way in which a business or its associated services are organized and conducted. Aside from the fact that the company knit in white yarn and dyed pieces to suit demand, Benetton was born of an innovative system of distribution. Zara's success arose out of a revolutionary logistical organization allowing 10 days' response to identified market needs. Ray Kroc founded McDonald's in 1955 and invented fast food. Prada began to make a name for itself through the use of nylon in the manufacture of its bags.

This was before the Internet. Since the early 2000s, we have witnessed the most revolutionary phenomenon impacting consumption and the plethoric creation of new brands owing their existence to the Internet. It will be no surprise that the six biggest companies by capitalization in 2019 were all Internet- and technology-related: in descending order, Microsoft, Apple, Amazon, Alphabet, Facebook, and Alibaba. The branding evaluation done by Interbrand in 2019 was consistent with the company capitalization and gives Apple, Google, Amazon, and Microsoft as the first four most-valued brands. The Internet has unleashed infinite possibilities for business innovations.

In particular, the rise of e-commerce platforms is having a durable impact on the luxury business and has been the opportunity to launch new kinds of distribution brands. They function as virtual department stores and are having an important effect on the luxury industry. While most of the luxury brands have been developing their own e-commerce activities, they also use the e-commerce multibrand platforms such as Alibaba, Lazada, Amazon, Shoppe, Zappos, Amazon, and so on. Alibaba Group created Luxury Pavilion in 2017 that tries to bring the same feeling of exclusivity that a brick-and-mortar store would provide. Brands such as Burberry, Hugo Boss, La Mer, Maserati, Guerlain, and Zenith are currently sold on their site. Many of these new brands born on the Internet such as Farfetch, Yoox Net-a-Porter (acquired by Kering in 2017), and Bonobos (acquired by Walmart) are focusing on established luxury brands and are evolving fast. Yoox Net-a-porter is expanding from pure e-commerce distribution companies to service brands providing white label digital support to designer brands through its YNAP platform.

In the fashion business, illustrious personalities like Louis Vuitton, Carl Franz Bally, Enrique Loewe, and Guccio Gucci were not creators in the stylistic or technological sense of the term, but artisans who developed their industrial and commercial vision beginning in the mid-nineteenth century.

At what exact point does a brand become a brand? The question is somewhat rhetorical, but a few commonly used indices can be mentioned here:

- When the brand's creator dies and the brand continues to prosper.
- When advertising is no longer needed to sell the products.

- When a €40 million sales volume is reached.
- When new categories of products can be developed successfully.
- When more than 50% of the general public in a given country are familiar with the product/company's existence.
- When the product/company has established a presence in Europe, the United States, and Asia.

We feel that any economic activity has within it the seed of a brand that will develop if internal and external conditions are favorable. Most brands started with the activities of small-scale artisans or merchants. It is even more true today that the Internet gives the impression that you can communicate and distribute easily online and with minimum investment. There are also many brands that are not international and have low name recognition that continue to prosper.

The Growth of a Brand

In a growth phase, a brand will implement a strategy of expansion, both quantitative and qualitative. Most brands that are successful today are in this phase of development, and are characterized by two-figure growth rates as we have seen for Gucci and Saint Laurent.

On the quantitative level, the brand will try to establish itself in new geographical markets while expanding its presence in its existing markets. The logic of volume is more evident in this phase; more has to be sold in order to absorb fixed costs more easily. But, since communication is generally managed in terms of a percentage of sales, the greater the sales, the more the brand will communicate.

On the qualitative level, the brand will optimize its production and distribution tools, possibly improve its product, and use its growing reputation to move into new areas. Such extensions through launching new categories of products are, of course, a growth factor, but they also increase awareness of the brand by making it more widely accessible, thanks to multiple and/or wider distribution channels. They plant the seeds of future legitimacy in new sectors. The budget for communication and strengthening the brand's identity can then serve as an umbrella for several categories of products and becomes more easily justifiable.

The fact that there are multiple axes of development—sectoral growth, geographical expansion, the introduction of new product categories, the optimization of internal processes, and repositioning the brand—explains why this phase can last several decades. With the exception of sectoral growth, these are all ways by which a brand can take market share away from its most significant competitors.

Sectoral Growth.   Sectoral growth, selling more of the product category we are already active in, is the most immediate growth axis. This is the realm of product innovation. The most visible case of rapid sectoral expansion is the explosion in the market for mobile phones, where we have seen the double effect of the market expansion, as more consumers are acquiring a phone, and the continuous product innovation and fashion fads enticing existing customers to acquire the new models. However, this single axis cannot ensure stable growth in a market that is volatile or is rapidly reaching saturation.

Geographical Expansion.   As soon as a product is successful in one country, it is logical to think that it should sell well in other countries. Attempts to put this into practice are varied and take on a great diversity of forms. In some cases, especially in the mass market, the same product, with the same communication strategy, can succeed. This is the worldwide strategy of Coca-Cola and Pepsi Cola, for example. We are not strong advocates of universal communication, which we feel is now applied increasingly less; and even in the cases of these products, which rely on target populations sharing transnational values (youth, dynamism, a relaxed attitude toward adults), there is room for adjusting to local conditions. In the case of certain big advertisers, the central marketing teams send out a complete, flexible kit that, for example, utilizes the same strategy but with different approaches. Thus, each national team can choose the particular campaign that will be most applicable to its environment. The Internet has increased greatly brands' capacity for adapting communication to specific markets. There is nothing easier than opening a new URL for local operations.

This is also what is done with all fashion and perfume brands, a large percentage of whose sales are to overseas consumers. The advertising will generally be identical. In certain cases, however, it may have to be modified slightly for cultural reasons, for example, for the Persian Gulf countries.

In the cosmetics industry, the product will be identical, but the communication will vary depending on the country. In one country, the product may not serve quite the same function as in another. In the United States, for example, a Yamaha 125cc motorcycle is a leisure product; in Southeast Asian countries, it's a means of transportation. In such cases, the advertising will be different.

There are also cases in which the product is different while the communication remains more or less identical. For example, in the Asian markets, certain cognac producers market sweeter versions of their products. While the name remains the same and the advertising is similar, the formula might be adapted to meet the needs of local taste.

There are cases, in the detergent business for example, where both the product and the communication differ, but they are generally outside the luxury categories and therefore not within the purview of this study. One may also think, for example, of a shampoo for which the world communication (using a universally known actress) will be distributed all over the world, but whose formula will have to adapt here or there. In countries where the water is calcareous, it will be necessary to develop a certain type of formulation; in others with softer water, this will not be necessary. In some countries, the standard bottle is 8 or 12 ounces (236.5 or 320 ml); in others, it will only be 100 or 125 ml.

This diversity of situations is a good illustration of the many difficulties that can be involved in exporting a brand. Cases of failed geographical expansion are legion. Leaving aside organizational dysfunction related to a poor understanding of local conditions, a brand, or its product, can sometimes prove simply not to be exportable. There are products that have a cult following in a given country, but whose potential outside the national borders is limited. Pastis 51 and Suze, typically French aperitifs that are popular in France, are difficult to export. Martini is drunk in its red sweet version with a slice of orange in Europe and as a cocktail with gin or vodka and olives in its white version in the United States.

Another type of brand that is very strong in its own country but difficult to export is the department store. There is a lot of academic literature on the many failures as well as successes that have hit distribution brands. Walmart withdrew from South Korea in 2006 after eight years in the market and closed its 88 stores in Germany the same year after 18 years of operation. One of the most known and recent examples of internationalization failure is the withdrawal from China of the French retailer Carrefour (the second-largest retailer worldwide) in 2019, after 24 years of operations. Carrefour had its share of problems in Asia where it closed, after disappointing performances, its operations in Thailand in 2010 and Malaysia in 2012. It was one of the largest retailers in France (and the world), but it still had difficulties expanding into Asia. Mitsukoshi in the United States, Target in Canada, Marks & Spencer's in Canada in 1999 and in continental Europe in the early 2000s, Starbucks in Israel and Australia—the list is long of the exportation difficulties of the department store/supermarket format.

The French might wonder why the Galeries Lafayette stores have not succeeded in locating elsewhere—in New York, Singapore, Bangkok, or Berlin. The explanation is simple. The success of the Galeries Lafayette in France is linked to a certain French lifestyle, represented by a group of French brands that are known and liked by French consumers. In Berlin or New York, those French consumers are not present, and brands thought of as representing French chic are not necessarily available to the store; if they are very strong brands, they already have a presence in the target market, often through exclusivity agreements with other local department stores or with their own boutiques. The challenge is that of creating a French lifestyle abroad, without French customers and without the leading French brands. It's hard to build a strong case for the existence of such a store.

Zara is a special case. The company's growth has been happening without advertising (except for the sales period) and has been based on the opening of new single-brand stores outside Spain, relying on its skill in reading trends and its rapid logistical responsiveness. In 1975, Amancio Ortega created Inditex, the owner of the Zara brand and the biggest fashion group in the world today, with 7,490 stores in 93 markets worldwide with sales of €26.15 billion in 2018, 12% being made online.

In conclusion, while geographical expansion would seem to be the most natural dimension of development, it is also complex and requires time and heavy investments. In addition, the results are often unpredictable, as we have seen in the geographical expansion of retail chains. The process of development on the international level makes it a wide open, complex, and risky game.

The Internet is not revolutionizing the geographical game completely, as might have been expected. If e-commerce allows for an immediate ubiquity, it is still essentially dependent on other factors on the logistics aspects of business. The brands aiming at a universal unique e-commerce site soon discover that language, taxes, currencies, deliveries, returns, and after-sales services are geographically related and a major part of the success of the business.

New Product Categories.   It's natural to want to amortize communication efforts over a larger number of products. That is why the development of new categories has always been a favorite area for brands. One of the keys to success is a correct reading of the lines of relatedness between the original product and the area of diversification.

The Michelin Guide (1900) and roadmaps (1910) are an interesting historical example of this type of diversification. The promotion of automobile tourism by a tire manufacturer showed a concern for innovation, but also fit perfectly into the context of an industry that was in its infancy. At the time, the automobile remained a leisure item for the privileged classes rather than a general means of transportation.

If diversification seems natural in the fashion and luxury milieu, it's because couturiers became aware very early on of the importance of their brand. The famous No. 5 fragrance, launched by Coco Chanel in 1921, is still one of the world's best-selling perfumes in 2020. During the past decade, this trend has reached feverish proportions, with the launch of new products that are sometimes quite removed from the legitimacy of the original products.

The couture brands, without venturing too far from the original matrix, first moved into secondary lines: Rive Gauche for Yves Saint Laurent, Ungaro's Ivoire and Emanuel, Versus by Versace, "Emporio Armani," D&G for Dolce & Gabbana (then successively folded into the Dolce and Gabbana brand in 2011), Donna Karan's DKNY, and so on. Then, during the 1990s, they developed lines of accessories (luggage, shoes, silk articles, eyewear), a sector with higher margins and rates of growth and also an effective vector of communication.

Ungaro, after being taken over by the Ferragamo family in 1996, launched a line of accessories but was unable to develop them successfully. Louis Vuitton began offering shoes. Loewe did the same, only to discover that one doesn't become a shoemaker overnight, and that to succeed with a new category of products, one has to be able to get across to the consumer a message of seriousness and competitiveness, not only in terms of product quality, wealth of the offering, and service at the point of sale, but also, above all, coherence with the brand's values.

Going in the opposite direction, the accessories brands (Ferragamo, Gucci, Bally, Prada, Loewe, and so on) diversified into ready-to-wear. They developed (generally through licensing) a line of eyewear, perfumes, and, often, watches. Bulgari began as a jeweler, and then developed accessories and perfumes. Jewelry and watch-making took on importance in the mid-1990s. Christian Dior and Burberry developed some feminine lingerie around 2010.

Finally, the hospitality business is attracting the luxury brands. In 1987, Maruccia Mandelli (Krizia) opened its K Club hotel in Barbados. The Ferragamo family began investing in it in the mid-1990s, but without associating its brand with it. Armani, in the wake of the launch of its Armani Casa products and stores, invested in hotels in Sardinia. Bulgari has associated its brand most openly with the industry in a joint venture with Marriott International Luxury Group to create Bulgari Hotel & Resorts, in which Bulgari is in charge of decoration and Marriott handles management. There is also Versace, which opened the Palazzo Versace in Brisbane in 2000 and intends to develop in this sector. After all, creating a living space—if well done and compatible with the brand's values—should be an effective way of moving toward achieving the coveted status of lifestyle brand.

On the other hand, hotels, museums, and universities have been developing their souvenir merchandise for a long time.

Other types of companies have also taken an interest in the potential offered by diversification. Marlboro launched a line of clothing in keeping with the mythology of the wide open spaces of the West, on which it has based its advertising for decades. Coca-Cola has opened single-brand stores to sell a whole series of gift and souvenir items, from T-shirts to coffee mugs, including such items as trays decorated with advertisements from the 1930s. Disney, Warner Brothers, and even soccer clubs (Manchester United, Juventus of Turin, Real Madrid) have successfully developed this diversification toward gift and souvenir products.

Most automotive and motorcycle brands have started offering clothing and accessories more or less associated with the use of their basic products. The Pirelli brand was one of the first to move into shoes, watches, clothing, and, above all, calendars with the success we all are aware of.

A remarkable financial performance through products as well as customer-segment extension has been achieved by one of the most luxurious of brands: Ferrari. They licensed their brand to a limited and selected number of producers and retailers of luxury goods proposing sportswear, watches, accessories, consumer electronics, books, and so on, distributed through 20 directly owned stores and 24 franchised stores as well as on their website. It also ventured in theme attraction parks. The Ferrari World Abu Dhabi park opened in 2009, where an all-around Ferrari experience can be enjoyed. The second park opened near Barcelona in April 2017. More will follow. Out of the total 2019 revenues of €3.8 billion, 14.3% are generated by the new brand extension activities.

The motorbike brand Ducati is following the same strategic direction, showing more than 25 licensees on its website in 2020, with brands like Microsoft, Puma, Mattel, and so on.

For certain brands, such incursions can be regarded as being merely speculative, with no real development ambitions and far removed from the core products and the brand identity. Such is clearly the case with brand restaurants, which have met with varying degrees of success (Lustucru, Eurosport, and Nescafé in Paris). And one may also wonder what future there is in Harley-Davidson fragrances. Others, however, have succeeded over the years in developing new territories of legitimacy that have made them stronger.

Time is the essential factor here. In his determination to reduce the number of brands in his group, Edwin Artz, former CEO of Procter & Gamble, would urge his people to: "Find the way, the unique selling proposition or the reason for being, which will enable you to sell several products under the same brand."

The second key to the success of a strategy of product diversification is the brand's degree of conceptualization. The more the values expressed by the brand are conceptual in nature, the easier it becomes to adapt to different and seemingly unrelated product categories. This has led to the current vogue for the lifestyle brand, the natural culmination of the principle of diversification. The concept is a strong one. It aims at all objects and services people use every day—what they wear, eat, drink, and smoke—but also their residence or traveling environment, including furniture, bedding, wallpaper, decorator items, draperies, floor tiles, paint, tableware, luggage, and so on. The lifestyle is carried through to the hotel in which they stay, the car they drive, the way they travel, and even the friends they have. Having a single umbrella brand is a way of guaranteeing the profitability of all the investments made on the promotion of this all-encompassing identity.

For brands whose identity was originally founded on a lifestyle, product diversification is often easy. Such is the case of Ralph Lauren, which promotes the traditional New England WASP lifestyle. All the products, which incorporate tableware and entertainment as well as paint for customers' homes, are very well presented in stores, particularly in the flagship on Madison Avenue in New York, where the lifestyle being offered is very clear.

Other brands, whose identity is strongly linked to a product or to specific signs, have more difficulty or are more prudent. Missoni, which established its identity for a specific type of fabric and a specific chromatic palette, does not venture far from the domain of clothing, a few accessories, and home products. Their partnership with the Rezidor Hotel Group to open a Hotel Missoni in Edinburgh in 2009 followed by one in Kuwait will stop operating in June 2020.

Besides, the most original initiatives are not necessarily crowned with success. They may result in a temporary gain in fame for the brand, but without paying back the investment they represent. Consumers are always there to remind us that the further products depart from the domain of established legitimacy, the more difficult it is to score a quick success.

We cannot conclude this section on diversification without a mention of the new brand Fenty, created by the singer Rihanna with the financial support of the LVMH group and launched in 2019. The brand will offer ready-to-wear, shoes, accessories, and jewelry. It is not the first time that products are developed under artist names that have already gathered recognition. Stella McCartney (even if it was her father's name that was known), Picasso, Jay-Zee, Pharrell Williams, Kenny West, and so on have developed sizeable businesses in clothing and accessories.

Diversification, then, is an area that can be profitable if a general principle—intelligent relatedness—is adhered to. But this is not always obvious. It's important to take every precaution, to be skilled in piloting the evolution of the brand or the characteristics of the products over time, and, above all, to respect the limits of evolution of the brand's identity. Hermès's product category development strategy is an interesting model to draw inspiration from. Over more than a century, they have grown from saddles to leather goods, silk products, ready-to-wear, watches, shoes, jewelry, and fragrances. Now in 2020 they are entering the cosmetic field by launching in March the Rouge Hermès collection made up of 24 lipsticks.

Louis Vuitton just opened their first restaurant in Osaka, Japan on January 31, 2020, inside its new flagship store, offering Japanese food curated by chef Yosuke "Suga" Sugalabo.

Optimization of Internal Processes.   This is an area of development that is too often neglected because it is too difficult to deal with. It's easier to design and open new points of sale than to reduce the development time of a product. Yet optimizing internal processes is what often succeeds in taking market share away from direct competitors. In the fashion sector, receiving products from new collections promptly means increased sales and, above all, significant increases in margin. As an example, a one-week delay for a ready-to-wear shipment to one store means an average loss of 2.5% of sales of the season. This is based on the hypothesis of a 50% sell-through of the collection in the first five months in the store before the one month of discounted sales.

Reducing the development time for new products (that is, the time to market, the time that elapses between the initial concept and the availability of the product for sale) can be the decisive competitive weapon in numerous sectors, including automotive, food products, telecommunications, clothing, and accessories. An effective reading of market signals, product design oriented toward surpassing the competition and satisfying target customers, production that adheres to quality standards, and flawless logistics that supply distribution networks at the proper time all have a positive impact on brand performance.

Brand Repositioning.   In fact, the term that should be used here is adjustment. By repositioning, we generally mean the *great leap* (double somersault) that takes place when a brand exchanges its existing clientele for another one that strategists are more comfortable with. This operation is fraught with risk and obviously would not be undertaken by a brand in its growth phase. As we will see, it is a radical remedy, more frequent in phases of decline. In the case of a growing brand, the action is subtler. It aims at making the brand more attractive without alienating existing customers.

When Marc Jacobs was recruited by Louis Vuitton in 1997 to develop a ready-to-wear collection, many people were skeptical. The first fashion show got a cool reception from the press and the brand's hard-core fans. They had trouble seeing the connection with the art of travel or the conservative spirit that had come to be associated with the brand's identity. However, fashion, which had seemed incompatible with the brand at first, proved to be an unexpected source of dynamism. The fashion shows and the opening of global stores in Paris, London, and Tokyo expanded its media coverage, and the choices made for the collections proved to be a tour de force in rejuvenating the brand's identity without alienating existing customers. The sales volume of the fashion and leather-goods branch of LVMH—where Louis Vuitton represents the majority—increased from €3.6 billion in 2001 to €22 billion in 2019 and represents 41% of the group turnover. We estimate the sales of the Louis Vuitton brand in 2001 to be €900 million and, in 2019, €13 billion. French fashion designer Nicolas Guesquière replaced Marc Jacob in 2013 as creative director of the house.

This success is the result of a profound understanding of the brand's identity and of the way it is perceived. Louis Vuitton was able to find in its historical identity the elements of a fashion discourse. The values of tradition associated with his luggage connote not so much conservatism as excellence and distinction—the nostalgic evocation of a time when travel was still an adventure and the domain of a small circle of privileged individuals. Nostalgic exoticism abounds in the fashion magazines today, but style counts less than fantasy. The brand has made extensive use of this imaginary assets. In a time of massification and homogenization of leisure, where the trend is toward the search for originality and refinement, such distinctive signs have undeniable seductive power. Louis Vuitton itself perpetuates this tradition by publishing books that are appropriate to its brand territory. In 1994, the collection *Voyager avec…* (*Travels with…*) offered authors' travel accounts. The *Carnets de Voyage* (*Travel Notebooks*) presented the world's great cities in the form of colorful illustrations. The *Louis Vuitton City Guide*, launched in 2005, is becoming a must for high-end tourists.

What we call the turbo effect of fashion is also at work in the case of Coach, an American luggage brand with handcrafted origins founded in 1941. Designer Reed Krakoff was recruited from Tommy Hilfiger in 1997 to give Coach—known until then for its sturdy leather bags—a fashion aspect and, in the words of its CEO at the time, Lew Frankfurt, to "invent the classics of tomorrow." The brand has also introduced new categories of products (shoes, eyewear, watches) and the talent brought to bear has reaped success. In 2013, Stuart Vevers joined Coach as executive creative director. In 2019, Jennifer Lopez became the chosen celebrity to represent the company globally, confirming the solid anchoring of the brand into ready-to-wear and accessories. Now Coach has transformed into the multibrand group Tapestry, which bought shoemaker Stuart Weitzman in 2015 and Kate Spade in 2017 to reach a group turnover of $6 billion in 2019.

One of the latest examples of the turbo effect is the success that Burberry has been experiencing since 2001. Superb ad campaigns blending modernity and British tradition, a product offering with appropriate prices, the systematic use of the brand's famous tartan—all these strategic choices have paid off.

In these three examples, the turbo effect works because it is based on an intelligent transposition of the brand's identity values—its invariants—to the stylistic grammar of fashion. Far from being an obstacle, the traditional connotations of Louis Vuitton or Burberry become in themselves the sign of a certain imaginary world that can be reinvented, extended to other products, and adapted to the taste of the times. These successful adjustments show an accurate assessment of the brand's identity and of how it is perceived by the markets. Such strategies, when they meet with success, lead to substantial increases in growth rates.

Conclusion on Brand Growth.   The lessons to be learned from the examples we have looked at include the following:

- The less the values expressed by the brand's identity are conceptualized, the more difficult it is to adapt to new product categories.
- Time alone lends legitimacy to brands that penetrate new product sectors, but only to the extent that these new products fit within the brand's preexisting ethics and aesthetics (or cause it to evolve while

respecting a certain continuity) and where the brand shows tenacity, authenticity, and determination with its new offering.

- It is wise to approach any drastic change in brand identity with great circumspection in a growth phase. When the *great leap* is made, it is never clear whether the new clientele will more than compensate for the one that may be alienated. It's a risky exercise that is best applied to brands in decline.

- All growth areas have their limits. Maturity lies in wait for brands, as it does for human beings.

The Maturity of a Brand

This is the time of optimum cash flow, but also the time to wake up. Generally, the rate of growth has been in the single digits for several years: decline is approaching.

In ordinary language, we would say that a new lease on life needs to be found, and that is what brand managers of mass-consumption products most often work at. They try endlessly to improve the technical performances of their product. But they also introduce novelty in the form of product extensions, say, a lavender or lemon–lime version of a fabric softener or a room deodorizer. This diversity, of course, entails additional production and storage costs and, above all, a business volume that is averaged downward by the lower-selling products. This sometimes requires reworking the existing sizes to make sure that the diversity of packaging is matched by the performance of each of the new varieties.

The period of maturity, then, is a period of broadening and diversification of the product offering. One product may specialize in a single form and function while another is launched to cover another application, but care must be taken to avoid excess. When Pampers, for example, launched its disposable diaper differentiated for girls and boys, it seemed like a very creative idea; but what did mothers really think of it? This is perhaps best gauged by the fact that the experiment was quickly abandoned.

Chanel, which has been facing the challenges posed by maturity for several years, reacted by broadening its product offering and launching—with much effort and impressive results—a leather-goods line, then a line of watches, and finally a line of luxury jewelry. What can come next? Products for men. Besides the already existing neckties, cologne, and fragrances, ready-to-wear for men has been available in some stores since 2016 and can be seen in women's fashion shows.

In this maturity phase, the same possible growth vectors exist as in the preceding phase. The sole difference lies in the fact that certain brands are capable of anticipating their maturity and possible decline while still experiencing strong development, while others can only resign themselves to their fate.

Decline, Relaunch, and Death

Decline is announced by a progressive loss of market share and decreasing sales volumes. At this point, there are only three possible developments: continuing decline over a more or less long period, followed by the death of the brand, or its relaunch.

Continuing Decline.   This period can last as long as financial resources permit. Such is the relatively common case of brands that have been trying for several years to curb a decline that is not yet under control. Examples are numerous. In 2000, Bally's business volume had been decreasing since the early 1990s, and in that time, 12 top management teams and two shareholders had strenuously attempted to turn the tide. Losses had been accumulating. Since then the company has been sold by Texas Pacific Group, which acquired the brand in 1999, to Luxembourg-based JAB Holding, which in turn sold it in 2018 to the Chinese multibrand group Shandong Ruyi. At the time of this latest acquisition, indications were given that Bally was on the path to profitability—the turbo effect of fashion doesn't work for everyone. Escada is another long decline story. It filed for insolvency in 2009, changed hands several times, and has been owned since 2019 by Regent, L.P., a US private equity firm. Dunhill, Kodak, Robert Clergerie, Diesel, Charlotte Olympia, Jaeger, BCBG Max Azria, and many other brands have been attempting for many years to engineer an upturn, often without visible results and sometimes seeing an acceleration of their decline, like Roberto Cavalli, whose US operations went bankrupt in 2019.

In the digital world, the history of Second Life, the 3D online virtual world launched in 2003, is close to a perfect brand life cycle curve. The game saw rapid growth in the initial years, reaching a peak in 2007 of approximately 1.1 million regular users. Then growth stabilized and started declining. It is difficult to get accurate data on the number of users today. Different sources estimate it at between 500,000 and 800,000. It does not seem to be in expansion anyway.

Brand Death.   Death comes from a lack of financial resources, caused by the erosion of demand, or as a result of a management decision.

Management can condemn a brand to extinction at the time of its acquisition. When the Spanish department store chain Corte Ingles bought out its competitor Galerias Preciados from Venezuelan financiers, it kept the best sales outlets and got rid of the others, but put all the stores under the single Corte Inglés name. Overnight, the Galerias Preciados name disappeared, as also happened in France with the Nouvelles Galeries after their purchase by Galeries Lafayette. The stronger, more evocative name won out. In the department stores sector, we need to mention Barney's New York, which filed for bankruptcy for a second time in 2019 (its first filing came in 1996). The filing was in part due to the high rent requested by the landlord. Even if the name survives, it is not going to be the distribution brand we have known.

Decisions on product portfolio rationalization, motivated purely by economic interests, are not without risk. Particularly in the case of prestige products, such as automobiles or watches, whose added value is high and very apparent, disappointed loyal customers can expose a brand to harsh penalties. This was made very clear in the Peugeot group's tampering with the Simca brand in France. Simca represented a brand in its own right, with a network of dealers who were proud to sell the cars and serve customers who were devoted to the brand. Simca was more than a name on the hoods of cars; it was a world, a virtual universe. Thus, rebranding Simca as Talbot was bound to upset many customers who used to be emotionally involved with the brand.

Still, brands do die. The automotive world is a source of many examples: Panhard, Simca, Talbot, Hispano-Suiza, Studebaker, Mercury, and so forth. General Motors announced in February 2020 that it was "killing off" the Holden brand, which existed in Australia and New Zealand for the past 160 years. Brands are also disappearing due to strategic failures. The Hummer brand, having not found a buyer in 2010, dies victim of its positioning in frontal opposition to the ecological and peaceful sensitivities of the market and the impact of the 2008 financial crisis on General Motors.

The service sector is also not free from resounding disappearances. The case of Arthur Andersen was emblematic. A global benchmark among the five leaders in the corporate audit market disappeared into the whirlwind created by the 2001 Enron's bankruptcy scandal for betraying its own raison d'être.

The banking sector also has its brand casualties. UBS in 2002 announced the termination of activities under the prestigious brands of Warburg and Paine Webber, which would be carried out by the parent company under the UBS brand. The Lehman Brothers brand, for its part, disappeared in the whirlwind of the crisis of which it was the catalyst.

Fashion has seen also some resounding disappearances—not only fashion precursors like Paul Poiret (founded in 1903) and Louise Chéruit (founded 1906), but much more recent examples like Sonia Rykiel, which was forced into liquidation in 2019 as no investor showed interest in the brand and as the owner was unable to turn it around. The story is sad and quite educational. The brand was founded by the eponymous founder in 1968 and it rapidly prospered to reach a turnover of €84 million in 2011. It was acquired in 2012 by First Heritage Brands, part of Fung Brands, an investment group led by the billionaire brothers Fung of the Li & Fung manufacturing organization based in Hong Kong. They also bought Robert Clergerie and Delvaux. In 2018, the company sales had fallen to €35 million. A number of reasons have been given to explain such a loss: bad artistic decisions, wrong recruitment, mismanagement in general, technological myopia, disengaged investors, and a weak retail presence in China. For sure the magic rapport between the customer and the founder, a lady who designed clothes for the modern, working, and independent woman, an active proponent of women's liberation, had disappeared.

Brand deaths are obviously triggered also by technological obsolescence. Betamax, the Sony Walkman, and Kodak cameras have all fallen into the history pits.

Relaunch.   The last means for a brand to achieve growth is through what we have called the *great leap*, which, to date, few brands have succeeded in making. The term generally refers to a repositioning of the brand to encompass a programmed change of clientele. It applies to companies in decline that have already undergone heavy restructuring and improvements to their internal processes and products but without managing to reverse the trend.

The decline of a brand is always visible in an erosion of its relevance to consumers. The brand and its products are no longer interesting, or, rather, they are less interesting than those of competitors. The evolution of the brand's identity that results from a successful relaunching plan is a synthesis of the brand's response to this problem.

Gucci cases of spectacular relaunch have already been covered in section 7.1. It should be noted that each major relaunch was rendered possible thanks to a drastic change of brand identity. The brand managed creatively today by Alessandro Michele, where no specific ethics or aesthetic invariants can constitute a recognizable identity, bears little resemblance to what it was when Tom Ford took over as creative director in 1992. His action at the time abandoned the brand's traditional values—quality craftsmanship, the Italian jet set of the Cinecittà years—and were replaced by the universe of the Hollywood swingles. Seduction was central to all of the brand's discourses, whereas now we are dealing with eclectic and gratuitous surprise. In the two cases, the clientele, probably almost entirely renewed, has more than compensated for that which abandoned the brand.

The Sleeping Beauties: A Special Case of Relaunching.   While companies sometimes sacrifice their brand, its fame may survive indefinitely nevertheless. Names such as Panhard or Hispano-Suiza are still alive in the imagination of several generations, though the plants that produced the cars have long since disappeared. Such resilience can, in the case of most prestigious brands, also lead to their resurrection (as, for example, with Westinghouse). There is the case of the famous Orient Express, now a registered brand, the property of Belmond Ltd. (LVMH), a hospitality and leisure company involved in luxury hotels, train services, and river cruises worldwide, or Solex motorbikes, acquired in 2013, by the Easybike company.

The examples of reviving sleeping beauties have been increasing in the past 15 years: Goyard, bought in 1998; Roger Vivier, which we mentioned earlier in the chapter, in 2001; Vionnet in 2006; Schiaparelli in 2007; Moynat in 2010; Shinola in 2011. In the world of motorcycles, the classic Indian brand that was the principal competitor of Harley-Davidson until 1953 was bought in 2011 by the industrial group

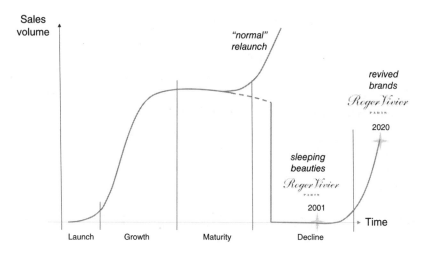

Figure 7.7   Reviving Sleeping Beauties

Polaris after two reactivation tests in 1999 and 2006, which ended in failure.

Once woken up, brands may go through several successive recovery tests—like Halston, for example, created by the American designer Roy Halston Frowick (1932–1990), who dressed the most elegant Americans like Lauren Bacall, Elizabeth Taylor, Jackie Kennedy, and Liza Minnelli. After Halston's death, a dozen revival projects were attempted with new designers without proven success.

As shown in Figure 7.7, the brand life cycle allows an effective visual representation of cases of relaunching sleeping beauties.

Other Possible Uses of the Brand Life Cycle

Figure 7.8 shows an example of how a private equity company whose objective was to acquire luxury brands could present in a schematic way the types of luxury brand it was interested in acquiring, highlighting on a single diagram sizes, stages of development, and geographical locations.

The Identity Prism

We are going to discover that a limited number of nonsemiotic tools exist to analyze and formalize brand identity. In 1992, Jean-Noël Kapferer

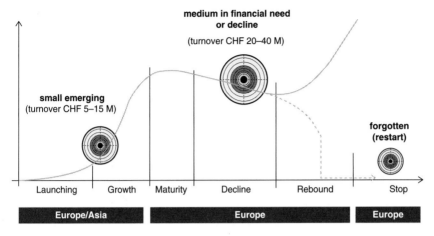

Figure 7.8 Typology of Targeted Companies by a Private Equity Fund: Emerging, Declining, and Forgotten Brands

introduced the first comprehensive analytical tool for dealing with the complex area of brand identity: the identity prism,[1] which is presented in Figure 7.9 (applied here to Hermès) and functions with six dimensions positioned around a prism.

The *physique* of a brand relates to the concrete elements that come immediately to mind when the name of the brand is mentioned. It is a set of sensory and objective characteristics, exemplified by the following:

- Aubade: women's sexy lingerie.
- Hermès: a Kelly crocodile handbag and a silk carré.
- Levi's: a pair of blue jeans, with a distinctive label.
- Toblerone: a chocolate bar in a yellow and red package with a triangular section.
- Brioni: an expensive Italian men's suit
- Ferragamo: Vara women's shoes with a grosgrain bow.
- Bally: a pair of shoes
- Tod's: moccasins with rubber plots
- Ferrari: a red racing automobile
- Ducati: a red motorcycle with a tubular trestle frame

---

[1] J. N. Kapferer, *Strategic Brand Management*. New York: Free Press, 1994.

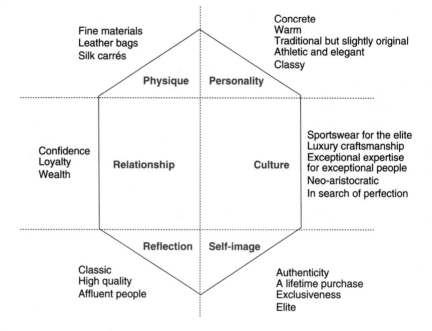

Figure 7.9   Brand Identity prism applied to Hermès (2020)

- Opinel: a pocketknife with a wooden handle, fitted with a safety catch
- Burberry: the tartan pattern

A brand's *personality* is apprehended by means of questions such as: If it were a man, what kind of character would he have? Professional, aesthete, performance oriented? Original, like Audi? Colorless and odorless, like Opel or Hugo Boss?

The brand's *culture* is linked to the original values of its creators, often the culture of the country, the region, or the city where the brand developed: Madrid for Loewe, Sicily for Dolce & Gabbana, Majorca for Majorica, Japan for Shiseido, Paris for Chanel, and so on. But the geographical dimension is not the only one expressed. Hewlett Packard, for example, puts forward the garage spirit of its two gifted pioneers and the spirit of an American entrepreneurial company.

Relationship involves the social communication of the brand. A brand with strong identity influences relations between individuals, first through signs of belonging to a group, and then well beyond.

What do people think when they see me stepping out of my Maserati or wearing the latest Zegna suit? Dolce & Gabbana strongly suggests seduction; Diesel, provocation; banks, confidence in general.

The brand's *reflection* describes the typical customer the market associates with the brand (the customer it imagines for it). This is not to be confused with the target customer: Kapferer is referring here to the market's perception.

The brand's *self-image* corresponds to the image consumers have of themselves when using the product. When a man lights up a Marlboro, climbs into a Porsche, or puts on an Armani suit, how does he perceive himself?

Kapferer's prism introduced a major innovation. It was a tool that, for the first time, made systematic study possible while showing the complexity of any approach to brand identity. Nevertheless, it does have limitations.

Self-image and reflection—the two sides of the mirror, as Kapferer calls them—are receptive in nature; they have more to do with the perception of the brand's identity than with the identity itself. As for the relationship dimension, it belongs more to the cultural domain. Personality and culture overlap. After having used it ourselves numerous times, our judgment is that the prism is a useful tool but tricky to use, in particular because of the lack of homogeneity in its categories. The physique, culture, and personality dimensions of the prism are directly related to the ethics and aesthetics of the brand as introduced in the previous chapter.

The Rosewindow

This is another nonsemiotic brand identity analytical instrument, created by Marie-Claude Sicard in 2002.[2] It is another model that we find very much in tune with our postmodern times: the rosewindow (see Figure 7.10).

The brand is considered as a trace (like a scar or a footprint). It is drawn from the field of cognitive sciences, in which each situation of communication is the result of the overlapping of seven contexts, namely:

---

[2] M. C. Sicard, *Ce que marque veut dire*. Paris: Éditions d'Organisation, 2002.

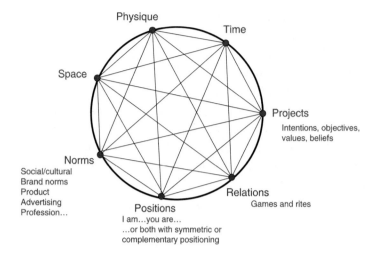

Figure 7.10   The Rosewindow (Marie-Claude Sicard)

1. Physical and sensory
2. Spatial
3. Timing/historical
4. Positional (of the two actors: the customer and the brand)
5. Relational (social context determining the quality of the rapport between the two)
6. Normative (the cultural context of socially shared norms and rules)
7. Actors' respective and perceived intentions (called projects)

These seven contexts are then represented as seven poles of equal importance, constituting a network where any impulse on one transmits to the whole system. Brands need to play on at least three poles, with at least one in each group. One group is made up of the tangible poles: space, physique, and time. The other poles are of a conceptual nature.

The more poles that are activated, the richer the brand identity. Strong brands use 7 out of the 21 possible itineraries (at least four poles). This model represents a major departure from the previously presented approaches, as it maintains that the brand itself has no soul, no nucleus. It is what the brand managers and the customers make of it. The brand identity is then made up of the most frequent itinerary taken by the brand among several poles during a given period.

We mention this model for its originality; however, the absence of a core to the brand identity, as we have defined brand ethics and aesthetics, makes it difficult to manage. Moreover, it does not define what good brand identity management should be.

For time, space, and affinity constraints, we will leave aside all the other models developed by the American school around the notion of brand equity, made of economic and symbolic values, which is based largely on the perception consumers have of brands in terms of awareness, recall, recognition, and associations. We don't use them and therefore don't feel qualified to discuss them fully.

The Semiotic Square

After the signifier/signified hinge and the derived EST-ET$^©$ diagram, a third semiotic tool can be used to make a more profound analysis of a brand's identities: the semiotic square, of which three types were already presented in Chapter 1.

The semiotic square is a visual representation of this developed articulation of a semantic category. The model "invented" by Greimas actually goes back to Aristotle's logical square, but it is reformulated here on the semantic horizon of languages and not on that of logic alone. It is based on two major differences: the qualitative difference of opposition on a specific semantic category and the difference by negation called contradiction relation.

When Jean-Marie Floch used the semiotic square in studying Ferragamo's brand identity in 1992, he was really the pioneer in the use of semiotics applied to luxury brands.[3] The square has since come into widespread use by advertisers, specialists in brand management, and trend agencies.

This diagram aims at describing a situation not in terms of static objects, specific events, and the like, but in terms of dynamic relations. To provide an analogy: in describing a boxing match, a commentator can concentrate on the actions, the physique, and the personality of each boxer but can also choose to concentrate on the flux of punches exchanged (contacts, acceleration, deceleration), since the dynamics of

---

[3] Jean-Marie Floch had also used the same technique in defining the layout of a hypermarket in the Lyon area in 1986.

the bout are what occupy our attention more than the identity or the presumed motivations of the fighters. Even if we know very little about the latter, this approach can still be used to describe the fight. In the same way, the power of the semiotic square lies in its ability to organize an abstract universe coherently, in spite of the fact that it is not recognized as being rational itself. It can point out meanings that are present, from a logical point of view, but latent, not yet active. It can also describe the way in which new meanings will appear.

This approach begins with Saussure's assertion in 1916 that any system of meaning is a system of relations and not only a system of signs.[4] These relations are established between semantic poles (a thing and its opposite form two poles united by a relation of opposition) to constitute semantic categories and axes of dynamic significance. For example, the category "gender" exists only to the extent that gender is articulated as a relation between masculine and feminine. Relations are considered as taking precedence over their terms, which are only the intersections of those relations. Therefore, in structural semiotics, there is meaning only if there is a differential between two terms and therefore that the relations between the terms prevail over the latter. According to this structural principle, which wants meaning to emerge only from difference, a category is therefore not a word but a relation between words, a relation of opposition, hierarchy, implication, and so on, which ensures the definition of the terms: "cold" means as opposed to "hot," "closed" only exists by virtue of "open," and so forth.

Faced with the universe of a brand, the driving concept, defining its identity, will therefore always be understood in a relational dynamic of difference and opposition. This is related to the dialectics we have introduced in the previous chapters. The control of latent meanings is a primordial issue in the management of a brand, and the semiotic square, developed over time by Greimas and Courtés (1979)[5] and Floch (1983),[6] has proven its usefulness.

---

[4] Ferdinand de Saussure, *Cours de linguistique générale,* compiled by Charles Bally and Albert Sechehaye, with the assistance of Albert Riedlinger. Paris: Payoy, 1916 (1995).

[5] A. Greimas and J. Courtes, *Dictionnaire Raisonné de la Théorie du Langage.* Paris: Hachette, 1979.

[6] J.-M. Floch, "The Contribution of Structural Semiotics to the Design of a Hypermarket," *International Journal of Marketing* 4, no. 3 (1988): 233–253.

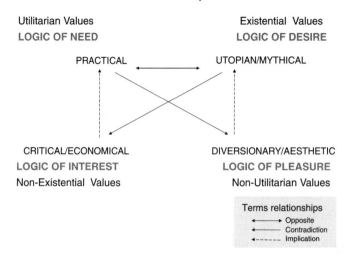

Figure 7.11 Semiotic Square of Consumption Values (J.-M. Floch)

Jean-Marie Floch (1983) considered the square to be "both a model thanks to which semioticians can represent the minimum conditions of meaning production and a precious tool for so-called 'qualitative' studies insofar as it responds to the triple scientific requirement of non-contradiction, completeness, and simplicity."[7] He has developed numerous squares in a large number of fields, but the most widely used (including by communication agencies) is that of consumption values (Figure 7.11). It is a fundamental methodological tool in the analytical panoply of semiotics applied to marketing. Floch used it in his studies for many brands in the most diverse fields (Ferragamo, Yves Saint Laurent, Lancôme, Chanel, Bally, Watermann, Loewe, Apple, RATP, Urgo, Opinel, Citroen, etc.), or even for the preparation of political programs or the analysis of works of art (Kandinsky, Boubat, Cartier-Bresson, Doisneau, Stieglitz, etc.) and comics (*Tintin in Tibet*, by Hergé). It is today the most widely used (and perhaps the most overused) semiotic tool in the world of communication and trend research. All the talent of the semiotician, applied to the understanding of the meaning production mechanisms of a specific brand, lies in his ability to discern the most relevant semantic axis (the category).

---

[7] Floch, "The Contribution of Structural Semiotics to the Design of a Hypermarket."

It is no coincidence that our "lifestyle hypermarket," as Gilles Lipovetsky describes our civilization as one of consumption, the square of consumption values highlights the four main motivations of the postmodern consumer. We observe that the majority of brands are striving today to develop the mythical and fun aesthetic dimensions of their offer and their identity, as this judicious square provides. It is true that, more deeply, this relationship between utilitarian values and existential values is not original: it refers to the old rhetorical topography of means and ends, and implements the primary mechanisms of all planned human action.

This type of analysis was conceived for structured stories, ones that are self-contained in a certain way. To apply the semiotic square to the analysis of brands, we must accept the presupposition that a brand can represent a micro-universe of meaning. Once this semantic axis, consisting of two opposites (practical—or convenient—and utopian), which applies ideally to the mechanisms of consumption, is in place, the semiotic square can be used to develop all its nuances.

Each of the contrary terms can be seen in relation to another term, differentiated by the absence of the characteristics of the first (contradictory). The contradictory to practical corresponds to the non-practical, that is, the diversionary, the playful, the aesthetic. The contradictory of utopian corresponds to the non-utopian: the critical, the utilitarian. On the left-hand side of the square, vertically, are two propositions where the term critical or non-utopian implies what is practical and utilitarian. On the right-hand side, vertically, we will find the utopian/mythical and the diversionary.

The power of the square lies in its capacity to organize an abstract universe in a consistent way. It allows the emergence of existing but latent meanings and the description of the way they are going to come up. Placing the accent on mechanisms of meaning is by no means superfluous where brands are concerned, because the problem here is that of defining the communication on which they base a large part of their relations with consumers.

We present here a study made of Salvatore Ferragamo in 1992 (Figure 7.12); it is remarkable how valid the study still is in 2020, proof that the brand invariants deserve their name. It was our first contact with semiotics. The study was conducted by Jean-Marie Floch and François Schwebel, who were then working with Creative Business, at

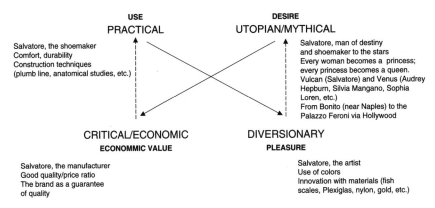

USE
PRACTICAL

DESIRE
UTOPIAN/MYTHICAL

Salvatore, the shoemaker
Comfort, durability
Construction techniques
(plumb line, anatomical studies, etc.)

Salvatore, man of destiny
and shoemaker to the stars
Every woman becomes a princess;
every princess becomes a queen.
Vulcan (Salvatore) and Venus (Audrey
Hepburn, Silvia Mangano, Sophia
Loren, etc.)
From Bonito (near Naples) to the
Palazzo Feroni via Hollywood

CRITICAL/ECONOMIC
ECONOMMIC VALUE

DIVERSIONARY
PLEASURE

Salvatore, the manufacturer
Good quality/price ratio
The brand as a guarantee
of quality

Salvatore, the artist
Use of colors
Innovation with materials (fish
scales, Plexiglas, nylon, gold, etc.)

Figure 7.12   Salvatore Ferragamo (1992–2020)

a time when Ferragamo was developing its ambition to become a global brand beyond Italy, the United States, and London.

The figure gives a general and structured picture of the evolution of the brand's positioning. It gave rise to a plan of action for products and communication. The choice was made to stress the right side of the square—the non-practical dimension of the brand. Note that the launch of the first Ferragamo perfume, with its heavy advertising, was meant to contribute to strengthening that mythic and aesthetic dimension. Strong brands in general are present on the four summits of the square, which means they are able to satisfy most of the purchase motivations.

The existential/practical semantic axis has been used extensively, but it is far from providing answers to all the questions relative to brand identity. Another axis introduced by Jean-Marie Floch proved highly useful in the case of Loewe and Bally. This semantic axis could be called authenticity/superficiality, that of perpetuating signs as opposed to producing meaning (see Figure 7.13).

Floch proposed a classification of luxury brands into two major categories: those that produce their own meaning (the "substance" brands) and those that exploit signs (the "sign" brands). The brands that desire to be seen as authentic seek to position themselves on the upper-right corner of the square, especially those that have talented and renowned designers, such as Chanel at the time of Lagerfeld, Jean-Paul Gauthier, and Christian Lacroix when he was still in charge of his brand creations. Brands like Louis Vuitton, Goyard, or Burberry, which make a

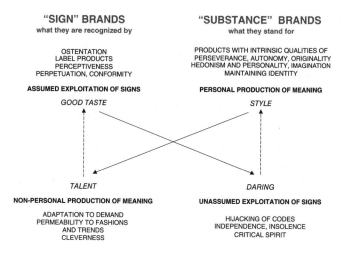

Figure 7.13   Two Basic Brand Positionings

systematic use of repetitive graphic codes (monograms), are positioned on the upper-left corner. Brands like Zara, which have the talent (or business system) of reading market desires, are on the lower-left corner. Eccentric brands like Paul Smith or Moschino are located on the lower-right corner.

Brands evolve over time, and although they are all present, with varying intensity, on the four corners of the square, some may drift from one corner to another, as Ferragamo did. It was originally positioned on the style corner (at the time of the founder Salvatore) and now finds itself on the good taste corner, because of the ubiquity of the "gancino" (the ubiquitous small decorative metallic hook) on many brand products.

The semiotic square renders possible the structuring of many paradoxes or dialectics of the types we have seen in Chapter 6. It can represent schematically the two major brand strategies we identified in the previous chapter: authenticity versus gratuitous design, as shown in Figure 7.15. But before reaching that stage, we have to introduce the two axes used in this diagram (Figure 7.14).

This diagram stems from the semantic axis built on "brands focusing on their identity (me and me)" versus "brands focusing on the markets (me and them)." We can geometrically cross the two contradictory axes of the semiotic square to build a diagram as shown in Figure 7.14. The vertical axis shows the notion of authenticity, here taken as being

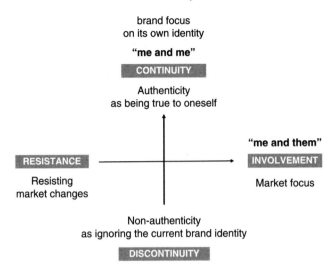

brand focus
on its own identity

"me and me"

CONTINUITY

Authenticity
as being true to oneself

RESISTANCE

"me and them"

INVOLVEMENT

Resisting
market changes

Market focus

Non-authenticity
as ignoring the current brand identity

DISCONTINUITY

Figure 7.14   Two Strategic Options: Market-Centered or Self-Centered Brands

true to a brand's own identity. It may be surprising at first to imagine brands not cultivating their own identity, but there are numerous examples today of brands doing exactly this and ignoring what and who they have been so far. Some mid-market fashion brands like Sandro and Maje or the Kooples are trying to serve their existing markets without having a strongly established brand identity beyond the values expressed by their existing customers. The horizontal axis represents the degree of orientation to the market.

The space is then divided into four quarters corresponding to specific strategies (see Figure 7.15):

Q1 is characterized by efforts to maintain both identity and the markets served, as achieved with success by brands like Ralph Lauren and Loro Piana.

Q2 shows brands that remain true to their identity while exploring new market possibilities, like Ferrari with its derived products and services. The area covered by Q1 and Q2 is where authentic brands are positioned.

Q3 is the interestingly very creative area of brands like Gucci and Loewe that are exploring new markets without any restraints from what the brand used to be.

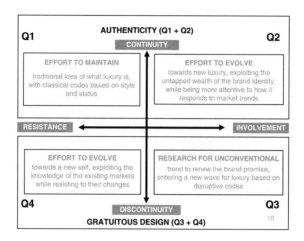

Figure 7.15   Authenticity and Gratuitous Design Brand Strategies

Q4 is where brands are more attached to their existing customers than to their own identities. CFOC (Compagnie Française de l'Orient et de la Chine) is positioned in this quarter. It proposes fashion, home products, food, and any other cultural "products" such as books, movies, or events, promoting Eastern historical and contemporary designs. The area covered by Q3 and Q4 illustrates the gratuitous design approach, gratuitous only because these brands are not trying to perpetuate or create aesthetic invariants for the brand.

Figure 7.16 presents some brands as examples positioned on the diagram. One of the applications of such a diagram can be of an instrument of internal communication, as we did at Jim Thompson in 2016 showing, with an arrow on the chart, the proposed change of strategic focus.

The semiotic square, by its nature, cannot offer exhaustive analyses. It nevertheless contributes to giving in-depth perceptions of domains that are too often neglected by the traditional instruments of marketing and strategy. Above all, it can structure universes, industry sectors, brand strategies, consumer behaviors, market trends, and so on.

A last example of utilization of the square should contribute to establish its versatility. We can apply it to Baudrillard's thesis on hyperreality,[8]

---

[8] J. Baudrillard, *Simulacres et simulations*. Paris: Editions Galilée, 1985.

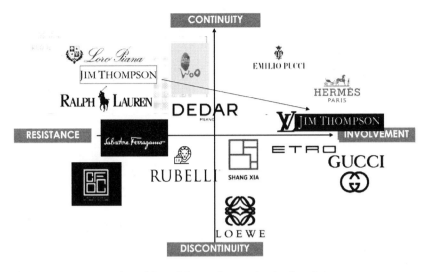

Figure 7.16   Examples of Brand Strategies on the Authenticity versus Gratuitous Design Brand Square

which we mentioned earlier to characterize designs without any signified dimension.

According to Baudrillard, the four successive phases of images are:

1. The reflection of basic reality
2. The perversion of basic reality
3. The masking of the absence of reality
4. Hyperreality with signs that have no referent and therefore are their own pure simulacrum

We can organize a semiotic square developed on the semantic axis to "show the existence of reality/show the absence of reality" the four propositions of relationship between representation and reality that the author proposes (see Figure 7.17). The semantic axis is an axis of transparency because the two poles expose existence or the absence of reality. Hyperreality shows the absence of reality through an image that no longer has any reference: it is transparency open to emptiness. The other two contradictory poles, "hide the absence of reality (playing with appearances)" and "hide the existence of reality (the bad appearance)," implement opacity.

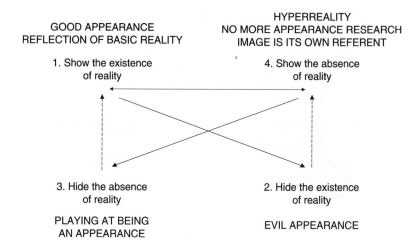

Figure 7.17   Structuration on a Semiotic Square of Baudrillard's Thesis on the Four Progressive Stages of Image.
Source: G. Mazzalovo, "Deus ex Opacitate: El administrador de sistema," in M. Serra and O. Gomez (eds.), *Transparencia y Secreto.* Madrid: Visor Libros, 2015. Acts of the seminar organized in Madrid by GESC (Grupo de Estudios de la Semiotica Cultural) in 2013.

Semiotic Mapping

Andrea Semprini takes the original semiotic square of consumption values introduced by Floch and turns it into a more malleable and more legible tool for marketers.[9] The principal semantic axis is transformed into the ordinate axis of a two-dimensional graph (Figure 7.18.). All the nuances of value, from the most practical to the most utopian, can be positioned on this scale. The coordinate axis (critical/diversionary) intersects the preceding one to form a semiotic mapping.

The advantage that mapping has over the square is that a spatial continuity is created on which each positioning is relative to all the others. Its author rightly insists on the fact that the mapping, like the practical/utopian square, presents consumption values, not attitudes and behaviors. These individual behaviors (passion, enthusiasm, indifference, rejection, and so on) will correspond to the strategies each consumer puts into practice to pursue the consumption values. Semprini analyzes in detail the four quadrants delimited by the two axes:

---

[9] A. Semprini, *Le marketing de la marque.* Paris: Editions Liaisons, 1992.

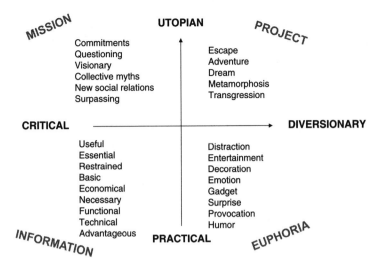

Figure 7.18   Semiotic Mapping of Consumer Values (Andrea Semprini)

- The northwest quadrant is called *mission*: the convergence of critical and utopian values leads directly to the will to surpass the present, projects toward the future, and seeks innovation. It is the combination of duty and a constant striving toward different worlds. Benetton in the late 1980s (at the time of the launch of the United Colors campaign), with its billboards showing young people of all races, characterized this positioning. The brand was offering an ideal world based on new types of social relations. The Body Shop and Dove, with their commitment to natural products, are other examples of brands located in this quadrant.

- The northeast quadrant, called *project*, conserves the willful dimension of the first quadrant, but the collective commitment is replaced by an individual quest for emotion. There is a strong propensity to embark on personal projects in the desire to find solutions to existential problems. Brands such as Swatch and Ungaro are positioned there.

- In the southeast quadrant, *euphoria*, the convergence of diversionary and practical values, is propitious for brands such as Oasis or Gillette, whose discourse is positive, reassuring, and relatively pragmatic. These are the brands that focus on the intrinsic attributes of their products: serenity, good feelings, and happiness for all. That, for example, is Calvin Klein's Eternity perfume. A variant of this quadrant is made up of brands like Moschino or Diesel that entertain using surprise, humor, and provocation.

• The southwest quadrant is the most immediately understandable. At the crossroads of the practical and the critical, the values presented are resolutely linked to the quality aspects of the products offered. The essential, the advantageous, the strictly necessary, the rational, and the useful are uppermost. This is the information quadrant, where mass-retail brands such as the Walmart and Kmart hypermarket chains are positioned.

Semprini also uses his mapping to analyze the brands' discourses concerning time, space, passions, relationships, and so on. The instrument proves to be just as powerful as the square, versatile, and more flexible to use. It introduces an infinity of combinations, focuses, and differentiations of consumption values that make it possible to comprehend a significant part of the complexity of brand identity management. Figure 7.19 presents an attempt at positioning several brands.

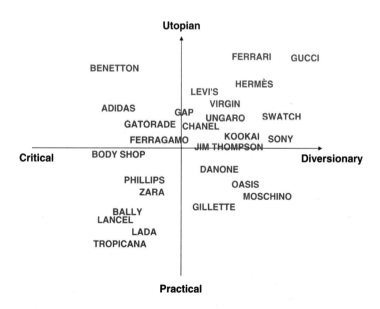

Figure 7.19   Positioning Brands on the Semiotic Map

The Narrative Scheme

At a time when storytelling is fashionable in academic marketing circles, this scheme originally developed by Vladimir Propp (1928) for the analysis of Russian fairy tales may prove to be a useful method for structuring brand speech. Propp's conclusions largely innervated the work of Greimas and structural semantics. The four episodes that make up the logical sequence of any story are:the contract, the skills (or expertise), the performance, the sanction (Figure 7.20.).

The utilitarian and existential values presented on the consumption square are in fact taken from narrative semiotic. In any story, the life values that give meaning to the hero's quest can be identified. These are generally existential universal values which motivate the hero's actions: good, beauty, glory, sacrifice, love, freedom, and so on.

The practical values, on the other hand, are secondary, instrumental, and represent the means necessary to the hero for attaining his existential objective. Example: the hero's search for a sword made of a magical alloy (a practical value) with which to kill the dragon and free his people (a life value).

In the first stage, the protagonist accepts a contract (challenge, promise, leaving to seek adventure); he or she then acquires

Contract	Competence	Performance	Sanction
Brand ethics	The company's	The company's	Brand perceptions
The company's	business areas	activities	Notoriety
philosophy	Its special expertise	Products offered	Desirability
Its world	Human resources	All consumer	Performance
vision	Distribution network	benefits	compared to
What it	Financial resources	Imaginary world	competitors
stands for	Patents, copyrights	offered	
	Management quality		
	and culture (vision,		
	coherence,		
	determination,		
	clarity, etc.)		

Figure 7.20   The Narrative Scheme (Jean-Marie Floch)

competencies (the classic initiatory stage); in the third, the protagonist successfully carries out the action or program with the aid of the competencies acquired, and within the framework of the system of values (contract) that defines his or her action. Finally, the protagonist is rewarded (or punished): the sanction is the measurement of performance of the initial contract.

The mention of the narrative scheme is not gratuitous, since one of the objects of semantics is to categorize the invariant elements of any form of discourse. If we can therefore assimilate a brand to a complex set of projects or actions that take place within the framework of a value system, then we are in the presence of stories, discourses, tales, to which we can apply the methods used in narratology.

The tool has less analytical power than the signifier/signified hinge and the semiotic square. It nevertheless constitutes a useful method of structuring a brand's discourse.

The Semionarrative Scheme

We could also call this tool the "generative journey" (Greimas and Courtés, 1979).[10] It is based on the hypothesis that the production of meaning is a generative process of complexification in a sort of "mille-feuille" (puff pastry) arranged in three consecutive strata. The first layer, the axiological level, is the deepest, simplest, and most fundamental level. It is also the least visible and requires research. It is made of values (elementary structure, semiotic square, position of the brand on life, death, justice, love, norms) that are the source of the brand identity, its meaning, and its duration and ensure continuity, permanence, and legitimacy.

The third layer, the most immediately visible, is the most articulated, specific, and superficial structure (discourses, images, figurative forms, enunciation). It is where the values are enriched with objects, forms, colors, persons, styles, logos, and so on. This level puts into life and context the underlying narrative structures that we find at the second intermediary level.

The second layer is composed of intermediate semionarrative structures (general syntax of modalities, actors and programs, scripts).

---

[10] Greimas and Courtes, *Dictionnaire Raisonné de la Théorie du Langage*.

The theoretical and operational challenges are to define the two "conversion" procedures between the three different strata, starting from the surface (the way which it offers itself to the eye) to go toward depth (the axiological base on which it bases its coherence) through three major operations:

1. The setting in values
2. The setting in narrative ("la mise en intrigue," the script)
3. The setting of the stage, the setting in signs ("la mise en signes," "la mise en scène," the brand manifestations)

Semprini (1992) applies the scheme to the development of the Régie Autonome des Transports Parisiens (RATP) logo (Figure 7.21).[11] RATP runs the Paris public transportation system (buses, tramways, and subway). It is present in 14 countries and is a global leader in urban mobility. Its values are humanistic and technology at the service of man's mobility.

Such a tool can be used for each individual manifestation, logo, event, advertising, product, and so forth. This is a simple model whose progressive logic allows the researcher to go back to the axiological

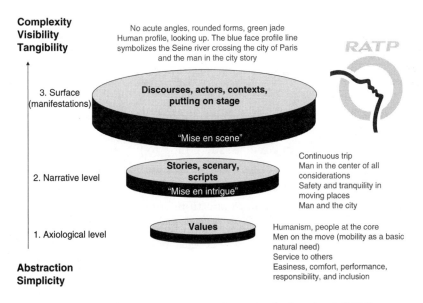

Figure 7.21 The Semionarrative Scheme Applied to the RATP Logo

---

[11] Floch, "The Contribution of Structural Semiotics."

invariants (ethical, technical, utopian, etc.) fundamental to the identity of a brand from its manifestations.

The intermediate stage of narrativization ensures the "ascent" from deep structures to surface structures. The relative weakness of this generative model stems from the fact that it only supports the content plan of brands' discourse and ignores their plan of expression. The brand identity hinge introduced in Chapter 6 fills this gap.

A Few Words on Semiotics

As *semiotic* has been used extensively in these last two chapters, we thought it would only be logical to spare a few lines on this discipline. Semiotics is about the study of the production of meaning. It analyzes the signifying structures that shape our discourses by considering them from the point of view of production and reception: its objective is to understand and to make people understand how we understand, when we read, when we see, when we hear—in short, when we perceive a text, an image, an object, a behavior, a space—and everything that makes sense to us. The semiotic gaze goes beyond the sign, but it passes through it.

If we consider, like Heilbrunn and Hetzel (2003)[12] that "marketing essentially refers to the intelligible management of a set of various signs (products, logos, commercial space, advertising documents, etc.)," we understand the privileged relationship that the two disciplines, semiotics and marketing, have developed since the innovative work of Roland Barthes, Algirdas Julien Greimas, and Umberto Eco in the 1970s, alongside Baudrillard's critical reflections on consumption. Jean-Marie Floch (1990),[13] one of Greimas's disciples and the first to develop a semiotics of marketing and corporate communication, considered that his discipline could serve as "an additional toolbox in the panoply of brand managers." Rossolatos also states that "the conceptual and methodological platform

---

[12] B. Heilbrunn and P. Hetzel, "La pensée bricoleuse ou le bonheur des signes: Ce que le marketing doit à Jean-Marie Floch," *Décisions Marketing* no. 29 (2003).

[13] J.-M. Floch, *Sémiotique, Marketing et Communication. Sous les signes, les stratégies.* Paris: Presses Universitaires de France, 1990.

for designing and managing brands as a sign system is the province of structural semiotics."[14]

From Semiotician to Manager

Most of the instruments presented so far are taken directly from the discipline of semiotics. We have pointed out that such tools require that we accept the following quite reasonable hypothesis: brands are systems of meaning.

From a manager's perspective, the tools we have described have a decisive advantage in that they elucidate and make the internal control of the brand's discourses possible. Paying careful attention to the brand's discourses and the meanings it intends to produce is an elementary part of a responsible manager's professionalism, and also of a responsible consumer's vigilance, since they are the primary recipients of the brand's messages.

The minimum of respect due to each of the stakeholders dictates that the brand make sense. This seems to go without saying. However, it's also a much simpler means of being competitive. Amid the media bombardment we are subjected to today, having something interesting to say is one of the conditions for effective communication. In fact, semiotics and advertising have had a privileged relationship from the start. After all, what is advertising's task if not the intentional production of meaning using signs?

All of the semiotic tools discussed must be used with an awareness of their limitations. Clearly, semiotics is incapable of the following:

- It is never able to create.
- It cannot invent a style or a best-seller.
- It does not attempt to substitute itself for the creativity of designers and publicists.
- It is never exhaustive in its approach.
- It is not a recipe for management problems.

However, it does deal with the mechanisms of the creation of meaning, and therefore can:

---

[14] G. Rossolatos, "Applying Structural Semiotics to Brand Image Research," *The Public Journal of Semiotics* IV, no. 1 (2012).

- Point up the brand's fundamental invariants, if they exist.
- Provide a framework within which everything that speaks about the brand, and therefore all its manifestations, must be situated: it determines the domain of the possible and that of the plausible.
- Manage the consistency among the different signals sent out by the brand.
- Manage the consistency between the brand identity and all the brand manifestations.
- Facilitate the strategic choices directors of brands must make.

Semiotics is at its most effective when it is coupled with analysis from other disciplines, like trend surveys on consumption on the chosen consumer segments, specific consumer behaviors analysis, competitor monitoring, and so on. In cases where semiotic analysis doesn't initially show solid results in identifying the brand's ethical invariants, other elements taken from market studies must be brought in. Semiotics is then used to rework these elements and draw practical recommendations.

We can affirm that semiotics' major contribution to brand management is in consistency but is only marginally helpful in managing relevance. Even so, it is one of the rare tools that can get away from the subjective considerations of the different players and pose the question of the brand's identity objectively. This is in no way a guarantee of creativity, but in the context of the diverse collectivities any company represents, that objectivity already represents considerable progress.

Some Quality Criteria for a Semiotic Analysis

What makes a good semiotic analysis? It is a frequent question. In order to help marketing researchers, brand managers, and readers of semiotic articles to form an opinion, let's see how we can recognize a quality semiotic analysis study from a less complete, detailed, or relevant one. Three main criteria can be used for this purpose: suitability or adequacy to the object, generalization beyond the object, and the capacity for questioning that the study opens up.[15]

---

[15] D. Bertrand and G. Mazzalovo, "Méthode sémiotique: de la structure au sensible," chap. 11 in *Méthodes de recherche qualitatives innovantes*, edited by Pierre Romelaer and Lionel Garreau. Paris: Economica, 2019.

1. Suitability (or adequacy). The analysis models used must allow entering into a more intimate proximity to the object studied, identifying the hidden meaning mechanisms but also the weaknesses in consistency and main issues raised by the object of study.

2. Generalization. Beyond the knowledge of a particular object (e.g., packaging), the study must allow a progressive extension to all the manifestations of a brand to reveal its different dimensions (in terms of expression and content). The results of this first generalization ensure comparability with other entities in the same sector. One of the capacities of semiotics is to allow the analysis of dense and complex corpus, to extract the threads of meaning production, and to lead to a synthesis whose condition of credibility is the objectivity of the analysis.

3. Questioning. The results of the analysis must lead to operational recommendations, justified by the analysis itself, hierarchical (that is to say, part of a strategy) and open to confrontation, in the case of multidisciplinary studies (e.g., semiotic and qualitative studies). But the essential lies in the "black boxes" whose secret world a successful semiotic study is capable of exposing: it must, from the fine and rigorous observation of its objects, reveal the unexpected, identify a weak signal, anticipate an emerging problem, explain the implicit. The ability to raise new questions is without doubt one of the most important criteria for a successful semiotic study. It thus contributes to the strategic thinking of companies, mobilizing, beyond the objects, all the components of meaning, and offering, beyond immediate operativity, a possible prospective vision.

Two other analytical instruments derived from semiotics, the exhaustive list of brand manifestations and the chain of communication, are shown, respectively, in Chapters 8 and 9.

Chapter 8

Creation and Merchandising

Whave insisted in previous chapters that creativity is one of the basic success factors and characteristics of the luxury industry. The high intensity and the broad scope of the creative activities are the foundation of most luxury brand success stories, if a certain number of conditions are met in terms of relevance, organization, processes, and business model. In simpler words, creative talents are necessary but not sufficient; one still needs to make money from this creativity. The luxury industry is famous for believing too often that the designer's genius transcends any market considerations. It may take the long years of experience of Christian Lacroix in the LVMH group—from the creation of his maison de couture in 1987 until its sale to the Falic Fashion Group in 2005, a period in which no profit was ever realized and where the cumulative losses reached more than €200 million to prove that sheer recognized and original creative talent needs to be framed by a competent business prescriber. Even the Falic brothers have not found the solution to transform Christian Lacroix's creative talent into an actually viable economic venture. In 2009, the fashion house was declared in default.

Most frequently, the creative process in the luxury business starts with a specific market segment being identified as promising by those in charge of the business or commercial part of the company. We refer to the people identifying the market opportunities as *prescribers* because their function is similar to that of an architect prescribing the use of certain materials or a doctor recommending a certain cure. The prescribers in turn commission the product, giving the creative department a list of descriptive specifications regarding number of product groups, function, price, and expected volume. In US and Anglo-Saxon companies, the marketing prescribers are known as merchandisers. We find in US department stores the position of general merchandise manager (GMM), with the responsibility of defining the merchandise strategy, leading the buyers' team, defining product assortments, prices, and expected sales volumes per retail location. This is the acception of the term *merchandiser* that we will use.

Figure 8.1 shows the typical sequence that a luxury product follows, from its concept to its presence in the distribution networks. For the design of technical products, the prescriber can be the marketing or commercial department or the CEO, depending on the type of organization. There, the creation function would be split among product concept, design, and engineering. We will focus on the model shown in Figure 8.1, which is prevalent in luxury ready-to-wear or accessories, whereby the prescription emanates from the merchandising manager. For mass-market brands or in most non-Anglo-Saxon brands, it would come from the position called product or collection manager.

What is common to any typology of product or service is that the design/creation activities always and systematically follow a business idea; this may be often true for artists too.

We can see in Figure 8.2 a typical representation of the value chain of a luxury brand and a simplified version of the luxury business process. The scheme has been around for a while since its introduction by Michael Porter in 1998,[1] but in our case it helps present the basic organization we have been adopting for the brands we have managed and that we recommend in the luxury industry.

---

[1] M. Porter, *Competitive Advantage: Creating and Sustaining Superior Performance*. Free Press, 1998.

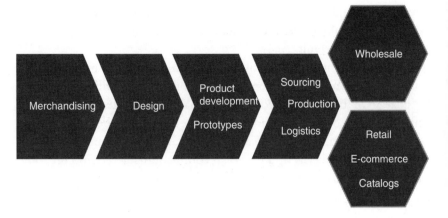

Figure 8.1 Luxury Products Business Process

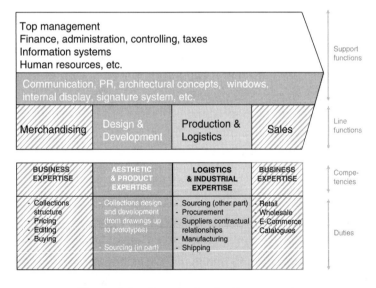

Figure 8.2 Organization by Competencies

The company organization is being built around the specific competences requested by each function:

- Business expertise resides with the merchandiser and sales executives (when these functions are not merged).
- Aesthetic expertise is with the creative director and designers.

- Product expertise is assigned to the product developers.
- Logistic, production, and sourcing goes to the procurement, industrial, and technical experts.

In this chapter we will naturally start where the business starts, that is, the merchandising function, before continuing to the creation phase and concluding with further considerations on brand aesthetics.

Merchandising

The Merchandiser's Responsibilities

The merchandiser is the brand businessman, responsible for sales, gross margin, and inventory. He is also constantly taking the pulse of the market, knowing the customers, closely following the competition, and gathering all the performance data from the company's own retail, e-commerce, and wholesale networks as well as data from the competitors. All these data are then gathered into a collection plan, which describes the number of groups, models, occasions of use, expected sales volumes, places, and prices at which the products can be sold. The price indications determine the maximum cost at which the product can be manufactured because the retail and wholesale direct gross margin cannot fall below certain limits. When competent, these merchandisers are today continuers of the post–World War II US department stores' great merchants like Gimbels, Marcus, Filene, Harris, and so on.

There is also a more restrictive usage of the word *merchandising* to define the way products are presented in a point of sale. In general it has to be specified as visual merchandising. This aspect is covered in Chapter 11, but we will not use this restrictive utilization.

There are two crucial moments in the merchandising process:

1. The preparation of the collection plan and calendar
2. The buying decisions

Figure 8.2 shows that the business expertise is needed at the beginning and at the end of the process. Once the merchandiser has formalized the collection plan, the design and development process starts. When the collections are presented in the form of prototypes, the merchandiser buys into them, selecting what will be manufactured internally or ordered externally and which will be sold in the stores as well as the sample collections that will be presented to the buyers from third-party retailers.

The merchandiser therefore has full responsibility for the merchandise throughout its life. He decides what goes on sale at the end of a season as well as what is going to be continued in the next one. He keeps monitoring the collection's development to ensure that the timing of the presentation of the samples will be respected and making sure that the decisions made by the designers and developers are compatible with the retail price targets.

As the merchandiser is fully responsible for sales, the gross margin, and inventory, it happens often that he is also given full responsibilty for the retail operations. The alternative is to split the retail operations (human resources in terms of recruiting and training, lease negotiations and management, contracts, implementation of window and internal displays, landlord relationships, store construction and maintenance, etc.) from the management of merchandise, including prices and inventories, which remain with the merchandiser.

The Collection Plan

There are two key documents that govern the whole product design and development process: the collection calendar and the collection plan. The latter consists of a detailed description of the products requested to be created and developed in terms of:

- The number of product subcategories and groups, comprising those kept from the previous season and new products. A product group is a homogeneous set of products with similarities of material, form, occasion of use, and so on, such as, for instance, a set of small leather pieces for men made with lizard skin and with a particular metallic decoration or lock.
- The number of products for each group and of models for each product.
- The occasions of use of the various group products (formal, casual, evening).
- The expected volume of each model per specific point of sale (POS).

- The expected retail price and therefore the maximum direct cost of production. This will often include technical specifications for construction or the type of materials required because this will have a direct impact on the manufacturing costs and design choices.

The collection plan is prepared for each major product category and frequently provides supporting analysis based on previous sales statistics, competitors' successes, and the respective positioning of the various groups.

Let's take a real example from the men's ready-to-wear (RTW) world. For reasons of confidentiality, we will call this Spanish brand Don Juan. While the name has been changed, the data used here is drawn from the real world. The brand promotes an identity centered around its Spanish origins and tries to be trendy and up-to-date without being perceived as excessively fashion forward. We will focus on the plan and some documents prepared by the merchandiser for spring season (SS) men's suits.

Figure 8.3 presents Don Juan's position compared to its reference competition with respect to the basic dimensions of price and fashion

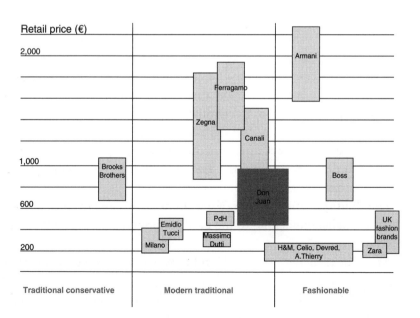

Figure 8.3   Don Juan Suits Competitors Price/Fashion Map

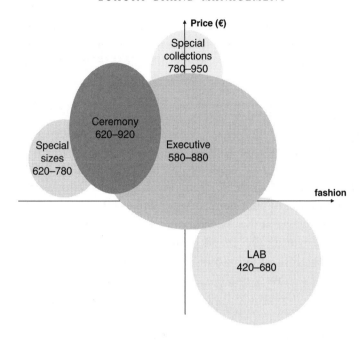

Figure 8.4   Don Juan Suit Collection Structure

content. It is important to monitor the market on a constant basis, and know where the brand wants to compete. The figure clearly shows that Don Juan is positioned between the mass brands competing on price and the global luxury leaders. The fact that it is the only brand daring to promote its Spanish roots as a main differentiating element of its brand identity is seen as reinforcing this unique positioning in a field held traditionally by Italian, US, and British brands. The second document, shown in Figure 8.4, maps the five groups of suits proposed by the brand according to their occasion of use. The size of the circles is proportional to the expected volume of sales.

The third document in the case of Don Juan is a general brief giving more detailed guidelines to the product designers and developers, as shown in Table 8.1.

As can be gathered from the Don Juan example, the merchandiser is the executive really driving the whole development process of the collection, and he needs to have the tools to ensure that all the departments involved are informed and coordinate with each other. There are also other documents covering, for example, the expected volume of sales

Table 8.1   Detailed Merchandising Briefs for Each Subcategory of Suits

---

Suit Collection Development Guidelines for Spring–Summer Collection
- Strong drive toward improved quality and more style.
- Continue the search for quality Spanish fabrics, in addition to Italian and British. Negotiate more exclusive fabrics.
- Continue developing a strongly Spanish modern style, with more recognizable details on the products (lining, stitching, labeling).
- Respect scrupulously the three sub-collection shipments to the stores.

EXECUTIVE collection:
- Only semi-traditional construction.
- 30 different new fabrics. Continuation of the five permanent fabrics.
- Keep the two- and three-button models. Start working on a double-breasted model for next Fall–Winter collection.

LAB collection:
- Only fused construction.
- 25 different new fabrics. Five to eight can be in common with EXECUTIVE.
- Extend the concept of the younger LAB line concept to all the other products for Fall–Winter.

Special sizes:
- Only plain basic suits. Both industrial and semi-traditional construction. Limited to 15 fabrics.

Special collection:
- This season it will be designed by the famous Spanish architect, "X." A special design team with members of both parties is being set up.

---

for each product and each individual model, by point of sale. This information, which can only be estimated, is probably the most difficult to quantify and the one with the most financial consequences. Commitments on fabric orders are taken very early in the process and drive the business gross margins. This is the exercise in which the real professional merchandisers stand out.

The collection plan is the contractual document binding all the departments involved in the development process. It can vary in its format and in the information given, depending on the type of merchandise, the type of brand, and its competitive environment. The plan can take very different forms according to the product category. For a ladies' shoe collection, there are likely to be lines instead of groups, classified by construction, occasion of use, specific soles, or materials. Each line will specify the desired retail price in the reference market, the heel height, and all the different materials that can be applied to it.

For a handbag collection, there are likely to be diagrams of groups positioned with respect to price and occasion of use, from the more formal to the more casual.

For a tie collection, things will be simpler. There will generally be two big categories separating printed silk from jacquard (woven), with a number of repeated and new patterns. The selected manufacturers, when there is no internal manufacturing, will also determine the quality of silk and fabrication and therefore the price.

To highlight the variety of approaches that brands have to the structuring of their offer, here is another real-life example of a men's RTW collection plan, presented in Table 8.2, for a brand that we will call Thomas for confidentiality. Contrary to Don Juan, Thomas is not focused on suits, but proposes a broader men's product offering. The table highlights the degree of details that needs to go into the document. The last column normally shows the total requested volume for each product group, but the data have been removed.

The presentation by the merchandiser of the seasonal collection structure to all parties involved (designers, product developers, retail executives, e-commerce and wholesales managers, communication executives) is the official beginning of the season's work and is a major internal communication opportunity to insure consistency and mobilization of resources toward the season objectives.

One can notice the focus on the number of stock-keeping units (SKUs) by subcategory and the mentioning of the permanent items. One of the crucial decisions to be made by the merchandiser at the moment of drafting the collection plan is the selection of the products that will be continued and those that will be liquidated.

In the case of Thomas brand, the presentation of the merchandiser contained additional detailed documents explaining the logics sustaining the requested collection plan, that is:

- The menswear sales performance in quantity and money for the two previous SS seasons (2018 and 2019), in order to see the dynamics (growth, decline, best-sellers) of each category, group, and SKU.

Table 8.2 Collection Plan for Thomas Brand Menswear SS 2019

Collection Structure – Menswear SS 2020

Category	Material	Patterns	Colors	Details	Permanent Items	SS20 SKUs Needed	Max. Costs/ Unit US $	Expected Volume
Men's Tops								
Men's Shirt	Silk	5	3	Plain + Print Silk Shirt (but prefer no floral prints)	2	10	90	
Men's Shirt	Plain silk	1	1		0	4	70	
Men's Shirt	Cotton	4	3	Print but small scale, not many detailed prints then make easy-to-wear, able to mix & match for all outfits	21	6	35	
					23	20		
Men's Bottoms								
Men's Pants	Silk	2	2	Not too slim fit a style & able to match with blazer for work outfit	0	2	140–180	
Men's Pants	Cotton	2	2	Plain color, may be with different jacquard print that is different from other collections & easy to wear	3	2	40–70	
Men's Shorts	Cotton/Linen	2	3	Loose-fit pants for easy to mix & match with tops/ men's linen shirts	6	2	30	
Men's Shorts	Silk	2	2		0	2	70	
					9	8		

Category		Fabric		Notes			
Men's Outerwear							
Men's Raincoat	1		2	New design. Trench	0	2	120
Men's Jacket	2	Silk, Cotton/Linen	2	Prefer fit & a little bit bigger, a bit heavier a fabric	6	2	100–150
Men's Kimono	2	Silk jacquard	2	Light fabric that is highlighted with silk + jacquard	0	2	60
Men's Kimono	1	Diamond weave	2		3	2	60
Men's Blazer	3	Silk wool, silk jacquard	2		1	4	150
					10	**12**	
Men's Knits							
Mens T-Shirt	5	Pima cotton, silk jersey	3	Need new small print, plain in pima cotton fabric	46	10	10–35
Men's Polo	4	Cotton, pique, silk jersey	3	Plain color + prefer silk with print fabric	14	8	15–40
Men's Sweater	2	Silk wool blend	3	Not-too-thick wool & able to wear with daily life	0	4	20–40
					60	**22**	
Men's Leisure							
Men's Pajamas	3	Silk	2	Silk fabric with print pattern	0	4	100
Pajama Pants	3	Silk	2	Silk fabric with print pattern	0	4	100
TOTAL SKUs REQUIRED – SS2020 MENSWEAR					**102**	**70**	

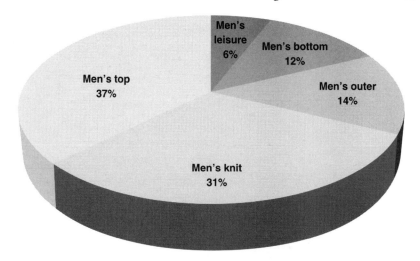

Figure 8.5 Overall Proportions of Thomas Brand Menswear Subcategories for SS 2020

- Detailed store feedback on SS 2018 as well as AW 2018 (important for the permanent items).
- An overall proportion by subcategory of menswear for SS 2020, as shown in Figure 8.5.
- The overall quantity for each SKU (i.e., single specific model; e.g., one color variation is a SKU) for each POS. As a simplification, the retail network is structured into different clusters of POS with similarities in terms of size, display space, typology of customers, and so on.
- Data on reference competitors' best-sellers and prices.

The Crucial Link to Strategies. The collection plan is one of the operational links ensuring the implementation of some major strategic elements. In the case of the Thomas brand, one of the most important strategic directions was to trade up (or reinforce its luxury positioning).

As an example, Figure 8.6 represents the strategic brief given in 2016 for Thomas's necktie business, whereby a whole range of new price positioning between US$100 and $200 was identified as an opportunity and price increases recommended. The merchandiser presented the diagrams of Figure 8.7 to highlight the progress made in following the

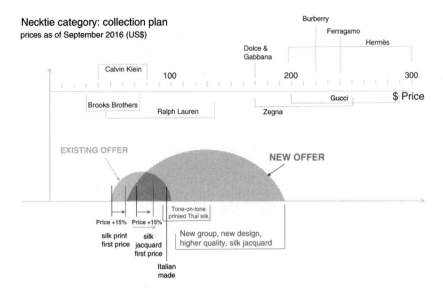

Figure 8.6   Strategic Collection Plan for Thomas Brand's Necktie Category

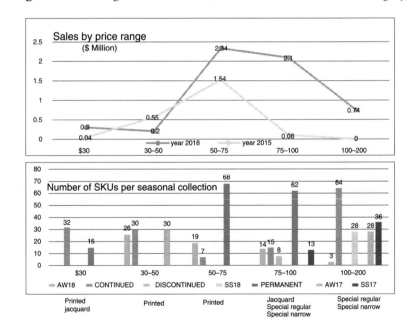

Figure 8.7   Sales of Thomas Brand's Necktie Category between 2015 and 2018 and Number of SKUs by Price Range

2016 strategic recommendations and the new business developed in the new targeted price range. This type of information on sales by SKU number per price range over a period of time makes it possible to monitor one of the most difficult exercise for luxury brands: growing into its luxury positioning.

It should be noted that the essentially strategic decision to add a new category of products—say, shoes for a RTW brand—to the brand offer would be analyzed within the merchandising department.

Pricing. The price indications determine the maximum cost at which the product can be manufactured. The prevailing margin standards in the RTW and accessories luxury industry are 55% gross margin at retail and an absolute minimum of 30% at wholesale. Table 8.3 illustrates a simple price structure scheme. This would have a direct impact on the choice of the quality of leather for a handbag or of the fabric for a man's suit, decisions typically made by the design team with control from the merchandiser.

Table 8.3 Theoretical Price Structure for Luxury Ready-to-Wear and Leather Accessories

Theoretical retail price:	$317.46	$100
Minimum theoretical retail margin:	174.55 (55%)	55
Wholesale price:	$142.85	$45
Minimum wholesale margin:	42.85 (30%)	13.5
Direct costs:	**$100.00**	**$32.50**

Table 8.4 Minimum Number of Final Prototypes to Be Produced Every Season for a Multiproduct Brand Following a Seasonal Collection Calendar

Ladies' ready-to-wear	150 pieces
Men's ready-to-wear	100 pieces
Handbags	50 pieces
Other leather goods	100 pieces
Silk	100 pieces
Total	**500 pieces**

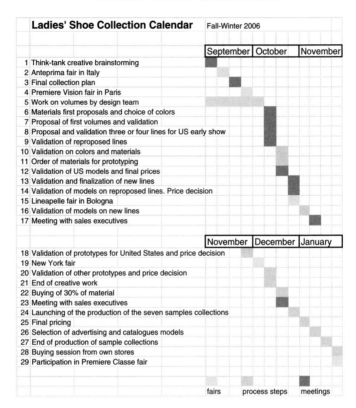

Figure 8.8   Collection Calendar of an A/W Ladies' Shoe Collection

The Collections Calendar

The collections calendar formalizes the important moments in the collections development process agreed to by all the departments involved: ordering materials for samples and for production, intermediate meetings to review the design progress, final editing of the collection, ordering from the stores, organizing the buying sessions for third-party distributors, fair participations, and so on. It is the most shared common tool of all the departments involved in collections development.

Figure 8.8 illustrates a real example of an Autumn/Winter (A/W) ladies' shoes collection calendar of a French brand, showing all the different steps involved. It appears clear, for example, that the prototype validation is a three-step process, with the lines and models requiring approval before their final realization as a prototype.

Table 8.5 Performance Indicators for Product Empowerment Teams

Volume	Sales
Profitability	Sell-through
	Net gross margin
Immobilized capital	Inventory turns (FG, WIP, RM)
Speed	On-time delivery
	Time for reassortment
	Time to market
Quality	Returns
Costs	Team operating costs
Team effectiveness	Initiatives and problem solving
	Interfaces with retail, wholesale, communication, and others
	Team cohesion, communication, atmosphere … fun

The number of professional fairs attended by the designers and merchandisers is also indicated, as well as the regular involvement of the commercial department right up until the presentation of the sample collection to wholesale clients and merchandisers (or store buyers, in certain cases).

Brands that have no wholesale business are generally laxer in managing the products' time to the stores. Third-party distributors, especially the US department stores, are rightfully extremely strict in respect to deliveries, as any delay impacts the sell-through performance.

Figure 8.9 presents a more complex picture of a brand proposing ladies' ready-to-wear (RTW) as well as textile home furnishing products. What becomes evident is that two to three main collections of RTW are being simultaneously managed at any given time. For instance, in September 2017 there is the Think-tank for AW 2018, which is the official launch of the collection, gathering all the designers around the creative director and sharing their creative ideas. This occurs at the same time that the merchandisers are buying the Spring/Summer (SS) 2018 collections from the samples presented by the development teams and while the 2018 Holiday collection is about to reach the stores. One can notice that complements of collections are mentioned on the diagram. These are specific additional developments that are requested to improve the season's performance by introducing additional designs, based on the initial performance of the collection in the early months

Top calendar

COLLECTION						OCT. 16				NOV. 16				DEC. 16				JAN. 17				FEB. 17				MAR. 17				APR. 17				MAY. 17				JUN. 17				JUL. 17			AUG. 17	
	34	35	36	37	38	39	40	41	42	43	44	45	46	47	48	1	2	3	4	5	6	7	8	9	10	11	12	13	14	15	16	17	18	19	20	21	22	23	24	25	26	27	28	29	30
AW 2017 PERSONAL GOODS	TT	THINK TANK																																											
				AW '17 COLLECTION DEVELOPMENT																																								
																						PRE-BUYING/BUYING/PRODUCTION														AW '17 IN-STORE									
SS 2017 COMPLEMENT			COMP. SS'17 DEVELOPMENT																																									
								PRE-BUYING/BUYING/PRODUCTION																	COMP. 'SS17 IN-STORE																		
SS 2018 PERSONAL GOODS																							TT		SS'18 COLLECTION DEVELOPMENT																				
SS 2018 HOME FURNISHING																								SS'18 HF COLLECTION DEVELOPMENT																					
AW 2017 PG HOLIDAY																							HOLIDAY AW '17 DEVELOPMENT																					
																													PRE-BUYING/BUYING/PRODUCTION															

Bottom calendar

COLLECTION			SEP. 17				OCT. 17				NOV. 17				DEC. 17				JAN. 18				FEB. 18				MAR. 18				APR. 18				May				JUN. 18				JUL. 18			AUG. 18	
	31	32	33	34	35	36	37	38	39	40	41	42	43	44	45	46	47	48	01	02	03	04	05	06	07	08	09	10	11	12	13	14	15	16	17	18	19	20	21	22	23	24	25	26	27	28	29	30
SS 2018 PERSONAL GOODS	PRE-BUYING/BUYING/PRODUCTION									SS '18 IN-STORE																																						
SS 2018 HOME FURNISHING	PRE-BUYING/BUYING/PRODUCTION									IN STORE CHRISTMAS		IN STORE SS' 18																																			
AW 2017 PG HOLIDAY				HOLIDAY '17 IN-STORE																																											
AW 2018 PERSONAL GOODS			TT	AW '18 COLLECTION DEVELOPMENT																																											
AW 2018 HOME FURNISHING				AW'18 HOME FORNITURE COLLECTION FLOW															PRE-BUYING/BUYING/PRODUCTION													AW '18 IN-STORE											
SS 2018 COMPLEMENT				COMP. SS'18 DEVELOPMENT														BUYING AND PRODUCTION											IN STORE AW '18													
							PRE-BUYING/BUYING/PRODUCTION										COMP. 18 IN-STORE																												
SS 2019 PERSONAL GOODS																				SS'19 COLLECTION DEVELOPMENT																										

Figure 8.9   Collection Calendar of Ladies' Ready-to-Wear and Home Furnishing Collections

(additional colors, expansion of best-selling products, etc.). This is called design-in-season, and even though the products only arrive in the last months of the season, they still generate additional revenue.

Once the collections plan and calendar, which constitute in effect a comprehensive business plan, have been released, the design and development work can start. This is a characteristic of the luxury industry: competitive advantages are often born at the interface of merchandising and creation.

Creation

Needless to say, creativity and innovation in products, services, and business functions are the main sources of competitive advantage in all industries, and even more so in the luxury business whereby the customer naturally expects a great deal of originality and newness within what he perceives to be the aesthetic characteristics of the brand. He also expects the product to be recognizable and carry a part of the dream inherent to the brand.

Managing creative people has never been a simple task (sometimes even for themselves). In this section, after presenting a description of the nature of creative activities for a luxury brand, we will delve into the organizational matters related to it, with real-life examples of design structures and their underlying logic. This will show how product management interfaces with the creative work. We will also propose some insights into how the notion of brand aesthetics can help in solving some creative management issues, and finish the chapter by talking about the bridges that exist between brands' creative activities and arts. In this fourth edition we add a few considerations on the notion of style as well as on the creation process (think-tank meetings and creative briefs).

As indicated in Figure 8.10, the creative function is the confluence point at which commercial, financial, image-related, technical, and logistical considerations come into play as well as the most natural constraint within which the designers have to work: the respect for, and constant upgrade of, the brand identity. The invariant aesthetic components of the brand identity are still rarely formalized and it is left to the designers' talent and sensibility to interpret the aesthetics of the brand, to keep it relevant with respect to fashion and longer-term social trends, and to ensure that it continues to reflect the brand values. A clearly formalized

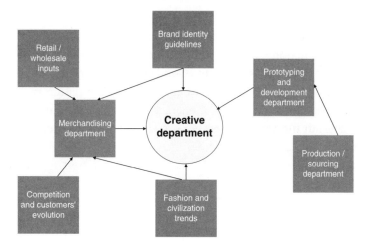

Figure 8.10   Inputs and Constraints Applying to the Creative Department

brand identity, expressing the invariable elements of what we have called the ethics and aesthetics of the brand, acts like a brand Bible and should be on every designer's desk, from the office junior to the creative director.

Adding to the complexity of luxury creation is the sheer volume of creativity required of the design departments of multiproduct brands, such as Gucci, Vuitton, Loewe, Celine, Bally, Coach, Burberry, Jim Thompson, Ferragamo, and so on. For a brand aiming at a lifestyle status, the minimum number of products to be presented in each collection every season is approximately as shown in Table 8.4.

For any model chosen for the season's collection, we estimate there will be an average of three prototypes. This happens twice a year. That is, for any brand with ambitions to reach a lifestyle status, at least 3,000 products have to be conceived and prototyped every year. In order to create such a volume of products within a demanding time limit, functional constraints require a rigorous coordination of resources. The number of samples can be much higher for the core business category of leading brands, especially for the preparation of the fashion shows.

The basic conditions of success for a creative team derive directly from Figure 8.10:

- Respect and enhancement of the brand identity
- Relevance of creations

- Proper organizational structure
- Efficient business processes
- Strong integration with the product developers
- Good knowledge of materials and suppliers … and plenty of talent and imagination

Creation in the realm of service brands (restaurants, hotels, resorts, cruises, air travel, and so on) focuses more on the physical comfort provided to the customers, on spaces, location, decoration, original and exceptional services, food, and communication.

Organization of the Creative Function

After receiving a specific assignment from the merchandising department, the design team, working closely with the company's own prototyping department or with those of contracted manufacturers, will need to realize the samples of the products they design.

Design and Development. The efficiency of the link between design and prototyping is a main source of competitive advantage for the luxury industry. Since most of today's designers do not have the technical knowledge to transform their own concepts into real objects, the need for efficient *modelisti* (prototypers in Italian) is acute. *Modelisti* are handicraft professionals who are able to interpret the designs (often in 2D) and ideas of the creative team and transform them into real products. They are specialized by product and are increasingly difficult to find. (Numerous great Italian shoe and handbag *modelisti* are spending their retirement as consultants for Chinese manufacturers.)

Gone are the Salvatore Ferragamos and Cristobal Balenciagas who could construct their creations with their own hands. Today's designers are visual, draw in 2 and 3D, and therefore need talented product developers. When the prototyping activity is integrated into the company, we often see the design and development departments merged, as the competencies are complementary. The product development phase is not made of pure prototyping capabilities. In the case of shoes, for instance, the fit is a whole science, jealously protected, and rarely formalized, mastered by only a few individuals who come into play at the time of prototyping and preproduction of small series. The prototyping department is also responsible for integrating the production constraints, as illustrated in Figure 8.10.

There are as many organizational models as there are luxury brands. A great deal depends on the number of product categories, the cultural approach to design, the simplicity of the brand aesthetics, the existence of strongly recognizable graphic codes, the designer's reputation, the size of the company, and so on.

To get an idea of the diversity and the organizational importance of the design function, we look next at how this works at some leather-goods brands, at different stages of their brand life cycle.

Leather-Goods Brands Michel Vivien, *chausseur à Paris*, designs women's shoes under his own name. He has them prototyped and manufactured by an Italian factory and sells them to the market himself through professional fairs. He has one design assistant, to whom he gives creative direction, and he does much of the creation himself. Not only does he directly control all creative activities, he manages all other functions as well. He probably sells fewer than 50,000 pairs a year.

At Robert Clergerie, where the volume of shoes produced is stable around several hundred thousand pairs, the prototype and design group in the early 2000s consisted of four people, and, as the company also had ambitions to move into the handbag and small-leather-goods sectors, an external handbag designer was contracted. The company also used an external consultant as a creative director.

Loewe's turnover in the early 2000s was in the region of a few hundred million Euros from activities spanning from leather goods, ready-to-wear, silk accessories, and gift items to fragrances for men and women. All products were designed in-house. The design function was spread within each of the four business units (leather goods, ladies' ready-to-wear, men's ready-to-wear, and fragrances) and comprised 20 people. In 1997, Narciso Rodriguez was hired to design the ladies' ready-to-wear, and the CEO, for lack of an overall creative director, functioned as brand identity manager, coordinating all these creative talents as well as the communication and retail departments. Since then, after two successive designers, Jonathan Anderson arrived in 2013 and the organization's structure has evolved drastically.

In the early 2000s, Bally was losing money, with a declining turnover of around $500 million. The sale of the company to the

Texas Pacific Group, a US private-equity fund, provided a good opportunity to restructure the brand to enable it to realize its ambition to become a lifestyle luxury brand reflecting perennial Swiss values. The management started by clearly identifying the main culture and the competencies needed to reach these objectives. Figure 8.2 presented at the beginning of this chapter explains the rationale underlying the revised Bally organizational chart, where the business expertise belongs to the merchandisers. It is important to establish the rule that merchandisers never get involved in aesthetic matters, leaving 20% of the collection to be defined freely by the designers with no constraints whatsoever. The logisticians produce and move goods. Decisions regarding suppliers, whose selection may be of strategic importance, are made in conjunction with designers and merchandisers. Then, all activities requiring a strong aesthetic sensibility, such as creation and communication, are regrouped.

In Bally, the organization chart for everyone involved in the creative activities in 2000 was structured along the lines of what is shown in Figure 8.11. The design and development functions were merged under a single responsibility to ensure a maximum fusion between 2 and 3D designs and prototyping. The editors–at–large, fashion reference personages or opinion leaders in the luxury world, were appointed in Paris, Hong Kong, and New York to keep the company informed on recent fashion trends, on what the competition was doing, and to provide feedback on past and current collections. Not counting these or other outside staff, such as the PR offices and the design departments dedicated to the watch and golf shoe licenses, a total of 31 internal creative staff were involved in the process. The financial effort needed to sustain such a multiproduct brand strategy is sizeable, but this is what the global lifestyle brands have to face.

The design and development organization adopted for Jim Thompson in 2016 was a variation of Bally's chart with the difference that a development director covering all product categories with specialized teams was reporting directly to the CEO and liaising daily with the group of designers also specialized by product category. The creative director was supervising the communication and all the designers as well as a group especially created for graphic design. The situation was a bit more complex because the textile design and development function was serving two business units: personal goods and home furnishing.

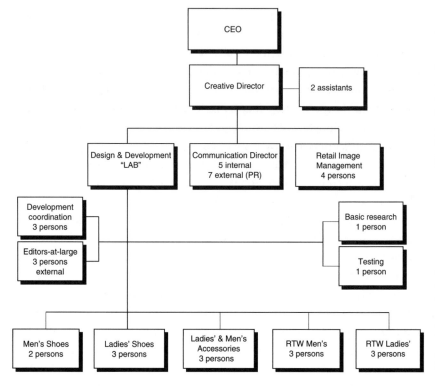

Figure 8.11   Bally Example of Design and Development Department Organization Chart

Mass–Market versus Luxury Brands.   These examples drawn from the leather-goods industry highlight the numerous models that can coexist within the same sector. Looking at the luxury industry as a whole, the number of organizational solutions is almost equal to the number of brands, and this, we believe, stems from the difficulty of rationalizing the aesthetic dimension of the brands. Within this abundance of organizational solutions, we can identify two extreme and opposite models that both avoid the issues surrounding the management of intrinsic brand aesthetics without really solving them.

The first model is found in major luxury brands such as Dior and Chanel, where the aesthetic keys are handed to a talented and proven designer (respectively, Maria Grazia Chiuri and Virginie Viard, in 2020) and the CEO has little power whatsoever in the creative function. The designer and the CEO seldom meet except perhaps at cocktail parties.

The second model belongs to mass-market brands like Gap, Zara, H&M, Celio, Springfield, and so on, where the design team (an army of anonymous individuals) works under the close supervision of the product manager, who imposes price and fashion constraints, and whereby creativity is reduced to following rigid commercial plans and what is currently hot in the market. This solution does not exclude specific initiatives with celebrities or even haute couture designers as the H&M Fall 2019 collection designed by Giambattista Valli or the special Fall 2006 collection orchestrated with Madonna. The product manager is frequently referred to as the collection manager or, as at Cortefiel (now called Tendam, Spanish and one of Europe's leading fashion retailers operating in the specialized chain segment), the buyer, which clearly reveals the main focus of their task. In this sector, the overall organization is quite simple. Besides the usual financial and HR functions, there will normally be three departments: the product department (merchandising, creation, sourcing), the communication department (advertising, PR, showroom management), and the retail/franchise department. The brand identity tasks are spread across the organization chart.

The basic difference between the two solutions is in the importance given to the creative function and thus to the decision-making power granted to the designer, which in turn reflects the brand's basic culture and way of competing. Each of these systems has created legends. The luxury model thrives on the geniality and talent of designers like Tom Ford and Alessandro Michele at Gucci, all the famous French couturiers, or Karl Lagerfeld at Chanel. It becomes much more difficult when the serving designer does not have these exceptional talents. The second model has given birth to extraordinary success stories such as Zara or H&M in the past 20 years—successes based essentially on good merchandising and on an extraordinary logistical capability that can reduce the product time-to-market to 10 days.

Nonetheless, the optimal solution is more balanced, where brand aesthetics are more coordinated and better oriented toward the constant reinforcing of the brand identity. How can these goals be achieved given the complex set of brand manifestations, all promoting the brand identity, performed by so many typologies of competencies? Figure 8.12 presents most of the manifestations through which a brand can be perceived by the market. They represent what could be called all the occasions of interface between the brand and its potential customer. We can recognize

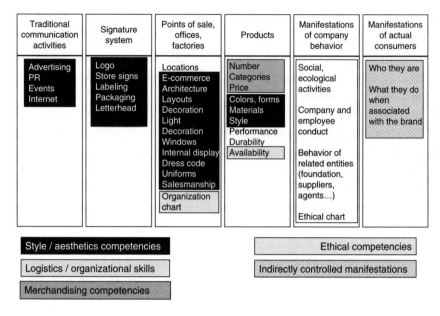

Figure 8.12   Brand Identity Manifestations—Different Competencies

Kotler's 4 P's, as price, products, promotion (advertising), and place are positioned in the scheme. However, the figure introduces more detailed activities as well as manifestations linked to the customers that are in fact not directly controllable by the brand. The figure reveals the multiple competencies necessary to carry out the brand activities. At the end of the game, who is really in charge of a brand's aesthetics? Who has the broad view necessary to span the range of brand manifestations and the power to act upon them?

The ultimate brand aesthetics manager can only be the CEO. He is in a position to really balance the sometimes competing logics of business and aesthetics and make the necessary tradeoffs between them. Not that we are asking him to be Giorgio Armani; such talents are given to very few. Neither are we suggesting that he be involved in actual design. Nevertheless, the CEO should be capable of working with both sides of the brain, and have proper aesthetic preparation and sensibility. In addition, a transparent and constructive attitude from all members of the top management team would help in producing an optimal aesthetic decisionmaking system.

Between the two extremes (creativity often given free rein in the luxury industry, and a systematic undervaluing of creativity within mass-market brands), there is room for more balanced organizational solutions whereby the respective logics informing the merchandising and creative processes can coexist and reinforce each other. The Bally or Jim Thompson solutions presented earlier are, we believe, close to achieving that difficult balancing act.

The Product Empowerment Teams.   Despite all the examples of monitoring tools and reports, more often than not the different cultures and specific operating objectives of different departments give rise to a lot of friction in the development process and, ultimately, to poor quality, late deliveries, higher costs, and higher prices.

To reduce the possibility of such problems, in the early 2000, Bally decided to launch what was called the PET (Product Empowerment Teams) project. The intent of the project was to focus people's attention on the virtues of teamwork and to streamline the product development process. A multifunctional team was created for each product division (men's shoes, ladies' shoes, men's accessories, ladies' accessories, men's ready-to-wear, and ladies' ready-to-wear). Each team, coordinated by the divisional merchandise manager, comprised the category head designers, the category developer, and a member of the supply management team, and each team worked in conjunction with retail operations and the wholesale, communication, information system, and finance departments. The focus of these teams was to make things happen quickly. In order to give substance to this setup and make the team responsible for the performance of the division, we introduced financial incentives based on the objectives of the overall project, with the CEO directly monitoring the team performances.

Table 8.5 shows the key performance indicators introduced. The efforts were worthwhile, as they rapidly reduced shipping delays, improved product quality, and remained within the planned prices.

It becomes clear from this section that putting the right product in the right place, at the right time, at the right price, and in the right quantities is not a simple task.

Creative Process

In a multiproduct-category brand, where there are many designers participating in the design activities, it is essential to be able to harness their often wild imagination and desire to be bold into an orderly process ensuring consistency for the brand. We have seen examples of how to achieve that goal through the organization of the design function. The process is as crucial as the structure.

The development of a seasonal collection starts with the think-tank. The creative directors gather all the designers of the different product categories to a freewheeling meeting where everybody shares his or her own views and ideas on what the next season's guidelines could be. The meeting lasts about one day and is the subject of a formal document a few days later. This is one of the rare gatherings where the CEO is not welcome. One month later each designer finalizes with the creative director a seasonal brief covering the main aesthetic guideline for the season. Together with the collection structure and calendar received from the merchandiser, each designer then has his seasonal roadmap.

The brief is the second essential piece (the first one being the collection plan, as seen in section 8.1. of this chapter) in translating strategies into actions. Seasonal colors are defined along the institutional ones, new materials, decorating elements like prints, jacquard patterns, degree of newness, aesthetic innovations, new monogram patterns, new labeling, and so on.

The brief is particularly relevant when outside creative work is being mobilized. Architects, capsule collection designers, freelance designers, communication agencies, and so on need aesthetic guidelines in addition to the scope of their work. The brief can indeed be very brief. When Pininfarina started to conceive the electric city car for the Bolloré group in 2008, four words were to guide the design team: iconic, agile, premium, and Pininfarina.

Designers and Style[2]

In the case of a single designer like the couturier, we tend to talk about his or her style rather than about brand aesthetics. The two expressions

---

[2] Some parts of the text on the designers and style section are extracted from a conference given by Mazzalovo ("Yves Saint Laurent: Questions de Style," organized by Fundacion Mapfre on the occasion of the exhibition "Yves Saint Laurent: Alta Costura, Alta Cultura." Madrid, October 2011. Text published on www.ec-aiss.it (official site of the Italian Semiotics Association). Video of the presentation available at https://www.youtube.com/watch?v=Vh4DrbdVdy0.

may be considered synonyms. The metamorphosis of a company bearing the name of a famous designer into a brand capable of thriving after his disappearance is a relatively common challenge in the clothing and sometimes also accessories industry. Chanel (twice), Lacroix, Dior, Ferragamo, Ungaro, Balmain, Givenchy, Céline, Robert Clergerie, and others have gone through this process with varying degrees of success.

Several problems may arise:

- To ensure a certain continuity, there is a need to analyze and formalize the creator's style in terms of allowing for its interpretation by other creatives.
- It is also a time to change vocabulary. We go from the style and personality of a designer to the aesthetics and identity of a brand. To conduct this passage, an in-depth analysis of the current designer's style and a formalization of its sensory invariants is necessary.

Style is a concept that is not always precisely defined. It has many semantic variants. Dictionaries' definitions emphasize above all both aspects of formal consistency and distinctive way of representation or action, that is, perceivable, durable, and differentiated expressive features. The dictionary *Trésor de la langue française informatisé*[3] gives these definitions, among others:

- Category of aesthetics allowing the characterization of the organization of verbal, plastic, musical forms, that the history of art has identified and described as having marked its era or as being characteristic of a particular artist.
- Set of means of expression that translate in an original way the thoughts, the feelings, the whole personality of an author.
- Personal way of using certain artistic means (choice of subject, shapes, lines, play of colors) that allows an artist to be recognized through his works …

The three components of what constitutes a style are presented:

A vision of the world (or values)
A way of doing things (or a way of being present and acting in the world)
Formal constants

---

[3] http://atilf.atilf.fr/tlf.htm.

We could make a parallel with the three levels of Semprini's semionarrative scheme mentioned in Chapter 7, section 7.8, where it is shown that the sense is produced through three layers going from the simplest (the values) to the more complex external manifestations. We thus find in these definitions elements of the semiotic definition of the aesthetics of a brand, of its "approach to the sensory," as Floch (1995) said,[4] and its function of representing a specific vision of the world. When Panofsky (2006) writes " ... a style is defined not only by what it expresses but also by the way it expresses it ... ,"[5] he certainly groups in the word *way* both the permanent plastic elements and the way of doing that produces these sensory results. It is the whole process of moving from a vision of the world (when it exists) to its expression that can be identified in the sensory world that defines style. "Identity is defined by its mode of production" (Floch 1995).[6] Style can be understood as a journey, a series of connections of elements, disconnected at the start, that ultimately create meaning. We can extend this definition to the production process of the aesthetic treatment of an object, that is to say the creative process in a broad sense. It is often the way of doing (or of not doing) that leads to the characteristic results of a creator. It also directly reflects his values, to the extent that brands and consistent individuals act according to what they believe in. A chosen lifestyle, as in the case of lifestyle brands, can only be the product of an ethical approach.

Two of the three components of style constitute the signifier: the formal constants and the way of doing (the professional expertise, among others) and being in the world are both observable. If the style, the *coup de patte,* is associated with a characteristic and therefore recognizable way of treating the sensory (it is a painting by Cézanne, a Dior dress, an Armani costume, or a Rolex watch), the stylistic analysis will naturally focus on finding these sensory invariants. However, studying the historical corpus of a creator's works or of a brand's manifestations sometimes leads to the finding of the nonexistence of identifiable aesthetic invariants or simply demonstrating an inability to identify them. This was the case

---

[4] J.-M. Floch, *Identités visuelles*. Paris: Presses Universitaires de France, 1995.

[5] E. Panofsky, *Ikonographie und Ikonologie: Bildinterpretation nach dem Dreistufenmodell*. Dumont, 2006.

[6] Floch, *Identités visuelles*.

with Loewe in 1996. No consistent approach to the sensory was identified, despite—or because of—150 years of history. The management then made legitimate and differentiating choices, built on a baroque aesthetic capable of expressing all the Spanish energy and sensuality. What is the style of Jean Nouvel (Pritzker Prize 2008)? Eclectic works, where it is very difficult to find aesthetic invariants. What is visibly common between his projects? Other architects, like Frank Gehry or Zaha Hadid, or designers, like Marc Newson or Ron Arad, have chosen a more formal expression. Their styles are more easily recognizable because recurring plastic elements are quickly identifiable in their creations.

This difficulty in identifying formal invariants is often encountered with ready-to-wear designers. The *Financial Times* article by journalist Vanessa Friedman's 2009 article about designer Marc Jacobs' Spring/Summer 2010 collection, "The Creative Confusion of Marc Jacobs" (September 19–20, 2009), is significant. It says that you cannot put the designer in "a stylistic box, because you never know what his style will be one season to another."

The ease of identifying sensory invariants will be defined by the degree of opacity (or transparency) of the style of a creator. But how deep should we look for these invariants? How to identify this "generating principle which allows the diversity of phenomena to be reduced to the unity of the concept" as defined by Jean Molino in the preface to Panofsky's *Idea* (1989).[7]

YSL brand was in that type of generational passage in 1999 when the brand was acquired by the group that would become Kering. Floch was called to analyze Yves's style in order to help his successor, who in that particular case was Tom Ford. The task was arduous given the eclecticism, paradoxes, and ambiguities of Yves's creations. There were many paradoxes and apparent contradictions generating an impression of great confusion. "I admire in him the abyss of his contrasts," would say Andrée Putman, French interior and product designer (1925–2013).

We will briefly mention the main results of Floch's analysis of Yves Saint Laurent style in the following section. We will just highlight here that Yvess' style was defined by the semantic axis *Here/Elsewhere*, which was applicable both at the ethics and aesthetic levels of brand identity.

---

[7] E. Panofsky, *Idea: A Concept in Art Theory* (1924). French translation, Paris, Editions Gallimard, 1989.

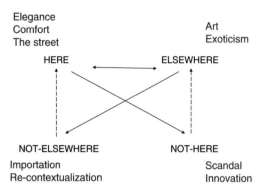

Figure 8.13   Application of YSL style definition to his creations

The square developed from this semantic axis (Figure 8.13) demonstrated its relevance, as it would structure not only Yves's creations, but also the couturier's life and his customer's profiles.

The lesson to be drawn from Floch's work on YSL's style is that it is not sufficient to identify colors or shapes used preferentially, but that very often one needs to dig deeper, not only in the immediate aesthetic expression but also in the underlying values and methods of designing.

Of the three components of style, "the way of doing things" is often neglected in stylistic analysis. In the example of Pininfarina mentioned in Chapter 6, sections 6.2 and 6.5, we have shown the brand ethics and aesthetics of the possible Pininfarina brand for monobranded products (Figure 6.2). In the course of the study, we also developed what we have called the Pininfarina creative sequence, as shown in Figure 8.14.

Brand Aesthetics

In Chapter 6 we introduced a definition of brand aesthetics that differs from the usually accepted philosophical meaning of a discipline dealing with beauty. We took a semiotic approach, using the term to encompass all the permanent brand elements belonging to the sensory world: the brand manifestations, which not only include the visual elements (forms, colors, light treatments, etc.) but also sound, taste, touch, and odor. The brand manifestations were introduced in Figure 8.12 and can be classified into four aesthetic fields: product, communication, space, and behavior.

	Invisible to the public			visible to the public	
brand ethics	project	process	plastic features	effects	
progress	concept (object, purpose, contexts)	nothing gratuitous (technological, function, & esth.)	volumetric coherence	elegance beauty simple / sober	
humanism	project briefs (market, techno, usage, eco, style,...)	start with vol. forms, then surfaces, textures and models, then details (lines as consequence of vol. decisions)	perfect surfaces	refinement harmonious proportions	
luxury			simple / essential		
harmony	client identity		the whole before the parts	strong personality	
Italian	innovation opportunities		dynamic and pure lines	emotional and meaningful objects	
first bodymaker		search for harmony	balanced proportions	user-friendly objects	
	ethics applicability	innovation as an aesthetic opportunity	few colors	long lasting	

Figure 8.14   Pininfarina Creative Sequence

The creative activities of a luxury brand operate at the center of the brand's aesthetics. However, is the brand aesthetics notion really relevant for brand management?

Relevance of Brand Aesthetics

There are three main factors that establish the relevance of brand aesthetics. First, there is a strong trend within society toward aestheticism: Consumption is getting aestheticized. This is a characteristic and an easily perceivable phenomenon of our time (Lyotard 1984, Baudrillard 1985, Featherstone 1991, Firat and Venkatesh 1995, Postrel 2003)[8-12] that the semiotician Andrea Semprini (2005) defines as "the general-

---

[8]J.-F. Lyotard, *La condition postmoderne*. Paris: Editions de Minuit, 1979.

[9]J. Baudrillard, *Le miroir de la production ou l'illusion critique du matérialisme historique*. Paris: Galilée, 1985.

[10]M. Featherstone, *Consumer Culture and Postmodernism*. London: Sage, 1991.

[11]F. Firat and A. Venkatesh, "Liberatory Postmodernism and the Re-enchantment of Consumption," *The Journal of Consumer Research* 2, no. 3 (1995): 239–267.

[12]V. Postrel, *The Substance of Style: How the Rise of Aesthetic Value Is Remaking Commerce, Culture and Consciousness*. New York: Harper Collins, 2003.

ization and trivialization of the aesthetic paradigm in the context of the development of postmodern brands."The formal treatment of products and services—understood here in the broad sense of materials, textures, sounds, smells, plastic and chromatic aspects, and so forth—so far considered as marginal, tends to become the fundamental competitive element as confirmed by the success of brands such as luxury fashion global leaders but also outside of the luxury field, as Absolut Vodka, Custo, or Desigual, for example.

During the modern industrial period, the aesthetic aspects were the object of what one could qualify as benign neglect. Today, we are witnessing a proactive management of the sensory dimensions of brand manifestations. Annie Le Brun (2018) writes: "There is nothing that we see, touch, wear, cross, eat which has not been aestheticized beforehand."[14] This is part of what Lipovetsky and Serroy (2013) observe as "the generalization of the strategies of aesthetic seduction."[15]

This is easily noticeable in the consumption of products and services. From the birth of design in the early 1950s, initially applied to small series or industrial machines, to the arrival of the likes of Ikea, Conran, Alessi, and Habitat, this phenomenon is clearly manifest. Today, design is everywhere. There are no successfully competitive products that have not been submitted to an aesthetic optimization. This is most evident in the extensive use of color on such traditionally plain objects as refrigerators, electrical plugs, radiators, cutlery, suitcases, fire extinguishers, cell phones, personal computers, and so on, which have risen in a few years to the status of fashion accessories or lifestyle identifiers.

Second, the simple fact that certain forms, colors, contrasts, or harmonies are more noticeable and easier to memorize than others, or trigger emotions in those exposed to them, proves the importance of aesthetics. Isn't the objective of any creator and communicator to generate emotion and memories to the target customers? An advertisement showing a young lady with a nail in the forehead (Nell & Me) or monsters and mutants (Brema, Lee Cooper, Thierry Mugler's fragrance, Alien, and so on) generates uneasiness, rejection, fear—all effects desired by their creators. There are proven statistical preferences for rectangles obeying the golden mean ratio. It has been medically proven that colors and light have

---

[13] A. Semprini, *La marque, une puissance fragile*. Paris: Vuibert, 2005.

[14] Annie Le Brun, *Ce qui n'a pas de prix*. Paris: Stock, 2018.

[15] G. Lipovetsky and J. Serroy, *L'esthétisation du monde*. Paris: Gallimard, 2013.

a physiological and psychological impact. There are an infinite number of examples that show that mastering brand aesthetics can assist in managing a certain brand's effects on its public.

The third aspect of the relevance of the notion of brand aesthetics is its ability to untie some tight corporate knots, as developed in the next paragraph.

Examples of Issues Treated with the Notion of Brand Aesthetics

We are convinced that the notion of brand aesthetics can go a long way in helping to resolve issues related to creativity in brand organizations. In fact, the aesthetic notion allows us to tackle, with an innovative approach, communication, organizational, and cultural issues.

Communication Issues.   The willingness to manage brand aesthetics in a systematic and rational way leads to some simple and immediate questions:

- Is the brand's aesthetic (or a specific brand manifestation) contributing to communicate the brand ethics efficiently and therefore consolidating the brand identity?
- Is the aesthetic treatment of a specific brand manifestation serving the brand's communication purpose (visibility, ease of memorization, special message to convey, specific emotion to generate, etc.) while remaining compatible with the brand aesthetics?
- Are the brand manifestations coherent among themselves?

Organizational Issues.   We saw earlier how difficulties in rationalizing the management of brand aesthetics can lead to two opposite and equally unsatisfactory organizational models: one giving full and unchallenged decision-making power to the designer, the other submitting the designer to the constraints of strict commercial rules. Rationalizing brand aesthetics would provide the necessary tools to allow a more fluid, balanced, and open rapport between all the direct and indirect participants in the process of creation.

Cultural Issues: The Missing Dictionary.   Design personnel tend to hold the merchants in perfect contempt. For their part, the merchants do not hesitate to criticize the bad design of a collection when sales do not meet expectations. Meanwhile, the production and development people look on everyone else as extremely frivolous and unprepared as to what a good product should be. These legitimate tensions often end up at a higher hierarchical level and affect the relationship between the head designer or creative director and the CEO or COO. In the confrontation between the manager—who lives among figures, statistics, budgets, consumer-behavior theories, board meetings, and financial analysts—and the creative designer—who is aware of the glamor of the position, sensitive to fashion and taste, mixing with the fashion elite and the press, and perhaps dreaming of imposing a specific aesthetic viewpoint to the world, the relationship is not always naturally easy and rarely allows for a rational and constructive dialogue.

"Why do you do that?" asks the CEO. "Because I feel it!" replies the designer. The main reason for such an unconstructive conversation is that neither has really been educated in how to discuss brand aesthetics rationally and that very few tools exist that would allow them to establish a common vocabulary for doing so. Given this, it is no surprise that most of the great designers have always had at their side a trusted person with whom they have had an exceptional symbiosis that has rendered unnecessary the need to explain. Yves Saint Laurent and Pierre Bergé are perhaps the best example of such a duo.

The work developed at Pininfarina in 2007 is a meaningful example of how a brand identity formalized together with the design teams helped in improving the relationships among them (see Mazzalovo's 2016 article).[16]

Possible Tools for Managing Brand Aesthetics

The analytical instruments introduced in previous chapters—the brand hinge, the semiotic square, the communication chain, and the brand manifestations—are efficient at framing all the complex processes by which a brand produces meaning, but they are not necessarily adequate to tackle the plastic dimension (light, color, composition, lines, and so on) of brand aesthetics.

---

[16] G. Mazzalovo, "Resolving Tensions among Creative Departments through Brand Identity Definition: The Case Study of Pininfarina," *Business and Management Studies* 2, no. 1 (2016).

There are a number of tools and methodologies that exist for managing the aesthetic dimension of brand manifestations, studied and elaborated by art historians, that can be used by artists, designers, and creative directors. We saw in Chapter 6 how entering into classical and baroque considerations helps in treating light, forms, and volumes and, above all, that these aesthetic elements relate to specific brand ethics. The brand aesthetics analytical grid introduced in the same chapter and that we applied to Jim Thompson is another practical tool. Finally, Riegl's three ends to aesthetic treatments introduced in Chapter 7 opens the analytical field and positions the brand identity elements into a broader view.

For the benefit of professors, students, and practitioners interested in deepening their knowledge of brand aesthetic management, we provide a succinct bibliography by aesthetic subject in complement to the preliminary one we mentioned in Chapter 6.

Light treatment

- To Heinrich Woelfflin's (1888) work on classical and baroque expression already mentioned,[17] we can add Jean-Marie Floch (1995)[18] and the very original work from Eugenio d'Ors (1935).[19]
- Neobaroque by Omar Calabrese (1987)[20] and postmodern baroque by Maffesoli (2008).[21]

Forms and lines

- In addition to William Hogarth's book (1753) on the serpentine line, which, according to him,[22] generates more perceived beauty because of its versatility, we can mention Aloïs Riegl's (1899) crystalline and organic lines, which respectively characterize the harmonistic and naturalist visions of the world.[23]

---

[17] H. Wölfflin, *Renaissance et Baroque*. Brionne: Editions G. Monfort, 1888; French re-edition in 1985.

[18] Floch, *Identités visuelles*.

[19] E. D'Ors, *Du baroque* (1935). Re-edited in 2000 by Gallimard Education (Folio Essais).

[20] O. Calabrese, *L'Età Neobarocca*. (Rome: Laterza, 1987.

[21] M. Maffesoli, *Iconologies. Nos idolâtries postmodernes*. Paris: Albin Michel, 2008.

[22] W. Hogarth, *The Analysis of Beauty* (1753). Re-edited in 1997, Yale University Press.

[23] A. Riegl, *Historische Grammatik der Bildenden Künste* (1899). French translation, 1978: *Grammaire Historique des Arts Plastiques. Volonté Artistique et Vision du Monde*. Mayenne: Klinckseick.

- The SINC square (sinuous/straight/angular/single-curved lines semiotic square) was introduced by Mazzalovo (2012)[24] to analyze the meaning related to the perception of these lines as well as the market preferences for them.

Composition

- There is ample multi-century literature on the golden mean and its simplification used in photography, the two-thirds rule.
- Rudolf Arnheim (1969) on the power of the center.[25]

Colors

- The law of Simultaneous Contrast of Colors by Eugene Chevreul (1839),[26] who, in his position as director of the Gobelins Manufactory in the middle of the nineteenth century, was one of the first to analyze scientifically the different categories of chromatic harmonies. He exercised a strong influence on the painters of his time (Pissaro, Seurat, Signac, Van Gogh, Delaunay).
- The chromatic square by Mazzalovo (2008), which classifies the Western colors meanings on a semiotic square.[27]

Contrasts and contradictions

- The semiotic square is in itself a precious tool. In general, each time one can find a semantic axis whose intrinsic contradiction can define a brand on both the ethical and aesthetic plans, we are likely to be able to develop a full semiotic square. Floch showed the way in

---

[24] G. Mazzalovo, *Brand Aesthetics: The New Competitive Front in Brand Management*. Palgrave Macmillan, 2012.

[25] R. Arnheim, *Visual Thinking*. Berkeley and Los Angeles: University of California Press, 1969.

[26] M. E. Chevreul, De la loi du contraste simultané des couleurs et de l'assortiment des objets colorés (1839). Translated into English by Charles Martel as *The Principles of Harmony and Contrast of Colours* (1854). Newer edition by M. E. Chevreul and Dan Margulis, *On the Law of Simultaneous Contrast of Colors*. Atlanta: MCW Publishing, 2020.

[27] G. Mazzalovo, "Exemples d'applications de la sémiotique de Jean-Marie Floch à la gestion des marques," *FICTIONS, Studi sulla Narratività* VII (May 20, 2008).

his pioneer approach of photographic analysis applied to a nude of Edouard Boubat published in his first book (1985).[28] He introduced a certain number of semiotic squares constructed on semantic axes such as plain/modelé, nature/culture, and so on, demonstrating their usefulness in visual analysis in general.

One of the last works Floch undertook was on the formalization of Yves Saint Laurent's brand identity at the time the couturier stopped designing ready-to-wear in the early 1990s. As mentioned earlier, Floch identified the semantic axis made of "Here/Elsewhere" as the dialectic driving and defining the couturier's life, his creations, and his customers. A full square was then developed. The work was not published at the time, but thanks to Andrea Semprini's help (he was working with Floch on the project), Mazzalovo was able to present it in an article in 2011, where a lot of apparent paradoxes and ambiguities that characterize Yves's life and the eclectism of his clothes coalesce to create an understandable universe of sense.[29] The square structures this universal theme of escape, the search for dreams, artificial paradises, and other evasions of reality.

There is also a great deal of literature on textures, tactile properties, symmetries/asymmetries, transparency/opacity, bright/matte, and so on that can be activated based on specific needs but that space does not permit us to treat here.

We are obviously not trying to be exhaustive. There are many particularly interesting insights in art history literature. For those who might be interested in digging further, here are a few names of painters, critics, professors, and art observers in general: Lomazzo (1538–1592); Du Fresnoy (1611–1665); De Pile (1635–1709); Schiller (1759–1805); Van de Velde (1863–1957); Kandinsky (1866–1944); Klee (1879–1940); Worringer (1881–1965); Panofsky (1892–1968); Arnheim (1904–2007); Gombrich (1909–2001), among others.

---

[28] J.-M. Floch, *Petites Mythologies de l'oeil et de l'esprit: Pour une semiotique plastique*. Paris: Editions Hadès-Benjamen, 1985.

[29] G. Mazzalovo, "Yves Saint Laurent: Questions de Style" (2011). Text published on www .ec-aiss.it (official site of the Italian Semiotic Studies Association). Video of the presentation available at https://www.youtube.com/watch?v=Vh4DrbdVdy0.

Conclusion on Brand Aesthetics

Introducing the notion of brand aesthetics as a possible management tool presents a double challenge. The first of these challenges is to prove that the notion is powerful enough to introduce a new approach to solve real issues. The second revolves around the audacity of thinking that brand aesthetics can be managed. This is itself dependent on a basic axiom, a certain vision of the brand business world, a notion of corporate ethics that asserts that there is no such thing as a no man's land within a company where rationalization has no room. Entrenched within such a notion is the idea that everybody must be able to explain the decisions they make and demonstrate how their choices are coherent with the company strategy and culture and how they make the brand more competitive.

Our considerations on brand aesthetics lead us naturally to the rich and complex relationships existing between brands and arts.

Art and Brands

Given that both brands and artistic activities share a central core of creativity as their raison d'être, we may expect to find certain similarities between them. We may think that the main difference between the activities of the commercial designer and the artist is that the latter generally does not have a business prescriber like the merchandiser we have introduced earlier. While this may be so in some cases, we should not forget the role of sponsors, patrons, agents, and galleries. The commercial dimension has never been absent from artistic activities and there is indeed a big overlap between the two worlds which, we are going to see, is growing today.

The most expensive painting in the world (Leonardo da Vinci's *Salvador Mundi*) was sold at Christie's for $450.3 million in 2017 (at the time of our second edition in 2012, the record was held by Cézanne's *The Card Players* at $284 million), which is sizeable but only a fraction of the leading luxury brands' yearly turnover. It is obviously negligible when we consider that the Chinese retailer Alibaba Group Holding Ltd.'s sales for its 24-hour Singles Day shopping blitz hit a record $38 billion in November 2019. But coming back to more terrestrial figures, is there a real difference in the commercial nature of the activities between the painter who has an exhibition every two years and sells his work through galleries or auction houses and the ready-to-wear designer who stages a fashion show twice a year and sells his goods through monobrand and department stores? Are there big differences in their commercial objectives and in their sales and marketing processes between contemporary art fairs and fashion fairs?

Was there ever a time when the artist created independently of any money or power considerations? Artists, designers: Where is the border now that brands fully compete with movies, television, and literature in proposing new ways of dreaming and possible worlds? To analyze the convergence of the two worlds of art and brands, we first examine how each one borrows from the other.

From Brands to Arts

Brands came to a rapid understanding of the benefits of being associated with artistic activities. Having a strong cultural dimension can never have an adverse effect on a brand's identity. On the contrary, this is very much in the spirit of our times as the affluence of cultural institutions, such as galleries and museums, has never been so great and the level of education is steadily increasing. For a brand not to develop the strong cultural dimension that art provides to its identity puts it at risk of losing competitive ground.

The designer's work has a lot in common with the creative artistic process. Both the artist and the designer need to make decisions regarding shape, form, and color. The genuine ones have their own style and both have concerns, ideals of beauty, ethics, and values that they try to express through their work—as well as target customers.

The associations between brands and art take several forms that can be classified according to the depth to which the brand's involvement with art penetrates its brand identity. It may start from the merely episodic association of circumstance with a known artist or art piece and progress to having an art dimension fully embedded in its brand identity. Daum, the French Lorraine crystal brand, is an adequate example of a brand whose identity is strongly linked to art through its heritage and participation to the École de Nancy in the early 1900s as well as the rapports with artists for whom they make crystal pieces they have designed.

From episodic associations to an art-based brand identity, designers and communicators in the luxury field have long had recourse to art works, either to compensate for their own wavering inspiration or simply to pay homage to the artist.

We listed the major brands/arts associations in the previous editions, but the examples of products, advertising, and events that have taken their inspiration from works of art have increased exponentially, and we will mention only some of the most recent and meaningful.

All art disciplines have been referred to the following:

- **Painting** has been an easy choice because of its visual properties and worldwide exposure of the most famous masters. One of the earliest examples of art and fashion association are Yves Saint Laurent dresses inspired by the painter Piet Mondrian released in 1965 and which became icons in Western fashion history. Saint Laurent continued to pay tribute to master painters throughout his creative life, invoking Picasso (1979), Matisse (1981), Van Gogh (1988), and Warhol. Paul Gauguin was used by Elena Miro in the early 2000s. Watteau, Boucher, and Ingres were used in Vanessa Franklin's work for Converse sport shoes in *Wad* magazine in 2005. In 2016, Jim Thompson made an agreement with the Thai national abstract painter Ithipol Thangchalok by which the silk firm reproduced five of his paintings on silk. When asked by journalists whether this was not another example of "merchandization" of art activities, like we will see later with the museum products, the artist replied that he had been painting on 2D frames and that the silk of the Jim Thompson scarves was giving a new dimension to his works and that ladies could even wrap themselves up in them, rendering more intimate the rapport between his art and the public. In 2010, Jean-Michel Basquiat's motifs were used by Reebok on its shoes and an exhibition was organized at the Museum of Modern Art in Paris. Sometimes the use of the artist's name and his signature are sufficient, as the Picasso cars (Xsara, C4, etc.) for Citroen have demonstrated since 1998.
- **Architecture.** The associations of major luxury brands with renowned architects to conceive their flagship stores are mentioned

in Chapter 11. Some brands are even calling the architects for product design, as happened in 2006 when Tiffany announced an agreement with architect Frank Gehry, who designed the extraordinary Bilbao Guggenheim museum, to create six exclusive jewelry collections.

- **Cinema** has been the main source of cultural legitimacy for a lot of new brands. It conveys modernity and movement, and the public can identify easily with the famous actors, who have themselves become a resource much used by television and the Internet. Events such as the Cannes Film Festival are very coveted fashion platforms for the luxury ready-to-wear brands, with actresses commanding astronomical prices to wear a specific brand. Canali's links to the Hollywood movie industry are promoted on its website, which lists the many recent movies in which its clothes have been worn. But the use of the cinema is by no means a recent phenomenon: Tod's famous campaign showing Cary Grant, Steve McQueen, and Audrey Hepburn wearing its loafers went a long way toward establishing the brand as an iconic product.
- **Poetry** was not left untapped. In 1995, a Loewe scarf was illustrated with a drawing and verses of Garcia Lorca.
- **Photography.** A recent example is given by Raf Simons presenting a menswear Spring/Summer collection in 2017 at Pitti Uomo inspired by Robert Mapplethorpe, transforming the master's transgressive photos into fashion pieces.
- **Music.** The most visible example of a brand/artist collaboration, going beyond a specific one-in-a-time collection is the rapport that Chanel is building with the very successful American singer Pharrell Williams. Since his appearance in a memorable advertising campaign in 2015 with Cara Delevingne and then in 2017 for the launch of the Gabrielle bag, he had developed a close relationship with the brand and the late creative director Karl Lagerfeld. He is now launching a unisex Chanel Pharrell capsule collection to be sold in some selected Chanel stores. His world made of hip-hop, art, and design is inspiring his creations and allows Chanel to achieve two objectives: entering the menswear field strongly and opening to customers it had never been able to reach before.

Louis Vuitton, in a lot of ways, has been a pioneer since the 1980s in the collaborations with artists. In the 1980s, it launched a series of scarves designed by artists and designers such as Philippe Starck, Sol Le Witt, and James Rosenquist. A very visible project was Stephen Sprouse's graffiti on the traditional monogram canvas in the late 1990s, but one of the most prolific collaborations has been with Takashi Murakami, who worked for several seasons on new versions of the monogram and who produced animations and exhibitions. High moments have also occurred in 2012 with the fruitful collaboration between the French artist Daniel Buren and Marc Jacob, LV's creative director at the time, and with the Japanese artist Yayoi Kusama, with whom an extensive capsule collection and windows were developed.

The most spectacular coup occurred in Spring 2017, when Louis Vuitton launched the "Masters LV x Jeff Koons" collection of women's handbags, backpacks, charms, and scarves and the accompanying shop window concept, which displayed five paintings from the Western canon of art history: *Mona Lisa* (1506) by Leonardo da Vinci; *Mars, Venus, and Cupid* by Titian (1546); *The Tiger Hunt* by Peter Paul Rubens (1615–1616); *Girl with a Dog* (1770) by Jean-Honoré Fragonard; and *A Wheatfield with Cypresses* (1889) by Van Gogh. On the bags, a copy of an extract from each painting constitutes the main design with the original artist's last name featured at the center of it in gold-plated letters (silver for *Mona Lisa*). The LV logo, the JK initials, and some motifs from the monogram patterns are spread on the image. The bags are then adorned with elements of the Jeff Koons brand, a bunny and flower from his *Inflatables* series. The improbable association of today's most powerful luxury brand with a major contemporary painter and five giant Master painters from the past is unique in contemporary history. This operation has been praised by some critics who see in these tripartite pieces the symbol of the contemporary creative word where remix is a key specific process. Demystifying what the *bourgeois* venerate, trivializing the symbols of past cultures, giving the impression that art can be owned by everybody (still, the price of a handbag is between $1,000 and $4,000), falls perfectly within the current trend of the creation of signs with no signification of the gratuitous design strategy mentioned in Chapter 7 (in Figures 7.15, 7.16, and 7.17).

Marketing experts were overwhelmed with admiration and screamed genius. However, a few critics, like Annie le Brun (2018),[30] qualified the process of a *cultural butchering* (*Dépeçage* in French). We have no information on whether the bags were a commercial success. Some can be found on eBay at approximately the same price as the retail one. We still see more monogrammed Louis Vuitton handbags being worn than the Jeff Koons versions.

Foundations. One of the earliest and most common manifestations of the links between brands and the art world has been the cultural foundation: for example, *La Fondation Cartier pour l'art contemporain* was created in 1984 and is dedicated to promoting the development and awareness of all contemporary art forms, such as painting, video, design, photography, and fashion. Another example, though on a smaller scale, is the *fundacion Loewe*. Created in 1988 with the objectives of encouraging the creation of music, drawing, and poetry among young people, it has instituted a coveted prize for poetry in the Castilian language. In fact, most of the major brands are involved informally in sponsoring artistic activities. The last major initiative belongs also to LVMH. In 2006, the group created the *Fondation Louis Vuitton*. The building itself was inaugurated in 2014 with a commitment to the contemporary arts within a historical perspective. The American architect Frank Gehry designed an impressive glass building dedicated to culture in the Bois de Boulogne on the outskirts of Paris. "A new space that opens up a dialogue with a wide public and offers artists and intellectuals a platform for debate and reflection," declares Bernard Arnault on the foundation's website (https://www.fondationlouisvuitton.fr).

It should be noted that the Kering Corporate Foundation created in 2008 has no art-related activities. It has been created to fight violence against women.

The utilization of art and artists by luxury brands has, in general, been quite successful and it is hard to see how such an association can harm a brand in any way. It helps attract the press and public attention, it reinvigorates brand creativity, it brings a new relevance to the brand when it is associated with current celebrities from the world of art, and it provides proof of the brand's sensibility to aesthetics. Therefore, we

---

[30] Le Brun, A. *Ce qui n'a pas de prix.*

are sure that the interest demonstrated by the brands toward the arts is bound to continue to increase in the years to come.

In fact, we are now at the stage where certain brand creations are reaching art status. New York's Guggenheim Museum was the first one to break that taboo when it organized an Armani exhibition in 2000. The 2003 exhibition of Guy Bourdin's photographs from the 1970s advertising for Charles Jourdan are a good example of this change of status. Keep in mind that, 20 years ago, the word "fashion" was almost obscene in art circles. The continuing rise of photography as an artistic activity has contributed to this change of perception, as well as the spread of fashion and design-related museums and exhibitions.

The similarities between brands and arts and their current convergence is very much a two-way street.

From Arts to Brands

Contemporary art has tried relentlessly to demystify the classical notion of artistic creation based on academicism, ideals of transcendental beauty, harmony, and so on. In the process, it has been instrumental in introducing into it elements that had never been incorporated before. Marcel Duchamp was a precursor to this when, in 1913, he presented a bicycle wheel on a stool as an artistic creation. He began incorporating into his artwork technical elements such as doorknobs, plastic bottles, and day-to-day objects. This was not completely new, however, as Picasso had already utilized the handlebar and saddle from a bicycle in representing a bull.

Duchamp refined his logic to incorporate ready-made art pieces and the famous 1917 urinal. Here, the artistic position evolves into a purely editorial role, selecting objects from daily life and choosing the moment and place of the exhibition. Is this so different from the way some current designers work, selecting from myriad prototypes made by their junior assistants, the pieces that will appear on the catwalk? This extreme approach indeed leaves little room for real creativity.

Artistic activity reduced to the discovery of an original concept and leaning heavily on the techniques of provocation (all familiar words in the communication world) is something at which Andy Warhol was a master. He piled up Coke bottles, produced colored pictures of celebrities, and painted the famous Campbell Soup can. The artwork reproduced the branded object without adding anything to it. Warhol himself recognized that there were no messages in his work, that he was a *commercial artist*, and that, in fact, business was the most artistic activity of all. The difference between Warhol's signed poster of the Campbell Soup can and the actual product lies only in the discourse to be had about it. It is the art theory that makes the art piece.

Without knowing the theory, you cannot possibly know it is art. You need to be part of the avant-garde, this restricted group who know; hence the importance of communication in contemporary art. If you do not know that a particular brand is hot, you are out of fashion. The artist is exploiting a concept that has proved successful exactly as most brands are trying to do. Postmodernism is crossed by a strong relativism. Everything is art, just like everything is communication.

The new brand Fenty is an interesting new case of an artist becoming shareholder and CEO/creative director of a potentially luxury brand. This is not the first time hip-hop artists have developed their own brands of clothes and accessories. Jay-Z has built a sizeable business with the brand Rocawear that he created in 1999. The particularity of Fenty is that the LVMH group has partnered with the artist Rihanna (Ms. Robyn Rihanna Fenty) to create a new luxury Maison based in Paris. Fenty is managed by Rihanna, who is developing her own vision in women's ready-to-wear, shoes, and accessories, including commercialization and communication of the brand. Fenty debuted in Spring 2020. It already launched its first collection at the legendary New York retailer Bergdorf Goodman in February.

Museum Business.   Another taboo is disappearing. In the great rush to cash in on any little piece of reputation or notoriety that companies, institutions, or individuals may have gathered over time, the past 20 years have witnessed an incredible fever of brand-extension activities that have led many brands to propose the most bizarre and sometimes illegitimate product offerings.

The great museums were among the first to open little souvenir shops within their own facilities, selling posters, art books, slides, and postcards to the cultural tourist. For institutions with names such as Le Louvre, the Museum of Modern Art (MoMA), and El Prado, the temptation to extend these activities is enormous, when all the competition is doing it and when it has no harmful effects on the customers' brand perception.

Now, in downtown or airport boutiques we find an eclectic range of articles: impressionist ties, Van Gogh mouse pads, Mona Lisa T-shirts, Picasso refrigerator magnets, and Velazquez aprons. It did not take long for business to realize the potential of these activities, and brand logic invaded arts when specialized brands—Museum Musei, for example, with its slogan, "The art from all over the world"—were specifically created to promote art-related articles. This is certainly a form of democratization of the arts, though it is not universally appreciated. After all, isn't the single most obvious and most necessary determining characteristic of a museum the presence of objects within it?

The tangible museum boutique has also been made virtual through the Internet. Museumshop.com is a leader in offering thousands of products from hundreds of museums as well as its own inventions. The artists themselves were among the instigators of such moves. Salvador Dali—whose strong commercial sensibility was such that his surrealist colleagues called him Avida Dollars, an anagram of his name—churned out prints and lithographs during his lifetime. His heirs allowed for the successful development of a sizable perfume and cosmetics business under his name. Paloma Picasso developed an accessory collection and, for the past few years, anybody can drive a Citroën model bearing the name of the artist.

At the end of these converging processes of contemporary art proposing branded products as masterpieces, genuine masterpieces placarded all over day-to-day consumer goods, and brands borrowing creative legitimacy from the artistic world, the frontier between art and brands has become blurred.

Indeed, the two worlds converge at a number of points:

- The nature of their creative activities.
- Their commercial aims.
- Their customers.
- The fact that contemporary art is becoming another element of lifestyle.
- The brand logic applied to their business in terms of differentiation, ethics, aesthetics, and the use of communication and distribution to serve their commercial objectives.

We have to recognize that there are now many ambiguities on what distinguishes art from the world of brands. Both are indeed competing on the common ground of communication, trying to generate cash out of entertaining activities, offering both real and virtual experiences, trying to make people dream, and helping them escape reality. This ever-growing fusion between the two worlds is not happening by itself. Specific actors understood long ago all the advantages to be drawn from this ambiguity. Luxury visionaries like Bernard Arnault and Francois Pinault are both collectors and respective owners of the art auction houses Phillips and Christie and have been quite instrumental in favoring the symbiosis. It's now the same business, to the point where bridges between the two worlds may no longer be necessary: their territories are definitely overlapping.

We have focused in this section on what is common to art and brands and their dynamic approximation. For those interested in delving into the nature and functioning of the works of art, and by the differences of the brand manifestations themselves, we recommend reading Nelson Goodman on "When Is Art?,"[31] whose title is already a choice of an approach that avoids the more traditional question of "What is art?"

We conclude this chapter on merchandising and creation with a few considerations on the impact of the development of rapid digital technologies. After communication and sales, the design and development function is one that has benefited most from the rapid digital evolution. All junior graphic designers are designing on computers (although some of them are still able to draw by hand). Prototyping with 3D printers connected to computer-aided design (CAD) has literally exploded and allows for more efficiency in terms of costs and speed. The link with suppliers for samples and production is also more efficient through the use of common software. The functions most impacted by the digital development have been marketing and sales—the topic of the next chapter.

---

[31] N. Goodman, "When Is Art?," in D. Perkins and B. Leondar, *The Arts and Cognition.* Baltimore: John Hopkins University Press, 1977.

Chapter 9

Communication in Digital Times

I t has been 25 years since CERN (The European Organization for Nuclear Research) made the Word Wide Web technology available to everyone on a royalty-free basis. Since then, the world has changed drastically for the major part of the world's populations in terms of how we spend our time, how we relate to others, and how we get access to information. We have seen new business activities being created, financial empires being built, companies' markets disappear, and the surging economic and geostrategic importance of the East. Some compare the digital revolution to the invention of the printing press, others to an industrial revolution where data and communication bring enormous productivity benefits. Dominique Cardon (2019) has a simple definition that retains that the digital explosion is a rupture of the ways our society produces, shares, and uses knowledge.[1]

A small set of recent statistics can define the situation. This Digital 2020 report from Datareportal published in partnership with We Are Social and Hootsuite, released on January 30, 2020, shows that digital activities are now an essential part of everyday life across the world.[2] On a global world population estimated at 7.8 billion, 4.5 billion (58%) are using the Internet, while social media users have reached 3.8 billion (49%). The trend continues to grow.

Luxury brands have not ignored this prodigious trend and most of them are heavily involved in the digital world. At the end of 2018, online sales already made up 9% of global luxury sales,[3] and they're growing faster than the total sales of luxury goods. All the leading luxury brand names are investing heavily in e-commerce and digital marketing. Even Hermès is selling online.

In this chapter we will describe first the main characteristics of these "digital times," come back to the nature of communication with new logics that digital technology brought about, and end up with a few reminders on traditional communication, which remains a relevant part of the engagement director's responsibility.

Digital Times

How can we characterize *digital times* in an extremely synthetic way?

Immediate universal access, everywhere, for all information, to everybody, who are both receptor and transmitter.

This statement stresses the speed and ubiquity of the connectivity but its terse form might not stress sufficiently the power to act that is being given to everybody, nor does it mention all the new values and businesses that this hyperconnectivity is generating. In this section we

---

[1] D. Cardon, *Culture Numérique*. Paris: Presses de Sciences Po, 2019. Dominique Cardon is professor of sociology at Sciences Po, Paris, and director of Medialab. He has published extensively on the digital world, and we have referenced his latest book extensively.

[2] https://datareportal.com/reports/digital-2020-global-digital-overview.

[3] https://www.digitalcommerce360.com/2018/10/23/luxury-brands-aggressively-turn-to-e%E2%80%91commerce/.

will try to keep a broad view on the ways the Web has changed and continues to change our daily lives.

A Brief History

The Internet was born in the United States in collaboration with researchers in the United Kingdom and France, as a project of inter-connecting computer networks. As with most revolutionary inventions, the Web as we know it today is the result of a long process with an increasing speed pattern as it approached the end result:

- **The predigital pioneers**. The earliest known computing machine (now called computer science) attempt goes back to French Blaise Pascal's arithmetic machine (la Pascaline) in 1642. In 1834 British Charles Babbage, together with Ada Lovelace, invented a pro-grammable machine, which, though it never worked, is considered to be the first configurable calculator. The Boolean logic invented by the British George Boole in 1854 served as the basis for the digital language logic with its three basic principles of conjunction (and), disjunction (or), and negation (no).
- **1936** is the year the British scientist Alan Turing published his famous article giving the theoretical groundwork to build a com-puting machine working on the basis of decomposing information in 0s and 1s, which is considered the birth of the binary language of digital computing.
- The Cold War context of the **1960s** eventually led to the formation of ARPANET (the Advanced Research Projects Agency Network) by the US Department of Defense.
- In **1973,** Vint Cerf at Stanford University and Bob Kahn at ARPA published research, including the design concepts from the French Cyclades project directed by Louis Pouzin that evolved into the Transmission Control Protocol (TCP) and Internet Protocol (IP), the two protocols of the Internet protocol suite.
- **1983** is considered the Internet's official birthday. On January 1, ARPANET and the Defense Data Network adopted the TCP/IP protocols in order to allow different computers on different networks to "talk" to each other. All computers and networks could now be connected by a universal language.

- Commercial Internet service providers (ISPs) began to emerge in the very late 1980s.
- **In 1990** Tim Berners-Lee invented the World Wide Web while working at CERN (Centre Européen de recherche nucléaire, or The European Organization for Nuclear Research) in Switzerland. The Web is a communication protocol allowing the connection between pages through the well-known hypertext link http:// www. The Web is included in the Internet and is one of several ways to retrieve information from it, simplifying its utilization, while the latter includes many other things like SMTP, IRC, FTP, Gopher, and Telnet protocols. You probably will not need these protocols, as many Web browsers allow users to access files using most of the protocols.
- On April 30, **1993**, CERN renounces its copyrights on all Web software and protocols, publishes the source code, and all html technologies become open to the public.
- **1995** is the date recognized as the beginning of widespread public utilization of the Web made possible by browsers like Internet Explorer, launched the same year.

"Internet is born as a political utopia and the Web as a commercial promise," writes Dominique Cardon (2019).[4] It may be the proper place to highlight the dual philosophical nature of the digital world that evolved from a certain Californian hippy culture of the 1970s to a prevailing individualistic merchant and egocentric spirit in the twenty-first century. This paradox continues these days under different forms, with dialectics like community/individual, open/restricted, cool/loud, libertarian/controlled, and so on, still very present on the Web as we experience it today and something that brands have to keep in mind.

A glossary of some of the basic digital expressions is to be found in Appendix B.

Overall Impact of Digital Technologies

"Digital revolution is a rupture in the ways our societies produce, share and use knowledge," writes Cardon.[5] It is generating deep changes in

---

[4] Cardon, *Culture Numérique*.
[5] Cardon, *Culture Numérique*.

ways of thinking and acting; it is challenging established authorities, redistributing power, and developing a genuine new culture.

The simple exercise of listing all the functions that are concentrated today into a mobile phone might give an overall idea of where we have gotten in terms of digitalization and the consequential changes it has had on our daily life. This is far from an exhaustive list as apps are numerous and continue to be created every day, but it may give an idea of many objects and services that are physically disappearing from our lives and how differently we behave:

> Telephones; calendars; watches; stopwatches; alarm clocks; calculators; typewriters; voice recorders; dictionaries; encyclopedias; flashlights; door keys; archiving; taking notes; money; banking transactions; maps; transportation, travel, and entertainment advisors; weather forecasts; travel agencies; translators; watching movies; listening to music; visiting museums; post offices; pictures and video cameras (taking and retouching); reading books; designing/drawing/painting; purchasing; shopping; making presentations; learning; playing; watching TV; reading newspapers; teleconferencing …

Table 9.1 is an attempt at summarizing the broad effects that digital technology is having on our societies, the consumers, and the brands. The most optimistic digital advocates promote the idea that the digital world is a mere prolongation and augmentation of the ordinary social rapports and activities and not necessarily a cultural change. We tend to disagree. You do not spend an average of 6 hours and 43 minutes (2020 data)[6] every day in front of a screen (that means 100 days per year being connected) and live with the comfort that all the human knowledge is available in a few clicks without a major rearrangement of the ways your brain works.

The Web has given eyes, public voice, and power to act to a crowd of ordinary citizens and granted them the power to know, connect, share, act, create, and express their opinions, talents or defects, personality, moods, life events, and so forth.

One of the success factors in the development of the Web has been that a large number of services seem to be offered for free, whether you

---

[6] https://datareportal.com/reports/digital-2020-global-digital-overview.

Effects	Knowing, Connecting, and Acting	Consequences and Examples
In general	Increasing power of individuals More capacity to know, connect, share, act, create, and express	Searches, bookings, buying knowledge, products, and services Digital art, co-creation Collective thinking, intelligence, and creation
	Surging of new collective projects Creating new business activities Improving old business models	Exchange platforms (social media, e-commerce, etc.) Self-organized communities Maintaining the Web
	Changing distribution of power and value creation	Relative obsolescence of numerous objects and services (paper geographical maps, encyclopedias, travel booking agencies, etc.)
	Instant spread of information Instant connection everywhere in the world Instant access to expertise and knowledge	Exponential exposure to volumes of information
	Thinking *vs.* knowing Different human brain utilization Weakening of past basic skills (memorization, mental arithmetic, etc.) Surge of new specialized vocabulary	Less use of memory Emergence of a more creative and collective intelligence Reduced capacity for integration and synthesis Weakening of handwriting
	Reinforcement of individualization Underutilization of tactile sense	Thirst for "high-touch" real contacts (real face-to-face presence) to compensate for excess screen rapports
On Customers	Engaging the brands, sharing opinions/experiences Transacting online More pre-purchase preparation	Blogs, social media feedback Co-creating with brands Becoming a personal medium
On Brands	Capacity to engage customers Capacity to gather information on each customer Easier specific customer-targeted communication New powerful market research techniques More efficient prospective techniques	Competing for customers' attention CRM development Quicker market/product testing Quicker feedback on products/services Ability to quantitatively analyze all digital contacts

purchase products and services, connect with family and friends, search for employment, or gain access to information and news. In fact, the commercial successes of Google, Facebook, Twitter, and so on are based on a business model that generates revenue through advertising and uses the collected data to profile and customize communication.

This has raised concerns on privacy and protection of data. The European Union developed the General Data Protection Regulation (GDPR) requiring websites to notify visitors of the data they collect and giving visitors the ability to consent to information-gathering.

The profound digital transformations have also triggered the creation of numerous companies based on improved secular businesses like Amazon and Alibaba or completely new activities like messaging, intermediary technological companies, and an overwhelming number of apps.

TikTok is an interesting and recent example of the creative space generated by the Web. TikTok is a video-sharing social networking app owned by the Chinese company ByteDance. It is used to create funny short dance, comedy, and show videos of a maximum of 60 seconds. It was first launched in China as Douyin in 2016 and then as TikTok in 2017 for iOS and Android in markets outside of China. It became available in the United States in 2018 after merging with musical.ly. It was the most downloaded app on the App Store in 2018 and 2019. That a short video application could reach 800 million active users[7] in so short of a time even when YouTube basically could be used for the same purpose is part of the digital magic and the surgical segmentation it allows.

WeChat is the more successful example of an Internet service combining a large number of features. It combines the functions of a call or video call, social media, chat, location sharing, file transfer, e-commerce, and payment. It is the equivalent of a brand's website, loyalty program, payment gateway, social campaigns, and advertising all in one and it reaches 1.1 billion monthly active users in 2020.

Another interesting example from China is Mr. Bags. He is one of China's most influential fashion bloggers, who has more than 5 million followers on Weibo and more than 850,000 followers on WeChat. He has collaborated with Givenchy, Chloé, Longchamp, and Burberry. For

---

[7] https://datareportal.com/reports/digital-2020-global-digital-overview.

Tod's, he managed to sell RMB 3.24 million worth of handbags (a limited co-designing edition for the Chinese Year of the Dog) on WeChat within six minutes from his e-shop, called "Baoshop."

Impact on Consumers

There are four major impacts on consumers' relationships with brands stemming from the resonance of the Web public space, the interconnectivity with the brands, and the e-commerce possibilities:

The consumers have an increased influence on the brand decisions (logo changes, products, etc.) and brand behaviors. It endows the customers with powers that existed only embryonically before. The advent of the Web has been to connect in real time the customer, not only to the brands but to all the actors active on the Internet (family, friends, virtual communities, brands, institutions, platforms, news, etc.). This wide connected network of brands and consumers has multiplied the power of the latter. As an example of this power, an Internet campaign by Greenpeace in 2010 led Nestlé to change a palm oil supplier that was destroying large areas of tribal ancestral rain forest. The influence exercises also within the digital world. In 2012, Netflix had planned to raise its subscription fees by $6 without proposing any service upgrade. Criticism from consumers was so intense that the company backed away from its decision.

Co-creation. A great number of consumers want to express their own creativity. An interesting example was the 2016 initiative of the Manchester City Football Club, which organized focus groups, surveys, user tests, and prototype designs with supporters in order to improve the look of both the Web and mobile experience, resulting in a mobile-first, video-rich experience with modern design and more relevant content.

The consumer takes more time to mull over their purchases because they have more means to obtain information and opinions as well as to make comparisons among competitors. We will see later in this chapter more details on the pre- and post-purchase phases of the customer purchase journey.

Consumers can purchase online at every moment of the day or night and from everywhere.

Impact on Brands

"If I displease a customer, I lose a salotto," used to say Salvatore Ferragamo, who was blessed with a rare combination of creative genius
and shrewd commercial sense. A *salotto* meant the group of four to six
ladies usually gathering for tea at 5 o'clock sharing, among other things,
their latest shopping experiences. Well, the *salotto* now is so much bigger, made up of the the Facebook friends of the group of ladies and all
the digital communities they belong to, compounded by an exponential
effect as each person relates to several others, and so on. There are five
main areas where brands have benefited from the Web:

The capacity to gather information on each customer
Easier specific customer-targeted communication
New powerful market research techniques
The capacity to engage customers
More efficient prospective techniques

In fact, it is characteristic of the fourth phase of the historical evolution of brands, as shown in Table 9.2.

Brand Evolution: A Historical Perspective.   Most of the twentieth century until the 1970s was a relatively low-tension competitive
context, and brands developed to foster identification and memorization of products. In the 1970s, the brand appeared as a subelement of
communication and rapidly developed into a new communication alternative to traditional product-focused advertising. Viewing product and
brand communication as mutually exclusive alternatives probably contributed to delaying a proper understanding of their respective natures.
This was the period in which Philip Kotler's 4 *P*s were presented as the
most relevant marketing analytical scheme.[8] It relied on the adaptation
and coordination of Products, Price, Promotion, and Place for achieving
effective responses to the customers' needs. This is what is still commonly
called the *marketing mix*. Brand at the time was only one element of the
products' activities, together with product line, quality, packaging, and
services.

---

[8] Philip Kotler, *Marketing Management*. Prentice Hall, 1967.

Table 9.2 Brand Historical Evolution (note that the dates are approximate as there is no real sudden discontinuity in the described periods)

Period	Brand Evolution Phase	Selling Values	Nature
1900–1950	Birth of the modern brand phenomenon	Products	Identification/differentiation
1950–1990	Explosive growth	Products/brand values	
1990–2010	Brand portfolios consolidation Branding logics spread	Brand values more intangible	Vector of meaning
< 2010	Antagonistic forces of: • Rationalization of portfolio • Ease in creating Internet–related brands • Relative decrease of brand identity strength	Accessibility and quick fads competing with brand identities Capability to engage customers	Existential Influencer and influenced

In the 1990s, there was a very clear shift toward intangible values expressed by the communication and associated with the products. Symbolic and semiotic values became crucial. The brand seized power. We moved from the modern brand that held sway from the 1950s to the 1990s, which was a mere communication instrument to promote the product, to the postmodern brand, which proposes meanings and possible worlds, establishing complicity with the customer beyond the product and often anchored in services. The brand became a project of meaning, where the product was only one of its manifestations. The postmodern brand proposed (and continues to) fantasy worlds, dreams, and values that give a specific meaning to the brand product or service consumption. It enriches the purchase experience. This is the period where we witness the omnipresence of brands in social life, where brand logics invade most social territories, extending to art, politics, education, NGO, and so on.

Around 2010, the spread and maturation of the possibilities given by the Web put another turbo on the postmodern brand. Without really changing its nature as a project of meaning, the multiplication of commercial and communication activities online has increased in parallel both the weight of the customers in the managing of the brand, including through the iterative process of brand identity building, as well as the relative weight of the brand as a social influencer itself. One of the most salient emerging features for brands has been the possibility of coming closer to its customers by engaging them, symmetrical to what happened for the customers with respect to the brands. Due to the constant increase of people's digital-related daily lives, customers have become major influencers on brands' identity and behavior. The Web has reinforced all connected individuals' capacities to act and interact. Meanwhile, brands have become major influencers in people's lives and beliefs.

Brand behavior. All brands are now trying to engage the consumers, influence them. They do not simply push products and communication anymore; they exchange and listen to their targeted Web users. This is why the concept of conversation is spreading so rapidly in marketing these days. We will come back to it in the Conclusion at the end of this chapter. In 2017, Adidas's move to create running shoes made from ocean waste is a good example of listening to the consumers' aspirations for sustainability and well-made sneakers. They sold over a million pairs in 2017.

One of the positive effects of digital times is the simple fact that everything is fast becoming public. With all the resonance power of the Web, brands have to behave with integrity, be true, and be authentic.

Another effect on brands is that because of all the "noise" created by the volume and flow of information on the Web, brands need to have bold, surprising messages and initiatives. This is not always easy for the major consolidated luxury brands that tend to have a more subdued approach, except those whose brand identity is anchored into provocation, like Roberto Cavalli for instance.

Luxury brands and e-commerce. Contrary to the mass brands, which quickly understood the potential that the Web was representing, the luxury brands were initially reluctant to use the Web. After all, one of the specificities of luxury is precisely the multisensorial experience available only in a monobrand store. Initially, some specialized sites, such as eLuxury, launched luxury brands on the Web. This commercial site, pioneer of online luxury business, launched by LVMH in 2000, presented a wide selection of apparel and accessories for prestigious brands like Dior, Emilio Pucci, Céline, Marc Jacobs, Versace, Dolce & Gabbana, Fendi, Tod's, and Louis Vuitton. In a sign of the times, the site closed late 2009 probably because of the opening of their own commercial sites by most of the brands. It has since been transformed into a Web magazine called *Nowness*, which is now "a video channel premiering the best in global arts and culture across Art & Design, Culture, Fashion & Beauty, Music and Food & Travel."[9] Art never harms a brand. Then, mid-2017, LVMH launched a new proprietary multibrand luxury online store called "24 Sèvres," the address of its Parisian luxury department store Le Bon Marché. It features not only LVMH's own portfolio of brands but also curates luxury fashion, accessories, and beauty products outside of the group. Even though the name is somewhat reminiscent of the Hermès fragrance 24 Faubourg (Hermès's Paris flagship store), the concept is quite innovative as it puts the products in context. Contrary to the specialized luxury multibrand e-commerce sites such as Farfetch Tmall Pavilion and Yoox, Net-à-Porter and Farfetch rely on glossy editorial content and fast delivery. 24 Sèvres focuses on

---

[9] https://www.nowness.com/.

digital "storefront" windows and is an attempt at rendering the online experience of shopping as close as possible to the one experienced in a physical luxury department store.

Traditional multibrand distributors have also quickly understood the need to be active in this new market. In 2010, Saks Fifth Avenue launched its e-commerce site, which 10 years later can ship to 206 countries[10] within a maximum of 14 days' delivery, offering most of the categories of products found in its traditional stores. There was, therefore, little sense for luxury brands not to directly control their sales online, especially since they already had active communication websites and were already present on social networks regardless of their will.

Faced with the rapid development of multibrand sites, and especially with the popularity of certain segments of the market for online purchases, luxury brands started opening their own commercial websites.

Thus, Gucci, in 2010, launched its online shop with great fanfare; Ferragamo had already been operational for some time. Louis Vuitton has been one of the pioneers in exploring the frontiers of digital activities. Its website contains an e-shopping feature that allows purchasing online, but the brand also multiplies the electronic addresses. These multiple websites not only increase the presence and the possibilities of contact with consumers, but allow many correlations among all the vectors of the overall communication strategy.

Most of the big players (Van Cleef and Arpel, Dior, De Beers, Hermès, Tiffany, Cartier, Guerlain, etc.) are selling online, as well as the smaller ones that need all the distribution power they can harness.

Chanel remains one of the last luxury brands having second thoughts about the relevance of the use of the Web for commercial transactions. Their executives seem not to be convinced that e-commerce is necessarily the way to connect to younger generations, or maybe it is not part of their core target. Still, at the end of 2016 they started selling fragrance, beauty, and eyewear products online. The announcement in 2018 of a strategic partnership with the global luxury e-commerce platform Farfetch to develop new digital initiatives may indicate a change of approach.

---

[10] https://www.saksfifthavenue.com/International.

Rolex is still not available for sales online as "New and genuine Rolex watches are exclusively sold by official Rolex Retailers," declares their website.[11]

The multibrand commercial platforms have also become major actors in the online sales activities. We will mention only the biggest one: Alibaba, Amazon's Chinese competitor, which was founded in 1999. Its online sales (US$34.7 billion in 2019) and profits surpassed all US retailers (including Walmart, Amazon, and eBay) combined since 2015. Considered reluctantly by the established luxury brands, it created Tmall Luxury Pavilion for premier brands in 2017. Since then the list of luxury brands eyeing the voluminous Chinese market present on the site has grown tremendously. As of February 2020, there were more than 150 luxury brands like Burberry; Hugo Boss; La Mer; Maserati; Isabel Marant; Valentino; Versace; Ermenegildo Zegna; Tod's; Moschino; Giuseppe Zanotti; MCM; LVMH brands, like Guerlain, Givenchy, Tag Heuer, Kenzo, and Zenith; Kering Group brands, like Qeelin and Stella McCartney. Richemont-owned prestigious jeweler Cartier was the latest luxury brand to join. Luxury's leading brands, such as Louis Vuitton and Gucci, have not come around to Tmall yet.

Meanwhile, in Europe, the Richemont group acquired Net-à-Porter in 2010. This commercial website, created in 2000, was then merged in 2015 with Yoox, the Italian online fashion retailer, to create the Yoox Net-à-Porter Group. On April 27, 2020, Yoox co-founder Federico Marchetti relinquished his role as CEO because of the poor performance in the recent years, sales falling short of a €4 billion 2019 revenue target and losses accumulating.[12]

In terms of communication, the rise of the social networks has had a seismic effect on the growth of Web power. One tells about his life on Facebook, shares one's pleasures and worries on WhatsApp, seeks a partner on Meetic, features in video on YouTube, gives one's opinion on Twitter or in multiple specialized forums, makes an appointment on Foursquare, and so on. We will see later in a special paragraph the role of social networks in luxury brand communication.

---

[11] https://www.rolex.com/watch-care-and-service/buy-rolex-watch.html.
[12] https://www.businessoffashion.com/articles/news-analysis/yoox-net-a-porter-federico-marchetti-steps-down.

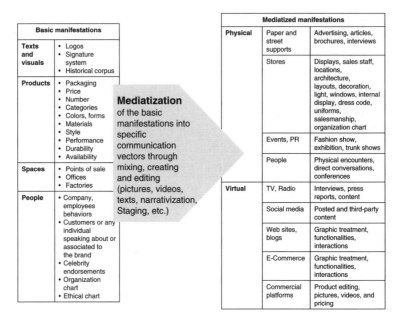

Figure 9.1　Basic and Mediatized Manifestations

There is no doubt, for any of the actors, that the Internet has revolutionized both trade and communication. Its capabilities allow brands to intensify and disseminate their presence, in a controlled manner (or not). The Web opens the possibility of interactivity in real time, of an increased exposure and multiplication of all brand manifestations, and, consequently, of a formidable management complexity. More than ever, the screens (computers, television, electronic tablets, mobile phones, kiosks, and videos) and the ways they are used hold the key to the future of many brands

Communication, which used to be one of the links in a chain, has become the chain itself. Kotler's legendary 4Ps have given way to brand manifestations (Figure 9.1) and the communication chain (see Figure 9.2) that we are going to see in next section .

Engaging Customers

Since one of the main impacts of digital times on brands has been to make them realize that push-communication has definitely been replaced by

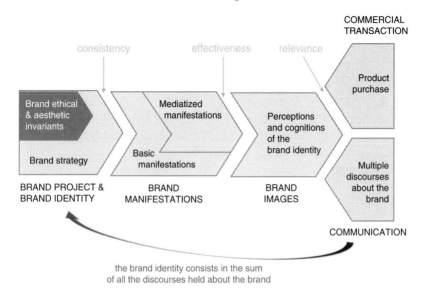

Figure 9.2 The Communication Chain

engaging the customer, we thought it relevant to go back to the word *engage* so widely used in communication these days.

We referred to Webster's 1913 dictionary,[13] which gives six main meanings, five of which perfectly describe ways brands must engage customers today:

1. The origin of the word is French, coming from "mettre en gage" (i.e., *to put under pledge; to place under obligations; to do or forbear doing something, as by a pledge, oath, or promise; to bind by contract or promise*). We find here the concepts of brand promise and brand contract that have been around in marketing circles since the 1980s. Without a brand promise that creates positioning and expectations, a brand cannot expect to reach and engage its customers.

2. *To gain for service; to bring in as associate or aid; to enlist; as, to engage friends to aid in a cause.* This is also relevant for brands today. Being able to motivate customers and mobilize them for social and sustainability causes or, more simply, to engage them as brand unconditional fans is an efficient way to create privileged links between brands and consumers. We have seen a great number of initiatives from brands

---

[13] https://www.websters1913.com/words/Engage.

during the early phase of the coronavirus pandemic in 2020, such as offering non-government organizations (NGOs) free access to brand sites and raising funds or help from Web users for specific causes.

3. *To gain over; to win and attach; to attract and hold; to draw.* This is indeed the ultimate brand goal in communication.

4. *To employ the attention and efforts of; to occupy; to engross; to draw on.* This is the meaning related to the expression of engaging someone in a conversation and is very valid for brands.

5. *To enter into contest with; to encounter; to bring to conflict*—like in engaging the enemy. This is the only meaning not applying to brands that have no interest in developing an antagonistic attitude with the consumers. It could apply to the rapports with the competition.

6. *(Mach.)* To come into gear with; as, the teeth of one cogwheel engage those of another, or one part of a clutch engages the other part. This meaning taken from technical gears serves as a good metaphor of the common work and results achievable by two components that need each other to function.

This is indeed a proper basis for a comprehensive engagement plan.

Communication

There are lots of theories on communication, and we would go beyond the purpose of the book to try to describe them. To go to the essence of the phenomenon, we will remain at the very general statement that *everything is communication* because any experience or encounter with the world by human beings generates perception and cognition.

Brand Manifestations

The occasions of experiences and encounters between brands and consumers are generated by *brand manifestations*. They are all the possible sensory interfaces with potential and existing customers. The recently introduced notion of touchpoint is quite similar to manifestations when defined as the ways that a brand interacts and displays information to prospective and existing customers. The manifestation notion is brand focused, multisensorial in nature, and does not necessarily generate an interaction with the potential customer, even though this is the ultimate purpose. Kevin McTigue (2019) proposes a definition that fits perfectly with our version of brand manifestation meaning: "Brand touchpoints are any point where your brand intersects with the consumer. They are the multiple places you see, hear, touch, speak with, and experience a brand."[14]

The manifestation scheme presented in Figure 8.12 in the previous chapter is adequate to highlight all the multiple and different competencies involved in communicating about the brand. However, if it was valid 10 years ago to also develop a comprehensive approach to brand communication activities, it fails to grasp the complexity that the digital communication introduced into communication management. There are many more types of manifestations, and many more actors not belonging to the brand giving their opinions and creating therefore more manifestations not directly controlled by the brand.

We have tried to come to terms with this new complexity by expanding the previous manifestation scheme (Figure 8.12) and categorizing the manifestations into basic and mediatized (see Figure 9.1). We have highlighted the fact that there are some fundamental, simple "brand life" elements like the product or a space, for instance, which are then mixed and exposed to the markets after creative and editing treatments and choice of media to reach and engage the customers. This is a process of mediatization of the simple basic manifestations bricks. It is also the opportunity to stress the importance of the Web in the communication process without forgetting what the content is made of.

The basic manifestations, fundamental bricks out of which to compose the communication, are the same as in the previous edition: products, spaces, people, and preexisting texts and visuals. The people's part has been expanded to take into account the intense activities of Web surfers. It felt important to show the intricate itinerary that communication takes and separate the decisions that are mainly of a creative nature in constructing the elementary building blocks of any communication from the narrativization and staging activities (*mise en intrigue* and *mise en scène*) that lead to the mediatized manifestations. We can refer

---

[14] K. McTigue, "Leveraging Touchpoints in Today's Branding Environment," in *Kellogg on Branding in a Hyper-connected World*, edited by A. M. Tybout and T. Calkins. Hoboken, NJ: John Wiley & Sons, 2019.

to Semprini's semionarrative scheme presented in Chapter 7 in Figure 7.21. The mediatized manifestations belong to the superficial level of the meaning construction process.

The mediatized manifestations are classified in physical and digital. The physical part contains what used to be called traditional communication (paper and street advertising, PR and events, stores, and people associated with the brand encountered face to face, not through a screen). The digital part is also classified by channel (media) and covers everything visible through a screen by all the Web established players (e-commerce and commercial platforms, social media, websites, and blogs; TV and radio having also been classified in that category).

The simple truth for the communication director (or better called now, the engagement director) is that he needs to guide and coordinate all the possible brand interfaces with the market. This consideration stems from a basic postulate that more arrows being shot at the same target are more efficient in generating sales than a random shotgun approach. In reality, there are several possible strategies available to the director. We can use a musical metaphor to describe the engagement director's responsibility. He is like a musician sitting at a keyboard, able to control (or at least influence) all of the brand manifestations, composing and playing—hopefully with success—the brand music, that is, the coordinated use of all the brand manifestations. There are four possible strategies:

The repetitive strategy, whereby, for reasons of efficiency, similar messages are expected from each manifestation. Even though fragmentary in essence, each of them should contain most of the identity values. This is a simplistic approach not able to exploit the rich array of possible manifestations, each of them having its own specificity and communication power.

The complementary strategy, by which different messages begin to make sense when merged, as, for instance, when classic store architecture highlights the baroque aesthetics of the products.

The cacophony strategy (or better, the absence of strategy), which unfortunately is still very frequent, where each manifestation tells its own story without overall coordination with the others.

The symphonic strategy, where each type of manifestation is used to its maximum efficiency in order to contribute to the easiest possible perception and understanding of the brand identity and its commercial offer. We know, for instance, that the Web can communicate more comprehensively and exhaustively on conceptual matters than the product, and that advertising can communicate more easily than architecture on brand ethics.

Adding to the difficulties of the engagement director's task is that the "noncontrolled" manifestations, such as all the information on the brand exchanged on the Web by users, has become so huge in number and therefore in influence. This is where the use of influencers can play a big role. They are included in the basic manifestation category under "people: customers or any individual speaking about or associated to the brand," with a main difference with respect to the usual customer posting on Facebook: they are remunerated for their posts.

The Communication Chain

In order to present the overall communication process from the formalization of the brand strategy of which the brand identity is an essential component to the act of purchase via the brand manifestations, we have updated the previous edition's communication chain scheme. Figure 9.2 illustrates the comprehensive sequence.

It all starts from a clear willingness to propose a brand project to the market. This is followed by all the perceivable elements of the brand, which we have called the *brand manifestations*. This is the sensory world of the brand, where its aesthetics are supposed to pursue the three purposes seen in Chapter 6 (see Table 6.6, Three Purposes of Aesthetic Treatments): representation, decoration, and functionality . As seen in the previous paragraph, this second tile of the process regroups both the basic and mediatized manifestations. Some of the basic ones sometimes have a direct access to the public without being mediatized. An example is the special rapport of an individual with a product such as a pair of shoes or a fragrance.

The passage from the first to the second link of the chain (known as the *consistency transition*) lies in the scripting and staging of the brand ethics into discourse and images (the *mise en intrigue* and *mise en scène*). The third step of the sequence comprises the multiple perceptions that these manifestations generate within the market, which lead in turn to the last link of the chain, split between the actual purchase and the multiple discourses about the brand visible by the Web users. This split last tile of the process is due to the fact that the communication process does not always end up in a purchase but very often in further communication induced by Web users. The passage between the second and third links is called the effectiveness transition: How effective are all the manifestations in conveying the desired brand identity? The passage between the third and fourth tiles is called the *relevance transition*, as no purchase or further communication is likely to occur if the customers are not interested in what they have perceived.

This scheme is a powerful analytical tool that can serve multiple management purposes. An example of an immediate use of the communication chain is to serve as a methodological framework for a brand communication audit. Another one is to use the framework to manage the seasonal communication plan.

The arrow from the "multiple discourses about the brand" back to "the brand project and identity" represents the fact that this is the dialectic between the brand and the market, which contributes to build the brand identity. The influence of the markets through the Web are more visible than ever. No need to stage real brands boycott manifestations as occurred in the 1970s, the Web has an enormous resonance and is proving now and again the power of the customers. It should be clear, however, that in the co-construction iterative process of the brand identity, both sides operate with different decision-making power and intervention tools. It is the brand that takes the initiative to cancel a new logo under the pressure of the Web, as happened at GAP in 2010. It could have stuck to the new version and taken responsibility for the market consequences. It is always the brand's decision to integrate—or not—the feedback from the markets.

Converging media. The linear presentation of the communication chain is mainly aimed at understanding the itinerary of the elements of communication that travel from the company and then are fed back to it. It also highlights that some communication elements are not directly controlled by the company. In front of this evolving communication field, media have started to be classified in three parts:

1. The owned media that the brand fully controls, like its own website, controlled blogs, and proprietory social media accounts.

2. The paid media that the brand pays to use its services, like traditional and digital advertising, paid searches, and sponsorships.
3. The earned media where customers are the channels and where the brand hopes to generate word of mouth, buzz, and possibly viral reactions.

It seems clear from the recent evolution that the three types of media will eventually converge. Many brands are already integrating elements of the earned media (favorable tweets or Facebook posts) into their own websites.

Communication Strategy

There are seven main starting points of a communication strategy:

The state of the brand reputation
The existing customers' profiles and states of mind
The desired customers
Internal aspects that the brand wants to make public (hiring of a new designer, a change of CEO, opening of new stores, new websites, etc.)
Products and services to be promoted (new product categories, new businesses, new services, etc.)
Strategic objectives that the brand wants to make public
Reference competitors' communication strategy

The first three elements of the communication strategy deserve some discussion.

Brand reputation. One great advance that digital technology brings to brands is the capacity to actually measure and therefore monitor brand reputation, which, in the past, necessitated substantial and expensive market research. Now, by blending Web and social media monitoring, SEO reputation, and surveying data on what people say, think, feel, and expect about the brand, we can constantly measure the brand reputation and have feedback on any initiative.

Existing and desired customers. Wertime and Fenwick (2008) advocate the obsolescence of the notion of market segmentation, arguing that "It is an outdated term which does not reflect that people now interact with the multiplicity of channels around them. What is required is a more contemporary and holistic way to think about your consumers and how to generate sustained engagement with them."[15] This leads to what they call a *Participant Print*, which is supposed to "capture the essence of the group of people who comprise your customers." This print includes the general profile made of psycho- and demographic data; the digital profile, composed of three digital data: the digital usage habits; the content consumption preferences; and a very new type of data, the consumer's content creation profile (avatars, virtual sport leagues participation, own blogs, etc.); the third component of the Participant Print is made up of the individual profiles of high-value consumers.

Sasin example. We present in Appendix A the work done on the Sasin School of Management brand identity. The subsequent developing of the communication strategy is a recent and relevant example on the path to follow for a higher education institution. It was prepared with a clear awareness of the current reputation, knowledge of the essence of the group of people who comprise Sasin customers, and in general the seven basic elements mentioned earlier on communication strategy.

First the underlying logics were formalized:

- Increase Sasin overall awareness outside of Thailand.
- Reinforce the impression of renewed dynamism and innovation at Sasin with alumni and potential Thai students.
- Announce all the deep changes occurring at Sasin.
- Increase Sasin local visibility and interactions.
- Attract intelligent and socially/ecologically sensitive students.
- Communicate Sasin brand identity, focusing on the three basic tenets "Global Thai/action oriented/human centered," of which entrepreneurship and sustainability are the most representative.
- Increase consistency among all the brand manifestations and in particular in graphic creative production.
- Increase frequency and volume of content online.
- More intense engagement of potential students.
- The economic and geopolitical importance of Asia and SEA.
- Thailand as a better alternative than China or Singapore.
- And so on.

---

[15] K. Wertime and I. Fenwick, *Digimarketing: The Essential Guide to New Media & Digital Marketing*. Singapore: John Wiley & Sons, 2008.

Table 9.3   Comprehensive Media Plan

		Activities	Weekly Calendar
Content production	**Products**	Primary focus (high margins, more representative of the brand, etc.)	
		Secondary focus (big investment products, special occasions, etc.)	
	Events	Fashion shows, participation in shows, etc.	
	Others	News stories, interviews, articles; webinars, blog post developments	
Media category	**Paid/organic search**	Keyword search, analytics, SEO improvements	
	Social media	Planning content and distribution to the selected media (banners, video, etc.)	
	Influencers	Search, evaluation, and control	
	E-mail marketing	Defined specific information, recall, testing, and promotional campaigns	
	Paper press and other traditional media	Planning content and distribution to selected media	

Then, specific content was developed in terms of key vocabulary, slogans, and graphic environment. Ultimately, a comprehensive communication plan was developed crossing all the different stakeholders with all the digital and traditional initiatives similar to what is indicated later in Table 9.3.

The frequency of revision of the communication strategy has increased notably and is more likely to be at least on a quarterly basis now.

Specificities of Digital Communication

I could not imagine then the miracle of the cellular phone, where sigh and confession cross the space like the light, whatever the gap and the distance. Emotions respond, feelings merge.

—Michel Serres, 2017[16]

Obviously,[16] digital times are revolutionizing and complexifying communication management, rendering obsolete a certain number of antiquated tools and inducing the introduction of more adequate ones.

In this section we will cover the following subjects:

* The powerful consumer decision journey scheme
* The new look of the communication plan
* The new key performance indicators
* A classification of the main social networks
* The new notion of digital identity
* The changing landscape of advertising
* An example of a new organization structure

The Consumer Decision Journey

We used to have a linear model of consumers' purchasing behaviors (often called *the funnel*), of which many variations exist. We were considering that the customer had to go through a sequence of states, such as *awareness/memorization/attitude/familiarity/preference/purchase intention/ actual purchase/loyalty*. We used to complete the consumer's behavior model by adding the brand meaning as the necessary first step, triggering the chain reaction leading to the act of purchase. We still believe that brands are complex systems that need to generate meaning to be competitive. As Marie-Claude Sicard has pointed out, communication is what provides meaning to information.[17]

However, the advent of digital, like in many other aspects, has completely changed that linear sequence. Nowadays, in the initial pre-buying considerations, the average customer knows how to utilize the proliferation of media and products to help him in his decision

---

[16] M. Serres, *C'était mieux avant!* Paris: Le Pommier/Humensis, 2017.

[17] M.-C. Sicard, *Ce que marque veut dire.* Editions d'organisation, 2001.

journey. His post-purchase behavior in terms of loyalty is also richer than before.

The consumer decision journey is a more relevant scheme to integrate the new conditions. This is an itinerary that consumers undertake, integrating touchpoints with the brand and general key factors affecting their purchase decision, including pre- and post-purchase behaviors. It is not linear, but rather iterative and random in the pre-purchase phase as consumers navigate the plethora of options and information available. It is more of a zigzag course among the possible sources of information, opinions, experiences, commercial offers, advertising material, and guiding or comforting messages from familiars.

Figure 9.3 indicates the many possible touchpoints that consumers may activate in their decision-making process. They are both digital and nondigital in nature. According to *Forbes* (2019), an average sale requires 7 to 10 pre-purchase touchpoints with the brand.[18] It can only be a very wide average, as this number will vary according to the industry. You do not buy a car like you would a fan or a fragrance.

The pre-purchase phase will include the initial considerations that have led to a known need or desire and the evaluation process of the various options. It is an open process in which brands appear and disappear along the flow and treatment of information. Obviously the customer's previous brand awareness plays a crucial role in the initial considerations, as rarely can anybody afford to do an exhaustive search.

Survey experts and marketing consultants have developed methodologies to investigate this itinerary, defining for specific industries, products, or services the number and nature of touchpoints activated in the journeys. Brands should have a maximum knowledge of this purchasing process and adjust their communication initiatives to it. As McKinsey already recommended in 2009, "Marketers must move aggressively beyond purely push-style communication and learn to influence consumer-driven touch points."[19]

---

[18] https://www.forbes.com/sites/ryanrobinson/2019/03/13/how-sales-has-changed/#199bbb593985.

[19] D. Court, D. Elzinga, S. Mulder, and O. J. Vetvik, "The Consumer Decision Journey," *McKinsey Quarterly*, June 1, 2009, https://www.mckinsey.com/business-functions/marketing-and-sales/our-insights/the-consumer-decision-journey.

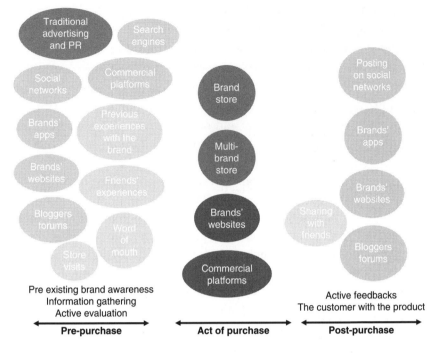

Figure 9.3   The Consumer Decision Journey

The obvious commonsense move is to be present on all touchpoints that are relevant for your products, preferably based on a preliminary survey.

McKinsey research found that two-thirds of the touchpoints activated during the pre-purchase phase are consumer-driven, such as Web reviews and opinions from family and friends, as well as in-store interactions and past experiences. It is not unusual to see consumers, while standing at the shelf in a store, use their mobile phone to get additional information from other sources. It is somewhat paradoxical that many people trust the input received from total strangers more than that from the brand itself. It is a big task for brands to regain customers' trust.

The challenge for communicators becomes how to manage the ever-increasing and changing number of digital touchpoints and learn how to influence customers on these media whose majority are nondirectly controlled by the brand.

Quoting Thomas Romieu, digital director of LVMH Group in 2013, McKinsey[20] notes that what luxury goods shoppers really want is a streamlined experience that minimizes the number of decisions they have to make and that luxury brands should therefore focus on a reduced number of five key touchpoints:

The city store: Even in the digital age, experiences in physical stores still heavily influence luxury customers. It remains the most important point of contact with them.

Person-to-person word of mouth: Luxury shoppers care about what their peers think. Such interactions can be traditional conversations with a friend or more modern digital dialogue like emails, texts, or Facebook comments.

Online search: Luxury brands invest tremendous effort and resources to create visibility in the offline world, starting with beautiful stores in the best locations. Being visible online is just as important.

Salespeople: A great experience with a salesperson can have a lasting impact on a customer, and vice versa for a poor one. The question is how digital technologies can help better train associates as well as enhance their interactions with clients.

The brand's website: A customer's experience with a brand's own site is a determinant of how they perceive that brand. Does the messaging feel authentic? Is there enough information about products? How original or exceptional is it?

This evolution calls for brands to think of offering flexibility and new product discovery at every step of the pre-purchase phase. Proactive personalization is an example of what brands can do, using the available customer data (internal or external) to propose individual customization options.

Added new adjacent services offered to the customer based on the mining of existing data is another way to engage him during his journey.

A third of the touchpoints involve brand-driven communication activities, showing that traditional marketing, which belongs to this category, has still a role to play.

---

[20] McKinsey & Company, "Back to Basics: What Luxury Customers Really Want from Digital," August 1, 2013, https://www.mckinsey.com/business-functions/marketing-and-sales/our-insights/back-to-basics-what-luxury-customers-really-want-from-digital.

The consumer's decision journey demands that a brand also focus on the post-purchase phase and develop better communication tools in this somewhat neglected part of the journey. Amazon was one of the first examples of submitting to customers new books to purchase based on previous transactions. Beyond the usual loyalty programs, there are many initiatives that luxury brands can take to engage customers in the post-purchase phase, like testing new products, asking opinions and suggestions, and making them part of the brand life.

The Communication Plan

The communication naturally follows the communication strategy as shown in the previous section.

A comparative analysis of what a media plan around 2010 for a luxury brand was and what it is today speaks better than a lot of demonstrations. The media plan used to be a simple advertising calendar of the next six months' season where the vertical axis was the list of all the paper-based fashion magazines, daily newspapers, and special supports such as street advertising (billboards, scaffolding on big worksites, recently arrived street electronic screens, etc.), where the main photos of the seasonal advertising campaign were displayed. The document was necessary to organize the distribution of the advertising material, as advertising spaces needed to be reserved beforehand.

Then digital communication management rapidly became the control tower of all communication activities. It has been like an ogre needing to be fed with always more frequent material (preferably video). It is the sheer volume of content and its increasing frequency that drastically changed the kind and number of resources needed in the communication department. It has also been a major cultural revolution as the attention to the quality, the relevance of the content, and the respect of the brand identity have often been sacrificed on the altar of speed and volume.

The traditional advertising media plan gave space to a comprehensive document attempting to plan the overall seasonal communication activities, both digital and traditional (some also call it the integrated media matrix or the master communication plan). It is normally programmed by week, and the long vertical axis is composed of many more topics than just the paper-supported media we had in the predigital media plan (see Table 9.3).

The new comprehensive communication plan, following the multitude of new media offered by digital technology, obviously contains higher complexity. It is becoming a combination of bar charts and photo album.

What remain as the backbone of the document are the major seasonal moments and the link to the product merchandising objectives. The fashion shows are now more a basis from which to extract a maximum of content that will feed all the various media. However, a lot of new material now feeds the "monster" with interviews, texts, reports on cultural events or artists, subjects not necessarily directly related to the brand and its products, and the great disruption comes from the constant engagement of customers on social media, which requires manpower; trying to keep interest at all time, coordinating with merchandise arrival in the stores, inventing promotional activities on the e-commerce site, and so on.

The communication plan has become more of a rolling tool of activities, with some timely anchor points and then a lot of initially unplanned activities. It is managed by being constantly reviewed, while the brand communication team seizes new opportunities and develops new ideas.

Key Performance Indicators (KPI)

The communication strategy and plan being implemented, the need to keep track of whether the objectives are being reached arises. As one of the characteristics of the digital world is that any type of move on the Web can be tracked and quantified, there is a plethora of new performance indicators. We have therefore chosen to focus on the commercial websites because most of them in luxury fashion and accessories are both informative and transactional. Brands came to realize early that there was no reason to separate the two functions and that the ultimate brand goal is to generate profitable sales.

In order to present efficiently the most meaningful KPIs used with commercial websites, we start from the basic brick-and-mortar retail equation that sales are the compounded results of three variables: the store's walk-in traffic, the visitor's conversion rate (i.e., how many of them buy), and the average transaction values:

$$\text{Sales} = (\text{total walk-in traffic}) \times (\text{conversion rate})$$

$$\times (\text{average transaction value})$$

As is shown in Table 9.4, this basic equation is applicable both to retail and e-commerce and allows for a simple classification of KPIs.

The first set of data are all those common to or equivalent in digital and retail activities. The data related to sales and merchandising apply to both digital and physical sales with the same vocabulary. The notions of sell-through and level of inventory apply only if there is a dedicated stock of products for the e-commerce activities. They lose their meaning if the inventory is shared between the retail network and the commercial website.

In terms of traffic monitoring, the reach is the number of people who visited the website and is almost similar to number of persons coming to the store. The number of page views is also almost equivalent to walk-in traffic.

The number of visitors making a purchase divided by the total number of visitors applies to both activities.

The second type of data are those enabled only by digital technology and relevant to retail activities. The sales per country where an online order emanates (for internationally accessible websites) from a foreign country is the equivalent of the customer nationality, which is normally captured at the point of sale.

The traffic-measuring data are much more developed in the digital world, getting data that could be interesting for retail but are seldom gathered because of implementation difficulties. To mention a few of them:

- The session duration is the equivalent of the time spent by customers in the online store.
- The pages per visit are the equivalent of the time spent in the online store on each product category.
- The bounce rate is the percentage of visitors who leave the site after viewing only one page and is equivalent to retail customers leaving the store without purchase.
- The repeat visitors.
- The average time on-site is equivalent to the time spent in the stores.

Table 9.4 Comparative Analysis of Retail and E-commerce KPIs

Sales	Traffic	Conversion	Value/Transaction
Data common or equivalent in digital and retail sales			
Sales statistics: Per product category Compared to budget Number of SKUs sold Number of orders **Merchandising data:** Sell-through Inventory	Reach: number of people who visited the website similar to number of persons coming to the store Page views	Number of visitors making a purchase	Average transaction or order value
Data enabled by digital technology, but relevant to retail activities			

Digital	Retail	Digital	Retail	Digital	Retail		
Sales per country	Sales per nationality	Session duration Pages per visit Bounce rate Repeat visitors Average time on-site	All have retail equivalent	Visitors to lead Lead to purchase Visitors to purchase Bounce rate	All have retail equivalent		
Exclusively digital KPI							
		Direct traffic Referred traffic Organic traffic					

355

In terms of conversion rate, the notion of *lead* is introduced in digital marketing to designate a prospective customer who has shown interest in a product or service and has provided contact information. A lead will potentially become a future client and can be reached for promotional activities. The notion has a reduced relevance in retail as customers' data are in general captured at the cash register only when a transaction is realized.

- The conversion from visitor to lead is when the customer data are given, which rarely happens in the store except when the customer cannot find what he wants and needs to be contacted when the product is available.
- The conversion from lead to purchase is the percentage of registered potential customers purchasing a product for the first time.
- The conversion from visitors to purchase is equivalent in both digital and retail. The digital conversion rates[21] vary greatly by industry, from 0.80% for men's and women's clothing to 3.60% for hair and beauty products in 2020. For high-end luxury e-commerce sites, conversion rates are probably below 1%.
- The bounce rate is also meaningful in the conversion analysis. It is between 20% and 40% on e-commerce sites. Note that the bounce rate is calculated on leaving after the first page and does not account for those visitors viewing more pages but not buying on the site. In retail stores, the conversion rate obviously varies according to the brand reputation and seasonal attractiveness and can go from 30% to 50% for mainstream mid-traffic brands. Duty-free boutiques show higher performance around 70%. Gucci and Louis Vuitton probably reach close to 90–100%.

The third set of data are exclusive to digital activities and have no meaning in the retail world.

- Direct traffic is the number of visitors who come directly to the website by typing the URL into their browser or clicking on a link from an email or document produced by the brand.
- Referred traffic or referral traffic describes the flow of people who come to a brand website from other sites, without searching on Google.

---

[21] https://www.irpcommerce.com/en/gb/ecommercemarketdata.aspx?Market=1.

- Organic traffic is generated by search queries from persons who do not have the precise intention to contact the brand.

We are far from being exhaustive in our presentation of KPIs, but some of the basics have been introduced. All these data need to be regrouped and monitored on a continuous basis. Figure 9.4 presents some extracts from the digital dashboard that the Thomas brand used in 2018 to monitor the results of their digital efforts, where most of the KPIs introduced are present.

We have avoided presenting what Clo Willaert (2019) calls *vanity metrics*, which she qualifies as "hollow and meaningless."[22] Indeed, the number of social media followers is not necessarily representative of the degree of engagement of brand customers. At best, when compared to competitors, it is an indication of the relative interest in the brand. Moreover, the number of "likes" is not correlated to the sales that a post can generate. In 2016, one of the most-seen videos of neckties of the Thomas brand received several million likes while the sales of the new products being promoted just remained in line with a normal season's volume.

In addition to the commercial activities generated on the website, pre- and post-purchase activities will have to be monitored, in particular on the social networks, focusing more on the meanings exchanged than the volume of visitors.

Social Networks

The Web has revolutionized public spaces by giving voice to new participants and providing them with new listeners. Anybody can talk and listen on the Web. Access and visibility have been completely democratized.

However, this is the advent of the social networks (or social media) becoming really relevant around 2003 (LinkedIn was created in 2003 and Facebook in 2004), which has been the main engine of the growth of Web utilization. See Figure 9.5 for the latest data on the number of users of the most-used social media.[23] In February 2020, the number of Facebook users is close to 2.5 billion; YouTube is in second place,

---

[22] C. Willaert, *Digital Marketing Like a PRO: Prepare. Run. Optimize.* Tielt: Lannoo Publishers, 2019.

[23] https://datareportal.com/reports/digital-2020-global-digital-overview.

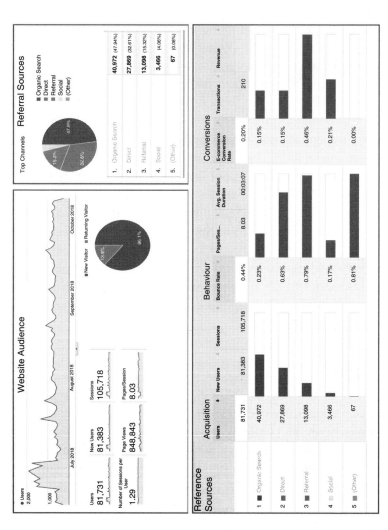

Figure 9.4 Example of Thomas Brand's Digital Dashboard (2018)

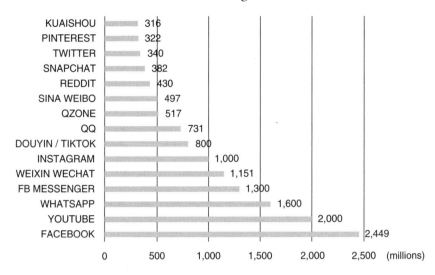

Figure 9.5   The World's Most-Used Social Media.
Sources: Digital 2020 Global Overview Report from Datareportal, We Are Social, and Hootsuite (February 2020).

with 2 billion monthly active users; WhatsApp is third, with 1.6 billion users around the world; launched in 2010, Instagram is sixth, with 1 billion monthly users; the most recent addition is the Chinese TikTok, placed seventh with 800 million users, and so on. These numbers are staggering and naturally brands have quickly realized the potential of social networks.

A social network is a dedicated website or other application that enables users to communicate with each other by posting information, comments, messages, images, and so on. In a nutshell, it is, simply, one personal page with the possibility to connect with other participants.

For example, all major luxury brands have opened official accounts on WeChat. An official account on WeChat can be used to raise brand awareness in Asia through regular posting and advertising, to sell online, to manage a community of loyal consumers, and to assess your performance through user profiling and article and advertising performance reporting.

For brands, it becomes essential to understand these numerous and impactful digital actors in order to be able to use them in an optimal way to meet their own communication and business objectives. Cardon presents a classification of social networks based on two axes defining the aspects of digital identity that Web users want to render visible.[24] One is the axis of *self-simulation* going from the *real self* toward a *projected* one. The other axis is of *subjectivization* going from *being* to *doing*. These two axes determine four quadrants, which define four categories of social networks:

1. The **Screen** is located in the quadrant "real/being." The data given are factual (name, birth, education, profession, physical description, pictures, etc.). Dating sites, such as Meetic, are the most representative social networks of this category. The platforms are designed to offer a progressive unveiling of yourself as you grow in confidence with interlocutors through preliminary exchanges of messages.

2. The **Clair-obscur** quadrant corresponds to "projected/being." Facebook and WhatsApp are the most representative. Content can consist of very personal dreams or desires and is shown only to a controlled public. The name given by Cardon reflects the fact that visibility can be adjusted. Most of the messaging applications are in this category, which is by far the biggest category of social networks and obviously where brands will be willing to be present.

3. The third group, **Lighthouse**, corresponds to "real/doing." Everything is visible to everybody. The contents is very specialized and oriented toward actions. Users show a very specific aspect of their identity, their interest in specialized fields (cooking, fashion, handicraft, aviation, cultures, employment, education, politics, etc.) where people sharing the same passion, opinion, or taste will flock. Sharing specialized content is the aim and brands will also be interested in this social network positioning.

4. The fourth quadrant shows the **virtual worlds** and corresponds to "projected/doing." This is the realm of all the video games, avatars, and virtual worlds as Second Life, where people never show their real self, but rather a utopian creation to play with.

Going beyond the digital identity framework underlying the four categories of social networks, we can describe them in a more direct way based on three characteristics: content shown, visibility of the source, and targeted public, as indicated in Table 9.5.

---

[24] Cardon, *Culture Numérique*.

Table 9.5 Cardon's Typology of Social Networks

Four Types of Social Networks		Screen	Clair-obscur	Lighthouse	Virtual Worlds
Three characteristics of Social Networks	**Content**	Factual Real	Emotions Feelings Personal	Specialized Specific Factual	Utopian Theatrical Virtual
	Source visibility	Revealed progressively	Known Identified	Fully visible	Visible but disguised
	Targeted public	Open	Restricted Controlled	Sharing passion, interests	Sharing interest in projected identities
Social networks		Meetic Tinder Grindr Gleeden	Facebook Snapchat WhatsApp Messenger Skyblog WeChat Line	Instagram Twitter Pinterest Flickr Linkedin	Second Life YouTube Myspace World of Warcraft TikTok

*Dominique Cardon's nomenclature.

361

Now brands will have more information to help choose which social network they want to focus on. Given the enormous amount of users the main social networks are commanding, most of the brands are using them all. However, in terms of time and resources dedicated, some social networks will be more efficient at reaching the brand communication goals than others.

Besides the particularly relevant features introduced by Dominique Cardon, there are also social network performance indicators that are being taken into account when brands prepare their communication plan.

Instagram is of particular interest, deemed by the Web the king of social engagement. A study led by Forrester in 2014 demonstrated that Instagram posts generated a per-follower engagement rate (number of likes and comments on Instagram; number of shares, likes, comments, reactions on Facebook) of 4.21%, 58 times more engagement per follower than Facebook and 120 times more than Twitter.[25] Recently this statistic decreased somewhat to around 2% as Instagram undertook a solid exercise of purging fake accounts. In any case, today, Instagram still remains the most engaging social media platform.

Every brand is leveraging the social networks' global reach. Their power as well as their specificities demand a clear strategy of their utilization. This is in fact a subset of the overall brand communication plan seen earlier.

Digital Identity

As mentioned in the previous section, *digital identity* is a notion that Cardon uses to build his social network categories. He starts from Erving Goffman's work, which maintains that a person's identity is multifaceted and is observable through mimics, attitudes, manners, and gestures.[26] Without challenging the value of the study, which leads to very fruitful developments like the social network categorization presented earlier, this behavioral approach is drastically different from the semiotic approach we have promoted on brand analysis in Chapter 6.

---

[25] https://go.forrester.com/blogs/14-04-29-instagram_is_the_king_of_social_engagement/.
[26] E. Goffman, *La mise en scène de la vie quotidienne*. Paris: Minuit, 1973.

These multiple facets of people's personality are variable in nature and are not part of the ethics and aesthetic invariants used in the semiotic approach to identity.

However, it raises the question of what happens to a brand identity on the Web. Today, nobody will challenge the need for brands (still debated for individual use by a few irreducible) to exist on the Web. The digital identity, in our sense, will be determined by the part of the brand identity invariants that are going to be visible on the Web. The multiple means of expression employed by brands on the Web create new categories of brand manifestations that have to demonstrate their competitiveness in a very crowded and fast-evolving environment while enhancing the brand identity.

If, for an individual, the need to make oneself visible to others is born from a need for recognition, it is even more true for brands, which need to start being recognized in order to generate sales. The Web serves, therefore, to reveal the collective nature of the identity-building process, where one needs others' attention and feedback in order to define itself. True for brands and individuals, the identity-building process is collective and iterative.

Obviously, there will be differences in the online and offline presences and perceived identities. To emerge as a winner in the constant online fight for the attention of the users, one needs to shout louder than others. That can be achieved through a high volume of messages, surprising content, provocations, exaggerations, extreme language, humor, and so on that traditional communication and products could not tolerate. A proper balance will need to be found between truth, authenticity, and the creativity that the Web needs because of its overcrowded nature. The dilemma is even more serious for luxury brands that cannot easily express all their luxury content due to the many graphic and time constraints imposed by the social media technologies.

It should be noted that the term *digital identity* is also utilized on the Web to describe the authentication technology designed for businesses and individuals to transact safely online. This has nothing to do with our considerations.

Advertising

In 2020, statistics from the site eMarketer[27] show worldwide digital advertising at US\$341 billion compared to US\$379 billion[28] for all traditional ads; that is, 47.3% of the total spent on advertising. The forecast before COVID-19 was 49.6% for 2021. The growth has been phenomenal since the first advertising banner went live in 1994.

Today, we can say that there is almost as much paid advertising on the Web than on traditional media (print, radio, and television). Digital (or online) advertising is placed with search engines, social networks, websites, apps, music streaming services, and so on. Note that the eMarketer statistics include all the digital advertising appearing on desktops, laptops, mobile phones, tablets, and all devices connected to the Internet, but excludes MMS, SMS, and P2P messaging type of ads.

Google and Facebook have the lion's share of this pie, holding, respectively, 37.2% and 19.6% of total US digital ad spending. Worldwide (excluding China), it is bound to be an even bigger share. Their strength is even greater on mobile phones (which account now for half of Internet use), where they account for 90% of advertising activities. It is the magic of the digital world to see two new entrants (Google AdWords was born in 2000) taking such dominant positions in a more than century-old consolidated industry like advertising. To all effects, advertising has become the fuel of the Web. It is the predominant business model and represents 90% of Google's revenue and 97% of Facebook's.[29]

There are two main types of Web advertising:

Display advertising, that is, the banners that are a mere transposition of what is being done in the traditional ways and that can be posted on social media (Facebook, Twitter, LinkedIn, etc.), mobile, and so on.
Search advertising, that is, the Google way, which under Google Ads is the real innovative approach at the basis of the success of digital

[27] https://www.emarketer.com/.
[28] These statistics may vary according to the sources. What remain firm is the share of both advertising categories.
[29] Cardon, *Culture Numérique*.

advertising. Without going into too many details, what Google proposes is a configurable, automated auction system where the words that the Web surfer writes in his browser are put on auction (a real-time bidding system) to advertisers, which pay only if the Web user clicks on their site. All of this is technically feasible thanks to the ultimate spy: the cookie and the fact that the communication never appears as advertising but is information. Other search engines such as Bing, Yahoo!, and so on are involved to a lesser extent than Google.

There are also other types of digital advertising like video and email marketing, which often overlap with the two main categories.

A lot of antagonistic forces are at play in this very lucrative data business. One of the major threats remains the rapid development of advertising-blocking software. In certain European countries half of the Web users are already using it. The reaction is being prepared: you can already see on the Web promotions for ad-blocker-proof advertising services.

Old and New.   The existence of these old and new ways to reach the consumer are all benefits for the brands that want to communicate more efficiently with their customers.

Traditional advertisement is certainly less targeted but has the capacity to connect with larger audiences. A Super Bowl or Oscar ceremony ad is likely to generate more exposure than a lot of digital ads. This obeys the basic law of volume of readers, listeners, and viewers more than whether the persons reached are the right target. Once clear on the desired target, the brands have to figure out the most adequate media and when and how to reach the target.

Now with the digital ways, instead of creating a broad message for an approximate audience, the message can be tailored to a precise audience the brand believes its products are right for. Brands can now target (and retarget) their potential and existing customers with ads based on their demographics, websites they visited, things they have searched for, and so on. We have gone from general practitioner to highly specialized surgeon.

Another advantage of the digital way is the ability to rapidly and cheaply test how people respond to a whole array of ads and monitor the results. This is a major development for smaller brands.

The role of traditional advertising is weakening, comparatively anyway. The main function of many magazines is to distract people in the dentist's waiting room. The number of publications; the increase in the number of paper pages of advertising; the constant race toward more provocation, which alienates the majority of people; advertising on public and mobile media; and, above all, the Internet, all contribute to diminishing the influence of this type of brand manifestation. Zara (though not in the luxury category) is a fine example of a successful brand that grew thanks to an enormously competitive business model and without advertising. Positioned in the intensely competitive mass-market clothing sector, Zara had annual sales of €28.3 billion in 2019, all virtually without advertising (its advertising is restricted to newspaper ads twice a year to advertise sales).

Even though they differ significantly, digital and traditional advertising must be managed jointly in order to optimize the advertising strategy. It is the mix of both, with consistent and complementary messages and visuals, that will make the brand customer engagement effort successful. A bus shelter's traditional ad campaign is usually reinforced by banners on the transportation company's website and apps and active directed discussions on social media, forums, and blogs.

Content.   We will see later in the section on organization that content production is becoming a strategic function in communication. For the seasonal luxury businesses, the advertising campaign of the season still remains, together with the fashion show, the main source of content. Pictures, video, carousels, and texts extracted from the seasonal campaign are the basic ammunition for the traditional media as well as for all the Web brand manifestations. Instead of selecting a limited number of pictures from the shoot for the paper media and the catalogues, much more content is being produced. Pictures and video of onstage and backstage, of the making of the campaign, narratives on the designers, the models, interviews of the art directors, and so on, will feed the digital "monster" so avid for content. Live streaming allows also shows and interviews to be in real time on the Web.

The Advertising Agencies.   The traditional communication agencies have adapted and developed the necessary expertise to provide digital services, while a huge number of new agencies have emerged, very often specializing in specific types of digital services. They provide advertising strategies to reach users in search, via ads, on their website and more, including SEO (search engine optimization), PPC (pay per click), marketing via email, social media, and content marketing, and web design in general.

In addition to guiding companies in the complex world of communication, the agencies (especially those born before digital) provide creative services to the luxury brands in presenting a more precise and better formulated brand identity than their counterparts that deal with mass-market brands. Often, the main choices regarding the photographs and models to be used and the creative direction are made by the brand itself. There is a certain comfort in selecting the most famous photographers, top models, or architects, as the major luxury brands have been doing and continue to do. They may not get a super-differentiated image, but it at least reduces the chances of blunders. There are examples where the agency becomes a de facto creative director. The US agency Doyle Dane Bernhach (DDB), for example, has been creating Volkswagen advertising since 1959 and has contributed to building the brand identity almost as much as the products.

Email Marketing.   While email existed long before the Web, it really took off as a powerful marketing tool thanks to its technical capability to send pictures, video, and many types of files, as well as to the Web capabilities of generating leads. The contact information collected on the Web allows for some basic engagement activities like:

- Announcements about new products and services
- Making special offers
- Sending personalized recommendations based on past purchases and searches
- Invitation to events
- Asking customers to leave the story of their own experience, and so on.

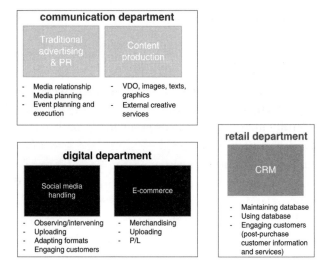

Figure 9.6   Initial Organization of Thomas E-commerce Activities

Possible Organization Structures

The advent of the Web has forced most luxury brands to adapt to the added complexity of the brand communication processes. Some have been quicker than others, but all have had to drastically reorganize their communication activities.

The case of the Thomas brand that we have introduced in the preceding chapters may provide some insights in the process. Thomas, a real but disguised brand for reasons of confidentiality, is European, with a turnover of around US$150 million, and involved in luxury personal goods for men and women (ready-to-wear and accessories). In 2012 its digital presence was limited to an informative website. Having decided to develop its digital presence, it hired an experienced digital director to lead the process.

The first decisions were to activate a social media presence with Instagram and Facebook and to launch an e-commerce activity, which was very rapidly merged together with the informative website. Figure 9.6 illustrates how the company operated in terms of customers' engagement.

Three separate departments were involved in dealing with trying to reach customers:

The traditional communication department dealing with the press, organizing seasonal campaigns, shootings, and fashion shows, reporting directly to the creative director, and having the role of the brand identity guardian. It was also the author of the initial website.

The digital department running the e-commerce activities (including uploading visual material, merchandising, and dedicated stock) and the social media presence.

The customer relationship management (CRM) was traditionally handled by the retail department.

Problems arose rapidly because of the fragmented structure but also because of the existing cultural differences between the "geek" mentality of the digital personnel and the traditional approach of the retail and communication departments. The digital department complained about not receiving more content and not rapidly enough. The traditional communication department despised the members of the digital department for lack of sensibility to brand identity considerations. Endless debates occurred about who had the final decision-making power on uploaded content. The clashes increased to the point where the position of customer engagement director was created to take direct control of all five of the functions previously organizationally fragmented.

The crisis revealed the importance of two aspects of managing communication in digital times:

1. The need to strengthen the content production capacity, clearly establishing the preeminence of the digital logics.
2. The need to mobilize a maximum of resources to engage customers, replying systematically to all comments made directly on the brand websites and social media presences, as well as forums, blogs, review sites, and so on.

The selected organization were Thomas choices at the time; however, the organization structure options are many and depend greatly on the size (and means) and culture of the companies, their position on the brand life cycle, and their immediate communication objectives that are normally an essential part of the communication plan.

Not Forgetting "Traditional Communication"

We have seen earlier that half of total worldwide advertising is still of a traditional nature and that the way to manage advertising today is to blend the best of both digital and traditional ways. Other traditional activities, while still impacted by the digitalization of the communication world, have been transformed to a lesser extent but are still very relevant in brand communication. We will cover only what we feel are the two most relevant communication activities: PR and the product.

PR

PR used to be called public relations, before the fashion industry changed it into press relations. As the name indicates, the PR director is mainly responsible for establishing and maintaining the company's rapport with the most influential journalists dedicated to luxury brands, even though the number of articles that appear in any given magazine is proportional to the brand's advertising budget allocated to that magazine. The logic is valid for online and offline activities.

The global brands lean on a worldwide network of PR agencies, and it is not unusual for them to contract six or more worldwide. This requires strong logistical capability: if the various magazines and newspapers around the world are to take pictures of products, obviously, they have to have those products available to them. To meet this need, the brands specifically manufacture numerous samples and send them to their selected PR agencies. The costs of this worldwide structure and of the sample collections make this prohibitive for the small brands, which need to rely on other brand manifestations.

Creating the Buzz (i.e., Going Viral).   The vocabulary changes but the phenomenon is the same. The other fast-growing function of the PR office is managing celebrity endorsements, the social relationships with the taste and opinion leaders of this world: movie actors, artists, architects, designers, singers, bands, sport celebrities, journalists, politicians, bloggers, influencers in general, and so on. Much has been written about how to create the *buzz*, the magical momentum that gets everybody talking about the hottest new product, brand, store, designer, event, and so on. While it is still a mystery to most, it is essentially a social and communication phenomenon that depends on moving in the right circles, mixing with influential people, and activating the digital "conversation mill."

Events. Events are generally, directly or indirectly, managed by the PR office and fall into three categories.

First are those that are directly organized by the brand: fashion shows, store openings, brand foundation awards, exhibitions, and so on.

In the late 1990s, the LVMH group with Galliano's fashion shows for Dior were the pioneer in transforming these events into real entertainment events much like movie premieres (the seating of the guests has become one of the most perilous of the PR director's duties). Their overall costs—of the dresses and accessories, the fees for the top models, the venue rental, the air tickets, hotels and fees offered to invited celebrities, gifts to journalists, and so on—can vary from a few hundred thousand euros to a few million.

How, then, is the success of a fashion show to be measured? If it were purely on the value of the articles published the following day, it would not be worthwhile. The show itself is ephemeral and would have little durable communication effect beyond the video replays shown in the boutiques if it were not for its utilization as digital content all over the season.

The advent of the Internet has already revolutionized the use of fashion shows as media events. For the past 20 years, we have seen unknown young people at the forefront of fashion shows with a notebook on their lap. They are influential bloggers, recognized by brands as essential elements for the dissemination of opinions about the brand. Live streaming allows also for real-time multiplication of the exposure of the event.

The opening of a store is generally a major event for luxury brands, matching in lavishness the investment made on the construction.

A second category comprises sponsored events such as the Louis Vuitton Cup or the *Grand Prix de Diane* sponsored by Hermès for 25 years (interrupted in 2008 and replaced by *Le Saut Hermès at the Grand Palais de Paris*), reinforcing its link to horses, competition, tradition, and aristocratic behavior. The March 2020 event was cancelled because of COVID-19, rescheduled for 2021.

The third category comprises events or ceremonies such as the Cannes Film Festival or the MTV and Grammy awards where the brand has high visibility. When, in the 1990s, Madonna showed up wearing Prada clothes to receive one of her 21 MTV awards, it had an incredible impact for the then-emerging brand. Competition between the brands to have high-profile celebrities showcase their clothes is fierce, placing such activities well out of the reach of the smaller brands. The climbing of the red-carpeted stairs of the *Festival de Cannes* by movie actresses and directors has become the most famous fashion show in the world.

Product placement, the introduction (for a considerable fee) of specific brands and products into movies or television shows, also figures large in this category. Sarah Jessica Parker and *Sex and the City* made Manolo Blahnik into a household brand with deep resonance among a younger generation initially not familiar with these sexy shoes.

Influencers.   Influencing is not really a new activity. This is the lady that Salvatore Ferragamo was afraid to lose, as she would drag a complete "salotto" with her. The PR department has always been in charge of the relationships with the famous. The only difference today is that the fame is also based on the number of visitors to Facebook or Instagram accounts. Bloggers started to be invited to fashion shows already in the early 2000s. An influencer is any person who inspires or guides the actions of others—more specifically in the digital world, a person who is able to generate the interest of potential buyers in a consumer product or service by promoting or recommending the items on social media, against some form of remuneration.

The Product

The product has a special place among the most meaningful brand manifestations. First and foremost, it is the basis of economic results. At the fourth step of the communication chain process, it is the product that is bought and determines the success of the overall brand project. Beyond this essential role, the product carries more communication content than most of the other manifestations, for a number of reasons. For example, as seen in Figures 9.1 and 9.2, the product is one of what we have called the basic manifestations that can enter into direct contact with the customer without necessarily going through a mediatization process. Besides its tangible features, it entertains special relationships with its owners, displays efficiently the creative power of the brand, and is always in context.

Tangible Attributes. The product is advertising in its most direct, evident, multisensory form and therefore generates immediate impressions through several tangible dimensions, conveying messages about the brand identity:

- *Aesthetics:* colors, forms, materials, textures, style. An Armani suit, with its cut, fabrics, labels, and price, tells you all about the Armani brand identity.
- *Functionality:* reliability, durability, reproducibility. Ferragamo's ability to consistently offer the same fit across different shoe models is part of its brand identity and allows for catalog and online sales.
- *Workmanship:* especially important for the high-end luxury brands, whereby it is still a cult and is a basic tenet of the brand identity. The product is the foundation of the brand's legitimacy in a specific sector. It is proof of expertise in a business area and a guarantee of the brand's authenticity.
- *Availability:* it has an impact on the way the brand is perceived, but can work both ways. Large distribution can increase brand awareness but work against a certain rarity inherent to genuine luxury. The creative work done by various designers on the Louis Vuitton monogram fabric could be interpreted as an attempt to fight this possible lack of originality. The product is therefore one of the main foundations of brand awareness. The more it is sold, the better it is known, especially if the product is wearable and identifiable from across the street. This explains the use of logos, materials, colors, metal accessories, and other style codes that are aimed at facilitating identification.
- *Merchandising and packaging:* collection structure, number of categories and models, prices, and so on are product communication elements. Tiffany's collections are not structured or presented in the same way as Agatha's.

For luxury brands, the product is the ultimate authenticity test. A Daum vase carries all the brand mythology of l'École de Nancy, but is also a specific crystal (*pâte de verre*): no two pieces are exactly the same and they will not be found anywhere else under another brand name.

Relationship with the Customer. The product spends a lot of time with its owner (certainly more than the distracted attention the consumer gives to a banner on his or her mobile phone or a page of advertising in a magazine) and develops the tactile (or olfactory) relationship between the two. An affective tie develops. Brands of cars, motorcycles, perfume, shoes, and coffee know this well. The product may also be the source of repeat purchases and is the key to confidence or disappointment that is created between the consumer and the brand.

The Principal Dimension of Brand Creation and Innovation. It is on the product that the bulk of research and creative efforts are concentrated. It is also where they are most visible. Stylistic and technological researches go hand in hand. Audi is a brand that has concentrated its efforts in both areas, with visible success.

Always in Context. At least in the store, the product is encompassed within the brand retail architectural concept—the windows and internal displays and the music—and promoted by dedicated sales staff in uniforms. In that sense we could say that the product is being mediatized.

We can summarize the product communication power by stating that bad advertising or negative Web comments *may* deter a faithful customer, whereas poor product quality *always* will.

Conclusion

To conclude on communication in digital times, what comes first is the harsh reality of the Web, where it is becoming increasingly difficult and complex to excite and inspire audiences who are overstimulated and often overwhelmed.

Besides the incredible positive impacts that the Internet has brought about and as mentioned in the first section, we could list some of the perverse effects that the Web is imposing on everybody, as even non-Web users suffer the possible negative consequences of the rise of digital. Luxury brands need to be fully aware of these negative effects in order to mitigate them somewhat:

- The nature of the Web can be qualified with a few adjectives: immediate, ubiquitous, fast, ephemeral, anonymous, virtual, plethoric, ever changing, and therefore favoring superficiality, rhetoric effects to the detriment of depth of analysis, encouraging egocentrism, privileging the deep-pocket players, and so on.

- The realm of everything, now and here, even if virtual, is changing mentalities. What to learn when I have all knowledge reachable through my mobile phone? Instagram Stories, launched in 2016, is the epitome of the Web. It allows users to post photos and video, add effects and layers, and all the uploaded content is wiped out after 24 hours.

- Given the time spent on screens, people are starting to long for more tactile relationships or at least for real-life exchanges without screen intermediaries. An example of brand awareness of this reactive trend is given by Amazon opening to the public its first Amazon Go Grocery store in 2018.

- Connection is not relation, as many confuse them. The connection has no value in itself. It is a banality to affirm that it is what you make with connections that matter. Relation building is what counts—what we have called engaging in the first part of this chapter.

- The course to high volume and high frequency content has been favoring the big brands to the detriment of companies with fewer financial resources. We see the same phenomenon in human resource management. The big players can attract the best talent with offers difficult to refuse. The GAFAM (Google, Apple, Facebook, Amazon, and Microsoft) are famous for recruiting the outstanding academic talents from the best universities.

Brand used to communicate in order to inform, to draw attention, to generate positive attitudes and desires, to be preferred, to be remembered, and eventually to enter into people's lives, to create a certain level of intimacy through common experiences. A new brand concept is emerging where brands, like all Web users, by the way, are becoming another medium themselves. Editing and publishing tend to overwhelm the genuine creative activities.

Digital has now become the engine of the luxury experience. The utilization of artificial intelligence and big data are bringing customer knowledge and relationship management to a new level, and luxury brands can now use technology to reconcile high-tech and high-touch and provide customized services. But the biggest evolution is likely to come from stores becoming part of the digital world. It goes beyond the omnichannel distribution idea. Digital has been generating continuous excitement and is not only a sales or communication channel anymore. In effect, Instagram has become the new store window, more powerful and versatile, and accessible at all times and everywhere. Digital can now be considered as the source of inspiration for reinventing the role of the store and the customer experience. The most recent and exciting experience that a consumer just had online sets the bar for the next online shopping experience, but also for the kind of experience the consumer expects when shopping. The physical store is becoming one of the components of an overall experience that is essentially digitally driven.

Experts predict that the Internet is on the way to becoming the fifth institutional power, after judiciary, executive, legislative, and media.

Chapter 10

Managing a Global Brand

For the client, the brand must be available everywhere in the world, supposedly thanks to a very large number of subsidiaries. In fact, brands are sold thanks to a large number of distribution opportunities, including "travel retail" ones.

To be a global brand, one must use department stores everywhere in the world, but also independent importers or agents. This setup incorporates, of course, the stores where the products are sold, but also the systems used to take the products from Paris or Milan to everywhere in the world.

In some cases, for example, in perfumes, the brand is present thanks to a completely different operator. An Armani perfume is not manufactured and distributed by Mr. Armani, but by L'Oréal. A Tom Ford perfume is not developed exclusively by Mr. Ford, but by Estée Lauder; and a Ralph Lauren watch is designed, manufactured, and distributed by

Richemont, which specializes in watches and jewelry. This is the world of licensing that is described in this chapter.

Managing a global brand means taking all the available opportunities to extend the brand everywhere and in different categories without weakening its status and its excellence.

International Distribution Systems

We said earlier that the luxury businesses are worldwide activities, which may give the impression that companies such as Givenchy or Max Mara have their own fully owned subsidiaries and their own stores in which to present their products to consumers. In fact, in much the same way that manufacturing is often subcontracted, so too is international distribution often handled by others.

In Figure 10.1, we start with the original company, which distributes its goods through distribution systems that include outside distributors, joint ventures, or subsidiaries. It may also sign license contracts for products it cannot or does not want to manufacture and distribute directly. The licensees, in turn, select their own distributors around the world. As a result, the original company has a presence in territories and in product categories that it does not directly control.

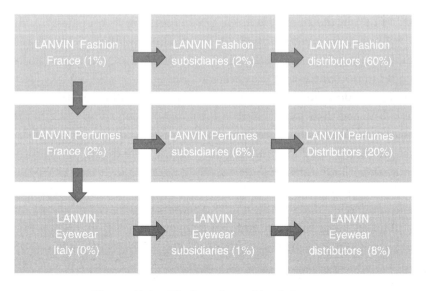

Figure 10.1 The Brand's Worldwide Presence

We move now from the simplest to the most complicated systems.

Exclusive Sales from Paris or Milan

This is how brands get started on exporting their products at the outset. They present their collections at the international fairs—in Paris, Milan, or Frankfurt, for example—and sell them on the spot to individual stores or department stores in a given city or a given country.

Most sectors have such fairs on a yearly or twice-yearly basis. In addition to the fabric and fashion fairs, there are also regular events for leather goods, jewelry, watches, optical frames, shoes, and so on. Here, distributors from around the world come looking for new ideas or new products. If they are attracted by a new brand, they may enter into an agreement, exclusive or otherwise, to sell the products in their stores or ask for an exclusive distributorship in their home country.

In the luxury ready-to-wear sector, the different brands present their fashion shows in the same week or in the same fortnight, and all major purchasers come to town with their purchasing budgets (or "open to buys"). The fashion brands pay particular attention to purchasers from Chinese operators, or American and Japanese department stores that can sometimes purchase large quantities of goods. At the end of the show, firm orders and cash down payments are taken for the goods to be delivered later in the year: at the end of this process, fashion houses have a precise idea of their sales for the coming season.

Before they come to Paris and Milan, department-store purchasers will have prepared their open-to-buy budgets based on each individual brand's performance over the previous couple of years. Because budgets are predetermined, new brands experience difficulty unless they have discussed their ideas with the department stores or the distributors beforehand. Without this, budget constraints would restrict the quantity that purchasers could buy, even if they were to love the new collection. Thus, the selling must be done well in advance and, if possible, at the headquarters of the main national department stores or distributors in major countries.

The exclusive sales system has many advantages. It is very low risk because generally there is a cash down payment with the order, with the balance being paid by letter of credit on the date of shipment. With purchasers from department and multibrand stores coming around every year looking for new brands and new ideas, it requires a minimum investment. In this way, brands can end up in some extremely-high-end department stores, where their products can sell easily and at full price.

Of course, the disadvantage of this is that the brand has very little control over the choice of stores or distributors and is dependent on the goodwill of one or another of the major operators. When a brand wants to grow, it must combine such sales with additional, more targeted, points of sale in large countries and specific alternatives if it wants to be represented in smaller countries.

Subsidiaries

It is a common misconception that fully owned subsidiaries are the most common system of distribution for luxury goods. This is seldom the case, however, and the majority of business is not done through subsidiaries.

Subsidiaries are great because they can do a good marketing job. They also have the advantage that their sales are consolidated at full value (wholesale price), rather than at export price. A company with many subsidiaries appears bigger and more impressive at home than a company without subsidiaries, and top management is very proud of managing or chairing, at a distance, a US, Japanese, or Chinese corporation.

However, in many countries in the Middle East or Latin America, not to mention Indonesia, foreign companies cannot hold 100% of the shares of a subsidiary dealing solely with the distribution of products manufactured and imported from abroad. In some cases, such subsidiaries are forbidden. In other cases, the majority of the shares must be held by a local partner. In countries like Russia or China it is possible to have a fully owned subsidiary, but it is generally advisable to take a local partner that will, among other things, be responsible for dealing with local authorities.

Second, subsidiaries, depending, of course, on the size of the country and the type of products involved, are often expensive. For example, having a subsidiary for a perfume brand does not make sense if expected sales are not reaching €4 million. Below that figure, the gross margin resulting from sales will not be sufficient to cover overheads and salaries. Also, budgets tend to be generally optimistic, but sometimes sales fall; a once-profitable subsidiary can then become a nightmare.

Third, subsidiaries require cash: the local inventory of products and the accounts receivables have to be financed by headquarters. When cash is tight, a subsidiary is not necessarily the best way to operate: growing through a system of subsidiaries is slower than with a network of distributors.

There is also a misconception that subsidiaries are easily controlled and therefore unlikely to initiate parallel businesses or *gray-market* operations. However, specialists in this area say that the easiest sources of products are general managers of subsidiaries that are behind their yearly budgets and who may be tempted to unload some products without controlling where they would end up.

For very large, established firms, subsidiaries may work well, but for small luxury-business firms this is certainly not the most common distribution system.

Local Distributors

Local distributors purchase the products with their own money, build local inventories, and sell in their own country. This is, of course, a low-investment approach for a luxury company looking to expand internationally.

A local distributor is generally granted an exclusive right to distribute a product or a brand in a given territory. Distributors generally represent several brands in order to spread the cost of their sales force between them. This also gives them better bargaining power with department stores or individual outlets, which can be an advantage for a smaller brand.

Local distributors assume all financial risks on the brand locally. They generally know how to negotiate for the best location in a department store and how to arrange discounts on media advertising tariffs. All in all, they can generally handle a brand's day-to-day activities very effectively.

There are limitations, of course, to the use of distributors. They are not always easy to control and may, in some cases, do their own marketing locally, rather than necessarily following what the brand would like. They may also vary the way they operate for the individual brands they handle.

Finally, when a brand is very strong in a territory, paying a percentage of wholesale sales to a local distributor can be much more expensive for the brand than having a subsidiary. Distributors are ideal for starting and developing a brand; but when sales reach, say, €10–15 million, it may make sense to start a subsidiary. But the move from a distributor to a fully own subsidiary may not always be easy, as we will see next.

The Joint-Venture System

Canceling a relationship with a distributor can sometimes lead to unpleasantness that may result in the distributor organizing a boycott of the brand among its closest customers. This has certainly happened in Japan when, for example, a particular department store had its exclusive distribution rights and master license agreements for a given ready-to-wear or jewelry brand removed when the brand decided to create its own subsidiaries.

The joint venture is a subsidiary that belongs in part to the brand corporation and in part to a partner who could be, for example, the former local distributor. The system provides an elegant way of smoothing over some of the potential difficulties involved in closing the relationship with a distributor and starting up a subsidiary by leaving open the possibility for the former distributor to play a major role through offering office space, back-office activities, and local market knowledge. Through such joint-venture agreements the way may be open for the principal to increase its shareholding over time and to gradually end up with 100% of the business.

Having said all this about the distribution avenues available to luxury-goods companies, the average luxury firm will probably deal directly with some department stores, will have up to 10 fully owned subsidiaries, between 5 and 20 joint ventures with former distributors, and probably 40 to 60 independent distributors around the world.

Price Structures

Prices are not set at random. They must take several factors into account. First, it is more expensive to distribute a product in the United States than it is to distribute it in Panama or a small island in the Caribbean. Second, some countries have import duties of up to 100%, as well as protective quota systems.

Luxury-goods companies try to harmonize their worldwide prices. They work on three different price zones, as shown in Table 10.1.

Table 10.1 Pricing in Different Zones (Perfumes and Cosmetics)

	Paris/Milan	New York	Beijing/Tokyo
Domestic market	100	85–105	120–140
Duty-free	80	68–84	96–112

Note: For fashion brands, New York domestic prices can be around 120 and Chinese or Tokyo domestic prices can reach 140 to 150.

The anchor is the Paris/Milan price, which we have put at an index of 100. Because there is no longer any duty in Europe, sales in other European countries are generally around 100 to 105 and duty-free prices are calculated at 20% below (that is, around 80).

For New York, the objective is to have retail prices at somewhere around 105, but in periods when the dollar is weak, such as we saw from 2000 to 2003 and to a lesser extent from 2015 to 2020, it is difficult to increase US dollar retail prices unreasonably, and prices often end up as low as 90 to 95. Latin America and Caribbean duty-free prices follow New York prices, and for some brands, still in 2020, they were below European duty-free prices.

In China or Tokyo, where costs of operations are high, and where import duties still exist in different product categories (with even an additional luxury tax in China), prices are generally in the 125–140 range. Duty-free prices are, then, automatically slightly more expensive than European domestic prices.

In countries such as Thailand or Brazil, where customs duties amount to 50% or more, retail prices would not necessarily be increased by that same percentage from the base of the price zone. The brand owner would look at the level of retail prices that would be acceptable to the local market and to tourists and would reduce its export prices accordingly, at the cost of a lower margin for them.

To understand how export prices and retail prices are set, one has to understand that the general rule is that there is not one given export price for everybody. In fact, the system generally works the other way around. The different partners first decide on the ideal retail price for a specific country, then estimate the logical margin on this price, and a specific export price resulting on these.

In fact, in the luxury business, there are often as many export prices as there are different clients. This approach is sometimes questionable, as in many countries price fixing is prohibited by law so that the price structure decided between the principal and the distributor must be considered only indicative, with only a suggested retail, but at the end almost everybody respects it, because it is more simple and makes more business sense.

The price structure will be based, as in Table 10.1, on a Paris/Milan retail of 100, and will start from the most logical or effective retail price for each given country. Taking into account the standard retail margin (which varies from one country to another) and the impact of different levels of value-added or other local taxes, a wholesale price can be calculated. From this, the agreed distributor's margin and the agreed advertising budget are deducted to give a landed cost, which is the basic agreement between the distributor and the principal. From there, it is necessary only to know the specific import duties for a given country and the other costs (freight and insurance) to be able to define what should be the right export price.

Table 10.2 provides an example of how this might work for two European countries.

For the purposes of discussion, we have assumed that Country A would sell at retail at 105 and Country B at 110. Wholesale prices are the result of the retailers' margins, which are 50% and 47.7%, respectively. Subtracting the respective margins and the advertising budgets from the

Table 10.2   Cost Structures for Europe (Perfumes and Cosmetics)

	France	Country A	Country B
Retail price	100	105	110
Wholesale price (irrespective of value-added tax)	50	52.5 (100%)	57.5 (100%)
Distributor's margin		25.2 (48%)	25.875 (45%)
Advertising and promotion budget		10.5 (20%)	8.625 (15%)
Landed price		16.8	23.0
Freight, insurance, and duty		0.6	0.6
Export price		16.2	22.4
Product cost	12.5	12.5	12.5
Gross margin	75%	22.8%	44.2%

wholesale price gives the landed prices of 16.8 and 23. It is then necessary to take into account freight, insurance, and duty, which produces an export price of 16.2 for Country A and 22.4 for Country B.

Although the cost structures in Countries A and B seem quite similar (distributors' margin: 48%/45%; advertising budget: 20%/15%), the final gross margin figures are very different: 22.8% in Country A and 44.2% in Country B.

In the French case, the gross margin is very high (75%), but this is not really a fair point of comparison because the firm sells its own products directly and does not use a different structure to cover distribution and advertising activities. It is clear, though, that activities in Country A are not very profitable, with a gross margin of 22.8%. There is a need for a very high margin in the French case to be able to feed the long distribution circuit as in Country A or B.

The advertising budget is generally integrated in the cost structure, and this money is at the disposal of the distributor to be used in that country.

In the case of Europe, the difference between landed and export prices is limited. As we will see later, this is not always the case.

In Table 10.3, we have taken the example of two countries with higher duties and different costs of operations.

In the case of Mexico, there is no major change from European cost structures except that, because of high import duties, the retail prices are much higher than in the United States.

For Japan, we have taken the case of an importer distributor who has no direct access to department stores or other outlets: very often

Table 10.3 Cost Structures for Japan and Mexico (Perfumes and Cosmetics)

	France	Japan	Mexico
Retail price	100	150	150
Wholesale price (second distributor)	50	67.5 (100%)	78 (100%)
Distributor's margin		37.125 (55%)	35.1 (45%)
Advertising and promotion budget		10.125 (15%)	11.7 (15%)
Landed price		20.25	31.2
Freight, insurance and duty		2.94	8.89
Export price		17.31	23.11
Product cost	12.5	12.5	12.5
Gross margin	75%	27.8%	45.9%

in Japan, the perfume counter, unlike the cosmetics floor, is not run directly by the department stores but is farmed out to someone acting more or less as a rack jobber and working on a 25% margin. This piling up of intermediaries—from retailer to wholesaler to distributor—is specific to Japan and explains in part the high cost of operating there.

Within these cost structures, it should be noted that percentages sometimes run in different ways. They are calculated from the retail or the wholesale price on one side. They are also based on the export price to assess the freight, insurance, and duty on the other side.

To simplify, people speak of the *coefficient* of a cost structure: the coefficient is equal to the retail price divided by the export price. Thus, in the Japanese cost structure the coefficient is 8.66 and for Mexico it is 5.62.

In discussions with different potential distributors in any given country it is necessary to compare the different price structures with which each of them wishes to work. Differences in the global coefficients are an indication of the economic advantage of working with one distributor or another. But it is also necessary to look at the advertising support included in the structure.

Advertising Structures and Advertising Policies

To follow on the previous paragraphs, in Japan's cost structure as outlined in Table 10.4, the export price is 17.31, while the advertising budget is 10.125—almost 60% of the export price. Why has the cost structure included a local advertising budget when this could have been added to the export price, and then spent directly by the brand owner? The only problem here is that, if the manufacturer were to invoice at 34.81 (rather than at 23.11) to include the advertising budget from Paris (as was done in the case of Mexico), import duties would have to be paid on the advertising money spent locally, which does not make sense.

This is why advertising budgets for perfumes and cosmetics are generally included in the cost structure. (For ready-to-wear, where the advertising-to-sales ratio is generally lower, a percentage of local spending is written into the contract even if it does not appear directly in the cost structure.) The direct consequences of this are:

- The brand owner (generally called the *principal*) feels it has reduced the export price of the products by this amount and therefore considers this advertising budget its own.

Table 10.4   Clients' Online Research Before Buying

Online Research by Country		Preferred Source of Research	
UK	54%	Multibrands full price	39%
United States	52%	Multibrands off-price	34%
France	51%	Department stores	34%
Japan	48%	Official brand stores	31%
Italy	45%	Luxury forum	29%
China	33%	Multibrand event	26%
Average	48%	Luxury bloggers	21%
		Facebook	15%
		Twitter	13%

Source: L. Dauriz, N. Remy, and N. Sandri, "Luxury Shopping in the Digital Age," McKinsey & Company, May 1, 2014.

- The distributor considers that it is paying the right price for the products and therefore feels that it is paying the advertising budget out of its own money.

The differences do not stop there:

- The principal is very interested in building brand awareness and its standing in a given market, so it tries to push for the largest part of this advertising budget to be spent in media investments.
- The distributor is more interested in the short term, so it prefers immediate promotional activities. It may also try to include in this advertising budget costs that are necessary to distribute the product but that it would have to spend anyway on things such as sales staff, promoters, or push money in the stores, which may also have immediate sales impact.

What happens when everybody believes that to distribute, say, a perfume brand in the territory, a budget of 15% of the cost structure is not enough and an additional couple of million euros must be spent? Here again the points of view may differ:

- The distributor considers that as it has no long-term rights in the brand, it is the principal's responsibility to meet these extra costs if it wants the brand to be better known in the territory.
- The principal considers that whatever happens in the local market is to the advantage of the distributor because it should have immediate

impact on its sales; therefore, any additional investment in advertising should be made by the distributor alone.

Such discussions have the potential to be discordant and disruptive to both parties and, fortunately, the standard rule is to split the costs of overspending equally.

It is clear, then, that the management of the distribution system requires a lot of time and attention. Most companies have to deal with a mix of structures involving a few subsidiaries and a large number of distributors. Subsidiary managers are simply company staff—albeit far from home—and should be motivated as such. Distributors should be considered individual partners, investing their own money for the success of the brand. Exclusive distribution contracts generally run from three to seven years and it is sometimes advisable to renew some contracts in advance so that a partner feels secure and motivated to continue developing the brand. There are also cases when joint-venture agreements must be discussed and signed.

Developing the distribution system is obviously the number-one activity for those who want to build a worldwide business and cannot afford to invest directly everywhere in the world. It is the responsibility of top management to know directly their distribution partners, in the same way that they should know personally the merchandising vice presidents of the major department stores in the world. This responsibility is particularly critical for perfumes and cosmetics and for wines and spirits activities.

Dealing with Online Operators

Distributors and franchisers are partners that can help anyone develop an attractive network of physical stores. But this is not the only way to distribute luxury products. They can also be distributed online.

In the next chapter, we will describe how a brand must organize a seamless online-to-offline system. In Table 10.4 we also predict that online sales will represent 25% of the total sales of a luxury fashion brand. But as far as the digital activities are concerned, should they also subcontract this logistical and technical activity or should they do it themselves?

What is sure is that starting in 2001 with Net-a-Porter.com, companies were created to act as digital retailers or Internet department stores and offered financial, communication, and logistical services to luxury fashion brands. In 2004, Net à Porter became profitable and was given the "British Fashion Council Award for Best fashion shop." It developed very fast, then was sold to Richemont, which later purchased Yook, and the new group, YNAP, reported sales of €2,262 million in 2019. This group acts as a digital department store: it generally takes the fashion pieces of a brand on consignment and sells them with a retail margin of 40%.

Another operator, Farfetch, also based in London, offers the same kind of services to luxury fashion companies, and, with a slightly different model, had sales of €1.968 million in 2019. They also work on consignment, and generally each brand has the responsibility to manage the distribution logistics. Also, because they are also operating worldwide, they can provide an international digital department store service to everybody.

The alternative for a luxury fashion brand is to directly operate their online sales system, or to subcontract this activity to YNAP or Farfetch or both.

One could think that customers alternate between online and offline, and if both systems are absolutely needed and complementary, it is not because one system goes down that the other system would automatically develop. For example, during the coronavirus development, one could have thought that as the physical stores were forced to close to respect the confinement measures, the digital sales would just go through the roof! Results for online luxury sales in March and April 2020 just proved the contrary and were very much below previous years' figures. As the luxury stores were closed, the clients were not in the mood to buy luxury fashion at all.

But one thing is certain: customers look at the products online and offline before buying.

What is clear is that luxury brand managers must be ready to offer physical stores and effective websites everywhere in the world, and this is another challenge in developing their activities to have a global brand.

390 LUXURY BRAND MANAGEMENT

Licensing Activities

Although it is a subject that is almost taboo, licensing activities play a major part in the economic balance of the luxury industry. Obviously, some brands are clearly against any licensing activities and never develop them, for example, Louis Vuitton, Hermès, or smaller brands like Robert Clergerie (Cartier could also be in the list, but they have cigarettes that are manufactured by a former sister company of Richemont, and after managing their optical frames business directly, they are now under license with Kering's optical frames division). For many years, Chanel had no licensing contracts, but today they have a licensing deal with Luxottica for Chanel optical frames.

By *licensing*, we mean a brand owner's farming out of the production and distribution of a line of products under its name. When they just use an outside manufacturer, we speak of subcontract manufacturing. When they give distribution exclusivity on a given territory, we speak of *distribution contracts* or *franchise agreements*. In this section, we will deal exclusively with the cases in which a firm subleases its production and its distribution to an outsider who is in charge of developing and manufacturing the product as well as selling it, using all systems available including advertising, promotions, and public relations.

This licensing activity sometimes represents a large part of a brand's income. For example, for Courrèges, Guy Laroche, or Wolfgang Yoop, license royalties can amount to more than 50% of total income. If they canceled all their licensing contracts, it would be difficult for them to make money.

In fact, licensing is the best way for a brand to develop its activities in a field that is different from its core business. This has been the case for optical frames for many years, as they require a special manufacturing know-how as well as an entry into specialized points of sale. It is often the case for perfumes, which are generally sold worldwide in selective department stores and that require special skills in terms of product development and manufacturing.

But despite an almost systematic use by luxury brands, licensing is generally downgraded. Some specialists believe that licensing prevents the development of a coherent brand image, although this problem does not result from licensing itself but from poor management and poor control of the licenses. Some representatives of French Luxury Firms explain the weakness of some French brands compared to Italian ones by the fact that "the French have developed licensing activities when the Italian have kept a system which is pure and without any license deals." As we will see in this section, Italian luxury brands use licensing as a way to develop their brand in additional product fields and they are still doing quite well.

People often blame licensing because it may result in an incoherent product offering and some products may be of inferior quality and promoted with low-prestige communication tools. To prove this point, people mention Pierre Cardin or Guy Laroche. But these same people forget to speak about Chanel optical frames with Luxottica or Gucci perfumes with Coty.

Another comment often heard is that licensing provides an opportunity for upscale brands to come up with lower-end and easy-access products that bring down the image of exclusivity and scarcity of their traditional product line. This would mean, for example, that Cartier cigarettes, manufactured by the Rothmans Group, are downgrading the image of Cartier. In fact, this is not necessarily the case, and maybe Cartier cigarettes, increasing the brand visibility, provide an additional luxury dimension to the brand, in a much lower price point market, but just as sophisticated.

In fact, licensing should only be criticized when it is poorly used, poorly developed, and poorly controlled.

In the first section that follows, to show that it is possible to develop a luxury brand under license, we will describe brands working almost exclusively under license. In the second section, we will describe business sectors that are specially fit for licensing activities. In the third section, we will describe some specific licenses to finish describing the way license activities should be followed and controlled; we end with our four-step approach.

Examples of Brands Developed Exclusively Through License Deals

A good example could be the German brand Joop, developed by the designer Wolfgang Joop, which works as a coordinated setup of independent licensees: ladies' ready-to-wear, perfumes, shoes, leather goods, underwear, and many others. However, even if this brand is very powerful in Germany, with several perfumes ranked in the top-10 bestsellers, it is not well known outside of Germany and it is not a good example of strong international development.

We are going to speak here of two brands that have known a very strong international development, without any upfront investment: Calvin Klein, created in 1968, and Hugo Boss, which was developed, starting from 1967, from the two grandsons of the founder; it was sold to a Japanese group in 1989, which sold it again in 1991 to the Italian group Marzotto, until it was purchased by a private equity firm, Permira. In these two cases, licensing has been the source of a fast and harmonious development, without any startup investment money.

Calvin Klein.   Calvin Klein, then 26 years old, developed his business in 1968 with a childhood friend, Barry Schwartz. When asked how he defines his business, he said: "We are a creative design and marketing studio." It is a nice way of explaining that all activities are subcontracted to licensees. But the reality is even stronger that that, as Mr. Calvin Klein is seldom involved in the design and development of products bearing his name.

In fact, starting in 2003, the brand is managed by the firm Phillips–Van Heusen (PVH). This company was known for its Arrow shirts, and is also the owner of Tommy Hilfiger. In its annual reports, it describes the activities of Calvin Klein as providing themselves sales level of €3.35 billion in 2018 and it claims their retail sales amounted to €10.6 billion for the same year.

Aside from PHV managing their women's ready-to-wear, bathing suits, and underwear themselves, they themselves license out perfumes, optical frames, watches, and other product categories.

Who invests in advertising? The licensees pay a large part of the total amount. Total advertising budgets are probably around €750 million but it is either spent directly by the licensees or paid by Phillips–Van Heusen with special contributions from these licensees.

Hugo Boss.   Hugo Boss, unlike Joop or Calvin Klein, is not an exclusive license brand, but it developed in the 1990s through a network of many license deals. For example, in 2010, license royalties amounted to more than 40% of net profit.

Their perfumes are with Coty, the watches are with Movado, and the optical frames are with Safilo.

The firm is very far today from its origins: from German army uniforms, they developed first a strong men's ready-to-wear, then a ladies' one. Contrary to Calvin Klein, the core of the business is not under license but it is to create fashion products, subcontract the manufacture of them, and manage their monobrand retail stores (in 2019 they had 1,113 of them, operated either directly or by a third party). Licensing helped develop their brand awareness and visibility in the beginning. It has also financed a very large part of the growth.

For Hugo Boss, licensing is a growth pattern accelerator and provides additional high-quality products.

Sectors in Which the Majority of Brands Use Licensing Deals

Three sectors correspond to this case: perfumes, watches, and optical frames. In these three sectors, products are relatively technical and are far away from the manufacturing and business models of ready-to-wear. Also, in these three sectors, the retail distribution is quite specific and requires a large number of points of sale and, of course, a specialized sales force that can visit these points of sale.

Perfumes and Cosmetics

In Table 10.5, we have classified the major perfumes brands in three groups:

1. Brands that have always been developed under license
2. Brands that have always been developed internally
3. Brands that are managed internally today, but that have been, at one time or another, under license

What is striking is that out of 32 fashion or jewelry brands, 25, or three-fourths, have either always been under license or used to be under license.

The point is quite clear: most perfumes are developed under license and a new ready-to-wear brand should be quite satisfied if it can sign a perfume license contract with a reputable perfume group.

Table 10.5   Perfumes Brands Under License or Developed Internally: The Situation in 2020

Brands under license	Brands developed internally today but which used to be under license	Brands always developed internally
Armani	Chanel	Bulgari
Boucheron[a]	Celine	Cartier
Burberry[a]	Dior	Hermès
Cacharel	Givenchy	Kenzo
Calvin Klein	Paco Rabanne	Loewe
Chloe	Thierry Mugler	Nina Ricci
Davidoff		Salvatore Ferragamo
Dolce & Gabbana		
Donna Karan		
Escada		
Gucci		
Guy Laroche		
Lanvin[a]		
Prada		
Ralph Lauren		
S.T. Dupont		
Van Cleef		
Joop		
Yves Saint Laurent[a]		

[a] Brands with an asterisk are under license today but have been managed internally at some time of their history.

Some cases must be explained. Chanel is today an internal perfume, but in 1921, Coco Chanel gave her perfume to the owners of Bourjois perfumes, who 25 years later purchased back the fashion house. Dior is also a special case, because today the perfume activity is part of the LVMH Group, when for many years the Christian Dior fashion group was a separate entity.

Why is it that no perfume brand that started and developed internally ever reached a very impressive development?

- Probably because the perfume and cosmetic sector is a different activity. The positioning of a new perfume is always quite difficult. The choice of a fragrance, which has, over time, a very strong impact, is the job of an expert. It is probably better if it is done by someone who really knows the business.

- Because the main perfumes markets (the United States, Latin America, or Middle East, for example) are different from the major ready-to-wear markets (Japan and China, for example).

- Because, as indicated here, perfumes and cosmetics must be sold in a very large number of points of sale in every country, and a fashion brand cannot easily reach the necessary volume to have a subsidiary or a motivated distributor in Brazil, Saudi Arabia, or Colombia. On top of this, department-store purchasers for fashion and accessories and for perfumes and cosmetics are always different.

- Because an important part of perfumes sales is done in duty-free, where, we will see later it is more effective to negotiate with several brands than just one to increase the necessary negotiating power.

What is certain is that, to launch a new perfume, it is better to have the support of one specialist and increase one's bargaining power. In Table 11.5, we have considered that Bulgari perfumes were managed internally. In fact, the brand belongs to LVMH and has not been included in the perfumes division of this group.

On July 1, 2008, Kering (then called PPR Gucci), the owner of Saint Laurent fashion, sold the YSL perfume business to L'Oréal. They probably thought that L'Oréal could develop the YSL perfumes brand better than they could themselves; we are very far from the anti-license hype of some self-appointed experts.

Watches. As an example, one could speak of Ralph Lauren, who created a joint-venture watch license with Richemont in 2007. The sales objectives were very qualitative, and the products that have been launched, starting at the Geneva fair of January 2009, have been quite beautiful. The brand was enlarged and today presents an impressive line of upscale quality watches.

Just like in the case of perfumes, some major brands like Louis Vuitton, Cartier, Chanel, or Hermès manage their watch business internally. But sometimes, like Cartier or Louis Vuitton, they belong to a group that already has a watch division, or sometimes, like Chanel, they have purchased a Swiss manufacturer to do it.

Gucci is again a different case: they started with a watch license in the early nineties with Wunderman, from California, but the group purchased it in 1997 and integrated it.

Some large groups like Swatch or Richemont seem interested in license deals. Groups like Movado seem to be the experts in this sector (with brands like Calvin Klein, Hugo Boss, Lacoste, Coach, and Tommy Hilfiger, for example).

Here again, the use of a license can result from different considerations:

- Watch-making is a specialized and technical activity.
- Production is extremely decentralized with different parts (cases, dials, hands, movements, etc.) generally subcontracted, then assembled. It is quite useful to know the different parts manufacturers to get components in time and at the right price.
- This business requires distribution systems everywhere and special sales forces visiting individual watch shops.
- There is a need for an effective after-sales service.

In the case of watches, the alternatives include finding a good licensee or investing in a structure that will have the credibility to negotiate with production subcontractors and the strength to set up a worldwide distribution system.

Optical Frames.   The business of optical frames is even more technical. The choice here is between selling sunglasses in one's own store or sign a license contract to have an expert do the manufacturing and selling optical frames in the most prestigious opticians worldwide.

But starting in 2017, things have dramatically changed. The Kering group decided to put all their optical frame businesses in an internal eyewear division, with a major factory and distribution center in Padova. They gathered all the 14 Kering brands, including Gucci, Saint Laurent, Balenciaga, and Bottega Veneta, plus the Cartier and Montblanc brands (this time under license from Richemont).

Most other luxury brands remained with their traditional licensees. One can mention:

- *Luxottica:* They handle Bulgari, Burberry, Chanel, Dolce & Gabbana, Ralph Lauren, Prada, Salvatore Ferragamo, Tiffany, and Versace.

- *Safilo:* They are licensees for Armani, Hugo Boss, Elie Saab, Jimmy Choo, Kate Spade, Marc Jacobs, Max Mara, Moschino, Pierre Cardin, Tommy Hilfiger, and Valentino.
- *L'Amy:* They handle Nina Ricci, Kenzo, Rochas, Chloé, and Chevignon.
- *Marchon:* They are licensees for Fendi, Pucci, Jil Sander, Calvin Klein, and Karl Lagerfeld.
- *Marcolin:* They used to handle Diesel, Moncler, Omega, and Tom Ford.

But this is not the end of the story. In 2018, seeing that Kering was integrating its optical frame business and organizing manufacturing and worldwide distribution systems, LVMH decided to invest a major percentage of shares in Marcolin (40%) and created a joint venture (51%) with Marcolin (49%), called Manifattura Thélios, in Longarone, concentrating all the optical frames businesses of the group.

Now the optical frames business becomes dual: the major groups (LVMH and Kering) have concentrated and internalized their business and the individual brands operate through license operations with Luxottica (now a part of the group EssilorLuxottica), Safilo, and Marchon.

Example of a Company Specializing in License Contracts: Children Worldwide Fashion

Apart from the companies described earlier (Richemont for watches; L'Oréal, Coty, or Interparfums for perfumes; or Luxottica for optical frames), it is interesting to describe a company dealing exclusively with children's ready-to-wear: Children Worldwide Fashion.

This a French firm, unknown by the public, that manages licensees of children's ready-to-wear for Boss, Chloé, DKNK, Givenchy, Lagerfeld, Lanvin, Marc Jacob, Timberland, and Zadig & Voltaire, among others.

The idea is that children's fashion does not sell ideally in ladies' fashion stores. They deal more with gifts.

The company had sales estimated at €250 million in 2018 and they manage 35 showrooms. They work in 56 countries and have 1,000 employees. Products are distributed in 2,700 points of sale or through company stores, as, for example, Youngly or *Les Ateliers de Courcelles*.

The Process of Development Under License

Selecting a Licensee.   In selecting a licensee, a brand needs someone who can develop a new product and distribute it everywhere in the world. Because the licensee is, in fact, investing its own money in such a venture, it must have sufficient financial resources to do so.

Product development can be quite expensive. A complete set of glass and plastic molds to create a full line of perfumes, together with its alcoholic line (perfume extracts and eau de toilette) and its bath line (soap, talc, powder, liquid soap, body creams, and so on) can cost up to €500,000 euros. This amount must be spent upfront, before any sale can materialize. Similar figures are also necessary for the development of a new line of watches before the first product reaches the stores. And this is just the tip of the iceberg.

Most of the investment to launch a perfume, a watch, or a new line of optical frames is a commercial one. Given that the original advertising and promotional investment can be huge and initial success is by no means guaranteed, the brand has to consider whether a potential licensee has the financial wherewithal to absorb any losses and invest in a second project. It goes without saying, of course, that the licensee will have access to the best raw materials and have its own production facilities capable of producing goods that meet all the requirements of quality and brand identity.

Product Development Under License.   Developing a product to the required standard may take 12 to 18 months. Distributing that product around the world may take a further 18 months. This obviously requires a long-term commitment from both parties. For products such as perfumes, contracts are sometimes affected for periods of 20–25 years. For watches, nothing can be achieved in less than 7 to 10 years. So, a licensing contract is almost always a long-term commitment for the licensee and a major long-term risk for the licensor.

What are the rewards? As a rule of thumb, a licensee pays royalties amounting to a standard 10% on the wholesale volume sold. There are exceptions: perfumes can be very large businesses and royalties are generally between 3% and 5% of wholesale and export volume. Products that are difficult to develop and to sell—men's and women's ready-to-wear, for example—can command royalties of 6–8%. On the other hand, products that are quite far removed from the licensor's usual universe or do not add much to the brand's overall image can sometimes justify licensing contracts with royalties of up to 12%. In addition, the brands may impose minimum sales (or at least minimum royalties) and minimum communication budgets per year.

It is important to differentiate the *investment* categories (perfumes, watches, optical frames, or ready-to-wear, for example)—activities that should improve the status of the brand—from the *consumption* categories (belts, underwear or handkerchiefs, for example), which consume the brand image without bringing much additional value to it. A good license portfolio should have a balance of investment and consumption activities.

A perfume license deal has another peculiarity: the perfume market is quite large, and this product category works on an advertising-to-sales ratio that can go as high as 20%, whereas that of the ready-to-wear business works generally on a 2–4% ratio. It is therefore quite common for investments in perfume advertising to be several times higher than those for fashion. This strong advertising presence in the perfume category can increase brand awareness and help develop a fashion brand. A case in point is Calvin Klein: when Minnetonka (since purchased by Unilever and now by Coty) started the perfume license, this fashion brand was almost unknown in Europe. It is the perfume advertising investment that conveyed the message of the brand and helped it in its ready-to-wear activities in this part of the world.

Japan used to be the number-one source of license income (excluding perfumes and watches). Generally, brands sign a master license agreement with a specialist that, in turn, signs sublicense agreements with different local companies.

In Table 10.6 we give a breakdown, unfortunately quite old, of license activities in Japan by product category.

The Control of Licensees.   A licensee will sometimes have a relatively short-term view of the brand: it wants its investment to be profitable. Also, when the licensee is obliged to pay, say, 10% royalties on sales, it may be tempted to understate its sales figures. Licensees sometimes consider, on their own initiative, that income from bargain sales or from factory outlets should not be subject to royalties. It is for this reason that license contracts generally stipulate a minimum royalty level that must

Table 10.6   Breakdown of Sales of Japanese License Activities by Product Category in 2009 (in € million).

	Sales for 2009	Percent of Total
Ladies' ready-to-wear	33.7	17.9%
Men's ready-to-wear	24.1	12.8%
Sportswear	26.6	14.1%
Shirts	3.4	1.8%
Swimsuits	2.9	1.5%
Children's wear	7.8	4.1%
Ladies' underwear	4.1	2.2%
Men's underwear	10.4	5.5%
Intimate apparel	2.7	1.1%
Ties	2.0	1.0%
Scarves	1.8	1.0%
Handkerchiefs	4.1	2.2%
Shoes	11.8	6.2%
Handbags and leather goods	12.7	6.7%
Belts	7.3	3.9%
Others	33.7	17.9%
TOTAL	189	100%

Source: Yano Research Institute, 2009.

be paid irrespective of actual sales. In our experience, for most contracts this is the only amount that will ever be paid.

Sometimes licensors find ways to control the volume manufactured under their brand: they may decide that they will control the printing of all labels bearing their name and the quantity of such labels issued to a licensee will be restricted to the licensee's specific volume needs. The licensor may also include in the label a watermark or other such device that makes it difficult to reproduce, in much the same way central banks do with the notes they issue.

But control is not confined to financial matters. Licensors must control the style and the quality of the final product, including the quality of the packaging and all aspects of the product environment—from presentation of the goods to warranty arrangements to after-sale service.

Many top brands provide a complete design and sometimes a real prototype of the product to be manufactured and distributed under license. Less-sophisticated brands sometimes leave their licensees to develop the product as well as they can on their own. When this happens, of course, the licensor has no real control over what goes on afterward.

It is crucial that brands understand just how important it is for the licensee to respect and enhance the licensor's brand identity. In the mid-1990s, for example, Ferragamo contracted a German company to develop its first fragrance under a license agreement. The contract had taken time to negotiate, as the brand was quite rigorous with respect to its identity. Despite numerous attempts by the licensee's creative teams, they were never able to come up with a concept, bottle, and name that the Ferragamo family found coherent with the brand identity. After several years of effort, both parties agreed to cancel the contract, and Ferragamo made a joint venture with Bulgari to develop its fragrance business.

When they provide the prototypes, licensors can control the product environment and insist on quality control of the final item. They must also control the product distribution. They sometimes specifically determine the distribution channels, if not the actual points of sale. They can also define prices and tariffs with the licensees.

Different Phases of Licensing Activities. Any criticism of the licensing concept seems to center around the experience of Pierre Cardin. Cardin develops very few products and seems to specialize in lower-middle-range license deals for suitcases or medium-quality kitchenware. But, as we saw with the example of Joop, there are other ways to develop products under license.

To clarify the issue and to ascertain the real value of licensing activities, it is necessary to consider this activity over the life cycle of a luxury brand.

Phase 1 As it gets started, a brand needs visibility. As it first sells its product, it must build awareness and its identity among a large group of consumers. Licensing deals are an effective way for a brand to increase its activities and general exposure.

At this very early stage, potential licensees will be reluctant to take on a brand that lacks sufficient awareness to help in the launch of a new product category. But if a ladies' ready-to-wear brand can sign a license contract for men's suits, this is certainly a good opportunity, provided that the brand identity can legitimize the new product category and that the product is of very good quality. It would also be an opportunity to establish major license deals for watches, costume jewelry, or optical frames.

For European brands at this early stage, license deals in a specific territory can help the brand's development at home and increase its visibility abroad. Asia, particularly Japan, has been an El Dorado for brands looking to raise their visibility or simply looking for cash. Japanese companies are very interested in licensing activities and have developed very specific and successful product categories (ladies' handkerchiefs with printed versions of larger scarves, for example) for their home markets.

As interest in master licenses has waned a little in Japan, China has stepped in to take up the slack.

Phase 2   When a brand develops and becomes more successful at home, it is time to launch another phase of licensing activity.

When the awareness of the brand makes it possible, worldwide license deals for such things as perfumes and cosmetics, watches, writing instruments, and costume jewelry become attractive.

It is through developing such licenses that the brand will increase its presence and its awareness. As mentioned earlier, advertising budgets for perfume are much larger than those for fashion, and having a perfume bearing its name gives a brand greater credibility. Lolita Lempicka is probably better known for its perfume license than for its fashion, and Guy Laroche is better known for L'Oréal perfumes than for fashion.

The selection of a perfume licensee is a very important part of the development of a brand. When Louis Féraud signed a perfume license contract with Avon cosmetics in 1982 for the United States, he made a big mistake. The perfume would be sold mainly from door to door and therefore would not get strong advertising support in major magazines. The fact that Avon was stronger in the United States than in Europe also made it difficult for the brand, which had its origins in Paris. Féraud would probably have done much better if it had entered into a licensing deal with L'Oréal or with Puig.

Phase 2 is the perfect time to develop a brand through licensing.

Through developing perfume deals in this second phase, a brand can establish a worldwide presence and develop additional business. If Alaïa had developed a successful perfume license 20 or 30 years ago, its fashion business would be much stronger today and better known by a wider range of consumers. An Alaïa luxury-watch line would also have reinforced the creative talent of this exceptional designer and transformed his image into a fully fledged luxury group identity.

It is when a brand starts to become well known that the launch of a perfume license makes most sense and can work as an amplifier and an accelerator for the brand. But this should not happen too early. When Christian Lacroix launched his first perfume, *C'est la vie*, in 1990, it was only two years after he created his fashion house. His name was very well known in Paris and New York, but much less so in Düsseldorf, Manchester, or Geneva, where his perfume had to be sold and purchased. The timing of this acceleration is critical to a brand's development. Christian Lacroix was always affected by that perfume failure in 1990. If it had waited another five years, who knows?

Phase 3 As a brand develops through different phases, the next step is to open freestanding stores in the major cities of the world. This objective can sometimes be in direct conflict with the development of licenses that have, by definition, a much larger distribution network. If a brand already has licenses selling underwear, belts, scarves, and leather goods in department stores and in multibrand stores, it will have difficulty selling the same products in its own boutiques, especially when department stores may be selling those same products at a discount. This type of uncoordinated distribution could send confusing and damaging signals to consumers.

Confusion would arise, too, if the brand had specialist boutiques that sold only, say, its ready-to-wear collections and left the accessories to a larger network of stores. And brand boutiques offering only a limited selection of products would have difficulty breaking even.

Phase 3 therefore represents a major change in policy direction. Brand managers must reduce the number of licenses so that individual stores can be opened and developed. But brands should not rush into this. It does not make sense to negotiate the immediate cancellation of existing licenses at great cost (as Saint Laurent found out when it was purchased by PPR Gucci). The move away from a strong license business to a strong boutique structure is not always easy, but it can be done, as the experience of Christian Dior shows.

Christian Dior was a very strong license brand in Japan until 2002. Dior management had probably been preparing for the shift years in advance. It opened freestanding stores, which could then not be profitable because of competition from its own licensed activities in major department stores. But when the master contract of the licensee, Kanebo, expired, it was not renewed and the brand was able to very successfully introduce direct import of its ready-to-wear and accessories. The groundwork for raising awareness of the Dior brand had been done over many years through the licensing arrangement with Kanebo.

Timing is of the essence: too early and the brand lacks the necessary awareness; too late and it has already lost momentum.

Phase 4 When a brand has its own stores in major cities in the world, it does not mean it should stop all license activities. If it has a strong perfume activity under license, it should go on as usual and this would be an additional resource. If it has licensing agreements for ties and optical frames, and its boutique stores cater primarily to women, again, there is no reason not to go on with license activities for men.

We mentioned earlier that even Chanel has a license contract. Valentino and Moschino also have license contracts. Valentino has perfumes with L'Oréal, eyewear with Luxottica, and watches with Timex. Moschino's handbags and leather goods are made by an Italian licensee, Borbonese. This is the new balance that must be developed in Phase 4.

So, licensing, at every stage of brand development, is necessary and is part of the global financial and identity balance. Those who speak against licenses have failed to understand that, in this activity, timing is almost everything; what is useful or even necessary at a given period may be useless at a later time.

The Special Case of Duty-Free Operations

A large percentage of luxury goods are purchased by people traveling: for perfumes, for example, it is estimated that around 15–20% of worldwide volume is purchased in duty-free outlets. For cognac and ties, too, duty-free purchases may sometimes account for up to 20% of worldwide sales.

An estimate by the specialist research firm Generation puts the total duty-free market in 2018 at €73.3 billion, with the following geographical split: Asia 49.2%, Europe 26.6%, the Americas 15.1%, the Middle East 8.0%, and Africa 1.1%. Of this total, wines and spirits represent €11.3 billion; fashion luxury goods and accessories €10.0 billion; and perfumes and cosmetics €29.3 billion. (Figures from the other research firm, Statista, are a bit different for the same year 2018: €72.9 billion).

The question is to imagine how this business sector will be affected by the coronavirus and the strong drop in airline travel. In many countries, the lack of convenient and unrestricted travel has decreased the number of business as well as tourist cross-country flights. People are now expecting the number of travel flights of 2019 not to come back until 2024 or 2025.

We will describe this activity here, because of its importance for the luxury sector, but the figures we present are those of the "old times," not of what will happen in four or five years.

Most duty-free stores are located in airports, where people generally have time on their hands and cash in their pockets. These stores are a good opportunity to provide discount prices and real customer savings in a sophisticated environment. When very few people traveled, it was a discount market reserved for the privileged few. Now that everybody travels, it has kept part of its luxury characteristics because traveling by plane—or on cruise ships—remains a relatively upscale activity.

Though duty-free stores are located in major airports, there is not always a direct link between the number of passengers and the size of the business, as shown in Table 10.7.

The Duty-Free System

Duty-frees operate on two basic conditions. As the products they sell have not really entered the country, they are not liable for import duties. As they are not sold within the country, they are not subject to a local distributor's margin. But while local duty-free operators do not pay import duties or local taxes, they do pay airport commissions, which can be two to three times higher.

Table 10.8 illustrates the workings of the duty-free system.

As Table 10.8 shows, if, for example, a perfume company sells its product in a store in Germany at a retail price of €105, its export price

Table 10.7 Estimates of Duty-Free Activities at Major International Air/Ferry Ports

	Sales 2018a (€ million)	No. of Passengers in 2018b
Dubai International	1,200	86,400,000 (2019)
London Heathrow	1,200	66,037,578
Seoul Incheon	1,000	28,000,000 (E)
Singapore Changi	800	37,203,078
Paris Charles de Gaulle	700	57,906,866
Silja Line, Finland	600	N.A.
Amsterdam Schiphol	500	43,570,370
Hong Kong	500	45,508,807
Bangkok	400	40,500,224
Frankfurt	400	50,932,840
Oslo	400	18,000,000 (E)
London Gatwick	400	35,000,000 (E)
Manchester	300	19,500,000 (E)
Tel Aviv Ben Gurion	300	12,000,000 (E)
Rome	300	33,723,213
Istanbul	300	30,000,000 (E)
São Paulo	300	13,699,657
Brussels Zaventem	200	15,000,000 (E)
Tokyo Narita	200	61,903,656
P&O Ferries U.K.	200	N.A.

[1] Estimates of Generation database and Duty Free News International (DFNI) database.
[2] International Airport Review, April 2, 2019.

Table 10.8 Duty-Free Pricing System

	French Retail Domestic (€)	European Duty-Free Retail (€)	German Retail Price Through Local Distributor (€)
Full retail price	100		105
Retail without value-added tax (20%)	83.33		
Duty-free retail price		80	
Wholesale price	50		52.5
Export price		32	16.2

Note: For the German prices, we have used the Country A figures from Table 10.2.

Table 10.9   Price Structure for the Duty-Free Operator

	Total Amount	Percentages
Airport retail	80	100%
Airport commission	32	40%
Operator's margin	16	20%
Export price	32	40%

may actually be €16.20; the difference is accounted for by a large distributor's margin and an advertising and promotional budget. When the product is sold directly to the duty-free operator at, say, Frankfurt Airport, the perfume company can invoice it at a price of €32; that is, at almost double the price it would sell for if it had to go through the German distributor's cost structure. Thus, everybody is gaining: the customer gets a better deal, and the manufacturer sells at a higher export price, even if there is no advertising budget built into the structure.

Table 10.9 explains how the system works from the duty-free operator's perspective.

When the duty-free operator purchases at 32, it receives only a 20% margin; most of the difference between the export price and the duty-free retail price goes on commission paid to the airport operators. In fact, airports have two major sources of income: landing and parking costs for planes, and duty-free commissions; in many cases, the latter provide more than half of the total airport revenues.

Duty-free operators work with an airport concession generally awarded to the highest bidder. Such concessions can last from three to seven years, but the majority are for seven. In preparing their bid, the major operators study their forecast volume of business based on the number of planes, the destinations and the nationalities, and the types of the travelers (tourists versus business travelers, for example), and commit themselves to give a commission (which can range from 35% to 55% of their sales) and sometimes also a flat minimum for each year of the concession.

In general, for a large-volume airport this activity is very competitive, with most of the worldwide operators bidding.

Operators factor into their bids considerations such as new slots that may be given for new destinations or new airlines, and they use their own estimates of nationality and travel-type mix for each of the luxury-product categories: Japanese customers smoke more than American customers, but they smoke mainly Mild Seven, the highest-selling cigarette brand in Japan. Americans buy whisky and cognac and, for cognac, their preferred brands are Hennessy, then Rémy Martin, and so on. Operators can then prepare a business plan with their best estimates of sales and the maximum concession fee they can offer the airport authorities.

Given the very high airport commissions (which can be more than half of the duty-free retail price), and in countries like Hong Kong, Guam, Singapore, and Panama where there are no import duties, it makes a lot of sense to build downtown duty-free stores or large downtown galleries because then the business model will work without the payment of large airport concession fees.

But in this case, duty-free operators are back to square one: they are in the official territory of the domestic distributors, unless they can pressure the brands and find middle ground. Of course, even these downtown stores are the result of the specific duty-free system that pertains in each country.

There are huge price variations from one place to another, but this is generally the result of differences in local prices (cigarettes are very cheap in the Chinese domestic market) and different retail price strategies of airport operators. For example, the operators of the Amsterdam Schiphol Airport prefer to work on a lower-percentage concession fee, provided the duty-free prices in many product categories are the lowest in Europe. This way, they believe they can attract more stopover passengers—going, for example, from Boston to Helsinki or from Houston to Hamburg—than London, Paris, or Frankfurt.

In 2019, it was found that for wines and spirits, one should buy in Kiev, Madrid, or Grand Canyon; for makeup, in London, Dubai, and Vienna; for perfumes, in Madrid, Porto, or London; and for cigarettes, Singapore, Hong Kong, or Bangkok.

The Major Duty-Free Operators

Eight or 10 major duty-free operators manage more than half of all airport volume in the world. There is obviously a strong advantage to size: the bigger the purchase potential, the better the duty-free operators can put pressure on their suppliers for better export prices. And the lower the purchasing prices they can get, the better they can win new airport concessions by offering a higher commission to the airport authorities. The major operators, ranked by size, are described here.

The Dufry Group.   The Dufry group, with sales of €8.4 billion in 2019, is the result of several major mergers: the purchase of Nuance in 2014 and the merger with World Duty Free in 2015. It operates almost all Spanish and British airports plus outlets in Basle, Milan, Panama, Mexico City, New York, Singapore, Moscow, Nice, and many other places. It has acquired strong Brazilian concessions. It manages 2,300 stores in 24 countries in 2019. It is also a ship chandler (duty-free operators in major harbors for cruise ships and others leaving domestic waters) in Barcelona, Colón, Panama, and Croatia.

Heinemann.   Heinemann is a family operator based in Hamburg, with sales of €4.5 billion for 2019. It operates all German and most Austrian airports, has major airport operations in Portugal, and has a presence in Miami and New York. The firm has developed very quickly in Eastern Europe (Warsaw, Budapest, Bratislava, Ljubiana, Moscow), as well as in Turkey and South Africa.

Its sales are divided as such in 2019: liquor, tobacco, and confectionery: 56% of sales; perfumes and cosmetics: 34%; fashion: 8%. By geographic area: Germany: 12%; other EU: 26%; other Europe: 37%; Asia: 19%; and the rest: 6%.

It is strong in food and tobacco products and has domestic distribution activities in Germany.

Lagardère Group (Aelia).   This group is difficult to compare with others because, with sales of €3.4 billion in 2019, it has several activities: sales of newspapers and books in airports and railway stations (Relay) and duty-free activities. On total sales of €3.4 billion, duty-free corresponds probably to a little more than €2 billion. This group is the result of an early joint venture between Air France and the Paris airports. In 2015, it purchased US Paradies, which gave it access to Atlanta, Dallas, Denver, Las Vegas, and other airports. The Paris activities seem to represent 40% of their total sales, but they still have 250 major points of sale, including

Roissy and Orly, but also in the United Kingdom, Poland, Ireland, and Spain.

DFS (Duty-Free Shoppers).   A division of LVMH, this activity was started in Hong Kong in 1960 by three individuals and was purchased by LVMH in 1996. It has estimated sales of around €3.15 billion for 2019. Most of its activities are in the Pacific region. The group headquarters are in Hong Kong and its major airports are San Francisco, Los Angeles, Bali, Singapore, and Honolulu, and it operates 150 stores located mainly in 15 Pacific cities, including Hong Kong, Singapore, Hawaii, San Francisco, Los Angeles, Bali, Guam, Saipan, and Abu Dhabi.

A specialist in Japanese and other Asian customers, the group has very strong negotiating power in dealing with suppliers. It is also very strong in its downtown activities, operating under the Galleria name.

King Power.   King Power, from Thailand, the biggest of the national duty-free operators. It was given the Bangkok airport concession in 2004 for 15 years and in 2019, it won the new concession until 2029. It had to offer a concession deal that would be better than the bids of, for example, Lotte World and Dufry. It also manages all Thai duty-frees. For 2018, its sales were of €2.23 billion.

Lotte World Duty-Free.   This a different operator in that it includes airport sales made mainly through Korean downtown department stores: purchasers can give their flight number and their departure date and have their purchases waiting from them on board. Thus, they can enjoy duty-free prices in the environment of a department store. Sales are estimated at around €2 billion.

Dubai Duty Free.   This airport duty-free wants to remain independent and products on sale in the airport are purchased directly from foreign suppliers. For 2019, its sales were €2.03 billion. Every month, it organizes a lottery in which a winner can get a new Ferrari. They are operating the airport duty-free to not only make money, but also to attract transfer passengers from Europe to Asia or from Asia to Europe with very interesting low prices.

Duty Free Americas.   This company, which belongs to the Falic brothers (the last owners of the Christian Lacroix Company before the bankruptcy), is based in Florida and had a turnover of more than €1.4 billion in 2019. It started by operating border shops between the United States and Canada and between the United States and Mexico. It also operates in 60 US airports like New York's JFK and La Guardia, as well as Chicago, Boston, Washington, and Detroit.

AER Rianta.   This Irish group is in fact the inventor of the airport duty-free system: they started in Shannon in 1947. They belong to the public authorities (they are a subsidiary of the Irish Airport Board) and have sales above €1.0 billion. They have always managed to have a trustful relationship with Aeroflot, starting in 1979 when they accepted Russian planes stopping over in Shannon for their refueling. With Aeroflot, they have joint venture agreements to operate Moscow and Saint Petersburg airports. In early 2020, they were rumored to be about to sell their shares in all Russian airports to their Russian partner. They also operate in Montréal, Ottawa, Winnipeg, Cyprus, Beirut, and Delhi.

In many other places, including Greece, Venezuela, and Argentina, small operators generally manage one or two airports and are often run with the blessing of the state.

The Negotiation

Negotiating with any one of these major operators is always difficult for brands. While the brand executives want to achieve both visibility and maximum volume in the airports, there is a high price to be paid for the privilege. First, they have to pay for each item to be listed and then for promotional support, which can include:

- Pricelist book advertising.
- Shelf location.
- Transparencies in the shop with the name of the brand, or an advertisement.
- A special promotional program for the brand.
- Push money for the sales staff.

In most cases, sales staff are employed by the brands themselves and have to be paid. Together, all of these factors mean that it is very difficult for small brands to break into the potentially lucrative duty-free market.

The Parallel Market: Reasons and Consequences

The parallel, or *gray*, market consists of quantities of products that are sold in stores that are not supposed to handle such products. Parallel operators purchase large quantities of products, if possible, in places where they are at the lowest possible price and bring them to stores that would not otherwise be able to get them. The parallel market is all the more developed for brands that have selective distribution practices that make their products hard to find and where prices vary greatly from one place to another.

The Reason for Parallel Markets

We must distinguish here between different product categories.

For **perfumes**, products are very easily transferred from one place in the world to another. Gray-market operators reason that if they can buy perfumes at wholesale prices in Panama at a very low price, it may be profitable to sell them in Japan, where retail prices are generally higher. These arbitrage activities are much the same as take place for currencies or for grain futures. Their only work is to take the perfumes from where they are available at good prices and sell them where they are in demand and at a higher price.

Perfume brands have built their image on the concept of selective distribution. Most brands make sure that their products are not available in supermarkets or hypermarkets in Europe or in US drugstores. Because they organize scarcity as part of their reason for being, they do not want to be found in huge display piles in a Carrefour hypermarket in the suburbs of Brussels the week before Mother's Day. This would damage their image of desirability and their exclusivity.

It is not easy for brands to keep their products out of drugstores and hypermarkets because in most countries there are laws to prohibit manufacturers from selecting their retail outlets. They are supposed to offer their products to every store without discriminating between retail outlets. So, perfume brands have defined policies stating that they will only sell their products to stores where the environment is exclusive and luxurious and where beauty consultants are available and knowledgeable about the products. They thus limit their sales to traditional perfume stores and beauty chains.

If they were to allow Carrefour to sell their products in the buildup to Mother's Day or Christmas, it would be quite unfair to the traditional perfume stores that carry the brand all year and would be unable to cover their distribution costs, losing out to supermarket sales.

In the United States, sales of perfumes and cosmetics are concentrated in department stores, where brands fight to get good locations and large counters, and large and sophisticated perfumes stores. If these products were also available in drugstores, it would dilute their overall image and reduce their negotiating power with department stores.

On the other hand, drugstores are interested in carrying top brands because this improves their image and broadens their product line into more glamorous categories.

So gray-market operators act as wholesalers and are ready to offer almost any perfume brand to the US drugstores. All products are available, but not at the same price. Brands such as Estée Lauder and Chanel that are difficult to get will be sold at retail or with a 10% discount on retail (which means that when drugstores decide to carry them, they are ready to sell without making money), while brands that are easy to get on the gray market—Pierre Cardin, for example—can be found with a 60–75% discount at certain periods.

Given that it is almost impossible for them to stay out of gray-market channels, the objective for perfumes is to be difficult to get—to be there at such a wholesale price that the retailer who handles the brand does so without making money.

For **accessories**, the history is a little different. First, because fashion dresses are unique, they are difficult to find in the gray market. Because they have a short shelf or store life, they are rapidly out of fashion. The main target for the gray market is accessories that are only sold in freestanding boutiques, such as those of Prada, Louis Vuitton, and Chanel.

Chanel or Louis Vuitton handbags often end up in the window displays of small leather-goods stores in Japan, for example. Clients are attracted to the stores because of these famous and exclusive brands, but once inside, sales staff do everything they can ("They are too expensive for the quality … I can show you a much more fashionable product … ") to move the sale toward other brands on which they make higher margins. So, the Chanel or Louis Vuitton products are there not to be sold but merely as an attraction.

For **wines and spirits**, the issue is complicated by the fact that, in most countries, heavy taxes are levied on such products and this is reflected in the prices in the stores. The issue here is not only the selective distribution aspect but also the way to avoid alcohol taxes. In some cases, products are smuggled into the country. To prevent this, some countries have tax stamps that are stuck on the collar of the bottles as proof that the tax has been paid. Of course, smuggled products are still available, but only from parallel, unofficial outlets, where customers buy at their own risk.

Collecting Products for Parallel Markets

Gray-market operators use all types of systems to gather merchandise. Some travel all over France or Italy in small trucks, visiting perfume stores and offering to purchase everything the store operators are ready to sell, at, say, retail minus 30%. If a store operator is behind on his budget or if his inventory is too heavy, he might be tempted to unload. Needless to say, distribution contracts between each perfume brand and the retailer prohibit any such activities, but it is not always easy to trace sales like this. There is a good lesson here for perfume brands and perfume salesmen: it is very dangerous to push store operators into purchasing too much merchandise. It may be a very common and effective practice in food supermarkets for mass-market products, but it is very dangerous for selective luxury products.

For Louis Vuitton, Prada, or Chanel handbags, the system is even easier. It is common practice for gray-market employees to pay passers-by to enter legitimate stores and buy different products for them. We estimate that for a brand like Louis Vuitton, more than €20 million-worth of merchandise will be bought from the different Paris stores each year and will end up in small, second-rate leather-goods stores, mainly in Japan. Some say that this system also involves getting official checks from small Japanese retailers to launder €20 million that will be put officially into a genuine Japanese bank account.

There are other sources of gray-market products. Distributors from countries buying at reasonable costs—Panama, Hong Kong, Paraguay, and Singapore, for example—all know some of the parallel buyers and might be tempted to unload some of their inventories. They are prepared to run the risk of not having their distribution contract renewed if they are caught. The brands themselves may sometimes sell their old inventories to jobbers.

What is certain is that luxury products can travel the world at a relatively low cost, compared to their value. Therefore, a perfume bought in Singapore or a handbag purchased in Paris may well end up in a US drugstore or a Japanese leather-goods store. In neither case will the products be sold in their normal environment.

How to Fight Parallel Distribution

When a gray-market product finds its way into a particular territory, a distributor or the manager of a local subsidiary will complain to the brand's head office, and with some justification. They say: "Those products come from your factory, so you should know where they went and what happened to them." They have a point.

Brands that are serious about reducing parallel activities must ensure that they keep proper track of their products. About 30 years ago, manufacturers began putting laser identification numbers on each individual sleeve carton to enable them to keep track of if and how things came to be in the gray market. The gray-market operators responded to this by discreetly removing all laser numbers from the cartons they acquired.

The next step, then, about 20 years ago, was for the brands to put a specifically located laser number on each perfume box so that each client would have a laser number. Then, even if the outer number were scratched, the client could still be identified. So the gray-market operators would also scratch other places on the sleeve, hoping perhaps to eradicate the identification of the distributor. While this was not always successful, it would often be sufficient to create uncertainty and make tracking difficult.

Today, the perfume manufacturers that really care use boxes that have systems that enable all products taken from the warehouse for shipping to a client to be recorded and tracked by computer and for each individual product to be identified by its destination.

Today, when a perfume appears in a store where it should not be, it is generally possible to identify the source. Although the distributor may not have acted illegally in allowing branded products to pass into the parallel market, what it has done is not good for the brand's standing. And in any event, in the absence of an invoice between a distributor and a wholesaler that has official links with a gray-market operator, it is still difficult to prove that a specific perfume comes from the distributor's stock. Needless to say, such invoices are quite difficult to get.

US Customs appeared at one point to have invented a very effective system to counter gray-market activities: only the distributor that had a right to the brand registration in the United States could import the product and pay duty. However, this still failed to take account of smuggling. What is certain is that the parallel operators will continue to disrupt the selective distribution system for many more years. For brands, therefore, the objective must be to limit the damage as much as possible—but the parallel market will probably always exist.

Chapter 11

Retail Management

For many years, the priority of luxury management was the creative process and the subsequent development of commercially viable products. The brands had their own home address that was a store in a large place at the origin of the business and that had a head office inside or nearby. Hermès had a very large store on rue du Faubourg Saint Honoré in Paris and Salvatore Ferragamo had a store on the Palazzo Feroni in Florence. Armani, as he developed his creations, wanted also to have a very large store in Milan, and Gabrielle Chanel on rue Cambon in Paris or Ralph Lauren on Madison Avenue in New York. They all wanted to have a major flagship store representing the concept and, if possible, presenting their complete collection.

Apart from this unique store that many top management members would visit almost every day, the rest of the selling and retail network would be less of a company priority. Abroad, many brands developed through department stores, but, around the year 2000, they realized that department stores were growing at an average of 2% a year when luxury brands grew more than 8% and had to shortcut them to develop faster.

Also, major brands' offices were visited by individuals from Moscow, Buenos Aires, or Taipei, who proposed building small replica stores in their home cities as franchises or through "exclusive distribution contracts," and it was an opportunity to develop wholesale sales from Paris and strengthen the worldwide presence of the brand.

Today, the worldwide setup of major brands is a mix of retail activities in major cities of the world, shop-in-shops in department stores in some cities, and exclusive distribution contracts or franchises, as well as wholesale activities geared at multibrand stores.

This move from wholesale to retail can be explained by Montblanc's history. Until 1990, Montblanc fountain pens were sold 100% at wholesale. They could be found in department stores and in office and school supply stores everywhere in the world. Sales were exclusively at wholesale, as was the case for the major competitors of Montblanc: Parker, Schaeffer, and Waterman. The president of Montblanc decided to start their first monobrand store in Hong Kong in 1990, then a second one in Hamburg, their home city. Today Montblanc has 350 monobrand boutiques in the world. Those boutiques helped them diversify successfully in watches, starting in 1997, then leather goods, jewelry pieces, perfumes, and so on. As of 2020, Montblanc has sales estimated at €650 million and a high level of profitability. Their competitors are no longer Parker or Waterman, but Longchamp or Longines. They are no longer in the same ballpark as the pen manufacturers. But while they were developing their own stores network, they had to be very careful not to jeopardize their wholesale activities, which were very profitable then, and still are today.

The Montblanc example shows how the business has changed in the past 30 years, but on top of that, the retailing activity faces a new challenge today: it has to move from a system of stores, to a mix of physical and online stores, and, from the point of view of the consumers, to a seamless continuum of physical and online stores (offline to online), which is the setup of the future.

In this chapter, we will start discussing the role of retailing today, then present the basic retail management ratios and discuss the issues of store location and store design, to end by describing the challenge of 2020 (offline to online setup).

Table 11.1 Stores and Sales History of a Selection of Brands

	2000	**2003**	**2010**	**2019**
Bulgari				
Sales (in € million)	376	759	926	3,200 (E)
Number of stores	126	182	273	259
Cartier + VC&A				
Sales (in € million)	1,500	1,994	2,688	7,083
Number of stores	250	250	364	398
Gucci				
Sales (in € million)	1,200	1,800	2,266	9,628
Number of stores	143	174	283	454
Louis Vuitton				
Sales (in € million)	1,500 (E)	2,200 (E)	5,000 (E)	13,500 (E)
Number of stores	143	317	440	448
Tiffany				
Sales (in € million)	1,334	1,600	2,167	3,966
Number of stores	119	141	220	275

Sources: Annual reports and authors' estimates.

Why Is Retailing So Important Today?

In Table 11.1, we give examples of the evolution of the stores of six luxury groups taken at random: Bulgari, Cartier (and Van Cleef & Arpels), Gucci, Louis Vuitton, and Tiffany.

For this selection of brands, the consolidated numbers of stores went from 781 to 1,834. It was multiplied by almost 2.5. We can estimate that today for the existing luxury brands there are more than 20,000 luxury premium monobrand stores in the world. And there is a need for 20,000 store managers, many store coordinators, country or area retail managers, not to mention visual merchandisers or luxury retail store architects.

In this section, we will start describing the present situation, show the differences between the wholesale and the retail models, and explain how the preeminence of a full retail model forces the total fashion and luxury model to change. This will then lead us to deal with the future of traditional retailing.

The Present Retail Situation for Luxury Brands

We should not give the impression that the luxury business has completely moved from wholesale to retail: it depends very much on the activities and the products.

Distribution for Fashion and Accessories or Jewelry

For fashion and jewelry, the process of moving toward a fully controlled store network is clearly strong. Traditionally, Louis Vuitton and Hermès were presented as brands whose policy was exclusively to sell in their own stores. It is really the case of Louis Vuitton, which seemed to have waited until niche perfumes were a viable alternative to mass selective perfumes, to launch their line of perfumes exclusively in their own stores. On the contrary, Hermès is clearly concentrating on their own stores, but their perfumes are sold in many multibrand locations. One should also mention Loro Piana or Chanel, which have a fully controlled retail system, except for their perfumes or eyewear.

But smaller brands like Balmain, Chloe, or Versace are still doing a large part of their activities at wholesale. This is of course the case for their perfumes or their optical frames businesses, but their ready-to-wear is still purchased by department stores to be put in their own counters or by the fashion multibrand stores of Brown's in London, Joyce (Lane Crawford) in Hong Kong, or Glamorette in Singapore.

For fashion, accessories, and jewelry, the most frequent system is a mix of directly operated stores, third-party-operated stores, department stores, and a few multibrand stores; this mix of distribution channels changes over time as those brands develop. Table 11.2 gives an example of the mix for three brands with different economic weights.

The message in this table is that even for a very strong brand like Chanel, directly operated monobrand stores are not the only way to distribute their fashion products. They still have, for the time being, 180 shop-in-shops in department stores, mainly in the United States and Japan.

The comparison between Givenchy and Balmain is also very interesting. Givenchy fashion has traditionally been considered a powerful

Table 11.2 Mix of Distribution Systems for Three Brands with Different Economic Weights (by number of points of sales) (2019)

	Monobrand Stores	Shop-in-shops in Department Stores	Multibrand Stores	Total
Chanel	240 (E)	180 (E)	0	420 (E)
Givenchy	65	68	120 (E)	253 (E)
Balmain	19	88	179	286

Sources: Michel Chevalier and Michel Gutsatz, *Luxury, Retail, and Digital Management.* John Wiley & Sons, 2020.

mid-range brand. They had enough investment money to work through 65 directly operated stores. On the contrary, Balmain used to be a small brand with very little investment money, and they have very few directly operated stores. Now, as the brand was purchased by the Mayhoola Qatari group, they have investment money to open their monobrand stores, and as the brand is selling very well, it has developed a strong presence in department stores and in multibrand stores.

We can expect Balmain to directly operate 75 stores in 2023 or 2024 if the demand for the brand continues to be very strong.

So, the retail development for a fashion brand is always a trade-off between the interest of that brand for multibrand retailers or the department stores and the money available (as well as the strength of the brand to reach break-even) to open directly operated stores.

The same analysis could be done for jewelry brands. Strong brands now have their own directly operated stores.

Some fashion brands differentiate their distribution channels as a function of their products: the full ready-to-wear collection for their own boutiques and a strong wholesale activity in multibrand stores for accessories like handbags or scarves. They can develop customer demand that way, in many places, where they could not afford to have their own stores and make money. Nevertheless, as soon as they strongly develop their own network of 100 or 200 monobrand stores, they have a tendency to close their multibrand accounts to concentrate the volume in their own premises, and in this way, their own stores can reach break-even more easily.

Distribution for Watches or Perfumes

Traditionally, watches and perfumes were sold though multibrand stores: customers expected to find everything in the same store. They would hesitate between Beautiful from Estée Lauder, J'Adore from Dior, or Gabrielle from Chanel: they would go to Sephora, spray them on their own skin, and then buy the smell that they preferred. In the same manner, one would go to a traditional watch store, put a Rolex, a Cartier, or a Breguet on one's wrist and buy the preferred one.

The Watches.   Today, the largest sales volume for watches and perfumes is done in multibrand stores. But Ebel, a pioneer, started to open monobrand watches stores in Hong Kong in 1994. It was too early and the brand was not strong enough to bring clients into those stores; it almost went bankrupt.

The idea was then picked up by other brands. Omega, for example, created a network of 200 stores in China; with 100 Omega monobrand stores and 100 multibrand retailers, and they are the leader in the country. Rolex developed their Chinese presence later, but they also have more than 50 monobrand retail stores in the country.

So how to sell watches? If one has a very strong brand and is ready to put a lot of money into the priority markets, monobrand stores could be the solution. Rolex and Omega are not alone: Piaget has 80 monobrand stores worldwide, IWC 79, Hublot 71, and Vacheron Constantin 63. Breguet, with its 35 stores, has a special strategy: most of their sales volume is through multibrand stores, but in a selected number of capital cities, they have a monobrand store, very well located, that acts not only as a retail store but also as a showroom for multibrand store operators or PR people.

One could say that watches used to be only sold in multibrand stores but that now, everything seems possible, according to the economic strength of each brand.

The Perfumes.   Perfumes, makeup, and skin care were generally considered to be traditional multibrand store products, and the development of the very big retailers like Sephora, Ulta Beauty, or Watson-Marionnaud and Douglas have given them most of the volume (probably up to 80% in some countries) that is sold in those multibrand outlets.

But niche perfumes brands like Annick Goutal, Jo Malone, or Frederic Malle are now developing a new perfumes segment, and the major perfumes brands like Chanel, Armani, Dior, and Lancôme are now creating collections of products generally not sold in their traditional outlets but through a new network of monobrand stores.

If this niche segment develops very fast, it would modify the situation, but so far luxury perfumes seem to be sold in a very large majority through multibrand outlets.

What would the full directly operated stores model change for the industry?.   If brands can fully control their distribution and sell exclusively their products in monobrand stores or in fully controlled online setups, would it change anything about the management?

For a fashion brand, fashion shows modify their reason for being. Traditionally, fashion shows were the opportunity for department store merchandisers and multibrands store buyers to see the collection for the next season well in advance and to select and purchase the items they would like to have in their stores six months later. But when a fashion brand completely controls its points of sale, it can decide for their stores what they have to sell: the fashion shows are then no longer necessary for the selection of items. This selection can be done internally or through computer programs, taking into consideration previous selling patterns for each store or each country. The fashion production calendar is then no longer necessary, as brands controlling their own stores can deliver as many collections a year as possible; 20 years ago, luxury fashion brands all had two collections per year (Spring–Summer and Fall–Winter), plus, eventually, two "cruise" collections. Now they could even copy Zara and their 26 collections per year if they see fit.

In that case, fashion shows are no longer part of a production and selling process and exclusively become a communication tool, which could take place, if necessary, closer to the selling season.

This change in operations requires a much more sophisticated logistical system. Production systems must be more integrated or more controlled if they are subcontracted. Products should be delivered to the stores and taken out as a function of their actual sales results and of their expected sales. Logistical platforms should also be organized and made very effective. Returns should also be handled and shipped back to other stores where they would have a higher probability of sale. The full logistical process can then be improved and made smooth and effective.

In a way, for their normal retail activities, brands should organize logistical systems so effectively and so fluidly that they would have internally what is also necessary to be successful online.

Basic Retail Management Concepts

Retailing corresponds to a certain number of reflexes that are useful to decide where to locate a store, where to measure the adequacy of a given location with the product one wants to sell, or how to control the efficiency of sales staff.

A Store's Reason for Being

The first question to ask is: What is the reason for being of a given store? Stores can be divided into three major different categories:

1. *Destination stores* are those that clients visit only a few times a year or even less. When a man wants to change his kitchen sink, he is prepared to spend a certain amount of time to visit kitchen fixture stores. He does not expect to find it very close to where he lives. He is ready to spend a part of his afternoon to visit different stores. He is making a destination shopping trip. He is ready to take his time so kitchen fixture manufacturers do not to need to open three or four stores in a large city: one or two will be enough and clients will make an effort to find them.

2. To the contrary, if one sells newspapers, one has to be very close to where people live or work: if customers don't find a newsstand easily, they will not purchase and read newspapers. Newsstands are therefore *convenience* locations. Clients will not go out of the way to find them.

3. A third category of stores are *interception* ones: if someone wants to make a copy of a key, rather than spending the afternoon finding a key store, one would put a Post-it on the refrigerator as a reminder that, the next time they go to the train station or shopping mall, they have to take the key to be copied. Those stores have to be located at some frequently visited interception spots.

One may think that luxury products are destination places. This is, in a certain way, the case when a Chinese tourist visiting Milan has put Prada and Gucci stores in their to-do list of shopping. Nevertheless, luxury brands can decide, for example, in New York or in Beijing to have a greater number of smaller stores than their competitors and to be more accessible than they are.

Basic Ratios.   Stores managers look at the sales and the **gross margin** of the day for their stores. But they also compare the daily gross margin to the theoretical one that would have been obtained if all products had been sold at full retail price, without any discount or special prices.

A very important criterion is the **conversion** ratio: the percentage of clients, among all those who enter a store, who purchase something. Even in supermarkets, this ratio cannot reach 100% because when two persons enter together, they are registered as two entries and would generally come out with only one sales ticket.

For the flagship store of a very strong brand, which many tourists have mentioned visiting in their to-do list, the conversion ratio can be well above 50%. In a fashion store, it can vary from 18% to 25%. For multibrand perfumes and cosmetic stores, it can reach from 20% to 33%. But for an art gallery selling paintings, it probably reaches less than 10/00.

For a given brand, this conversion ratio may vary from one country to another and also from one store to another, but the average conversion ratio can give an indication of what one could expect when one opens a new store somewhere. It can also vary by nationality of those entering the stores: basic behaviors may differ from one nationality to another.

Looking at the conversion ratio by store can also give a first impression of the efficiency of the sales staff or the coherence between its specific location and the type of products that are offered.

The **average ticket** is also a critical element, as it is the basis of many accounting analyses: How many people enter the store? What is the conversion ratio? With the average ticket, one can get the sales level for a given period of time. The **number of items per ticket** is also an index that can be useful, because it can give the average per sales staff, to measure how each one is able to sell a second or a third item to the average customer of, for example, a fashion or a shoe store.

There are two other useful sales statistics tools: the **sell-through** is the percentage of products of a new collection sold in the first month, then in the first two months, and so on. For fashion or seasonal products it gives an indication of the percentage of the new collection that has been acquired by the clients in, for example, one or two months, and it makes it simpler to predict the percentage of this stock that will remain after the four months of full-price seasonal sales and will have to be unloaded at bargain prices. It may force store managers to find special prices or special promotional programs that could be less costly before the bargain sales period and would therefore be more effective. After the fact, it may be interesting to also compute the percentage of sales at full margin and the percentage of sales at bargain prices.

The last useful ratio, particularly in shopping centers, is the **attraction ratio**, which records the number of people entering a given store divided by the number of people walking past the store. This measures the strength of the brand and the effectiveness of the show windows' decoration to convince people they should enter and see what is inside. It can also help in comparing the attractiveness of different shops next to each other in the same alley of a luxury shopping center and which one has the strongest pulling power.

How Do People Behave in a Store?.   Tracking studies, in particular those done by Paco Underhill,[1] have analyzed how clients behave when they are in a store.

They look straight ahead as they enter and only really start looking around after they've been in the store for several meters.

They believe they go straight ahead but they imperceptibly turn slightly to the right: they probably want to use their right hand to touch products. Because they slightly move to the right, the bottom left of a store is generally the least visited area: if the floor plan makes it possible, it becomes the ideal place to put the fitting room. This leaning to the right explains, for example, why supermarkets generally have their entrance not in the middle of the front, but generally on the right-hand side.

---

[1] Unless stated otherwise, all research findings presented in this chapter are taken from Paco Underhill, *Why We Buy: The Science of Shopping*. New York: Simon & Schuster, 2008.

In a store, people want:

- To touch products.
- To be able to speak to someone, but the staff does not always know how to start the first contact.
- There is a strong correlation between the time spent in a store and the probability of purchase (in other words, the conversion ratio). The more interesting the store, the more pleasant it is, the longer people stay, and the higher the conversion ratio.

One would like the clients to stay as long as possible in a store, but their behavior will depend on both inside and outside variables.

A study described by Paco Underhill measured the average time spent in a furniture store in the United States:

- A woman with another woman: 8 minutes 15 seconds
- A woman with a child: 7 minutes 19 seconds
- A woman alone: 5 minutes 20 seconds
- A woman with a man: 4 minutes 41 seconds

Other studies measure how the purchase probability can increase. For example, if the selling staff member initiates a contact with the client, the conversion ratio could increase 50%; hence the interest in training the staff to engage and start a positive and horizontal conversation with people entering their store. When this same staff member engages the client in a positive conversation and if the client tries on a piece in the fitting room, the probability of purchase increases by 100%.

Also, beware of people visiting the store and leaving! They might buy the next time they enter the store. They might as well buy online. If they leave the store unhappy, they would probably, then, decide not to buy through the Internet. It certainly makes sense to be nice to them all the way to the door and to make sure they have a positive impression of their visit.

Store Location

At first sight, it is very easy to choose a location for a store in a major luxury market: go next to a Gucci or Chanel store. But what kind of store should you look for? A very large one? A small one with a relatively small ground floor but a very nice space on the second floor? A store with an average location or with an outstanding one?

The first question is to understand what one wants to do with a store, then what it represents to its clients. In the following sections, we will first describe the different types of stores. Then we will look at the economic analysis of the locations. After that, we will finish with leasing systems.

Types of Stores

One must differentiate different types of stores. They can be classified by size. They can also be defined by their ownership or their position: Are they freestanding in a street? Are they part of a luxury shopping center, as is, for example, very common in China? Or are they part of a department store?

Classification by Store Size.   What first comes to mind are **flagship stores**. They were originally an institution for the brands. Now, the biggest brands have developed those very large stores (more than $1,000\,m^2$) in each major region in the world as, for example, Paris or Milan (often their home base), then Hong Kong, Tokyo, Shanghai, and New York. They can present their full collection but can also sometimes add a brand museum, or several stands where craftsmen could be working, or a workshop, where they could prepare individual made-to-order products. The objective is to be more than a selling place—to appear as a landmark in the city in which it is located and an entertainment destination.

We could then speak of **standard stores** of different sizes. They could measure, for example, more than $300\,m^2$ (type A stores, with the full product line), 100 to $300\,m^2$ (type B stores, with product lines only in the main categories), or less than $100\,m^2$ (small stores with a limited product offering). These groups and their reasons for being will change very much with the progress of the digital development.

Another group is **pop-up stores**. The idea was started by Comme de Garçons and was then copied and developed by almost everybody, including Prada, Dior, and Chanel. Brands were looking for large freestanding commercial space that could be available for three to four months at a very low rent while a large building or a complete block was being renovated. The store could be out of the way and would not require a top location as it would be a full destination place. The pop-up stores would then create an opportunity to host social events or PR activities that might include a museum, or special inscriptions in leather pieces, and so on. The idea was that, with a low rent, it was possible to create a very special PR place where clients could come and learn about the brand and where journalists could visit and write long articles on the products and their specificities. The ideal timing is to rent this space in September, organize it for opening late September, and invite journalists in early October so that they could publish articles in November that would suggest that their readers visit this place or other stores of the brand in November or December. The original idea was great, but little by little landlords realized the opportunity they had with small out-of-the-way locations and they started to increase the rent; the economics of the system then became more difficult.

Classification by Ownership. One should also differentiate stores by ownership. First, we can speak of **directly operated stores** belonging to the brand. But one could also speak about **third-party-operated stores**. These could be **franchised**, that is to say, owned and managed by an outsider who would respect the franchising rules, be committed to purchase a minimum amount of product each year, and pay a percentage of royalties on his retail sales. The most frequent outsider system, also in the category of third-party-operated stores, is the **exclusive distributor** contract for a given country, enabling an individual operator to distribute a brand in a territory and do it at wholesale but at retail as well.

The Case of Department Stores. Department stores are another way to distribute products. Historically they selected products, purchased them, and sold them at multibrand counters. Their job was to identify the best products at the best possible prices and to sell them branded, unbranded, or with their own department store brand. But over the past 50 years, their business model has moved toward shop-in-shops. A shop-in-shop is obviously a shop in a department store. The place is selected and decorated by the brand, the merchandise generally belongs to the brand, and the sales staff are employees of the brand and wear the brand uniform. When the client selects a product, he or she is given a sales slip that he or she brings to the department store cashier for payment. The department store will then take the total amount, deduct its retailer's margin, and transfer the wholesale amount to the brand.

It seems like a normal store but it is a joint activity of the brand and of the department store. The brand provides the products and the staff, and the department store attracts the clients and makes the sale possible.

Economic Analysis of Store Location

With the Internet, it is possible to know, for every block of housing in the world, the number of inhabitants, their average income, the number of mobile phones, the number of credit cards, or the number of houses broken into and credit cards overdue. It is also possible to look at the number of square meters of stores at a less than 5-, 10-, 15-, or 30-minutes drive from each block and to define the resulting trade adequacies and trade inadequacies.

It is therefore possible to identify where there is enough potential to come up with a new store and select the most logical locations.

The question is: When a customer is 20 minutes away from a store in a city and 20 minutes away from a store in another city, where would he or she go? A very old study, done in 1929 by Reilly, gives the answer: between two stores of equal distance in driving time (for example), the consumer would select the city where there is the bigger number of inhabitants or the bigger number of commercial stores. It is therefore possible to draw maps of equal attractiveness of the commercial zones of two cities.

This is the official rule, but some secondary variables can also affect the picture:

1. Clients are reluctant to cross a river to go shopping (for example, in large cities with a river in the middle, one needs to put in at least two stores).
2. Highways have a less systematic impact, but they also divide the geographic zones in the mind of the clients.
3. Railways provide a large number of potential clients, and not immediately next to the railway station but one or two blocks away can be a very interesting location for a department store, for example. Subway stations play a similar role, albeit to a lesser extent.
4. The two sides of a wide street are not equivalent. Generally, people prefer to walk on the sunny side and are much less tempted to

walk on the shadowed side. For high destination brands it does not make too much of a difference, but for little-known ones or convenience store products it can considerably change the potential of two locations, just across the street, one from the other.

Different Leasing Systems

Securing a top location in a major city is not an easy matter: they are seldom available and generally expensive. Very often, it is necessary to pay a large amount of key money upfront. There are several leasing systems that apply around the world, each with its own rules and peculiarities.

The **American lease system** generally does not include key money. The lessor rents a place for 9 or 10 years, after which the lessee has to negotiate a new lease, at market price, for a specified period. If the parties cannot agree on the new lease, or if the lessee wants to get out, no money is due either way.

The American system is balanced and very open, but there is a catch to it: where a store is losing money, or where sales drop dramatically overnight (as happened after 9/11/2001), the lessee is bound by the contract to continue paying rent for the entire period of the lease.

Many foreign luxury brands have found themselves in such a position and were sometimes even unable to sublet the premises. Even if the original contract does permit a sublease, contractual clauses governing product category and brand positioning can be very restrictive. In difficult times, lessees may be faced with the prospect of subletting at a lower rent and having to make up the difference for the duration of the lease.

If prospective lessees are careful, they organize an exit clause by creating a fully owned legal subsidiary for each store they open in the United States: if things go sour, they can bring the subsidiary to Chapter 11 bankruptcy and rid themselves of the rental commitment. But then, prospective lessors also have a way around this: when they see that a subsidiary is signing the lease, they ask for a guarantee from the head office.

In many parts of Southeast Asia, the American system prevails, but with only three- or four-year leases. While this probably makes the relationship between lessor and lessee more balanced than in the United States, it also gives the lessor the opportunity to increase the rent every three years in line with current demand for that location.

The **Japanese lease system** is even more to the advantage of the lessor. In Japan, leases are long (10 years), but on signing the lease, the lessee is obliged to pay a deposit equivalent to 10 years' rent. Though this deposit is returned at the end of the lease if the lessee does not wish to continue the arrangement, the lessee is, in effect, giving the lessor an interest-free loan. If the lease is renewed with a higher rent, the lessee pays an additional deposit to cover the difference in rental amounts.

Because the system works very much to the advantage of the lessor, many foreign luxury brands found it very difficult to move into Japan and open stores: they just could not afford it. To get around this, the brands developed through shop-in-shops with department stores. Louis Vuitton, which had a policy of opening only freestanding stores around the world, was forced to make an exception in Japan and move into department stores. At the end of 2019, Louis Vuitton had 45 stores in Japan, only 12 of which were freestanding: the other 33 operated as shop-in-shops within almost every Japanese department store chain.

The slowdown in retail development from 2000 to 2005 led to a reduction in the payment of key money from 10 years to 5. Also, luxury companies seem to have decided to purchase land and become owners of their own stores, but this, too, requires a lot of money upfront and easy access to bank loans.

Unlike these other systems, the **French system** works to the advantage of the lessee. The lessor rents a store for a period of nine years, but the lessee can exit unilaterally every three years. If, after nine years, the lessee decides to stay, the lessor must renew the lease for a further nine years, with a rental increase that is determined in line with a national construction cost index. Lessees have no obligations other than to stay a minimum of three years and have the right to stay in a place as long as they want. If the store is in an area much in demand, the rental will become much cheaper over time compared to that paid by more recent neighbors.

But the lessee also has another option: he may leave the place and ask for key money from a new tenant. Informing the landlords of the change is sufficient for all obligations to transfer to the second tenant.

This key money will appear as an investment in the balance sheet of the new tenant, who will hope to sell it at a much higher price later on. The lessee has the possibility of making money, and the system was probably created to give small shopkeepers sufficient money to live on when they retired.

To sum up: Selecting and renting a store in a major luxury city is always a long-term investment. It can cost huge amounts in key money—sometimes as much as the equivalent of several years' sales—and can prove very risky if, as in the United States, there is no way to cut costs when the location produces poor results.

For shop-in-shops or corners in department stores, the situation is quite different, as the stores provide floor space in a given location in exchange for a given percentage of margin. In the worst cases, department stores also demand a minimum payment each month. The brand has to pay for the decoration of the space, for the salaries of the sales staff, and for all promotional activities.

To conclude, this need for a worldwide store development program is probably due in part to a luxury business requiring more cash investment. This is obviously the case if one fully owns the building of the stores. It is also the case if one wants to be located in the very best parts of the cities and must pay very high key money amounts.

Budget, Planning, and Control

The planning system starts, obviously, with a budget. This budget starts with a sales target, then an inventory forecast so that the purchasing can be consistent with expected sales.

Sales Target

The sales target depends on the pulling power of the brand, the size of the store, and the width of the merchandise offering. The expected volume must be forecast for each month. (For fashion stores, there will be a higher ticket average for the winter season than for summer.)

For a new store, sales grow for at least two years and then plateau when it has found its base of repeat customers who are used to the new location. When a store is doing well, moving it elsewhere, even 200 or 300 meters away, could be a mistake because, again, customers would have to familiarize themselves with the new location.

For a new store, the sales budget is often preset at the level committed in the pre-opening financial analysis. As a rule of thumb, in Europe, rental costs should be less than 10–20% of sales. In Asia, rental costs can reach 20% and, in some cases, 30% of the sales target, but the overall profit-and-loss picture is different, with, in some countries, a more limited staff cost in percentage terms.

When, after six months, the store fails to meet its sales objectives, management has the tendency to remain optimistic and to wait for an improvement. Unfortunately, this improvement seldom comes unless the merchandising mix or the sales staff is modified.

Inventory Forecast

With the sales forecast and the gross margin target (which is different from the theoretical gross margin) in place, it is then possible to prepare an inventory forecast by month.

But this forecast must be divided into different product categories: ready-to-wear and accessories, and within accessories, leather goods and other accessories. Within the ready-to-wear category, the inventory should be split between the classics (which are there all the time and can be sold this year as well as next year) and the seasonal products (which have to be sold by the end of the season, either through bargain sales or in factory outlets).

Actual sales results and inventories should be followed up each month for each large product category and even down to the single-model level. Each store must have a scorecard each month against which remaining inventory is compared with budgeted monthly and cumulative sales. If, say, cumulative sales are 30% below forecasts and this trend continued until the end of the year, the scorecard would show the need for a dramatic reduction or a cancellation of orders for future deliveries, or for major changes in the selling approach. This monthly scorecard is absolutely necessary to enable the store to react very early to lower or higher sales than expected. It is even more necessary for fashion brands, where seasonal purchases are the name of the game.

As mentioned earlier in this book, department stores refer to the purchasing plan as their *open-to-buy*. For perfumes or permanent accessories, these are forecast on a monthly basis and are based on the sales forecast made on the previous year's sales. So, the system is very tough for brands that have lost ground in the preceding 12 to 18 months. Their open-to-buy is arithmetically reduced, and there would have to be a very good reason for this rule not to be respected.

The purchasing plan ensures that the store has enough merchandise to meet its sales target, but with a monthly readjustment between the planned sales target and the most probable sales level.

In luxury retail, an important driver of the nature of the seasonal merchandise purchased for each point of sale is the number of models or stock-keeping units (SKUs) that the internal display system allows. If, as should happen, all models purchased by the store are displayed, then the number of models purchased is directly dependent on the store's internal display setup. An 80- square-meter store will not be able to show the full collection that a 400-square-meter store can. Therefore, the number of models purchased will depend on the overall shelf space available at each point of sale. The depth of the purchase will depend on the open-to-buy budget.

Margin Control

As mentioned earlier, the theoretical and actual gross margins are not always the same. This is the result of bargain sales (if they have not been carefully forecast and accounted for), special discounts, and pilferage.

Special discounts are given by the sales staff to their favorite loyal customers. Brands such as Louis Vuitton or Cartier do not offer discounts at all, but some give loyalty cards to regular customers that entitle them to, say, a 10% discount. In many places, journalists or VIPs get up to 40% discount if they are on the right customer list. Such actions can significantly reduce actual margins, but it is a systematic process that is relatively easy to control.

A number of brands allow sales staff a degree of discretion (within predetermined limits) in offering individual discounts in circumstances when such an offer can make a difference in the customer's thinking or when there is a chance, say, of the customer purchasing a second item. But this must be carefully planned and controlled, on a day-to-day basis if necessary.

Pilferage can happen in the warehouse or in the stores. In department stores, it is believed that the majority of products disappearing from the shelves, from the warehouse, or from the counter are stolen by staff. In luxury stores, this is probably less so. But it is necessary to do frequent physical inventories (at least for each season and immediately after the bargain sales) to keep track of what is happening.

The Store Information System

In most luxury companies, the cash register of every fully owned store, wherever it is in the world, is linked to a global computer system. This gives the company an online inventory report that enables it to follow up on the inventory forecast and the products on order in real time. This is necessary to reduce working capital and ensure that all stores are working as efficiently as possible. With this system, for example, it is possible to organize product transfers from different stores in the same town, every day.

It is also possible to view the performance of each store online and to see how close they are to meeting their budget targets. The system enables accurate sales forecasts and streamlines the supply chain.

Staffing, Training, and Evaluation

Staffing

The tendency is to hire people who have worked for the competition and who can bring with them a good reputation and a good customer address book. But it is sometimes better to bring in new talent and to give them company-specific training. This may be the more difficult path, but new staff have no preconceived ideas of how things should be done.

The same is true for store managers. It is good to promote managers from within the sales staff, but several major brands are moving top university graduates into managerial roles to see how they develop in the company.

Training

Obviously, a sales person who is efficient will increase the conversion rate and the average sales ticket. This is a question of attitude, empathy with the client, and responsiveness.

In some of our retailing seminars in Paris, we sometimes send executives as mystery shoppers to visit luxury stores and assess the quality of the service. Often, the results are great, but what is very striking is that two different teams sent to the same store—one in the morning, the other in the afternoon—can sometimes come up with completely different impressions. It is likely that they have not spoken to the same people, but what is clear is that even for top luxury brands there is plenty of room for improvement in the area of customer service.

Sales training is one thing, but product training is something else again. Recently in New York we asked a salesgirl in a Coach boutique if a particular handbag was made in China (actually it was indicated inside, on a large label). She answered: "I don't know, but it may be the case because we are looking for top-quality craftsmanship, and I think, today, some Chinese workshops provide the very top quality." This was obviously a rehearsed response, but it was impressive nonetheless.

Product training is generally well done for a brand's main products. Montblanc's sales staff is very good on fountain pens, just as Longchamp's sales staff is very good on leather goods. But what about a Montblanc watch? Or Longchamp ready-to-wear? The level of staff expertise is not necessarily as broad and complete as might be expected.

The solution is, of course, frequent internal training (on the products) and external training in general sales practice and techniques. But this is not simple when the annual turnover of sales staff is 50% in Europe and is even higher in Southeast Asia.

Evaluation and Motivation

Every brand, particularly those that rely heavily on their own stores or their own department-store counters, looks for the best way to evaluate and to motivate staff. Formal evaluation should take place twice a year.

Incentive systems vary from one brand to another. Brands such as Louis Vuitton do not give commission on sales because they are very concerned about gray-market sales and want to ensure that staff never push for sales. There are other approaches, including:

- Commission incentives for individual staff or for the store staff as a whole, which can come into effect on every sale or start only after a monthly budget target has been met.

- A special bonus given when the monthly target (individual or at the store level) is met.
- A mix of the above.

The system chosen will depend on the brand's objectives. An individual incentive requires a system of turn-taking so that each sales person in turn has the first contact with the customer. But this system can lead sales staff to be unpleasant to customers they perceive as having little sales potential and thus to pick and choose the people they wish to serve. On the other hand, team incentives require a strong team spirit and a strong sales manager.

The Store as a Communication Tool

Because of its expected visibility, a luxury store is always a part of the overall image a brand can create for itself, and this is why store design is a very important part of the retailing process. Brands generally want their stores to use the same concepts and create the same atmosphere so that consumers, wherever they are in the world, feel as if they are in the main store in Paris or Milan.

There is an exception to this rule: Bulgari tried a completely different system and has achieved beautiful, bold statements through its retail architecture. Each of its stores is different and striking. Its New York Fifth Avenue store has nothing in common with its Tokyo store or its Beijing store. Prada did not go all the way with different designs for each store, but they also managed to build different and sometimes impressive stores.

Most of the other brands work on one concept that they adapt to the different shapes and sizes of their stores and to the respective customer flows. The same architect will be in charge of all the stores to ensure a continuity of look. Architects and designers, such as Peter Marino, Rem Koolhaas, Tadao Ando, or Anouchka Hempel, specialize in this activity, working to give the brands a distinctive style and atmosphere. Even when a brand strives toward having identical stores, this can't always be achieved, as concepts change over time and there may be periods of overlapping styles as a new design comes into play. Brands are careful, though, to ensure that design changes are not so marked as to have an impact on the brand identity, which changes very little over time.

But store design can vary as a function of the brief. Some brands want their stores to be primarily for ladies' ready-to-wear. Other brands want their stores to be for both men and women, which is quite a challenge. Others want the emphasis to be on accessories. Whatever the chosen emphasis, it is usually obvious to consumers as soon as they walk in.

Again, there are exceptions to this general rule. Take the case of Diesel Jeans stores (although this is not really a luxury brand, it's worth mentioning anyway). The company's objective is to present the merchandise in such a confusing way that customers are forced to ask the salesperson for assistance. It wants its customers to be disoriented and has created an unfriendly environment so that the customer has no choice but to interact with the sales staff. Only brands with strong customer awareness and a strong identity can force the customer to do it their way.

We said earlier that customers like to touch the products. Louis Vuitton or Hermès stores are almost like exclusive jewelry stores in that their products are presented inside glass counters and generally cannot be touched. To get a closer look at a product, it is necessary to ask the sales staff.

The concept and design of a store are very much a part of the brand identity discussed in Chapter 6 and can be a strong statement that the brand communicates to its environment in general, and to its clients in particular.

This is why the treatment of the space where employees and customers spend time has become the new competitive frontier. The ability to deal creatively with spaces, living 3D environments, requires a talent that does not often exist within a brand's general human resources. There are specific aesthetic and functional aspects to consider—often requiring enormous financial investments—in creating a context that expresses what the brand stands for, while generating the necessary revenues. Bernard Arnault has described architecture as a form of image-making.[2] It was no surprise, then, at the end of the 1990s to see the global luxury brands competing to attract the best architectural talent. This trend is now reaching much smaller brands too.

---

[2] Bernard Arnault and Yves Messarovitch, *La passion créative*. Paris: Plon, 2000.

Landmark Projects

Set out here is a summary of some of the most creative and spectacular retail projects realized in the past 20 years. This is a mere glimpse of what has been achieved and is by no means exhaustive.

New York

- In 1999, Christian de Portzamparc, winner of the Pritzker Architecture Prize in 1994, was chosen to create an original symbol of the LVMH group presence in the United States. He created the 23-story LVMH Tower on East 57th Street, with a very innovative fractal facade and the "magic room": a four-story glass cube at the summit. He later went on to create LVMH's new corporate headquarters on Avenue Montaigne in Paris.
- Rem Koolhaas, the Dutch architect and the winner of the Pritzker in 2000, designed the Prada store on Broadway. Opened in December 2001, the store, costing €32 million, has 2,300 square meters of retail space. Koolhaas was given great freedom by the owners, Miuccia Prada and Patrizio Bertelli, and went on to design Prada stores in Los Angeles and San Francisco.
- John Pawson, the British high priest of minimalism, conceived Calvin Klein's ice palace on Madison Avenue.
- Peter Marino, the US architect and decorator, was asked to remodel the Chanel store on East 57th Street in 2018. He changed everything in this 1,400-square-meter location, including the level of the floor.
- The same Peter Marino was asked to renovate the Bulgari 450-square-meter location. He was AIANY's 2018 best of year winner for mid-size retail projects.

Tokyo

- Opened in the Ginza shopping district in 2001, Maison Hermès is the brainchild of Renzo Piano. The architect's design is that of a traditional Japanese magic lantern. In daylight, the translucent facade gives a hint of what is beyond, the events and objects blurred by the thickness of the glass blocks. At night, the entire building glows from within. The tall, narrow, elegant building (45 meters long by 11 meters wide) is classical yet innovative and stands out like a piece of well-crafted jewelry. In terms of its location, respect for traditions, cosmopolitanism, and innovation, it would be difficult to be truer to the Hermès brand identity.

- Following the success of the Koolhaas store in New York, Prada continued its radically innovative retail architecture drive in 2003 with a store in Tokyo's fashionable Aoyama district. The intent behind Swiss duo Jacques Herzog and Pierre de Meuron's design was "to reshape both the concept and function of shopping, pleasure and communication, to encourage the meshing of consumption and culture."
- Armani asked Doriana and Massimiliano Fuksas to create a huge tower in Ginza in 2007.
- Dior asked Peter Marino and the studio SANAA to create their large store in Omotesando in 2014.
- Rimowa asked Stephan Vary to build the biggest Japanese store in Ginza in 2019.

Seoul

- Seoul should be mentioned for its excellence in luxury store design.
- Notable are the Hermès store, built by Rena Dumas in 2006, as well as the Christian de Portzamparc store for Dior in 2011 and the Frank Gehry store for Louis Vuitton, which takes a style very similar to the design of the Louis Vuitton foundation in Paris.

Milan

- Giorgio Armani commissioned Tadao Ando to design a spectacular fashion theater in the former Nestlé building in the canal district. Ando's 3,400-square-meter reinforced-concrete theatre (long pillared corridor and modular movable catwalk with seating for 680 people) leads into a dining area and water courtyard. The building incorporates Armani's showroom and commercial offices.
- For the design of the vast new Armani Casa housewares store on Via Manzoni, Armani chose Michael Gabellini, the minimalist American who rose to fashion fame as the creator of Jil Sander's limestone-floor temples in Milan and on Avenue Montaigne in Paris. Armani said that for his new stores he wanted a neutral background, not an architectural statement. "The problem with famous architects is that they become so instantly identifiable," he said. "It is better to work with different architects."

- Peter Marino rates a particular mention. His name is synonymous with excellence in design and quality in construction and he is internationally admired for his commitment to historical preservation and adaptive reuse of existing buildings in the pursuit of the integration of art, architecture, and interior design. He has the most impressive track record of any of the famous architects who have worked for luxury brands. His recent projects include five stores for Chanel; two stores for Fendi; four stores for Louis Vuitton; three stores for Dior in 2002; Armani's New York store; and many others.
- Smaller brands are starting to follow the trend, though with more limited investment capabilities. Nonetheless, there have been some recent success stories, including two spectacular projects completed by Future Systems: the bright, modular Marni store on Sloane Street in London, where the clothes become part of the overall composition and design; and Comme des Garçons in Tokyo.
- In 2016, Dolce & Gabbana asked the French architect Gwenaël Nicola to design their new store in Milan. Afterwards, they asked him to develop their next 12 stores around the world.
- In 2017, La Perla developed a new concept for their 270-square-meter store on Via Monte Napoleone. It was designed by Baciocchi.
- In 2018, the Japanese architect Kengo Kuma was selected by Valextra to design their store in Milan.

The big luxury brands have chosen to use outside architects and designers because of the reputation and kudos they bring, and because they are unlikely to create anything uninteresting. Furthermore, there is a natural dissociation between products and store creativity. The case or jewel box is of a different nature from that of the content. It is not sold. It is shown and it helps show the product. The store is a symbol of power and a permanent link to culture. For fashion moguls, architecture is the new strategic subject. Governments have long been the main sponsors of modern buildings, but it looks as if luxury brand owners may become the new renaissance princes of patronage. They have understood that architects (from serving clients with avant-garde tastes) tend to be one step ahead in aesthetic trends, which then filter down into product design and fashion.

The same logic applies to office and factory design. The factory of Forge de Laguiole, the legendary French knife, was designed by Philippe Starck, and its original architecture is attracting busloads of foreigners to the little town of Aubrac.

The Communication Power of the Store

The store's role in communication is unmatched by any other single brand manifestation. This communication power is made possible by several factors.

First of all, the store presents the product in context, where different brand manifestations converge to give the most complete brand experience a customer can get. Customers are under the simultaneous influence of the architecture, the product, and the sales staff aesthetics. It is also a multisensory experience, where products, music, odors, decoration, light, logo, and advertising materials are physically accessible. It is interactive by nature and should be the place where the customer can obtain the maximum of information about the brand and receive luxury service.

Nike Town, Disney stores, Hermès Tokyo, and Louis Vuitton Champs Elysées are places of entertainment, able to propose the most complete physical experience of the brand in an overwhelming and multisensory manner. The smallest Timberland boutique, with its well-planned and controlled environment (products, apple aroma, temperature, materials, colors, the feel of wood underfoot), can create and convey a feeling of being in a log cabin in the Himalayas.

The Don Juan brand example introduced in an earlier chapter showed how the table of brand manifestations can be utilized in communication management. In formalizing its identity and reformulating its competitive strategy, the brand established an overall communication program to frame all the messages it needed to convey and applied it to each brand manifestation to determine what part of the program each could most efficiently promote. In this systematic way, the company was able to orchestrate an overall communication drive where each manifestation had a specific role, while remaining coherent with the rest.

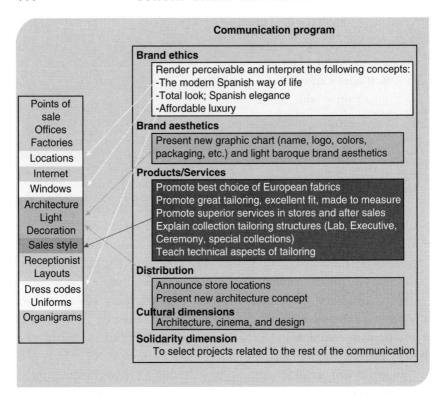

Figure 11.1   The Store as the Most Complete Experience for Virtual and Real Brand Elements

Figure 11.1 shows, in particular, the role of the points of sale in promoting the messages of the communication program. The same exercise could be conducted for each type of manifestation.

Personnel Communication.   It all starts with the doorman at the entrance of the store, the receptionist, or the customer-service telephone operator (very often outside-contracted). These very often form the first points of contact a customer has with a brand, and first impressions die hard.

One of the major features of the luxury industry that distinguish it from mass-market brands is salesmanship. The way luxury-store sales staff engage with, talk to, and deal with potential customers is very particular. They have to adapt to the customer, lending assistance when asked and knowing when to leave the customer alone. The aim is to establish a relationship that goes beyond the pure commercial transaction. Many personal relationships between sales personnel and their clients are born in this way. The sales staff is a very valuable brand asset. In 1999, when Texas Pacific bought Bally and decided to develop a luxury-lifestyle brand strategy, the first thing the CEO did was to cancel the retail policy in which sales staff were measured on their ability to sell a leather jacket to any customer who entered the store.

The uniform and grooming of the sales staff is always important but more so in the luxury industry. The makeup of a L'Oréal salesgirl should be as perfect as the shoeshine of a shoe-brand salesman or the CEO.

Internal and External Display.   Traditionally, in each city or each country there is a retailer with a reputation for having the most beautiful window displays. The Christmas windows of Saks Fifth Avenue in New York have enchanted generations of children; Loewe windows in Spain were eagerly awaited in the 1950s and 1960s; queues form in front of the Hermès store windows in Faubourg Saint Honoré whenever the display is changed. **This is a hallmark of the luxury industry.** Louis Vuitton has invested heavily in this field, hiring known artists to decorate and prepare complex and spectacular window displays that are genuine works of art. To replicate such displays in 450 stores worldwide requires a huge investment and complex logistical and advertising capabilities.

Windows are part of street advertising and have the same function as a billboard or a poster. In fact, advertising elements like campaign photographs and products are often on display. Internal display, which is usually the responsibility of the window-dressing team, involves rigorous training and strict adherence to the guidelines and rules set out in internal manuals.

The Challenge of the Seamless Online, Offline Process

Is there a future for physical stores? As online activities develop, one could fear that physical stores may become something of the past. In fact, the situation is slightly more complex.

The First Reactions to the Development of Digital Activities for Luxury Brands

In the 1980s, many outsiders considered that the development of online sales activities would have no impact on luxury products. They claimed that luxury customers wanted to touch the products before buying them, that they would like to try on the fashion outfits, and that they would not be interested in the possibility of receiving expensive items at home. They would also say that high jewelry pieces, because of their very high tickets, would not work online.

Another issue was often mentioned: online fashion retailers are said to receive 25% of what they deliver as returns from their shipments and have to sell them at discount in outlet locations. If the same percentage of Gucci or Chanel outfits were also sent back, and had to be sold at distressed bargain prices, the overall economic picture would not be very profitable.

Strangely enough, the percentage of returns on luxury online sales is estimated to be much lower than for mass-market outfits.

In fact, luxury online sales developed much faster and more easily than what was expected.

As far as the digital process is concerned, luxury brands are in a much better situation than mass-market products like soaps or shampoos: they generally have direct contact with their clients and often have their names or addresses. They have a good database, and they can organize direct contacts with their clients.

Also, the fact that expensive luxury products require a very sophisticated purchase ceremony did not fit with a basic mailman asking for a signature, standing on the stairs of one's standard housing unit. But it happened that jewelry deliveries, for example, could be done by uniformed and well-trained staff, and one could imagine a person presenting the piece that had been ordered, but also coming with other items, of the same basic price range, for comparison purposes and eventually for a possible different selection.

The Present Situation

Another surprise: Clients purchasing online are not forgetting about the physical stores. Hermès, for example, observed that online clients would visit physical stores more often than those never buying on the Internet.

For them, the system was not online *or* offline, but on- *and* offline.

A study by McKinsey on the age of digital published in 2018 (see Table 11.3) describes the process: before purchasing, the average French client has nine contacts with the brand. He or she has four contacts with

Table 11.3 Number of Online and Offline Contacts Before and During a Purchase

	2014			2016		
China	7	6	13	7	8	15
South Korea	6	5	11	6	7	13
Italy	5	4	9	5	6	11
Average	5	4	9	5	6	11
Brazil	5	3	8	5	5	10
Japan	4	3	7	5	5	10
France	4	3	7	4	5	9
United States	4	3	7	4	4	8
United Kingdom	4	2	6	4	4	8

Offline
Online

Source: Antonio Achille, Sophie Marchessou, and Nathalie Remy, "Luxury in the Age of Digital Darwinism," McKinsey & Company, February 1, 2018.

a physical store and five contacts with the online store. The purchase is made during the ninth contact with the brand, including physical contacts in a store. The point is to no longer fear that clients buying online would not have been able to touch the products. They have had the chance to do that during a previous visit, and now they know exactly what they want and are ready to buy it. They want to be able to do it immediately and in a way that is the most convenient for them at a given time.

So, doubts about the development of online sales were not unfounded; they just did not take into account the complete purchasing process. This process was not an online or offline one; it was a dual process in the face of sophisticated and flexible clients.

The Expected Future

In the recent book *Luxury Retail and Digital Management*, one of the co-authors of this book shows his estimates of luxury purchases from different types of outlets (see Table 11.4).

One could say that online sales were only 5% of total sales in 2010. There were probably 10% in 2019, and they would reach 25% in 2025. Actually, during the confinement in 2020, it already reached

Table 11.4   Percent of Sales of a Fashion Luxury Brand According to Different Distribution Setups

	1960	**1990**	**2010**	**2025**
Monobrand stores	20%	50%	65%	55%
Multibrand stores (including shop-in-shops in department stores)	80%	50%	30%	20%
Online stores	0%	0%	5%	25%
Total	100%	100%	100%	100%

Source: M. Chevalier and M. Gutsatz, *Luxury Retail and Digital Management*. Hoboken, NJ: John Wiley & Sons, 2020.

18 to 20%. This growth in percentage is of course very impressive, but physical sales will remain (with 75% of the volume) the biggest retail channel.

The point, as was mentioned earlier, is that a luxury brand that does not develop a strong digital system could not expect to keep a strong offline physical business: the client wants to move several times, from one system to another one, before making his or her final decision. If they cannot go back and forth and find a perfect seamless system, they may not be interested by the brand anymore.

In fact, clients expect a complete seamless system. They want to visit the physical stores and the online site. They may buy a Saint-Laurent pair of shoes online. Once they receive them, they realize that they are too small for them. Theoretically they could redo the packaging and mail the shoes back to the digital site. But it is easier and more secure to go to a Saint-Laurent store, return their shoes, and try on a bigger size. If they fit, they may want to be able to go out of the store with this new pair. They may also try on another pair of shoes. They want to buy them right away, but their size is not in the store. They should be able to pay for this second pair at the store's cash register and to receive it from the online site the following day in their home. Everything should be possible, and the system should be perfectly seamless.

It should be the same for returns, for after-sale services, or for any additional request or activity.

Each retail store should be able to handle returns, but the process of each store should be organized and expected. A client asking for a return should not have to know when he or she enters a store whether it belongs to the brand or is an outside franchisee. If he or she visits a department store, he or she should not be told that the shop-in-shop is not owned by Saint-Laurent and cannot take back the product coming from elsewhere. The store staff should take it anyway (and a special procedure, or a special financial agreement, has to be negotiated beforehand with the department store).

To develop a complete seamless system, all the stores or outlets should sell at the same retail price (what should one do about import duties?).

This seems to be the future. But it should be planned, organized, and managed right now. It is at least what young clients expect to obtain from any luxury brand.

The Online, Offline Setup.   To have a fully seamless distribution system, one should have both a good offline and a good online organization. Having a good offline one seems obvious; one needs a strong store network, with third-party-operated stores that are ready to accept the constraints of the seamless online, offline requirements; one also needs a special procedure of operations with department stores, so that they can offer the needed flexibility. Having this also requires a special organization and incentive for sales staff so that they have an interest in dealing with returns and after-sale services for products that were not purchased in their stores and total flexibility on services.

For online activities, things are a bit more complicated. A seamless system requires a perfect logistical system with warehouses, order preparation, shipment, and special delivery procedures in the clients' homes. It also requires an easily accessible online site. Can the client find it easily and use it smoothly and without effort? This is also a difficult issue.

The Present Online Setup.   Some brands, like Hermès, Louis Vuitton, or Prada, have their own sites with the capability to have many languages. Others prefer to use major fashion online operators.

The first successful one was probably Net-à-Porter, created in 2000 in London by Nathalie Massenet. Another was Yoox, created in Milan in 2015 and now merged with Net-à-Porter (to become YNAP), which belongs to the Richemont group. A third was Farfetch, created in 2008 by a Portuguese entrepreneur and based in London. These two groups (YNAP and Farfetch) have specially been created for fashion and luxury brands. They work more or less as a worldwide digital department store; they take products only on consignment and are ready to retail full collections. They have digital or logistical platforms in different places of the world and, generally, they work on a 40% retail margin on sales. This is almost a system similar to a department stores.

But they are not alone in proposing this kind of digital or logistical platform. Amazon in the United States and Alibaba in China are interested in the development of this service. Another system could be to be associated with any online operator, even if they are not selling luxury products today.

The Future of Luxury Retailing

As we expect luxury online sales to reach 25% of total sales, this means that for the younger generation, it would probably reach 30–40% of their purchases and become a major selling tool.

But will the major online traffic be done though the individual brand platform (as they click "Chanel" or "Prada"), or would customers prefer to have access to many brands though a Farfetch click? This remains a very big issue. If most of the business is done though individual brands, then those brands would have the upper hand in their negotiation with multibrand online sellers like Farfetch. If, on the contrary, most of the volume goes though multibrand online operators, those would become very powerful and the brands would have less control of the retail situation.

Today, brands try to keep all options open; they develop their own online site as quickly as possible, and they also test the big multibrand operators. It seems to be a type of race where everybody is trying to end up first in the long run and win the jackpot.

Is it possible to predict which is going to win the race? It is a bit early to say at this stage, but the answer to this question will certainly shape what the luxury retailing setup would be in the future.

On the other hand, the brands themselves will modify their store setup:

- The major brands already have the worldwide number of stores they need: around 450 to 500. They would probably not increase this number very much, but they would make changes and renovations in many locations.

- Those developing their physical network very fast would be the new-comers like Michael Kors, Kate Spade, Coach, or Tory Burch.
- The mix of the stores will vary. Today, major brands have three types of stores, as discussed earlier: Stores A, which are flagships and present the full collection of products; Stores B, which are major stores and present a large majority of collection items; and Stores C, which have a limited scope and only a small part of the collection (women's fashion but not men's, full accessory lines but only a little group of women's ready-to-wear, etc.).

In the future, every store will present some part of its full collection but would be able to take orders on the total brand offer and promise delivery the next day. All stores could sell the total collection and, in this case, Stores C are more profitable than Stores B because they have a lower rent. They represent the future.

Out of the 400 to 500 stores mentioned, for the very best brands, 300 could be C stores and 25 be very large flagships "retailtainment" stores. The B stores would be less needed and very often too expensive to operate. This last question is for the real estate experts: What should they do about their B stores?

What is certain is that luxury stores will keep providing beautiful landmarks in many major cities of the world.

Chapter 12

Sustainability and Authenticity

One of the ways to propose a relevant conclusion to this both macro- and microeconomic journey in the realm of luxury brands is to highlight the trends that we feel will shape its medium-term future.

The luxury market has increased 3.6 times since 1995, reaching, as we say in Chapter 2, an estimated total business volume of €297 billion in 2019. According to *Forbes*, Bernard Arnault, controlling owner of the LVMH group, became in 2019 the second-richest man in the world.[1] The luxury business has been good for many participants—the owners, manufacturers, and distributors— as well as on the consumers' side during that period.

---

[1] https://www.forbes.com/billionaires/.

Growth has not been steady because the luxury market is not immune to the economic environment. Volumes fell in 2002 and 2003 following the attack on the World Trade Center in September 2001 and the outbreak of avian influenza. There was a similar drop in 2009 due to the subprime financial crisis; it is taking a hit from the COVID-19 virus right now.

Still, the market has shown a lot of resilience, and much of what is substantial growth is due to improved global living standards and the emergence of the middle classes in many countries around the world. The growth of luxury has benefited from successive geographic engines. Ferragamo is a relevant example. In 1990, half of its turnover, which was around €100 million at the time, was generated by American customers. The founder, Salvatore, had started his activities in the United States and he had maintained privileged relationships with the department stores of this country after his return to Italy. In 1996, half of the turnover (just over €400 million) was made with Japanese customers. In 2019, 45.7% of the turnover is generated in Asia,[2] which, if we account for the purchases made by Chinese customers overseas, the percentage of sales to Asian customers could easily be in the range of 60–70% of the consolidated revenue.

Faced with the exhaustion of geographical reserves (it will be a long time, if ever, before India and Africa can become new and relevant luxury engines of growth), it becomes legitimate to try to anticipate the main trends that will mark the years to come. As with any prospective exercise, one can only attempt to extrapolate some of the current visible and understandable trends. The future developments that we have identified are presented in Table 12.1.

Each of these trends deserves to be developed further. Some of them (digital impact, Chinese customers' importance, luxury consumption evolution, the strengthening of mega brands) have already been described in the text, but the physical limits of our work do not allow deepening the analysis of each of them. However, we want to emphasize two of them—sustainability and authenticity—because they will continue to gain importance in the search for brands' competitiveness and because they are both under the control of brand managers, although heavily influenced by consumers' moods and values.

---

[2] https://group.ferragamo.com/en/investor-relations/financial-documents/2019.

Table 12.1   Medium-Term Luxury Market Trends

Strategic Context
• Continued growth of the middle classes and the "super rich" (HNWI, high-net-worth individuals). • Emergence of global Chinese luxury brands. • Deficiency of certain luxury materials (leathers, exotic skins, etc.). • Increased competition between luxury brands, especially from multibrand groups. • Mega brands become stronger to the detriment of smaller ones. • Data management (AI, big data, data analytics) revolutionizes the way business is conducted, skewing it toward prospective. • E-commerce continues its stride. • Sustainability is integrated in all strategic considerations.
Consumption in General
Certain characteristics of postmodern consumption will increase, such as the trends toward aestheticization, baroquisation, and product virtualization.
Luxury Consumption
Macroeconomic level
• Ostentatious luxury and real luxury continue to thrive. • Intermediate luxury is being swallowed up by mass luxury. • New luxury is more about experience than ownership. The exceptional takes precedence over the exclusive.
Microeconomic level
• The authenticity of the brand and all its manifestations becomes a fundamental value to maintain its competitiveness. • The values of sustainable development, while integrated into the identity and strategy of the brands, influence all the functional areas of the brand. • Intensive use of mobile technology and the Internet in all operational functions and especially in the constant search for engaging customers.
Products
• Intensive use of 3D printing. • Bespoke continues to develop, helped by technological progress. • Simplification of the interface with products (user-friendly). • Combination of technological materials and more precious traditional materials. • Intensification of the transition from product to experience. • Continuous development of the second-hand market.

Sustainability

The term *sustainable development* was defined in 1987 in the report *Our Common Future*, released by the Brundtland Commission. It was created in 1983 by the United Nations in order to unite countries in pursuing sustainable development together. This commission, formerly known as the World Commission on Environment and Development, is now referred to as the Brundtland Commission, after the chairperson of the Commission (Gro Harlem Brundtland, former Prime Minister of Norway). Sustainable development is supposed to meet the needs of the present without compromising the ability of future generations to meet their own needs. The strength and originality (at the time) of this definition is that it integrates the concepts of humanity and intergenerational equity. It introduces the notion of "needs," in particular, the essential needs of the world's poorest people and the idea of "limitations" imposed by technology and social organization on the environment's ability to meet both present and future needs. Sustainable development can be considered the organizing principle of sustainability, despite the apparent oxymoron, as some think that development is inherently unsustainable.

Trends in sustainable development are not specific to the world of luxury. This "green" push is present in all economic and cultural sectors and therefore also taken into consideration by luxury brands. Being sustainable is no longer an option for anyone. For all companies, this has become a prerequisite without which they risk losing competitiveness. The Hummer car is an example of a brand made obsolete by the push of ecological logics. Designed for belligerent activities, it was unsuitable for normal road service and its fuel consumption was excessive.

Compatibility Between Luxury and Sustainability

The luxury industry has often been accused of reacting belatedly to the growing awareness of the planet's environmental problems. Others have also argued that the two concepts of luxury and sustainability are incompatible. This apparent incompatibility is also one of the explanations for the relative delay of the sector compared to others in its awareness of ecological themes. It is necessary to put an end to this misconception. There are at least five reasons that invalidate this incompatibility:

First of all, there is no ontological incompatibility. If we take the definitions of the two concepts, it seems obvious that nothing opposes them in their essence. The generally accepted definition is "development that meets current needs without compromising the ability of future generations to meet their own"; there are no objective reasons why the luxury industry should not be able to operate under this definition, even if it involves additional costs. The definition of luxury given by Floch in Chapter 1 characterizes the ethics of genuine luxury brands as being based on "the rejection of the all economical," that is, the nonpursuit of the lowest costs. We thus find total compatibility between luxury and sustainability, even if ecofriendly operational processes may generally generate costs higher than those of nonecological brands.

True luxury is also the negation of "disposable." Many industries, especially those of mass fashion brands where the logic of volumes prevail, plan the obsolescence of their offerings. The genuine luxury industries base their success on the durability of their products. At Bally, for example, the high-end men's shoes of the Scribe collection launched in 1951 were resoled for free without a time limit. The practice was interrupted in 2001. Many luxury brands repair and repackage their products, particularly in the watchmaking field. Patek Philippe's advertisements clearly state the longevity of their products in their famous slogan: "You never actually own a Patek Philippe; you merely look after it for the next generation."

The use of natural products is part of luxury brands' identity. Linen, silk, cotton, cashmere, wool, wood, precious stones, and so on are integral parts of the identity of some luxury brands. The use of these materials generally consumes less energy for their production than synthetic products and, above all, they are renewable. A good example of an initiative in favor of sustainable development is that of Loro Piana, which has made its reputation precisely in natural and precious materials such as cashmere and vicuña. Loro Piana, originally an Italian family company, acquired in 2013 by LVMH, is the world's leading buyer of vicuña hair. This animal, which lives at high altitude on the Andean plateaus, is renowned for its very fine and silky coat. The vicuña's population, which had decreased to 5,000 in the 1960s due to poaching, rose to 220,000 between Peru and Chile in 2013 thanks to protective measures in which brands like Loro

Piana participated. In 2013, the brand acquired an 85,000-hectare estate to make a preserve for the white vicuña and ensure both the protection of the species and supply for the brand.

Preservation of ancestral know-how. It is the antithesis of the exploitation of workers without specialization and it allows the perpetuation of trades and cultures. Chanel, Daum, Lalique, Baccarat, Blancpain, and so on are good examples of brands that preserve ancestral trades, but Hermès is the best representative by pursuing its long-term strategy of developing projects combining creativity and exceptional craftsmanship.

The luxury/ecology incompatibility is therefore a misrepresentation of a reality that is exactly the opposite. When we go beyond the connotation of superfluity, which sticks to the notion of luxury, and to that of rusticity, which is still too often associated with the notion of ecology, we realize that, in fact, luxury is ecological in nature and should therefore be a natural and privileged promoter of sustainable development.

The growing sensitivity to ecological challenges has sparked the emergence of new luxury qualifications. Some are immediately understandable as green luxury or balanced luxury, whereas others require some explanations:

- *Deeper Luxury* is the title of the 2007 report that Jem Bendell and Anthony Kleanthous made for the WWF, which defines authentic luxury brands as those that identify their consumers as having the means and the motivations to respect both people and the planet. The authors urge luxury brands to face up to their responsibilities.
- *Intelligent luxury* is a slogan of the tourism companies Soneva Resorts and Six Senses Spas, which have facilities in the Maldives and Asia, and which is defined as a luxury of the highest international standard in an environment that feeds the indigenous sensibility in design, architecture, and services, merging nature with the experience of customers. Banyan Tree Hotels & Resorts was among the first brands to develop the concept of ecological hospitality when they opened their first hotel in Phuket in 1994 on land that had been occupied by a tin mine, which they fully cleaned and planted with 7,000 tropical trees. Since then, sustainability has been a defining element of their brand identity.

The number of sustainable initiatives is multiplying across the world, reflecting, especially in the younger population, a growing sensibility and sense of responsibility toward the planet's ecological and social evolution. The Web is a phenomenal space of resonance for these feelings and the capitalistic process of recuperation of all consumers' trends and moods is at work. In view of the multiplicity of sustainable initiatives, we have chosen to describe a limited number of them that seem to us particularly meaningful.

Indicators of Higher Sustainable Sensibility

While the level of engagement from boards and top executives on the issue of the environment still leaves much to be desired, most firms today routinely publish sustainability reports, work to increase their energy efficiency, and market more environmentally friendly products or services to customers who are more and more interested in brands' environmental performance.

Fashion.   The fashion industry has a bad environmental reputation. We have been accustomed for years to the protests against the use of fur, which managed to win some battles and influence some of the brands; however, there are much bigger issues:

- The underutilization of produced clothing and the lack of recycling bring about a loss of value of US$500 billion every year globally, according to the Ellen MacArthur Foundation (2017).[3]
- The fashion industry is not energetically efficient; it pollutes and produces a lot of waste. Fashion generates 20–35% of microplastic into the ocean.[4]
- Fashion's carbon footprint (10% of global carbon emissions) is superior to those of international flights and shopping combined.
- It is responsible for 22% of pesticide utilization.
- Often, luxury brands deliberately burn unsold ready-to-wear merchandise in order to maintain their exclusivity. In 2018, Burberry

---

[3] Ellen Macarthur Foundation, "A New Textiles Economy: Redesigning Fashion's Future," 2017.

[4] Imran Amed, Anita Balchandani, Achim Berg, Saskia Hedrich, Shrina Poojara, and Felix Rölkens, "The State of Fashion 2020: Navigating Uncertainty," McKinsey & Company, November 20, 2019.

declared in their 2017 annual report that it had destroyed £28.6 million of unsold merchandise.[5]

- Consumers' habits feed a noncircular economy, which favors bigger and more ephemeral consumption. Since 2000, clothing sales have doubled, while items are worn 29% less.[6]

Nevertheless, fashion hasn't yet taken its sustainability responsibilities sufficiently seriously. The best performers on sustainability are the very big players as well as some mid-sized, family-owned companies, while over half of the market, mainly small to medium-sized players, has shown little effort so far. The rest of the industry is somewhere in between. This is confirmed by the Pulse Survey (2017),[7] in which two-thirds of polled fashion executives have not yet included environmental and social factors guiding principles in their company strategy.

However, there is an increased awareness from consumers about the nonsustainability of the current fashion system, and this is the more sure indication that fashion brands are going to have to review their modus operandi.

Scrutiny is building and initiatives are multiplying:

- There were the usual environmental protests at the London Fashion Week in September 2019.
- More meaningful is the Fashion Pact launched in August 2019 by Kering chairman and CEO François-Henri Pinault, under the initiative of the French president, Emmanuel Macron.[8] It has been signed by approximately 250 brands in the fashion and textile industry (ready-to-wear, sport, lifestyle, and luxury), including their suppliers and distributors, in order to pursue key environmental goals in three areas: stopping global warming, restoring biodiversity, and protecting the oceans. The Pact was presented to the heads of state at the G7 Summit in Biarritz.
- In the Spring–Summer fashion shows that occurred in Autumn 2019, it seemed that most of the brands competed more on declarations of sustainable initiatives than on the products displayed.

---

[5] Madison Darbyshire, "Fashion That's Tailored for a Fragile Planet," *Financial Times*, December 5, 2019.
[6] Ibid.
[7] Global Fashion Agenda & Boston Consulting Group "Pulse of the Fashion Industry," 2017.
[8] https://thefashionpact.org/?lang=en.

"Forget Street wear. Sustainability was the hottest look of the day," wrote Vanessa Friedman in the October 12–13, 2019, issue of the *New York Times International*.[9] Gucci and Gabriella Hearst announced that their shows were carbon-free; Kering announced its commitment to reduce its greenhouse gas emissions by 59% by 2025; Louis Vuitton, Dior, and Alexander McQueen insisted on the reusability of the materials utilized for the shows, and so on. The British Fashion Council introduced its Institute of Positive Fashion to rally a group of brands in order to establish standards for green business.

Stella McCartney.   This designer has a particular position within the fashion industry. When, in 1997, Paul's daughter landed Chloé's designer job, replacing Karl Lagerfeld, her main nonnegotiable condition was "no leather and no fur." She established immediately the brand ethics she would give to the Chloé brand and established clearly what she believed in. Even though her no-leather policy drew a lot of criticism because the artificial leathers she uses are often petroleum-based, McCartney continued to develop her approach when she quit Chloé in 2001 and launched her own brand, with Kering holding a 50% stake. In 2019, she bought back Kering's half and LVMH acquired a minority stake in her brand. At the same time, she was also appointed as a special advisor on sustainability to LVMH's executive committee and to chairman and chief executive Bernard Arnault.

Recent Examples of Workers Protesting for Sustainability[10]. The fashion industry does not have a monopoly on protests. Even in the middle of the COVID-19 pandemic, in February 2020, thousands of cleaning workers marched in Minneapolis in what is probably the first union-authorized climate strike in the United States. Going beyond the traditional demands for better pay and working conditions, the protesters were pressuring their companies, such as Wells Fargo and United Health Group, to take action on climate change, that is, to share their values.

---

[9] Vanessa Friedman, "Fashion's Race to Sustainability," *New York Times International*, October 12–13, 2019.

[10] https://www.huffpost.com/entry/employee-activism-climate-change_n_5ea04b1ac5b6a486d082480d?nci.

Public concern about global warming, driven largely by millennials, is rising and companies are under pressure from all their stakeholders, including employees, to adopt clearly defined climate-related objectives for their products, services, and ways of operating. Employees are now asking companies to get committed to fighting climate change. The protests take different forms: walkouts, strikes, petitions, online discussions. In 2019, thousands of Google employees signed an online letter demanding that the company be more active in climate change initiatives. In part prompted by employees demanding more action, more and more corporations, like Alphabet, Microsoft, Patagonia Adobe, Amazon, and so on, are publicly declaring their sustainable commitments.

Sustainable Thinking.   This is the title of an exhibition organized by the *Museo Salvatore Ferragamo* in Florence from April 2019 to March 2020. The museum, which normally shows the brand heritage iconographic material as well as the historical shoe samples of the genial creator, was proposing, in collaboration with fashion designers, artists, architects, and other museums, a reflection process on sustainability. New ecological and recycled materials, contests for junior designers, initiatives with the participation of the brand's employees and the Polimoda School, art pieces from artists committed to diversity and a better relationship with nature, and so on.

The exhibition also served as a reminder that Salvatore Ferragamo was a precursor in the utilization of natural materials. During World War II, because of leather supply difficulties, he started using materials never used before in shoemaking, such as raffia, fish skins, cork, braided papers, cellophane, straw, fabrics, and so on.

Indices and Conferences.   For the past 25 years, we have witnessed an explosion of rating indices, fairs, and conferences dedicated to sustainability. A few can be mentioned:

- *The Dow Jones Sustainability Index* (DJSI World), launched in 1999, was the first index to monitor the financial performance of the companies most committed to sustainable development. It has now evolved into a family of indices that tracks the stock performance of the world's leading companies in terms of economic, environmental, and social criteria. The 2019 Corporate Sustainability Assessment represented 61 industries and saw the biggest increase in company participation and overall record numbers.

- Alphabet Inc. (Google) is leader in the categories media and entertainment, interactive media, and services and home entertainment
- Peugeot SA in automobiles
    A few industry leaders belong to the luxury industry:
- Montcler S.p.A. in textiles, apparel, and luxury goods
- Hilton Worldwide Holdings Inc. in hotels, resorts, and cruise lines
- Air France-KLM in airlines
- Kering was listed for the seventh consecutive year, recognized as one of the industry leaders within the textile, apparel, and luxury goods sector

- *The Sustainable Brand Index* was created in 2011 and shows how brands are perceived in terms of sustainability by their main stakeholders and analyzes how sustainability affects brand communication and business development. The study is conducted yearly from a consumer perspective and, since 2017, from a decision-maker perspective as well. The Index B2C focuses on more than 1,400 brands, 35 industries, and 58,000 consumers across eight countries (Sweden, Norway, Denmark, Finland, The Netherlands, and The Baltics). In fact, the main limitation of this index is the limited number of countries it covers. Hopefully, the geographical scope will increase over time. In the Netherlands report, apart from local brands we find Tesla in fourth position globally and the leader in automobiles, Ikea in 7th position, The Body Shop in 13th, Toyota 44th, Kia 85th, Volkswagen 87th, Peugeot 93rd, Mercedes-Benz 101st, Opel 112th, L'Oréal 158th.
- *The Global 100 Index*, which prides itself on being the most objective and transparent of the sustainability indices, is owned by the Toronto-based media and investment advisory firm Corporate Knights. Each year, the latest version of the index is announced at the World Economic Forum in Davos. Its methodology is based on 12 quantitative performance indicators such as productivity of energy, carbon, water, waste, innovation capacity, percentage of tax paid, CEO-to-average-worker pay, pension fund status, safety performance, employee turnover, leadership diversity, clean capitalism pay link (tying executive compensation to ESG criteria).

Some examples: Kering SA (apparel and accessory products) is 23rd in 2020, down from 2nd place in 2019; Adidas AG, 55th; Alphabet Inc., 52nd; Tesla Inc., 74th; L'Oréal is ranked 98th. One of this index's main limitations is that it deals only with 100 corporations and only considers groups with a market capitalization of at least US$2 billion.

- The English newspaper *The Guardian* launched a slightly different initiative. They created the *Planet Brand Index*, a classification of 100 brands that "could save the world"; not a recognition of results but a call to action. Three criteria are considered: the influence, the global scale, and their understanding of sustainable development. We will find there most of the American blue chips like Disney, Microsoft, Apple, and Avon, as well as Gucci, Louis Vuitton, Ferrari, L'Oréal, Zara, Burberry, Cartier, Mercedes-Benz, Starbucks, Adidas, Audi, Red Bull, Nike, and Canon.

- *1.618 Paris* is an agency that organizes an exhibition every two years on the theme of sustainable luxury. It started in 2011 and brings together an international community of brands, entrepreneurs, thinkers, nongovernment organizations, and artists dedicated to building a better world and who are trying to redefine luxury in the twenty-first century. Their definition (by negation) of new luxury is: "True luxury is not mass produced, does not destroy the environment and is not socially ignorant."[11] 1.618 is an approximation of the golden ratio. The fifth edition, in 2018, brought together 41 brands in multiple fields such as architecture, design, mobility, tourism, gastronomy, fashion, jewelry, and well-being. The sixth edition is planned for December 2020.

- *COP26*, which was supposed to take place in Glasgow in November 2020, has been postponed to 2021. COP stands for Conference of the Parties under the UNFCCC (United Nations Framework Convention on Climate Change). For almost three decades, world governments have met every year to forge a global response to the climate emergency. Under the 1992 United Nations Framework Convention on Climate Change, every country on earth is treaty-bound

---

[11] http://www.1618-paris.com/.

to "avoid dangerous climate change" and find ways to reduce green-house gas emissions globally in an equitable way. The annual meetings have reached various degrees of failures and successes. The US withdrawal from the Paris Agreement should be confirmed if Donald Trump is reelected in November 2020. Nonetheless, since 2015, when nations agreed to limit temperature rise this century to below 2 degrees Celsius under the Paris climate accord, the number of Fortune 500 companies pledging to reduce their carbon emissions has quadrupled,[12] with employee demands identified as their key drivers.

The list of events, initiatives, and rating systems could be much longer. What is important is that, now, most of the luxury brands are announcing their commitment to sustainable development. We have chosen LVMH, Kering, Hermès, and Ferragamo as a sample in order to illustrate the seriousness of their approaches to sustainability.

Sustainable Luxury Brands.   In 2007, the WWF commissioned a study that classified luxury brands according to their respect for the environment. The first in the rankings were L'Oréal, LVMH, and Hermès with a C+, followed by Coach with a D+, then Swatch, PPR (now Kering), and Richemont with a D, the last in the ranking being Tod's and Bulgari with an F. The study was not free from defects (reduced number of brands and multibrand groups, judgment based solely on communication, etc.), but it demonstrated a relatively low awareness on the part of the market and brands on the ecological theme.

Since then, the large multibrand groups have been much more involved in ecological and social causes—some, like LVMH, since the 1990s. Most have gone beyond the stage of specific initiatives and have integrated their efforts very early in their strategic choices, product design, and supply chain. Their annual reports leave a substantial place to their efforts for sustainable development.

In LVMH's 2019 Annual Report, published January 28, 2020, one can read in the general summary that "LVMH is driven by a permanent commitment to perfection and quality, and by a long-term vision combined with a sense of responsibility in all our corporate actions, notably in its commitment for the preservation of the environment, sustainability and inclusion."

---

[12] 2019 report from https://www.naturalcapitalpartners.com/company.

Four categories of commitments are highlighted: transmission and savoir-faire, leadership and entrepreneurship, art and culture, and social and environmental responsibility. In this fourth category, major initiatives are listed:

- The LIFE (LVMH Initiatives For the Environment) program was created in 2012 to elevate the environmental performance of LVMH and its brands. It is an integral component of each brand strategic business plan, with performance measured with key environmental performance factors. To intensify its actions, LIFE 2020 set out four objectives shared by all brands: improve the environmental performance of all its products, implement high standards in its supply chain, reduce CO_2 emissions, and energy reduction.

- The Environment Academy, created in 2016, is responsible for informing and training the group's employees in the protection of natural resources.

- LVMH launched in 2011 the initiative of the *Dîner des Maisons Engagées*, an annual fundraising dinner to finance the fight against sickle cell anemia.

- In 2007, EllesVMH was created in order to encourage the professional development of women in all positions and at every level of the organization through a variety of initiatives.

- The LVMH Group launched the website WeCareForModels.com to support the charter drawn up in 2017 jointly with Kering on working relations with fashion models, proposing expert nutritionists and coaches' advice for fashion models, as well as promoting responsibility, transparency, and empowerment in a sector that has witnessed a lot of abuses.

- Maison/0: LVMH and Central Saint Martins, the renowned London art and design school, invite young talents to identify disruptive solutions to address sustainable development and innovation in luxury.

The group now publishes an annual environmental report in which it recalls that their environmental commitment began in 1993 and gives the quantified results of all of their sustainability initiatives. During Paris Fashion Week in September 2019, LVMH announced a series of commitments for the environment and biodiversity, including a Raw Materials Sourcing Charter specifying a target of 70% of the group's leather to be sourced in Leather Working Group (LWG) certified tanneries, up from 48 currently.

On January 20, 2020, LVMH appointed a new environmental development director, Hélène Valade, an expert in the area. She will report to Antoine Arnault, who will oversee the group environmental department in addition to his role as head of communications and image for the group.

In 2013, Kering chose a name that phonetically means "attentive, benevolent, concerned about ...". On the group's website, the initial functional options are Group, Houses, Talent, Sustainability, Finance, Press, Join us. The sustainability approach is described as "'Luxury and sustainability are one and the same.' Reflecting this deeply held conviction of François-Henri Pinault, sustainability has always been at the heart of Kering's strategy. Far more than an ethical necessity, it is a driver of innovation and value creation for the Group, its Houses, and its stakeholders."

In terms of governance, sustainability is represented from the Board of Directors and the Sustainability Committee to the managers of the group's brands. A Chief Sustainability Officer together with some 50 persons are involved in the implementation of the sustainability programs. They have developed the Environmental Profit & Loss (EP&L) account as a key indicator of their sustainable business model. Since 2008, the Kering Foundation has made the combat against violence against women the focus of its actions. Kering published four reports in 2019: "Additional Information to Kering ESG Reporting 2019," "Kering Group Modern Slavery Statement 2019," Methodological note of social reporting 2018, and Methodological note of environmental reporting 2018.

A great number of their initiatives are listed on their website. Together with LVMH, they are probably the most active luxury group in sustainability.

For Hermès, whose brand identity is strongly linked to exceptional and often ancestral crafts, it is natural to be active in sustainable development. Two statements from the Hermès 2019 Universal Registration Document including The Annual Financial Report confirm that the brand is born sustainable and that, beyond specific initiatives, its identity itself is of sustainable nature: "Hermès's mission is to create unique and original objects to elegantly satisfy the needs and desires of its customers.

Its goal is the pursuit of excellence, in each of its métiers and services, with craftsmanship at the heart of its model." And later, "Though the decade has come to an end amid intense uncertainties and a general awakening to environmental and public health concerns, it is clear that Hermès' offering remains relevant and well-liked. This offering is based on the simple idea of creating objects designed to last."[13] Handicraft and timelessness are key to Hermès's identity.

Hermès claims to be a humanist company, deeply respectful of all those involved in its processes. They recognize that their "craftsmanship model leaves a careful environmental footprint." Biodiversity is taken into account in the construction of production sites, and in its indirect sphere, the Group has a positive impact on its supply chain, by preserving autonomous ecosystems and by participating in global initiatives. But above all, offering long-lasting, repairable objects is a sure way to reduce overconsumption and waste. Hermès is therefore an attentive, concerned, and committed player in exercising its activities while respecting its ecological, social, economic, and cultural environment.

We have seen the Ferragamo Sustainable Thinking initiative in an earlier section. The Florentine brand is clearly engaged in sustainability and its website indicates that it adopted six sustainable development goals broken down into concrete actions developed internally.[14] The Group is committed to good health, well-being, quality education, affordable and clean energy, decent work and economic growth, sustainable cities and communities, and responsible consumption and production. In 2018, the Group joined the United Nations Global Compact, the world's largest corporate sustainability initiative.

We have given examples of some of the biggest luxury groups. There are still a number of brands that lag behind what large multibrand groups do. This is in general due more to a lack of financial resources than to a lack of will to progress in the direction of sustainability. Other brands, even if they sometimes remain at the level of ad-hoc initiatives, are also seriously involved.

MBA Programs.   The growth of the sustainable MBA is another clear indication of the rise of sustainability sensibility. The common

---

[13] https://finance.hermes.com/var/finances/storage/original/application/059c282fc6a5e9e4eff1a6befa69a890.pdf.

[14] https://csr.ferragamo.com/en/responsible-passion/sustainable-development-goals/.

theme of these programs is the extent to which environmental and social sustainability can be achieved within a liberal economy. They help evolve the historical hard capitalism focused essentially on generating profits to shareholders toward a more human-centered vision of a business that would be part of a community and with responsibility toward the next generations.

Since the launch in 2003 of what is recognized today as the first fully integrated sustainability program of the Presidio Graduate School, with MBA programs in San Francisco and Seattle, there were 52 programs as of July 2020.[15] The sustainability MBA programs vary significantly from one school to another, and the list of 52 programs does not include traditional MBA programs that have incorporated sustainability-related topics into their curriculum, nor graduate schools, such as Sasin in Bangkok, which was a pioneer in incorporating the sustainability values in its identity, as well as in its programs, as early as 2000.

To conclude this list of indicators of higher sustainable sensibility, which have been selected for their relevance and recentness, we are comforted by the fact that everybody, both on the brands' and consumers' sides, is recognizing the need to work more efficiently at changing our rapports with nature and changing our consumption patterns; some with different degrees of commitment and results, but with a clear understanding that sustainable development is not just an option anymore.

Possible Consumer Segmentation

According to LinkedIn's 2018 Workplace Report, 86% of millennials would consider taking a pay cut to work for companies whose values aligned with their own. That says a lot about the role and state of mind of the younger generation toward sustainability.

However, age is not the only meaningful segmenting dimension.

The Sustainable Brand Index (Sustainable Brand Index[TM] B2C 2019)[16] that we introduced in a previous paragraph proposes an

---

[15] https://en.wikipedia.org/wiki/Sustainable_MBA.

[16] https://ssusa.s3.amazonaws.com/c/308477602/media/44735e465a2100c6724218169857 950/Official%20Report%20NL.pdf. This report is written by SB Insight AB, an insight agency based in Stockholm and founder of the Sustainable Brand Index[TM]. The study has been conducted yearly since 2011. In 2019, 50,000 consumers in more than 20 industries have been analyzed on sustainability. The study is conducted annually in Sweden, Norway, Denmark, Finland, and the Netherlands.

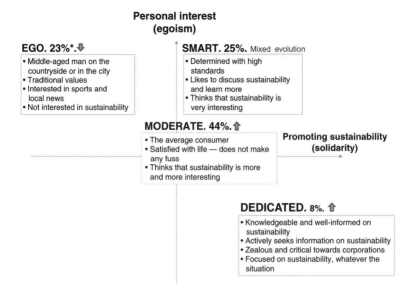

Figure 12.1   Four Types of Consumer Attitudes with Respect to Sustainability.

*Weighted average over the five countries (The Netherlands, Sweden, Norway, Denmark, and Finland).

Source: Extrapolated from Sustainable Brand Index™ B2C, Official Report 2019 (The Netherlands).

interesting and simple segmentation of customers' attitudes toward sustainability that may be useful for luxury brands. Figure 12.1 indicates the four typologies of customers on two axes: individual interest versus sustainability promotion. Although the analysis is done on a limited number of European countries, its framework is applicable globally.

- The **Dedicated** customer is a fan and pursues sustainability in all parts of his life. This customer represents less than 10% of the population but has almost doubled in the past seven years, with an increasing rate in the past three.

- The **Ego** customer is just not interested in sustainability. He is a conservator and traditionalist and prizes the price-to-value ratio in his purchasing decisions. This customer represents almost a quarter of the population. The percentage decreased 10 points in the past seven years, with an acceleration in the past three years. It probably feeds the moderate group.

- The **Moderate** customer is the largest group, with 44% of the population. This customer is the ordinary citizen, a follower of the trend and therefore slightly interested in sustainability because he feels it is growing in importance with some parts of the population. The number of this customer has decreased since 2015, but has grown slightly in the past three years.
- The **Smart** customer is pursuing what is good for him, but tries to combine it with what is also good for the world. He is in general curious about sustainability. This customer also represents a quarter of the population. The percentage of smart customers has increased by seven points in the past seven years.

It will be interesting to follow the continuous monitoring of these populations, hoping that more countries will join this relevant survey.

Greenwashing

Even greenwashing is not what it used to be. The higher awareness of climate change, combined with Internet virtual public space, has been changing the rules. People fact-check now more than ever and disclose and denounce the lies and empty promises. We have been used to so many companies making great declarations on ecological and social principles, claiming sustainable initiatives, and bragging about their beliefs. The quest for authenticity that we are going to analyze deeper in the second part of this chapter is real. Consumers want to see clearly that the sustainable initiatives disclosed by the brands are true and have a meaningful impact.

One of the latest examples in the energy field is given by the reactions to the cleaner energy BP advertising campaign launched in early 2019. BP's First Global Advertising Campaign since the drama of *Deepwater Horizon* has been accused of being deceptive and hypocritical by the not-for-profit legal group ClientEarth.[17] Under the "Keep advancing" slogan, BP's latest campaign promotes a broad and generic message about a company working to make all forms of energy cleaner and better. It

---

[17] Harry Dempsey and Anjli Raval, "BP Accused of 'Greenwashing' in Cleaner Energy Ad Campaign," *Financial Times*, December 4, 2019.

contributes to give the impression that BP is heavily involved in clean and renewable energy, when it is the object of only 3% of its capital expenditures, the rest being invested in traditional oil and gas activities.

As mentioned earlier, scrutiny is now everywhere to control the veracity of sustainable allegations.

Conclusion on Sustainability

"Not being prepared for a major crisis like COVID-19 has demonstrated how ill-prepared we will be for extreme weather events due to climate change," said David Levine, co-founder and president of the American Sustainable Business Council. The forced confinement and consequential interruption of many human activities caused us to be suddenly exposed to realities that we had either forgotten or simply never even saw or experienced:

- Dolphins in Venice's transparent waters
- The Himalayan mountain chain visible at 200 km away from India
- Deer in the middle of cities
- Whales in marinas
- The skies without white wakes of planes above cities
- Unseen solidarity reactions from individuals, private and public entities
- The beauty of empty city landscapes
- Silence
- Ourselves in a time of crisis and with time to reflect on it

Nature is taking back its rights and we can see clearly the consequences of many human activities. Coronavirus is acting as a revelator as well as an accelerator of preexisting trends. We may hope that these revelations will help reinforce the already growing sensibility toward sustainability and encourage the decision makers on both sides of the markets to take direct actions to promote types of consumption and production that are more respectful of nature and human beings.

We believe that luxury will prove that it is possible to sell dreams while respecting the planet and participating in activating sustainable development. Let's see the role that authenticity plays in this ambitious objective.

Brand Authenticities

Authenticity is one of the main requirements of current luxury consumers. It has been the subject of extensive literature since the 1970s (Benjamin 1969, Baudrillard 1976, Derbaix and Decrop 2007, Gilmore and Pine 2007)[18–21]. The concept is complex and is subject to many meanings. This polysemy makes it difficult to understand its nature and its mechanisms for producing meaning. It is therefore necessary to provide a certain clarity on the subject so that brand managers can better master and take advantage of this concept to which the market has become particularly sensitive.

This recent surge of interest should not hide the fact that authenticity has accompanied human history. Who appreciates the false? The fight against counterfeiting is as old as the appearance of the first coins in the seventh century BC.[22] For example, there was the trade of false relics in the ninth century and false Chinese porcelain from the seventeenth century. Albrecht Dürer at the beginning of the sixteenth century already won lawsuits against his counterfeiters.[23] Reflections on authenticity have been at the heart of considerations in many disciplines for several millennia. They have always accompanied men in search of truth and meaning in the face of their own representation activities. From the considerations of Plato in *The Republic* on mimetic art, to the considerations of Benjamin on the original in the face of reproductive technologies, passing by the authentic man advocated by the existentialist theses, the notion of authenticity spilled a lot of ink and applied to objects, subjects, authors, and experiences as well.

To return to the world of consumption, the brand manager, who listens attentively to the market, must be interested in the concept of authenticity and the most relevant notions of a sociological, ethical,

---

[18] Walter Benjamin, *L'œuvre d'art à l'époque de sa reproductibilité technique* (version 1939). Paris: Editions Gallimard, 2010.

[19] Jean Baudrillard, *L'échange symbolique et la mort*. Paris: Gallimard, 1976.

[20] M. Derbaix and A. Decrop, "Authenticity in the Performing Arts: A Foolish Quest?" *Advances in Consumer Research* 34 (2007).

[21] James H. Gilmore and Joseph B. Pine II, *Authenticity*. Boston: Harvard Business School Press, 2007.

[22] Musée de la banque nationale de Belgique. www.nbbmuseum.be

[23] Olivier Babeau, *Le Management expliqué par l'art*. Paris: Editions Ellipse, 2013.

cultural, philosophical, identity, moral, and strategic nature that irrigate it. Some statistics demonstrate this renewed interest. For example, the frequency of the use of the words "authentic" and "authenticity" in English-language literature scanned by Google gives an increase in use of 83% for the adjective and 200% for the noun since 1920.[24] The consumer world offers us many examples. On the supply side, we can note, among other things, the success of organic products, the slow food movement, the requirement for controlled designations of origin, the advent of activities based on nostalgia and based on belief that "it was more authentic in the past" (vintage fashion, cinema remakes, tourist parks with historical themes, etc.). On the demand side, there are many forms of exigency of authenticity from consumers: the search for transparency, honesty, originality, and vintage; adherence to values from the past, attention to geographic or cultural origin; the requirement to comply with manufacturing standards; sensitivity to consistency with an identity or a value system; the desire for real relationships with others, and so on. This quest for authenticity is found not only in the discourses of brands and the media in general but also in political programs and academic publications.

The probable causes for this new interest in authenticity are to be found in the reactions of consumers to many factors, of which we can make a nonexhaustive list:

- The increase in plagiarism
- The intensification of the use of simulacrum as a technique in communication and product offering
- The excessive dose of utopian and out-of-reach worlds for most consumers
- The increase in virtual experiences through social networks
- Consumer expectations regarding the social roles that brands must play
- The forces of homogenization of globalization

Despite the ambiguity and polysemy of the concept, one can try to introduce a generic definition. The notion of authenticity is normally associated with the values of truth, conformity, and legitimacy.[25]

---

[24] Google Books Ngram viewer. https://books.google.com/ngrams.
[25] Trésor de la langue française informatisé. http://atilf.atilf.fr.

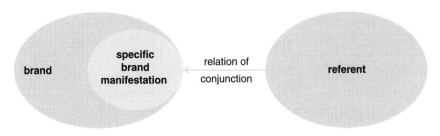

Figure 12.2   Components of Brand Authenticity as the Quality of a Relationship with a Referent

Authenticity is the quality of a relationship of an object, being, system, or concept with a referent. The rapport can be of conformity, coherence, adequacy, relevance, analogy, belonging, descent, ascent, filiation, and so on. Semiotically it will, in any case, be a relationship of conjunction, of greater or lesser physical or conceptual proximity. Figure 12.2 graphically presents the components of our approach to authenticity.

The nature of the referent and that of the relationship that links it to the entity that we want to qualify as authentic are the two dimensions that determine the type of the bestowed authenticity.

Referents as Sources of Authenticity.   Referents can be of different natures; they are the sources of authenticity and determine the type of relationship with the entity in question. External referents can be both tangible and intangible. Internal referents are largely related to the brand identity.

External Referents.   Table 12.2 presents 11 possible external sources of brand authenticity (Mazzalovo 2013),[26] as well as examples of brands that use them. The multiplicity of authenticity sources explains the plural we used in the title of this part of the chapter that we have called "brand authenticities."

This list of 11 typologies of external referents (Mazzalovo 2015)[27] is neither exhaustive nor homogeneous (innovation, for example, can

---

[26] Gérald Mazzalovo, *Autenticidades de las marcas.* Revista de Occidente, No. 404. Madrid, Funcion Ortega y Gasset. Gregorio Marañon, 2015.

[27] http://www.1618-paris.com/.

Table 12.2   External Sources of Brand Authenticity

	Sources	Typology	Examples of brands
tangible	**Geography**	Regional specialities and characteristics, location, place, garage	Baccarat, Laguiole, wines, cheeses, restaurants, Hewlett Packard
	Material	Use of special materials: cashmere, diamonds, crystal, "pâte de verre," braided leather, fabric with logo	Louis Vuitton, Baccarat, Daum, Tittot, Bottega Veneta, Svarowski, Loro Piana
	Performance	Banks, audit, restaurants, hotels	Red Bull, Rolex, Garmin, Suunto, Caterpillar, KPMG
	Process	Competence: "savoir-faire," knowledge ("tour de main, » recipe, formula)	Services, design, handicraft-based, Digital, Kentucky Fried Chicken, Coca-Cola, Starbucks, Google, Amazon, Twitter
	Design	Logos, colors, shapes, "coup de patte"	Kartell, Cassina, Muji, Swatch, LV, Montblanc, Chanel
Intangible	**Personality**	Brand founders, invented characters, historical figures	Karl Lagerfeld, Yves Saint Laurent, Mickey Mouse, Hello Kitty, Barbie
	Institutions	Associations based on nations, cultures	Comité Colbert, BBC, Red Cross
	Art	Museums, artists, movies	Moma, Louvre, Daum, Rocawear, Fenty, foundations
	Time	Brand history, year of foundation	Campbell soup, Kandahar, Label "China time-honored brands"
	Values	Sustainability, green, ecology, Women beauty canons	ONG, Unesco, Dove, the Body Shop; organic products
	Innovation	In all functions or other sources	GAFAM, Swatch, Yoox

be applied to many other sources such as design, materials, processes, etc.), but it gives an idea of the variety of possible authenticity references. Strong luxury brands build their authenticity from a multiplicity of referents.

It is through the referents of authenticity that market moods are being conveyed. For example, the success of artisanal products made according to ancestral processes that call upon referents of history, places, and processes results from a current need to return to a past perceived as free from the problems of today's life.

Calling on or relating to external authenticity referents can be as simple as writing "Made in Italy" on a product in an attempt to appropriate all the values linked to productive and creative Italian know-how, or indicating "Member of the Colbert Committee" on a website or brochure to situate the brand in the luxury world. But in the majority of cases, the credible establishing of authenticity referents requires the use of more complex and longer processes. The authenticity referents are expressed through the brand's discourses in the form of texts in the broad sense (images, writings, spaces, characters, etc.) and are then subject to market verification that tests their credibility.

An example taken from the Belgian leather-goods maker Delvaux illustrates the complexity that the mechanisms of building the authenticity of a brand can take from external referents. In 2008, the brand offered its Brillant bag, a best-seller launched in 1958, with a text written on the front of the bag: "This is not a Delvaux (*Ceci n'est pas un Delvaux*)." It is an example of the communication process based on simulacrum that brands often use. The simulacrum makes it possible to summon a referent through a double process of imitation and differentiation (Mazzalovo 2014).[28] In this specific case, the process summons three main referents. In order not to confuse them with the referents of authenticity, we will qualify them as simulacrum referents. These are:

1. *The Treachery of Images*, the famous 1929 painting by the Belgian surrealist painter Magritte (1898–1967) stating "Ceci n'est pas une pipe"

---

[28] Gérald Mazzalovo, "Simulacrum in Building Brand Myths." Article presented to the 9th Global Brand Annual Conference at Hertfordshire Business School in Hatfield, University of Hertfordshire in 2014. Available on the website of the Italian Semiotic Association, www .ec-aiss.it.

2. The Belgian painter Paul Delvaux (1897–1994)
3. All the trapezoidal bags

The goal of the Delvaux brand is to strengthen its positioning as an authentic luxury Belgian brand. Luxury brands often associate with the art world to assert their status and Delvaux thus calls on two Belgian painters. The trapezoidal shape of the bags is traditionally used by some luxury brands of leather goods (Hermès, Ferragamo). In this way, using three simulacrum referents, Delvaux succeeds in establishing two authenticity referents: luxury and being Belgian. It will then be up to consumers to judge its legitimacy.

Internal Referents.   A new acception of the concept of authenticity is emerging in academic and professional circles that is less linked to tangible or intangible external sources but rather to consistency with the true nature of a brand identity. Therefore, brand identity, as defined semiotically in Chapter 6, becomes itself an internal source of authenticity (see Table 12.3). The notion of internal referent is linked to the principle of self-realization, the development of one's potential, and is present in both Western and Asian philosophies. For brands, the question is both operational and existential. Is the first collection of a new designer (such as Yves Saint Laurent in 1958 when he presented his first collection for Dior or Marc Jacobs in 1997 or Ghesquière in 2014, both for Louis Vuitton) in line with the spirit of the brand or its founder? This is the dilemma of any designer working for a brand. Ideally, this conformity (or, at least, compatibility) should be able to express itself on both ethical and aesthetic levels. An authentic Hermès bag is not just a product actually produced by the brand, it is also a product that reflects its identity in terms of aesthetic invariants and projection of handicraft expertise as well as the elitist and aristocratic world that characterizes it.

Table 12.3   Internal Sources of Authenticity

Sources		**Brands**
Brand identity	Aesthetics	Absolut Vodka, Rolex, Desigual
	Ethics	Dove, Body Shop, Red Cross, United Nations

The concept of loyalty to oneself, presented here for brands, is not really new. It is found in other areas that also deal with authenticity, such as in leadership literature where the foundations of authentic leadership are built, among other things, on this loyalty (Walumbwa and Al 2008).[29]

As has happened in art history when eighteenth-century empiricists shift the notion of beauty, until then considered as an intrinsic quality of things, to a perceptual and subjective experience, the notion of authenticity is evolving toward no longer the quality of an object but the quality of the experience of the object. As Jorge Lozano (2013) says, "Authenticity is not an ontological problem."[30]

Constructivists in particular argue that authenticity is not the quality of an object, but a cultural value constantly reinvented through social trials (Olsen 2002).[31] Wang (2000)[32] introduces a notion of experiential authenticity, a state that can be caused by nonroutine activities in which people feel closer to themselves than in everyday life; an authenticity that would, therefore, derive from an escape from the constraints of everyday life and that would release an authentic feeling of oneself.

Once the authenticity based on objects, experiences, and identities is recognized, it is easier to understand the extension of the concept to brands. Authenticity qualifies the relationship of conformity that certain characteristics of a brand, such as its identity, its values, its products, and the experiences it can provide, can have with specific referents.

The introduction of authentic experience opens the way to the subjectivization of the referents that are the sources of authenticity. We have highlighted tangible and intangible referents, external to brands, internal referents to brands, linked to their identity. There are also referents internal to consumers and therefore of a completely subjective nature. Santos et al. (2014) present a relevant example in their study of groups of Vespa brand fans whose judgments of the authenticity of new

---

[29] Fred Walumbwa, Bruce Avolio, William Gardner, Tara Wernsing, and Suzanne Peterson, "Authentic Leadership: Development and Validation of a Theory-Based Measure," *Management Department Faculty Publications* 24, University of Nebraska, 2008.

[30] Jorge Lozano, "L'authentique n'est pas l'unique, mais quand même." Presented to the Executive Conference on Brand Authenticity organized by Kalaidos University of Applied Sciences in Zurich, June 21, 2013.

[31] Kjrell Olsen, "Authenticity as a Concept in Tourism Research," *Tourist Studies* 2 (2002).

[32] N. Wang, *Tourism and Modernity*. Amsterdam: Pergamon, 2000.

products are based on personal idealizations of what they think Vespa designs should be.[33]

Semprini (2013) further expands the concept when he declares that authenticity, in the postmodern period, is less a question of truth than of loyalty to one's own brand project.[34] For him, the main source of authenticity becomes a brand's ability to address someone's inner self, to offer new responses to their desires and needs for identity. Table 12.4 shows the evolution from a modern to a postmodern approach to brand authenticity.

This evolution from an initially purely objective and verifiable authenticity toward one of subjective nature, is a postmodern phenomenon. A study by Leigh, Peters, and Shelton (2006) summarize well how a feeling of authentic consumption is constructed through the sum of authenticities of diverse nature.[35] The authors analyze the behavior of MG brand car owners and demonstrate that it is the combination of the authenticity of the object, its possession, the driving experience, the construction, and confirmation of the owner identity that eventually lead to an act of consumption recognized as authentic by consumers.

Different typologies of authenticity therefore coexist. The brand manager must take account of this multiplicity and understand their

Table 12.4 Evolution of the Sources of Authenticity

	Modern	**Postmodern**
Time	Oriented to the past	Oriented toward the future (projects, dreams …)
Referents	Objective and verifiable	Subjective
Focus	Facts External elements	Personal emotions
Brand anchoring	Products, origins	Experience, identity, connections

---

[33] Fernando Pinto Santos, Anne Rindell, Anne and Ana Pinto De Lima, "Heritage and the Quest for Authenticity." Presentation made to the 9th Annual Global Brand Conference at Hertfordshire Business School in Hatfield (UK) University of Hertfordshire, 2014.

[34] Andrea Semprini, "Brand Authenticity: A Time-related Issue?" Presented to the Executive Conference on Brand Authenticity organized by Kalaidos University of Applied Sciences in Zurich, June 21, 2013.

[35] Thomas W. Leigh, Cara Peters, and Jeremy Shelton, "The Consumer Quest for Authenticity: The Multiplicity of Meanings within the MG Subculture of Consumption," *Journal of the Academy of Marketing Science* 34, no. 4 (2006), 481–493.

mechanisms to be able to possibly influence them. To overcome the complexity introduced by the different types of authenticity, it has become necessary to systematically qualify the term and specify which authenticity is being considered.

Overall Conclusion

By concluding this book, which covers both micro- and macroeconomic aspects of the management of luxury brands, one becomes aware of the complexity, vitality, and universality of the luxury sector. The fact that it is necessary to publish a new edition of this book every five years confirms the evolutionary rapidity of a set of industries that reflects the profound changes that agitate our society and the need to be a close, directly involved, and interested observer in order to follow its trajectory.

Luxury universality can be explained by the fact that it is both a driver and a consequence of globalization. It mixes investors, consumers, and distributors of different cultures and origins. European brands are owned by Asian capital; some Western groups are shareholders of Chinese brands. Asia manufactures for European and American brands and Europe does it for Chinese brands. Design teams are more and more multi-ethnic. Nothing very new, one could retort. The worldwide success of Chinese blue and white ceramics in the fourteenth century (probably the first global luxury items) would not have been possible without the cobalt oxide extracted from mines located in Persia and exported along the Silk Road. The Italian Jesuit Giuseppe Castiglione, who entered the court of Emperor Kangxi in 1714, painted the faces and horses while Chinese painters took care of the landscapes on paintings commissioned by the emperor.

For luxury brands in general, this mosaic approach, which integrates elements from different cultures in a common project, is made necessary by the imperatives of competition. Enlightened brand owners will now seek the elements, functions, and people most relevant to the success of the brand project, regardless of their geographic position, helped in this by technological advances in communication and transport. It remains to be seen what consequences COVID-19 and the relationship between the West and China will have on this multicultural approach. We hear a lot these days about the decoupling of the US and China economies, and the supply chain disruption brought by the virus may have durable strategic effects.

We can certainly consider as a cultural impoverishment the apparent standardization presented by the main shopping streets of all the big cities of the world. Only the strongest brands in the world can afford the rents of the best retail spaces or even the acquisition of buildings. Many online multibrand or monobrand e-commerce platforms are now facilitating worldwide access to brand merchandise without brands having to invest in prohibitive central retail places. Even if brands are naturally looking for an adequate international distribution, we should not be forgetting that each brand offers the values that configure its identity. Brands often reflect the cultural environment of their main decision-making center, where they generally grew up. It is natural that their identity borrows from the values of the region or country where they were born and have developed. Dior will always be associated with a certain idea of Paris, regardless of the nationality of the designer (who is Italian for the time being, Maria Grazia Chiuri since 2016). It is obvious to everyone that Gucci and Ferragamo have a product offering that reflects an Italian sensibility, just as Louis Vuitton and Chanel are brands expressing French culture, Coach and Chrysler an American way of life, and Shiatzy Chen and Shang Xia expressing Chinese values. Luxury brands can give the impression of a certain standardization of lifestyles, especially by their global distributive presence and sometimes by communication campaigns that converge in their visuals, but each luxury brand is first the expression of a specific identity. The brand's identity (*caractère identitaire*), which, by the way, is one of the five criteria for admission to the Colbert Committee (The French Luxury Association), is explained in Chapter 2.

The intensity and diffusion of the media activities of global brands contribute to the promotion of specific cultures from other regions. This phenomenon of awareness of other cultures goes in the direction of a better understanding of different values. It nurtures respect for difference. In fact, we come to realize that exoticism understood broadly as the encounter of different cultures is one of the main engines of the luxury business. This is a vast topic, subject to deeper studies and probably a source of future publications.

The universality of luxury is also based on the sharing of specific luxury values. All peoples aspire to excellence, qualitative perfection, beauty, the extraordinary, and rejection of the ephemeral. Luxury is a mirror that reflects our tastes, our moods, our expectations, and our ambitions. To observe it, to know it, to practice it as brand manager or consumer is to participate actively in the life of our civilization and to be on the front of its most creative innovations at technological, aesthetic, and strategic levels.

Cassandras have predicted for decades the inevitable decline of luxury consumption. The appearance of numerous second-hand luxury goods stores seems to them a premonitory sign of a saturation of the market. It is probably more a sign of the increasing sustainable sensitivity. We do not agree that luxury is declining; it has a bright future ahead. The rise of the middle classes worldwide and the natural human desire toward excellence and beauty continue to feed luxury growth, which is likely to become more organic than geographic.

Appendix A

Applying Brand Identity Analytical Tools

The Case of Sasin School of Business, the Leading Thai Business School, Chulalongkorn University (Bangkok, Phuket)

W e have chosen to prepare a special appendix for the brand identity work done in early 2020 on Sasin School of Management, where one of the authors is a faculty member and senior research fellow. He led the study, together with other faculty members and some MBA students.

This is the most recent example of the application of the brand hinge introduced in Chapter 6. This study confirms the versatility of the semiotic approach to brand identity. It is the second time we apply the methodology to a service brand (the first time was on Pininfarina); however, it is the first time we use it on a higher education institution.

Brand management applied to universities is still in its infancy, and semiotics applied to their identity is even rarer.

It was an opportunity also to reflect on what luxury is in education, as a Sasin ambition is to become a luxury institution. The question is rarely expressed in these terms. Excellence, efficiency, relevance, technology, and utilization are more familiar terms in the education field.

Without getting into too many details, we will outline the main axes that guided our reflection. In order to extrapolate the luxury notion into the realm of education, we used the following leads and some definitions introduced in Chapter 1:

- The academic rankings indicate in a quantified way the best institutions in the various education fields. They remain major sources of inspiration.
- Another immediate approach is to consider the quality and reputation of the professors and of the students and alumni throughout history. How many Nobel prizes, awards, patents, and so on have been granted to them? History provides examples. Aristotle and Alexander the Great are probably the most famous couple. Aristotle did not trouble his disciple with forming syllogisms or with geometry; he infused him with good precepts concerning valor, prowess, magnanimity, temperance, and the contempt of fear—all notions still relevant today. It also draws the attention to the value of one-on-one tutoring that Sasin is developing further.
- There is a huge literature dealing directly or indirectly with education that dates back to Athens and Imperial China. The fact that they are still studied is undeniable proof of the quality and relevance of their content. We all remember Montaigne's famous sentence on forming "heads that are well-made rather than well-filled" (Les Essais 1595).
- Luxury brand lessons (relevance, authenticity, consistency) (Chapter 2)
- New luxury and the moral definition based on coinvestment (Chapter 1)
- Luxury services

Sasin Brand Ethics

Sasin Graduate Institute of Business Administration of Chulalongkorn University was founded in 1982 under the initiative of the late King Bhumibol Adulyadej (Rama 9) through a collaboration among Chulalongkorn University and the Kellogg School of Management and the Wharton Business School. Sasin became the first school in Thailand to receive AACSB accreditation in 2010 and the first to receive EQUIS EFMD accreditation in 2010. Rama 9 bestowed the name on the Graduate Institute of Business Administration on his 60th birthday, December 5, 1987. The name comes from two Sanskrit words, "sasa" and "indra." Sasa, meaning "rabbit," represents the king's birth year in the Thai 12-year astrological cycle. Indra means "chief." Thus "Sasin" literally means "king of the rabbits."

Sasin is now the leading Thai Business School. It pioneered the use of visiting professors complemented by full-time Sasin faculty and other experts in Southeast Asia and offers MBAs, dual degrees. and PhD programs.

See Table A.1 for the results of the analytical work on Sasin brand identity.

As mentioned for the other Thai brand, Jim Thompson, here we also find the dialectic East versus West. The initial collaboration with Wharton and Kellogg is part of the founding principles of the school, which goes and fetches the best available resources around the world. Its programs are providing a Thai point of view on global and universal business issues.

Table A.1 also introduces a classification of the values of a brand. It derives partially from the psychosociologist Rokeach's work (1973),[1] where values are considered related to preferences having implications on behaviors. For him a value is a lasting belief that a specific mode of behavior or goal of existence is personally or socially preferable to another mode of behavior or goal of existence. The values thus defined can be further classified. When a value refers to ways of living or behaviors, it is an *instrumental value*. When it refers to a goal of existence or a

---

[1] M. Rokeach, *The Nature of Human Values*. Free Press, 1973.

Table A.1   Sasin School of Management Brand Ethics (2020)

Proposed brand ethics
Values and world vision
  1. **Essential values**
      - The richness and uniqueness of Chulalongkorn and Sasin
        history and heritage
      - Thailand/Thainess/Thai cultures
      - SEA/Asia Pacific/Asia/the world
      - New luxury (exceptional in many ways)
      - Pragmatism
          • Action learning and action research
          • Inductive logics
          • Worldwide selection of the best resources and ideas to
            meet Sasin objectives
      - Ability to get the best from specific sources, integrate and
        ultimately create innovative programs and methods (Thai
        absorbing, mixing, and creating genius)
  2. **Instrumental values (character features. Behavioral)**
      - Elitism
      - Generosity/empathy/compassion
      - True to oneself, true to the truth
      - Multiple authenticities
      - Pragmatism
      - Entrepreneurship
      - Freedom of thought
      - Quality exigency
      - Innovative in programs and methods
  3. **Teleological values (world vision)**
      - Sustainability
      - A smart and solidary world
      - A proper and forward-looking balance of Asian and Western
        philosophies★
  4. **Underdeveloped**
      - Sense of humor
      - Art
  5. **Dialectics**
Sasin identity emerges also in the ways it resolves some apparently
opposite elements:
      - tradition/innovation
      - East/West
      - formal/casual
      - technology/handicraft
      - action/reflection
      - inclusive/exclusive
      - nature/culture

world vision, it is a *terminal value* that we also call *teleological* value as it expresses an idea of finality.

We have added the *essential values*, which, for example, being Thai represents cultural values that could be distributed in the two previous categories but that we have kept separated for communication efficiency reasons. Then we highlighted the values to make an effort upon and finally the dialectics. Plenty of additional material supports the synthetic Table 6.2, which cannot be presented here for space limitation.

Sasin Brand Aesthetics

The work performed on the Sasin School of Management identity entailed a definition of the aesthetic invariants that are shown in Table A.2.

A particular aspect is that the school has the advantage of owning two logos (see Figure A.1):

Table A.2 Sasin School of Management Brand Aesthetics (2020)

Sasin brand aesthetics
Permanent sensory elements

Two logos: *Phra Kieo* and rabbit
Institutional colors (blue, yellow, dark blue, white, and black)
Graduation ceremony robes
Facilities in Bangkok and Phuket Phuket (aspects and
    locations)
All specific Bangkok and Thailand aspects
Permanent elements of the school vocabulary (mainly
    appearing in graphic form online or brochures):
    - MBA degrees, PhD, dual MBA
    - Sustainability and entrepreneurship
    - Research focus and methodologies (action research,
        inductive method)
    - Courses in English
Awards, accreditations (logos of EQUIS and AACSB)
Links with prestigious foreign schools and universities
    (Wharton, Kellogg, etc.)

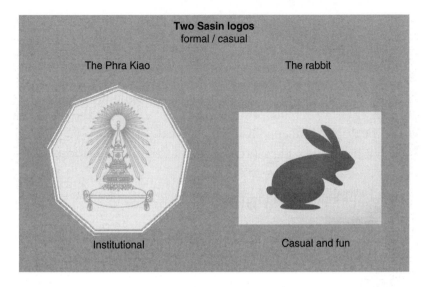

Figure A.1   Sasin Two Logos

- The Phra Kieo was King Chulalongkorn's personal emblem, which was authorized by King Vajiravudh to be used as an emblem for Chulalongkorn University (to which Sasin depends) when he gave it his father's name. It represents a Thai coronet, royal headgear for high-ranking members of the royal family. The Phra Kiao is inscribed into a yellow nonagon in reference to the late King Rama IX, the ninth monarch in the Chakri dynasty. Because Thais associate each day of the week with a color, yellow has become a Sasin color, since His Majesty was born on Monday represented by "yellow." This logo is very institutional in nature and subject to rigid rules of utilization (always at the top of a page, etc.).
- The rabbit is derived directly from the name of the school, as mentioned before in Sasin's brief history. If Sasin is chief of the rabbits, there was only one step to take to introduce another synthetic representation of the school, which brings more fun and is easier to use.

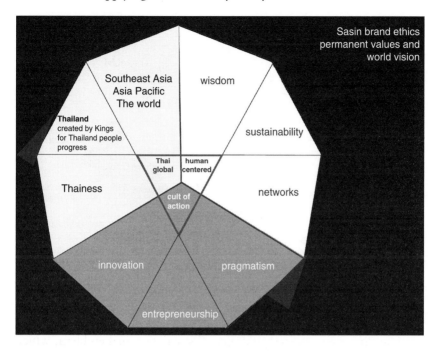

Figure A.2   The Nonagon Structuring Sasin's Brand Ethics

- The presence of the nonagon with its rich symbolism in many cultures has been an occasion to link more tightly the ethics and aesthetics of the brand. It helped structure the multitude of elements of the school ethics (Table A.2) by developing the ternary nature of the nonagon: $9 = 3^2$.

The three basic tenets of the brand ethics were formalized as being global Thai, human-centered (sustainability being the main axis), and action-oriented (mainly expressed in the entrepreneurship drive), out of which all the elements of Table A.1 would derive. The nature of the nonagon shape fits ideally to express all of the Sasin values, as can be seen in A.2 and A.3.

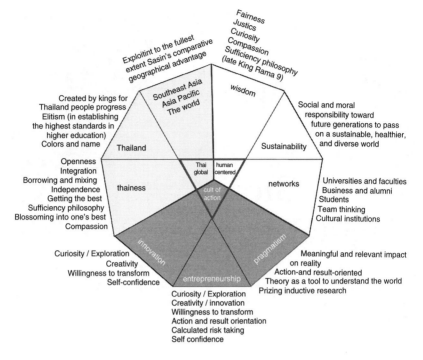

Figure A.3   The Nonagon Structuring Sasin's Brand Ethics (details)

The work on Sasin's identity continues. It is never over. As we have shown in Figure 6.5. for Jim Thompson, it serves as one of the basic components for all the brand manifestations' ethics and aesthetics and is helping prepare the creative briefs for architects, decorators, visual (web and paper) designers, and merchandise designers, as well as curriculum and pedagogical methodologies.

Appendix B

Glossary of Digital-Related Terms[*]

Ｗe thought it would be useful to have some of the basic terms constantly used in the digital world briefly explained.

---

[*]The main sources for the glossary are the following:

- https://www.merriam-webster.com/dictionary/
- https://en.wikipedia.org
- https://techterms.com/definition
- https://dictionary.cambridge.org/dictionary/english
- https://corporatefinanceinstitute.com/resources/knowledge/ecommerce-saas
- D. Cardon, *Culture Numérique*. Paris: Presses de Sciences Po, 2019.

App

Abbreviation for application. A computer program or piece of software designed for a particular purpose that you can download onto a mobile phone or other mobile device. Web app: an application that you can use on the Internet rather than having to download it.

CC

Creative Commons. This is a new type of license for software created by Lawrence Lessig in 2001, whereby the author does not abandon his rights, but regulates the conditions in which the software can be utilized by others.

Cookie

Invented in 1993 by Montulli, this is a small digital file placed in the Web user's browser that allows the site to recognize who is visiting it. The gathering of the information of the past navigation allows for the building of users' profiles.

Engagement rate

The engagement rate measures the level of interaction by followers from content created by a user. It provides a more accurate representation of content performance than absolute measures such as likes, shares, and comments. There are different calculations depending on the platform considered. The engagement rate is calculated differently depending on the platform. For Facebook, for example, we will use the total amount of shares, likes, reactions, and comments; for Instagram, the total amount of likes and comments.

Other KPIs can be seen in Chapter 9, section 9.3.

Facebook Ads

This is a Facebook product based on a targeting technology that allows advertisements to reach a specific audience. Advertisers can target their audience based on features like geographical location, gender, age, work, relationship status, personal interests, purchasing patterns, device usage, and so on.

GAFAM

The acronym referring to Google, Amazon, Facebook, Apple, and Microsoft.

Google Ads

Formerly Google AdWords, this is an online advertising platform developed by Google, where advertisers pay to display brief advertisements, service offerings, product listings, and video content. It can place ads both in the results of search engines like Google Search (the Google Search Network) and on nonsearch websites, mobile apps, and videos (the Google Display Network). Through its innovative bidding model, Google Ads offers services under a pay-per-click (PPC) pricing model. It has become the main source of revenue for Alphabet Inc., generating US$134.8 billion in 2019.

HTML

Hypertext markup language.

http

Hypertext transfer protocol.

https

Hypertext transfer protocol secure. It is the same thing as http, but it uses a secure socket layer (SSL) for security purposes. Secure websites use the https protocol to encrypt the data being sent back and forth with SSL encryption. A website is secure if its URL starts with https://.

Influencer

A person who exerts influence: a person who inspires or guides the actions of others. More specifically in the digital world, a person who is able to generate the interest of potential buyers in a consumer product or service by promoting or recommending the items on social media.

Internet

This is not the same as the Web. It is a communication protocol called TCP/IP (Transmission Control Protocol/Internet Protocol). It allows for computers to be connected through all possible network infrastructures. It started being developed in the 1960s by ARPA (the Advanced Research Project Agency), an agency belonging to the US Department of Defense, and was completed in its current form in 1983. A lot of scientists contributed to it; however, Vint Cerf and Robert Kahn were the main actuators.

Lead

A lead designates a prospective customer who has shown interest in a product or service and has provided contact information.

Meme

A meme is an idea, behavior, or style that spreads by means of imitation from person to person and often carries symbolic meaning referring to a particular phenomenon or theme. The word originated with Richard

Dawkins's 1976 book *The Selfish Gene*. An Internet meme is a concept that spreads rapidly from person to person via the Internet. The prominent form of such memes consists of image macros paired with a concept or catchphrase, often including surreal and nonsensical themes with parodies, remixes, or mashups.

MMS

Multimedia Messaging Service; it is a mobile phone service that allows users to send multimedia messages including images, videos, and sound files to each other.

Pagerank

Algorithm of Google research engine.

SEO

Search Engine Optimization. These are the activities aiming at finding the keywords that generate the optimal traffic to one website, making the website easily accessible to search engines.

SMS

SMS stands for Short Message Service. It is the most widely used type of text messaging, sending a message of up to 160 characters to another device. SMS is used to send text messages to mobile phones. It was originally created for phones that use GSM (Global System for Mobile) communication, but now all the major cell phone systems support it.

The Web

More recent than the Internet, invented by Tim Berners-Lee in 1990 while working at the CERN (Centre Européen de recherché nucléaire) in Switzerland. The Web is a communication protocol allowing the connection between pages through the well-known hypertext link http://www. The Web is included in the Internet, simplifying its utilization, while the latter includes many other things like SMTP, IRC, and FTP protocols.

1995 is the date recognized as the beginning of the widespread public utilization of the Web made possible by the browsers like Internet Explorer, launched the same year.

Troll

On the Internet, a troll is a person who quarrels with people by posting inflammatory, digressive, extraneous, or off-topic messages in online communities in order to provoke readers into emotional responses. Trolling is now often equated with online harassment.

URL

Uniform Resource Locator; it is the address of a specific webpage or file on the Internet.

Webinar

A seminar or other presentation conducted over the Internet allowing participants in different locations to see and hear the presenter, ask questions, and sometimes answer polls.

Wiki

Technology invented in the United States in 1995 by Ward Cunningham that allows anybody to write, delete, and correct Web pages.

Index